FEMINIST
INTERPRETATIONS
OF
DAVID HUME

RE-READING THE CANON

NANCY TUANA, GENERAL EDITOR

This series consists of edited collections of essays, some original and some previously published, offering feminist re-interpretations of the writings of major figures in the Western philosophical tradition. Devoted to the work of a single philosopher, each volume contains essays covering the full range of the philosopher's thought and representing the diversity of approaches now being used by feminist critics.

Already published:

Nancy Tuana, ed., *Feminist Interpretations of Plato* (1994)

Margaret Simons, ed., *Feminist Interpretations of Simone de Beauvoir* (1995)

Bonnie Honig, ed., *Feminist Interpretations of Hannah Arendt* (1995)

Patricia Jagentowicz Mills, ed., *Feminist Interpretations of G. W. F. Hegel* (1996)

Maria J. Falco, ed., *Feminist Interpretations of Mary Wollstonecraft* (1996)

Susan J. Hekman, ed., *Feminist Interpretations of Michel Foucault* (1996)

Nancy J. Holland, ed., *Feminist Interpretations of Jacques Derrida* (1997)

Robin May Schott, ed., *Feminist Interpretations of Immanuel Kant* (1997)

Céléne Léon and Sylvia Walsh, eds., *Feminist Interpretations of Søren Kierkegaard* (1997)

Cynthia A. Freeland, ed., *Feminist Interpretations of Aristotle* (1998)

Kelly Oliver and Marilyn Pearsall, eds., *Feminist Interpretations of Friedrich Nietzsche* (1998)

Mimi Reisel Gladstein and Chris Matthew Sciabarra, eds., *Feminist Interpretations of Ayn Rand* (1999)

Susan Bordo, ed., *Feminist Interpretations of René Descartes* (1999)

Julien S. Murphy, ed., *Feminist Interpretations of Jean-Paul Sartre* (1999)

FEMINIST INTERPRETATIONS OF DAVID HUME

EDITED BY ANNE JAAP JACOBSON

THE PENNSYLVANIA STATE UNIVERSITY PRESS
UNIVERSITY PARK, PENNSYLVANIA

The excerpt in Chapter 3 from *A Mind of One's Own: Feminist Essays on Reason and Objectivity* by Louise Antony and Charlotte Witt is reprinted by permission of Westview Press, a member of Perseus Books, L.L.C. Copyright © 1992 by Westview Press.

Library of Congress Cataloging-in-Publication Data

Feminist interpretations of David Hume / edited by Anne Jaap Jacobson.

    p.   cm. — (Re-reading the canon)
    Includes bibliographical references and index.
    ISBN 0–271–01971–9 (cloth : alk. paper)
    ISBN 0–271–01972–7 (pbk. : alk. paper)
    1. Hume, David, 1711–1776. 2. Feminist theory. I. Jacobson,
Anne Jaap. II. Series.
    B1498.F46   2000
    192–dc21   99-37479
                                                CIP

It is the policy of The Pennsylvania State University Press to use acid-free paper for the first printing of all clothbound books. Publications on uncoated stock satisfy the minimum requirements of American National Standard for Information Sciences—Permanence of Paper for Printed Library Materials, ANSI Z39.48–1992.

For my mother,
Frances Davies Jaap

Contents

Preface

Nancy Tuana

Take into your hands any history-of-philosophy text. You will find compiled therein the "classics" of modern philosophy. Since these texts are often designed for use in undergraduate classes, the editor is likely to offer an introduction in which the reader is informed that these selections represent the perennial questions of philosophy. The student is to assume that she or he is about to explore the timeless wisdom of the greatest minds of Western philosophy. No one calls attention to the fact that the philosophers are all men.

Though women are omitted from the canons of philosophy, these texts inscribe the nature of woman. Sometimes the philosopher speaks directly about woman, delineating her proper role, her abilities and inabilities, her desires. Other times the message is indirect—a passing remark hinting at women's emotionality, irrationality, unreliability.

This process of definition occurs in far more subtle ways when the central concepts of philosophy—reason and justice, those characteristics that are taken to define us as human—are associated with traits historically identified with masculinity. If the "man" of reason must learn to control or overcome traits identified as feminine—the body, the emotions, the passions—then the realm of rationality will be one reserved primarily for men,[1] with grudging entrance to those few women who are capable of transcending their femininity.

Feminist philosophers have begun to look critically at the canonized texts of philosophy and have concluded that the discourses of philosophy are not gender-neutral. Philosophical narratives do not offer a universal perspective, but rather privilege some experiences and beliefs over others. These experiences and beliefs permeate all philosophical theories whether they be aesthetic or epistemological, moral or metaphysical. Yet this fact has often been neglected by those studying the traditions of philosophy. Given the history of canon formation in Western philosophy, the perspective most likely to be privileged is that of upper-class white males. Thus, to be fully aware of the impact of gender biases, it is imperative that we re-read the canon with attention to the ways in which philosophers' assumptions concerning gender are embedded within their theories.

This new series, Re-Reading the Canon, is designed to foster this process of reevaluation. Each volume will offer feminist analyses of the theories of a selected philosopher. Since feminist philosophy is not monolithic in method or content, the essays are also selected to illustrate the variety of perspectives within feminist criticism and highlight some of the controversies within feminist scholarship.

In this series, feminist lenses will be focused on the canonical texts of Western philosophy, both those authors who have been part of the traditional canon, as well as those philosophers whose writings have more recently gained attention within the philosophical community. A glance at the list of volumes in the series will reveal an immediate gender bias of the canon: Arendt, Aristotle, de Beauvoir, Derrida, Descartes, Foucault, Hegel, Hume, Kant, Locke, Marx, Mill, Nietzsche, Plato, Rousseau, Wittgenstein, Wollstonecraft. There are all too few women included, and those few who do appear have been added only recently. In creating this series, it is not my intention to reify the current canon of philosophical thought. What is and is not included within the canon during a particular historical period is a result of many factors. Although no canonization of texts will include all philosophers, no canonization of texts that excludes all but a few women can offer an accurate representation of the history of the discipline, as women have been philosophers since the ancient period.[2]

I share with many feminist philosophers and other philosophers writing from the margins of philosophy the concern that the current canonization of philosophy be transformed. Although I do not accept the position that the current canon has been formed exclusively by power relations, I do believe that this canon represents only a selective history of the tradition. I share the view of Michael Bérubé that "canons are at once the location, the index, and the record of the struggle for cultural representation; like any other hegemonic formation, they must be continually reproduced anew and are continually contested."[3]

The process of canon transformation will require the recovery of "lost" texts and a careful examination of the reasons such voices have been silenced. Along with the process of uncovering women's philosophical history, we must also begin to analyze the impact of gender ideologies upon the process of canonization. This process of recovery and examination must occur in conjunction with careful attention to the concept of a canon of authorized texts. Are we to dispense with the notion of a tradition of excellence embodied in a canon of authorized texts? Or, rather than abandon the whole idea of a canon, do we instead encourage a reconstruction of a canon of those texts that inform a common culture?

This series is designed to contribute to this process of canon transformation by offering a re-reading of the current philosophical canon. Such a re-reading shifts our attention to the ways in which woman and the role of the feminine is constructed within the texts of philosophy. A question we must keep in front of us during this process of re-reading is whether a philosopher's socially inherited prejudices concerning woman's nature and role are independent of her or his larger philosophical framework. In asking this question attention must be paid to the ways in which the definitions of central philosophical concepts implicitly include or exclude gendered traits.

This type of reading strategy is not limited to the canon, but can be applied to all texts. It is my desire that this series reveal the importance of this type of critical reading. Paying attention to the workings of gender within the texts of philosophy will make visible the complexities of the inscription of gender ideologies.

Notes

1. More properly, it is a realm reserved for a group of privileged males, since the texts also inscribe race and class biases that thereby omit certain males from participation.

2. Mary Ellen Waithe's multivolume series, *A History of Women Philosophers* (Boston: M. Nijhoff, 1987), attests to this presence of women.

3. Michael Bérubé, *Marginal Forces/Cultural Centers: Tolson, Pynchon, and the Politics of the Canon* (Ithaca: Cornell University Press, 1992), 4–5.

Introduction: A Double Re-Reading

In the essays in this collection, Hume is doubly reread. One rereading, common to the volumes in this series, is a feminist one. Feminist philosophy has made available a variety of approaches in philosophy, and has introduced an array of topics and methodologies. Readers will find in what follows a rich mixture of feminist interpretations and reflections on a wide range of Hume's writings.

This feminist rereading introduces new themes into Hume scholarship. These include Hume's positioning of women in his philosophical texts,[1] the role of society in his conception of the human mind, and his conception of human nature in comparison to recent antiessentialism. The essays also address a great diversity of subjects in Hume's work, discussing his theory of knowledge, his conception of human inquiry and the human mind, his views on our knowledge of the external world and the future, his treatments of the passions, emotions, and virtue, especially including sympathy and justice, his conception of moral education, his views on aesthetics and religion, and his historical work.

The second rereading forsakes the old and convenient image of Hume as the enemy of constructive philosophy. In such a picture, Hume is an accessible target, one on whom Anglophone students were trained for generations. Indeed from his own time until very recently, Hume was read as an extremely negative philosopher. As Boswell tells us, "Goldsmith said David Hume was one of those, who seeing the first place occupied on the right side, rather than take a second, wants to have a first in what is

In preparing this Introduction, I was helped greatly by discussions with Cynthia Freeland and Rupert Read. Acute comments from Nancy Tuana improved the final version.

wrong."[2] Hume himself says, "I expected, in entering on my literary course, that all the Christians, all the Whigs, and all the Tories, should be my enemies. But it is hard that all the English, Irish and Welsh, should be also against me. The Scotch likewise cannot be much my friends, as no man is a prophet in his own country."[3] Hume adds, "I fancy that I must have recourse to America for justice," and insofar as North American scholarship dominates the recent reinterpretations, he is right.

The feminist rereading both participates in, and extends, the second rereading of Hume. In part this is because of the work of one of the authors in this volume, Annette Baier. Baier has been ovular in the community of Hume scholars who are reenvisaging Hume's work.[4] She has extended our understanding of the role of community in Hume's philosophy, among other things. At the same time, Hume scholarship as a whole still reflects the traditional neglect of feminist perspectives on the history of philosophy. An example of this is a recent volume that some feminists in the society of Hume scholars have labeled "The Gentleman's Companion to Hume."[5] I believe that the essays in the present volume show that the standard approach to historical interpretation excludes very valuable viewpoints and limits our understanding of the historical Hume.

In the following section, I will consider some of the reasons why Hume is no longer read as the completely negative skeptic. As we will see, they raise some central and feminist questions about the academy's treatment of the canon; however, most of our discussion of the new feminist considerations will be postponed until the third section.

Hume Studies

Although his writings have always been included in the canon, the shifting interpretations of Hume's work raise important feminist issues. I describe two of them in this section: adversarial philosophy and feminist questioning of the canon. Other related issues are described in the following sections.

Hume is widely regarded as the greatest philosopher to have written in the English language. He is thought to provide profound and original observations on an astonishingly wide range of topics, including metaphysics and epistemology, philosophy of language, philosophy of mind, moral philosophy, religion, and aesthetics. He is also more generally thought to be one of the great English writers, and he produced historical work that is still important.[6]

At the same time, traditional interpretations of Hume make his status puzzling. Drawing on Hume's already negative reputation, Thomas Reid set the tone for two hundred years of Hume commentators.[7] Hence, until very recently many historians of philosophy have seen Hume as a thinker whose genius consisted largely in revealing the deep errors in a theory of ideas sketched out by Descartes, and filled in by Locke and Berkeley.[8] In these accounts, one can see Hume as the bad boy of Western philosophy, whose once youthful skepticism, full of traps for the unwary, continually threatens our thought. Thus, reading about Hume often gives one the puzzling realization that our gallery of the great philosophers includes someone who is thought to have erected a monument to error and the false. (That this is so raises a question about the constitution of the canon that I describe below.)

Hume scholarship has changed greatly in recent years. One correction to the very negative picture is made by repositioning his moral philosophy.[9] The ethical writings present us with a philosopher clearly engaged on a positive project, one that pictures us as unavoidably social beings. When we consider Hume's ethical writings, it becomes much more difficult to see him as merely working out the implications of a wrong-headed theory of ideas. Baier's work has been very important here and with the third factor mentioned below.

A second correction is made by a more careful reading of the texts. For example, the view that Hume argues for the skeptical thesis that all science is impossible appears to ignore an obvious feature. Hume explicitly presents himself as developing a science of the mind, a project that, he assures us, can have significant successes. Whatever else is true, he cannot *simply* be a skeptic.

A third factor has been the discovery in Hume of a positive account that provides at least a sketch of an alternative to foundationalism. If we take foundationalism to require that knowledge be based on indubitable premises and valid derivations therefrom, Hume's seeming negative reflections on our knowledge can be seen as rejecting this conception of knowledge, rather than as claiming that we have no knowledge at all. On such a reading, Hume characterizes at least some of our natural belief-forming procedures as producing what we would consider knowledge. This "naturalized" reading of Hume originates with Kemp Smith, but its acceptance as a reading of Hume appears to have become more widespread as naturalized epistemology has been more fully conceptualized in our philosophical community.[10]

A fourth impetus for reorientation is created by a quite profound change in methodology in the history of philosophy. Anglophone philosophy often allows or even promotes what has been called "adversarial" philosophy.[11] For such adversarial philosophy, philosophical method, as I have heard it said, consists in one person's putting up a philosophical position and everyone else's trying to knock it down. ("If women don't like it, they should get out of philosophy," was the conclusion drawn, on the occasion I have in mind.) Such methodology means that we read for mistakes and errors, at least as we see them. Hume has certainly been a favorite practice target in philosophical training. However, as a methodology for understanding others' work, adversarial philosophy has great and obvious limitations, and its use in the history of philosophy is now generally eschewed, at least as regards historical figures, who are no longer—at least by good commentators—scanned for their suitability as targets. Somewhat ironically, those commentators who do treat historical figures as targets are likely themselves to become the targets of sometimes very negative reactions.

It is not true, however, that we can simply cast off the blinders of the past and now discern the truth about Hume. A very central question in contemporary Hume studies concerns how much of a correction to the negative picture should be made. The essays in this volume exemplify the wide diversity of current opinion. This is well illustrated by the first four, which are concerned with topics on which Hume has traditionally been thought to be skeptical, with the first two providing a reading that is considerably more positive than that of the third and fourth. A question I suggest for the reader below is whether there is a single right account of what Hume says.

In the following section I will describe the essays in this volume and we will be considering more specifically feminist questions in studying Hume's work, including those in the first four essays mentioned above. We should note, however, that the material in the present section illustrates a particularly important issue for feminist approaches to the canon. Feminist recommendations of adjustments in the canon have often enough been thought to be potentially harmful on a quite grand scale. It has proved tempting to many to insist that the canon merely consists in the greatest works ever written (or spoken), and that any educated person should know what they contain. It appears to follow that questioning the canon may damage Western education, among other things. This picture suggests that the canon is simply the result of a careful selection of the greatest works and that what the great contains is unproblematically accessible. The idea that the content is unproblematically accessible is shown to be highly questionable when we turn to Hume studies. It looks very much as though Hume was been badly misread for more than two centuries. Further, the misreading conveniently made him a foil for generations of philosophers who took it as no small accomplishment to triumph over him.[12] The values behind the selection of the canon and its interpretation are demonstrably not simply, if at all, a disinterested love of wisdom. As the officially anonymous author of the Abstract to the Treatise, who is commonly thought to be Hume, says, "The Author must be contented to wait with patience for some time before the learned world can agree in their sentiments of his performance. 'Tis his misfortune, that he cannot make an appeal to the people, who in all matters of common reason and eloquence are found so infallible a tribunal. He must be judg'd by the few, whose verdict is more apt to be corrupted by partiality and prejudice . . . and [who] are apt to form to themselves systems of their own, which they resolve not to relinquish."[13]

Feminist Resources

While there is now a rich tradition of feminist philosophical reflection on the canon of Western philosophy, Hume himself has not yet proved a site for extensive feminist evaluation.[14] This is particularly true of the Hume as recently constructively reread. It is important, then, that the essays in this volume show that feminist approaches have fresh and valuable things to say about Hume's work and his place in the tradition. Readers are very much invited into the resulting conversation. The authors in the collection offer us a number of different perspectives on Hume's work; evaluating one author's perspective, reconciling or adjudicating among conflicting views, and generalizing an author's approach are three of the ways one could join in. I will conclude this Introduction by describing in more detail some further questions readers might address.

Hume's major philosophical work, A Treatise of Human Nature,[15] is divided into three books, and the first ten papers in this volume follow his ordering of the topics. We start, then, with essays on Hume's metaphysics and epistemology. The first essay is by Annette Baier, a very major figure in Hume studies and in feminist philosophy, among other areas. As I noted above, she has been very influential in the positive rereading of Hume. She has been the leading figure in arguing that Hume's metaphysics and epistemology must be seen in light of his work on the passions (Book II) and moral philosophy (Book III). Indeed, Baier could be seen as arguing for a subversion of Hume's seeming priorities.

Baier notes that a fondness for Hume's writings may seem to indicate a failure to transcend one's education in the patriarchal tradition. However, she rightly points out that it would be self-defeating to dismiss "as hopelessly contaminated all the recorded thoughts of all the dead white males." Further, she maintains that Hume's outsider position and his goal of radically transforming philosophy should make him of interest to feminist philosophers. Many of the essays in this volume provide evidence for this last claim.

Baier addresses the question of Hume's theory of knowledge. While writers prior to Baier had begun to see the extent of Hume's naturalism, Baier extends the view in extremely important ways that bring in Books II and III. In doing so, she shows the extent to which the community is important to Hume in his conception of what counts as knowledge. An interesting theme in this essay, and in Baier's work on Hume more generally, is the way in which community and normativity are linked together. Baier sees this theme in Hume's epistemology, and relates it to recent feminist thought.

The second essay is by Genevieve Lloyd. The publication of her 1984 *The Man of Reason*[16] was an important event in feminist reading of philosophy's canon. Lloyd showed that Western philosophy operates with a thoroughly genderized conception of reason, one that places reason in opposition to the imagination and emotions, among other things. In her essay in this volume, she argues that Hume develops an integrated, nonoppositional conception of the mind, one with important implications for philosophical practice. Her essay skillfully traces this central theme through the *Treatise* and several of Hume's essays. The diversity of her resources give one a good picture of the Humean philosophy produced by an integrated mind.

In her discussion, Lloyd focuses on the love of truth. Taking Baier's work as a starting point, Lloyd traces Hume's development of an account of our love of truth. The account starts in Book I by taking truth-seeking as merely a natural propensity. It is enriched by passion and imagination in Book II, and in Book III sympathy emerges to give our intellectual life a social aspect. The painful and arid pursuit of the abstract becomes subservient to the practical and to public approbation. As Lloyd points out, the result is a reenvisioning of human intellectual life, one that engages in what is traditionally consigned to the feminine and in doing so abandons the stark oppositions of reason, imagination, and emotion that characterize still so much in philosophy's view of proper intellectual methodology.

The ideals of intellectual life are again examined in the third essay, my own, in which I consider Hume's treatment of causation, our knowledge of the unobserved, and the existence of an external world. These are topics he treats principally in Book I of the *Treatise* and in *The Enquiry Concerning Human Understanding*.[17] My overarching concern is with philosophical methodology. Feminists who criticize the ideal of philosophy as being perfectly consistently argued, disinterested reflection on abstract concepts are too often thought to be questioning philosophy itself and to be positioning themselves outside the tradition. However, as I argue, since the tradition includes Hume, it has already accommodated texts that flaunt the ideal. On this interpretation, it is a mistake to excise inconsistencies from the text in order to produce the one consistent view that Hume supposedly endorsed.

As I point out, some researchers in cognitive science are also giving us grounds for questioning philosophy's traditional ideal of the exercise of a pure rationality. A convergence between some recent cognitive science and Hume's philosophy is significant, since Hume is arguably engaged in an enterprise with which our cognitive science is continuous. Hume is giving us a science of the human mind. Susan A. Martinelli Fernandez's essay in this volume also places Hume in dialogue with contemporary cognitive science.

Hume's discussion of the existence of an external world is the topic of the fourth essay in this volume, by Aaron Smuts, who explores the ways in which gendered metaphors operate in Hume's discussion. According to Smuts, Hume's discussion of the external world is gendered, and shifting images of nature and woman signal Hume's shifting attitudes to the philosophical worth of having an opinion on the existence of an external world. Smuts traces in Hume's philosophy an opposition of reason to nature, and locates its place within a category of binary oppositions, including male and female. In the context of Lloyd's view of the development in the *Treatise* of Hume's conception of the good intellectual life, it is significant that Smuts finds a difference in the use of nature metaphors in the later *Enquiry*.[18]

Smuts also discusses more generally the role(s) of metaphor in philosophy. He surveys the diversity of views of metaphor that are present in philosophy, including philosophy not generally well represented in Anglophone philosophy departments. Drawing on feminist and more general deconstructive resources, Smuts shows the value of attending to Hume's metaphors. At the same time, as he points out, his aims are not deconstructive, since Hume's metaphors serve, and do not subvert, the aims of the texts.

Jacqueline Taylor's essay picks up topics from both Book II and Book III of the *Treatise*. She addresses Hume's treatment of emotions, particularly our moral sentiments, in his development of a science of the mind, and her discussion situates it in a current debate between realists and antirealists about values, both moral and aesthetic. Following Sabina Lovibond, Taylor maintains that the standard noncognitivist reading of Hume, in bifurcating fact and value, devalues the latter. Since, as other essayists in this volume have pointed out, there is a historical and cultural tendency to associate women with emotion, sensibility, and value, the bifurcation does not bode well for feminism.

In contrast, Taylor offers a reading of Hume's moral psychology that advances one of the goals of feminist philosophers; namely, to take seriously the social influences on the passions and the influence that the passions have in turn on our social and cultural sensibilities. She shows that the complexities of Hume's account of how we cultivate our aesthetic and moral sensibilities significantly differentiate his ethics from contemporary noncognitivist theories. Hume, on this reading, provides us with the resources to analyze critically the effects on character development of the sociocultural development of institutions, practices, and standards of value. Hume's ethics may, then, be fruitfully appropriated by feminist philosophers interested in moral psychology and the potential for a virtue-centered ethic to provide a practical political critique.

Taylor's essay involves a wide range of topics, including philosophy of mind, moral philosophy, and aesthetics. The next several essays address topics principally within the area of moral and political philosophy. The readers should notice that in these four essays, Hume's merits as a resource for feminists appear mixed. Hirschmann's essay particularly reminds us of the detailed resources developed in recent feminist theory, in comparison to which Hume's theory can be seen as less full.

In their essay, Joyce Jenkins and Robert Shaver address a notorious and genuinely shocking passage on justice in Hume's *Enquiry Concerning the Principles of Morals*. In this passage Hume maintains that gender and race can determine whether one has a right to just treatment. Race and gender are important for Hume's theory of justice because his theory at least apparently privileges the strong, and race and gender indicate contrasting degrees of strength. Benevolence, not justice, is the source for virtuous treatment of the weak.

Jenkins and Shaver address competing interpretations of how Hume's invocation of benevolence, rather than justice, is to be understood. Is Hume being Hobbesian, advocating a form of justice that accords rights only to those who can participate in mutually advantage interactions? Or is his conception based on more utilitarian considerations about how the weaker members of society are in fact best served? Jenkins and Shaver argue for the later interpretation and against the dominant reading of this passage. However, they do not use their arguments to let Hume entirely off the hook. Rather, invoking John Stuart Mill's *The Subjection of Women*, they catalog the defects in paternalistic benevolence.

An ethics of care is generally identified as the product of feminist reflection. Christine Swanton finds a powerful version of a standard objection about such an ethics in Nietzsche's work. The objection is that the result of compassion, pity, is in fact a pathological infection, and ultimately expresses narcissism, cowardice, and a kind of revenge. Focusing on Noddings's work,[19] and her conception of "engrossment," Swanton brings in the resources of an approach to Hume that draws on virtue ethics in order to address the Nietzschean objection. Swanton shows that Hume's account of empathy and benevolence can make an ethics of care less vulnerable to objections than is often thought. The Hume of this essay provides an account of altruistic virtues that has much closer affinities to an ethics of care than does any Nietzschean account of altruism.

Swanton draws on, among others, the work of Philippa Foot and Rosalind Hursthouse in her discussion of virtue ethics. Her account of what a Humean virtue is includes a discussion of the potential downside to Humean sympathy. She also argues forcefully that a virtue ethics approach to Hume's treatment of benevolence provides a very different picture from that of Hume as a precursor of utilitarian thought.

The political theorist Nancy J. Hirschmann is also concerned with an ethics of care, but her attention is on the insights of a number of theorists who have been working in that general area. She explores the feminist development of a picture of connected knowing; in doing so, she draws on diverse resources by authors such as Annette Baier, Carol Gilligan, Nancy Chodorow, Patricia Hill Collins, and Nancy Hartsock. A central question for Hirschmann is whether Hume develops a similar notion of knowledge. In particular, is Humean sympathy comparable to feminist empathy as she describes it? Hirschmann sees Hume's account as significantly different from that of recent feminists, and she suggests feminist resources that can resolve tensions in Hume's work.

Hirschmann argues that Humean sympathy is fundamentally more individualistic than feminist connected knowing. The latter places emotion at the foundation of knowledge, while, for Hume, sympathetic reaction is the result of knowing. As a consequence, feminist empathy posits humans as more intimately connected. Hirschmann distinguishes between skeptical and individualistic readings of Hume, and urges that we not disregard the individualism in Hume's philosophy that remains in place even when the skeptical reading is given up. She importantly traces the differences between Hume and feminists on the notion of political obligation, and maintains that Humean political theory is committed to a more conservative stance than is the feminist one.

Picking up some of the themes present in the previous two essays, Susan A. Martinelli-Fernandez turns our attention to the issues of moral education and social construction. Her intention is to consider how one can use some aspects of Hume's work to create a feminist narrative about ourselves that is inclusive of women's experience without maintaining that there is one female essence. She concludes that Hume can give us a theory of moral development that meets the worry that his work is fundamentally grounded in patriarchal suppositions.

Martinelli-Fernandez discusses questions that have played important roles in feminist discussions of ethics. For example, to what extent does a feminist perspective have either to employ an essentialist conception of woman or to depend on patriarchally constructed notions of the female? These questions are particularly important for a theory of moral education that draws, as Hume's does, on the need for models of moral behavior. Martinelli-Fernandez's idea of creating a feminist narrative addresses these problems by allowing space for a corrective diversity of perspectives. She finds in Hume a relational view of the self that provides a basis for such narratives.

Martinelli-Fernandez also considers how Hume's theory of moral development compares with some recent work in cognitive science. She isolates a problem in some recent theories; namely, accounting for the normativity of moral discourse. In this regard, Hume's work is seen to have positive advantages.

The question of social construction and essentialism appear in a different context in Sheridan Hough's essay. Hough compares Hume's empirical account of human nature to the antiessentialist view of Nietzsche. Both Hume and Nietzsche argue that female comportment is a social construct, and indeed a necessary artifice. This necessity, however, is viewed differently by each. Hume claims that the biological reality of childbearing (and the related difficulties of securing paternity) creates an educational imperative: women must be trained to be chaste and modest. Female anatomy does not provide feminine manners, but it does demand their inculcation. Neitzsche, however, denies that the facts of human reproduction establish anything as fixed as a 'nature,' for women, like men, have the ability to reinterpret themselves.

It would seem that Nietzsche's approach, despite his renowned misogyny, leaves open a possibility for women that Hume denies them. Hough argues against this easy conclusion. She maintains that Hume's notion of sympathy may provide a conceptual space in which to reconsider women's status. She examines one of Hume's essays, "On Love and Marriage," in which he retells the Platonic story of the androgynes—the female-male creatures who are equal partners in all things—in order to explore the emotion mechanism of sympathy. The androgyne becomes a useful emblem for considering the kind of imaginative exercise that a sympathetic review of women's lot would demand. Hough's work brings into Hume studies for the first time Neitzsche's critical tool of constructing a genealogy.

Christopher Williams's essay takes us on to Hume's aesthetic theory. Williams raises questions that are highly relevant to feminists in general, though his attention is principally on works of art. The question is how to assess the feelings of displeasure that offensive material may evoke. These feelings may be evidence of a laudable refinement or they may reveal an indefensible prudishness. We need to understand the difference between a flaw in the work, which moral enlightenment can reveal, and a flaw in the audience, which would show false refinement. This general issue is related to a range of feminist concerns, since women are often enough supposed to enjoy or appreciate "great" works that represent significant parts of the human race in demeaning ways, or worse.

For Hume a central question is whether the offensiveness in question is an offensiveness in manners or morals. Our moral feelings, and only our moral feelings, provide us with the means for a laudable rejection of a work of art because of its offensiveness. Further, for Hume, the moral inaccessibility of a work of art to an observer is always to be counted as a flaw in the work. Williams finds Hume's position in need of revision, and he explores how we might effect it. One motivating concern is to avoid a reactionary aesthetics. Hence, Williams also explores ways in which a development in morals or taste may yield laudable aesthetic reactions.

Kathryn Temple considers Hume's historical writings, delineating his association of gender and genre in his historical writings. Hume officially distinguishes between proper history and feminized romance, with proper history aligned with the masculine. It is masculine history that Hume presents himself as producing, and its order and linearity provide a reassuring view of origins of England. Nonetheless, Hume's historical work also employs the conventions of romance, and a debased subgenre of it, "secret history." Having officially aligned himself with the masculine history, Hume is safe to exploit the feminized forms and does so at various points to deal with elements that disrupt the linearity of his narrative.

Bringing in the work of Luce Irigaray, Temple explores the ways in which romance and secret history are linked to woman as the disruptive source of disorder and multiplicity. Temple's account of the association of woman with at times even chaos includes a detailed analysis of Hume's treatment of Frances Howard, who, like another woman Hume describes, is seen as "prodigal, rapacious, dissolute, violent, revengeful."[20] In addition to presenting her detailed treatment of Hume's historical texts, Temple discusses some of the more general issues that have featured in other essays in this volume. These include Hume's views on the nature of woman, and issues from his moral philosophy.

Jennifer A. Herdt's work is groundbreaking in bringing Hume's treatment of religion into the arena of feminist religious criticism. In her essay, she also brings into conjunction with Hume studies feminist writers not previously part of the discourse. Like Temple, Herdt reminds us of the fact that Hume can see women as dangerous. It is women, Hume maintains, who lead men into superstition. He sees women as trained to be "weak and timid" so that the social order may be maintained. However, he also takes such induced weakness and timidity as dangerously engendering superstition and religiously motivated violence.

Herdt maintains that we can take what seem to be negative reflections on women as the basis for a feminist critique of religion. Nonetheless, Herdt also sees in Hume a strongly conservative strain based on a preoccupation with the maintenance of social order and the absence of conflict. She argues that he fails to realize fully his own insights into the relations between repression and violence. She also provides criticisms of two aspects of Hume's discussion of religion: his discussions of artificial lives and his critique of hierarchical thinking. In both respects, she argues, Hume's discussion has serious weaknesses.

In Conclusion

The essays in this volume can easily be seen as constituting an extended conversation. A theme is picked up, it is elaborated, a dissenting voice appears, and so on. Feminists do not speak with one voice. In this section, I will describe at a very general level some of the most important feminist issues addressed. As I said at the beginning of the previous section, readers are very welcome to join in the discussion. I will try below to suggest some further ways it could be continued and enlarged.

The essays in this collection demonstrate the benefits of feminist readings of a historical figure. For example, one problem the constructive interpretation of Hume has posed is that of providing an acceptable account of Hume's positive picture of the human mind and its ability to acquire knowledge. Baier and Lloyd, in bringing in a fuller and integrated picture of the individual intellect, give us the most extensive picture yet of what this might be. They do so in part by stressing the social nature of the knower. In their essays, feminist sensitivity to the more subtle problems of Cartesian individualism has led to an understanding of the text that is arguably better grounded than any preceding it.

The feminist concern that theory accommodate the fact that human beings are embedded in a sociocultural context appears also in Taylor's and Martinelli-Fernandez's work. The results are similarly productive. Taylor gives us new ways of understanding Hume's moral theory, while Martinelli-Fernandez's essay fruitfully brings to Hume scholarship major contemporary concerns that have been influenced by continental philosophy. The anti-Cartesian themes of the self as constructed in narratives and the accompanying antiessentialism in Martinelli-Fernandez's work are echoed in Hough's, who brings to Hume a discussion of a central continental figure.

The authors just mentioned bring feminist perspectives to Hume in part to understand his work better and in part to understand better the philosophical issues they are addressing. My own essay also reflects this motivation. The overall result, I suggest, enriches our understanding both of Hume's texts and of the philosophical problems addressed. There is a difference worth describing. There are nontraditional topics that feminists have introduced to mainstream Anglophone philosophy; Taylor's, Hough's and Martinelli-Fernandez's essays are particularly rich in this regard. However, the first four essays of this volume show that feminists can have illuminating things to say about very traditional topics in epistemology and metaphysics. These essays are still distinctively feminist.

Bringing feminist concerns to an historical figure may enable us to understand and assess better what feminists are saying. Swanton and Hirschmann illustrate the fruitfulness of doing this. In both these essays we see again the extent to which Hume's philosophy situates the human being in society.

Another concern of feminist critics is the misogyny of so many figures in the canon. There are three ways in which one can consider the extent to which Hume's texts are misogynistic: how women figure as symbols in his texts, how Hume describes actual women, and what policies toward women he actually advocates. As we approach the question of misogyny, we should be pessimistic about the treatment of women in an eighteenth-century text by a male writer, and the news about Hume is not terribly good. Smuts and Temple address the metaphorical positioning of women. Woman is associated with disorder and disruption. Even kindly Mother Nature can turn out to be a whore.

Metaphors, as a sophisticated reader knows, are not mere decoration. The proof of this in Hume's case is the fact that his actual discussion of women often enough follows the metaphors. Thus, Herdt and Temple have powerful things to say about Hume's treatment of women's effects on society; here again, women are positioned as disruptive and disorderly. Jenkins and Shaver describe a distressing paternalism. Further, Herdt argues for several considerable flaws, including Hume's failure to adequately evaluate hierarchical thinking for its effects on women. While the view of Hume we get from these consideration is discouraging, it could be much worse, as Baier has pointed out.[21] Further, as Williams's essay makes clear, Hume is still addressing questions of very considerable importance to feminist thought. Indeed, Williams's discussion gives us ways to think about how to evaluate texts with what we regard as moral flaws.

Hume's metaphorical treatment of women may also relate to my view of his metaphysics and epistemology as lacking a kind of consistency. Some recent feminists have urged that we take the instability in a male philosopher's views about women to be a deep and important one that actually serves to sustain the texts.[22] If we so approach a text, then we can also ask whether the instability in metaphors about women tracks an instability in approach to the philosophical problems explicitly addressed. To some extent, the third and fourth essays, taken together, suggest that this is a potentially fruitful area of investigation. The number of topics important for feminists that might receive such treatment is very large. For example, the treatment of personal identity in Book I would greatly reward feminist investigation from this perspective.

There is a closely related question: How is Hume's thought gendered? We have to be careful with this question. As many have pointed out, it can easily be thought to bring with it a conception of what "the feminine" essentially is, both reducing the diversity possible for human beings, and once again positioning women as "the other." One approach to this problem is to ask, as I shall do, about the extent to which feminist theorists, or Hume himself, see(s) him(self) as identified with the masculine.

Because the question of whether Hume's thought is genderized cuts across questions already addressed, some of the discussion of this question has in effect already occurred. For example, Hume's picture of the integrated mind indicates a way in which his theory of mind seems not gendered; that is, it does not embody only "male" experiences or "male" ideals. However, the individualism Hirschmann discerns in it argues in a different direction, and indicates a disconnectedness that fails to reflect many women's experience. In addition to what we have already seen, we should note that the deeply gendered metaphors revealed in Smuts's discussion do raise the question of whether Hume's understanding of the philosophical problem is at least in part an enactment of his gendered relation to nature.

On the question of genderized methodology, the picture of Hume is, by now unsurprisingly, mixed. In my essay I allude to the possible paternalistic positioning of the philosopher who wants—at least at some junctures—to say that his theories show that most of our beliefs are false. Further, as Temple shows us, Hume enthusiastically embraces an officially masculinized image of at least some of his work. In contrast, a number of writers find Hume's methodology very feminist friendly. These include Baier, Lloyd, Taylor and, in some ways, myself.

This brief summary indicates the diversity of views that readers of this volume will encounter. Hume did have profound and original things to say about a great number of things. As Williams's, Temple's, and Herdt's essays show, his thought even possesses dimensions rare in the work of those today addressing standard philosophical topics. I hope that the essays in this volume will indicate that reading Hume is rewarding, for there is much work to be done and more voices to be heard. I want now to turn to consider in closing some of the ways in which the essays raise questions for readers. My discussion here is very partial, and many more interesting questions await the readers' discovery.

The essays do not give us a unitary picture of Hume. This is true in a number of ways, and readers might think about what the diversity in each of these ways shows. For example, Lloyd finds that Hume's views develop as the *Treatise* unfolds; if we take the later discussions of the *Treatise* to be much more constructive on their own than the earlier ones, should we use Books II and III to reinterpret Book I? And if we do, what are we doing? Do we see ourselves as getting at "what Hume really thought"? Or is it rather more like reconstructing Hume's texts in a philosophically valuable way? Or something else? For all of us, Hume is to some extent an outsider, an other. Historical interpretation might well benefit from feminist discussions of understanding the other that are found in cultural studies.

A similar question arises in regard to Hume's treatment of issues concerned with social order. Taken together, our authors could be seen as maintaining that Hume has a highly conservative philosophy that none-theless can engage with mechanisms for change, which he can acutely and favorably describe. Should we bring these two strands together? Is there an unambiguous view of Hume to be discovered?

A related area has to do with the amount of disagreement among Hume commentators.[23] What does this show about Hume texts? To what extent is it a matter of the goals of the community of commentators? The debates and disagreements about historical texts, including those in this volume, may constitute a form of social interaction that will reward feminist attention. These questions also relate to feminist concerns with the positioning of texts in the canon as the product of an apolitical perception of the great works.

As we move from Book I to other topics, the questions become even more diverse. The fact-value distinction, so famously thought to be clearly stated in Hume's work, is argued by Taylor to dominate in only unacceptably superficial views of Hume's work. Is she right? If she is, we need to rethink the way in which the cognitivist/ noncognitivist distinction is taken to Hume's work. Taylor, drawing on Lovibond, shows us that this topic coincides at least in part with the feminist concern to rethink the reason-emotion bifurcation in Western philosophy.

Is it fruitful to see Hume as a virtue theorist, as Swanton does? If so, how do we develop the utilitarian thoughts that Jenkins and Shaver find in Hume's work? And does virtue theory have resources that are particularly useful for feminists? This question is so far scarcely addressed in the philosophical literature, despite the significant presence of women in its development.[24]

The relation between some of these themes and Hume's work on religion and history raises further questions. For example, can we take Temple's discussion of Hume's motivated employment of his officially rejected 'feminine' style back to our other questions of seeming diversity in Hume's texts? As we turn to religion, we might ask how much Hume remains a bad boy, and so perhaps can be taken into a feminist reconceptualization of religion. Here, as indeed at many other points, we might welcome such companionship. However, perhaps we should remind ourselves that traveling with Hume will involve some shocking and puzzling encounters: "Revenge is a natural passion to mankind; but seems to reign with the greatest force in priests and women: Because, being deprived of the immediate exertion of anger, in violence and combat, they are apt to fancy themselves despised on that account; and their pride supports their vindictive disposition."[25]

Notes

1. This topic is simply missing from, for example, "The Gentleman's Companion to Hume." (See below and n. 5.)

2. Quoted in M. A. Box, *The Suasive Art of David Hume* (Princeton: Princeton University Press, 1990).

3. David Hume, *The Letters of David Hume*, ed. J. Y. T. Grieg (Oxford: Clarendon Press, 1932), no. 469.

4. See especially her *A Progress of Sentiments: Reflections on Hume's "Treatise"* (Cambridge: Harvard University Press, 1991).

5. See David Fate Norton, ed., *The Cambridge Companion to Hume* (Cambridge: Cambridge University Press, 1993).

6. David Hume, *The History of England* (1778).

7. Thomas Reid, *Essays on the Active Powers of the Human Mind* (Cambridge: MIT Press, 1969).

8. Most recently, Antony Flew, *David Hume: Philosopher of Moral Science* (Oxford: Basil Blackwell, 1986).

9. Many Hume scholars have made this point. The point is generally considered to originate with Norman Kemp Smith, *The Philosophy of David Hume* (Macmillan, 1941; repr. Garland, 1983).

10. Feminist contributions to this development include Loraine Code's two recent books: *Epistemic Responsibility* (Hanover: University of New England Press, 1987), and *What Can She Know? Feminist Theory and the Construction of Knowledge* (Ithaca: Cornell University Press, 1991).

11. Janice Moulton, "A Paradigm of Philosophy: The Adversary Method," in S. Harding, ed., *Discovering Reality* (Dordrecht: Reidel, 1983), 149–64.

12. Most notably, Immanuel Kant in *Prolegomena to Any Future Metaphysics*, ed. and trans. Gary Hatfield (New York: Cambridge University Press, 1997).

13. "Abstract Of A Book Lately Published; Entitled A Treatise Of Human Nature, &C." (London, 1740).

14. A mark of this is the relatively thin number of feminist works on Hume.

15. David Hume, *A Treatise of Human Nature*, ed. L. A. Selby-Bigge; 2d ed., rev. P. H. Nidditch (Oxford: Oxford University Press, 1978).

16. Genevieve Lloyd, *The Man of Reason: "Male" and "Female" in Western Philosophy* (Minneapolis: University of Minnesota Press, 1984; 2d ed., 1993).

17. David Hume, *An Enquiry Concerning Human Understanding and an Enquiry Concerning the Principles of Morals*, ed. L. A. Selby-Bigge; 3d ed., rev. P. H. Nidditch (Oxford: Oxford University Press, 1975).

18. However, in her essay Baier points out that the more positive assessment in this work is limited.

19. Nell Noddings, *Caring: A Feminine Approach to Ethics and Moral Education* (Berkeley and Los Angeles: University of California Press, 1984).

20. Hume, *History of England*, vol. 6, chap. 63.

21. Annette Baier, "Good Men's Women: Hume on Chastity and Trust," *Hume Studies* 5 (April 1979): 1–19.

22. See Penelope Deutscher, *Yielding Gender* (New York: Routledge, 1997), for a very useful survey of these views, among other things.

23. The disagreements on interpretation in this volume pale in comparison with some of the debates in the Hume scholarship community. See, for example, the forthcoming Rupert Read and Ken Richman, eds., *The New Hume* (London: Routledge, 2000).

24. There are certainly feminist discussion of virtues. However, the virtue theory that Swanton discusses has not received much feminist attention. This is so despite the prominence of Philippa Foot and Rosalind Hursthouse in developing it. Hursthouse's forthcoming book on virtue theory (Oxford University Press) should make the theory more available to the audience it deserves.

25. David Hume, Essay XXI: "Of National Characters," in *Essays: Moral, Political, and Literary*, ed. Eugene F. Miller (Indianapolis: Liberty Classics, 1985), n. 2. Quoted by Herdt in her chapter, this volume.

1

Hume

The Reflective Women's Epistemologist?

Annette C. Baier

We cannot reasonably expect, that a piece of woollen cloth will be wrought to perfection in a nation which is ignorant of astronomy, or where ethics are neglected.

—David Hume, "Of Refinement in the Arts"

Recent feminist work in epistemology has emphasized some themes that I find also in Hume's writings on epistemology, when these are taken to include not just Book One of the *Treatise* and *An Enquiry Concerning Human Understanding* but also his claims, in his "ethical" writings, about natural abilities and their relative importance. These themes are found as well in several of his essays and throughout his *History of England* (especially in its appendixes), where his concern is with the difference between relatively "ignorant" and barbaric societies and those more-civilized societies in which the arts and sciences have made some progress. I find explored there what might be called a social and cultural epistemology, an epistemology that should be of interest to feminists. Of course, women can produce and are producing their own epistemologists and thus they do not need to turn to kindly, avuncular figures like Hume for suggestions or for confirmation of their own views. Nor do women agree with one another in their epistemological views. Many will dismiss my fondness for Hume's writings as a sure indicator of my failure to transcend my philosophical upbringing in a patriarchal tradition. Still, the very emphases that some women epistemologists, such as Lorraine Code,[1] make on the cooperative nature of our search for reliable beliefs, and our shared responsibility for successes and for failures, should incline us toward a willingness to get helpful support from any well-meaning fellow worker, alive or dead, woman or man. (And my Oxford teacher, J. L. Austin, practiced as well as preached cooperative investigations in philosophy, albeit ones with a strong leader in charge.) To dismiss as hopelessly contaminated all the recorded thoughts of all the dead white males, to commit their works to the flames, could be a self-defeating move. At the very least we should, as Hume advocated, examine each work we are tempted to burn to see if it does contain anything that is more worth saving than patriarchal metaphysics.

Hume is usually labeled an empiricist, and he does talk a lot about what experience alone can teach us. For him, this instructive experience consists in the first place in repeated pairings in a succession of lively "impressions" preserved in idea copies. It includes not merely what our senses reveal but also what our passions and their typical *expression* show us. We know from experience what makes us and others angry, and we come to know whose anger we should dread. At the start of the *Treatise*, Hume gives a sort of apology for beginning his work on human nature with an account of the human "understanding"—our capacity to retain, retrieve, relate, and use "ideas," those less lively derivative perceptions that would be more naturally attended to, he says, after prior attention to the experience whose lessons they preserve. His "excuse" for putting ideas first in his philosophy (and he is surely the first to see any need for any excuse) is that the impressions that philosophers should be most concerned with, and that he will be most concerned with, are human passions, and they usually depend on ideas, so he has to deal with thought and ideas, in at least a preliminary way, before he can do justice to feeling and action. He repeats in the *Abstract* that the reason why relations of ideas, and in particular the "natural" relations that gently select our thought sequences for us, are so important is that "*as it is by means of thought only that anything operates on our passions*, and as these are the only ties of our thoughts, they are really *to us* the cement of the universe, and all the operations of the mind must, in a great measure, depend on them" (A *Treatise of Human Nature* [hereafter T.] 662;[2] first emphasis mine). Theoretical reason (or should we say "imaginative curiosity"?) serves practical reason (or must we say "practical good sense"?). The reason that Hume's treatment of ideas comes before his treatment of passions and actions is precisely what may be termed "the primacy of practical reason."

The vital job of ideas is to remind us what gave pleasure or was useful to whom and at what costs and to help us to plan for the successful satisfaction of our considered experience-informed preferences. Belief "influences" passion and action, so belief matters. Lively ideas that are not quite beliefs also influence passions (suspicions, misgivings, hopes, fears), so ideas and imagination also matter, even when such ideas are not maximally lively, when they fail to carry total conviction. "Images of everything, especially of goods and evils, are always wandering in the mind" (T. 119). Such wanderers have their effects on action as well as on passion and reasoning. Poets by their eloquence can rouse our passions, even when the vivid conceptions that their tales produce in our minds do not "amount to perfect assurance" (T. 122). The whole of Hume's epistemology, in Book One of the *Treatise*, is in the services of his philosophy of passion and action in Books Two and Three. This is said at the start; it is repeated in places like "Of the Influence of Belief"; it is implied by the conclusion of Book One, whose most despairing moment took the form of a failure to be able to give any answer to the practical questions, "Whose favor shall I court, and whose anger must I dread? What beings surround me? and on whom do I have any influence, or who have any influence on me?" (T. 269); it is reiterated in Book Three's section on natural abilities and in the *Abstract*. The famous words I have just quoted from Hume's moment of despair, or feigned despair, show that it is not just practical questions but practical social ones that Humean epistemology is to serve. Not just how to get things done, but how to win friends and influence people, to placate the right superior powers, to find one's place in a web of social relations involving favor, anger, influence.

The celebrated laments in the conclusion of Book One of the *Treatise* might be read as the expression of a member of a subject race, the Scots, who had just lost their independence. Hume—speaking English with a despised Scottish accent, writing English with awareness of his own deaf ear for his own lapses into "Scotticisms," hoping for an audience with a readership who did not treat him as really one of them—might also be seen to have been in a position a bit like that of a woman trying to make her way in a profession where she is suspect from the start, a "strange uncouth monster," unlikely to win acceptance from those already securely in possession of whatever "thrones" may exist there. Admittedly, whatever Hume thought he was doing in this celebrated "conclusion of this book," he surely did not think he was merely expressing a literary Scot's frustrations, let alone putting himself into women's shoes or sympathizing with the bluestockings of his day. (Hume's relations with Elizabeth Montague, whose stockings gave us this concept, were cool.) Nevertheless it is not entirely fanciful to see him, in his unsuccessful attempts to breach the academic fortresses of Scotland (the chairs of philosophy he failed to get at Edinburgh and Glasgow), as a suitable male mascot for feminist philosophers in at least the early years of feminism—those during which some feminist philosophers were feeling unappreciated, excluded, ill understood. Hume was, if you like, an unwitting virtual woman. Both his "outsider" position (in relation to the dominant culture whose favor he would have had to court if he had succeeded in his academic ambitions) and his radical goals for the transformation of philosophy should make him of some interest to twentieth-century feminists, quite independently of the interesting things he had to say about equality for women and about the means by which they might achieve it.[3]

As far as his understanding of our understanding goes, Hume is famous not merely for his empiricism but for his scepticism—for his debunking of rationalist pretensions to intuit causal necessity in individual instances and to turn reason on its own supposed workings in such a way that it articulates and endorses those pretensions, and for his challenge to rationalist pretensions to require reason to exert its quasi-divine authority to govern the motivational forces at work in human action and response. This debunking (outside a very limited domain) can be read as an attack on the whole patriarchal theological tradition and on its claims about the relative authority of various human voices—the voice of divine reason, the voice of passion, sometimes of "animal" passion, the voice of plain good sense; the voice of the backward-looking avenger of crimes on account of their odiousness versus the voice of the forward-looking magistrate inflicting punishment designed to be no more severe than necessary to produce obedience (T. 410–11); the voice of the warlike patriot condemning the enemy's devilish "perfidy" while calling his own side's treachery "policy" (T. 348) versus the voice of the impartial moral evaluator recognizing perfidy wherever she finds it; the voice of cruel inhumanity versus that of normal human sympathy; the rough masculine voice versus the soft feminine voice, and so on. But it is notoriously much easier to attack a view, and to criticize a culture based on that view, than to indicate persuasively what alternative would be, and would sensibly be predicted to be, better than the one in use. What is Hume putting in place of the rationalists' sovereign reason in all the realms where he topples its authority?

As far as validation of matter-of-fact beliefs goes, Hume's official answer, in the *Enquiry Concerning Human Understanding* (hereafter E.), is "custom or habit." After pointing out that even experience-informed reason cannot get the premises it would need to argue its way by its own rules of validity to a firm prediction about any future event, and that "there is a step taken by the mind which is not supported by any argument or process of the understanding" (E. 41), Hume goes on, "If the mind be not engaged by argument to make this step it must be induced by some other principle of equal weight and authority" (E. 41). That principle is said a page later to be custom or habit, and it is important to note that it is said to have authority, not simply to have causal influence. This may seem a disappointing answer. Indeed, we might take this to be part of the debunking enterprise, and many do read Hume's "sceptical solution" as a merely ironic one, as the final turn of his undiminished skeptical doubts about causal inference itself rather than about the rationalists' versions of it. But I do not think that he means "authority" ironically in the passage I have just quoted. He does see the natural association of events that in the past have been experienced as constantly conjoined, as carrying epistemic authority. He argues in *Treatise* that *all* our thought moves, even the more refined and controlled of them, are "effects" of the gentle and sometimes not so gentle force of natural association working on our minds T. 13). Thus if anything is to have epistemic authority, if any step taken by the mind is to receive normative endorsement, it cannot fail to be some sort of instance of associative thinking. What gives it its authority will indeed be a special feature not found in any and every associative thought move. The rationalists, Hume believed, had misidentified that special feature. He is offering another way of understanding epistemic authority, one that allows us to give authority to some habits that are not habits of deductive argument and to establish them as rules (T. 268).

The "habit" of trying to reduce any thought move that we regard as careful and disciplined to what Hume calls a "demonstration" of reason is a habit that Hume is doing his best to get us (or at any rate his contemporaries) to break. He offers us, as alternatives to demonstration and the habits inculcated by "our scholastic headpieces and logicians" (T. 175), his version of inductive or experience-based "proofs," complete with eight rules for proving (Section XV of the *Treatise*, Book One, Part III), and a special sort of arithmetic for arriving at experientially based probability estimates for those cases when our experience has failed to yield constant conjunctions. These are experience-tested and experience-corrected customs. By the end of Part III of Book One, Hume is willing to call them "reason." It is, however, our human variant of "reason in animals," not some quasi-divine faculty; even the rationalists' preferred thought move, "demonstration," is treated as a human (language-mediated?) variant of rigid animal instinct. The deductive logicians' rules, and the habits they inculcate, are shown to have a narrowly restricted field of application and authority, mainly in pure mathematics, and even that authority is redescribed by Hume as a special case of the more comprehensive epistemic authority that he is suggesting that we should acknowledge. Even in our demonstrative thought moves, he claims, the necessity that we take to license and require the move to the conclusion is like causal necessity in belonging "entirely to the soul" (T. 166), a projection onto our subject matter of "the determination of the mind" (T. 166) in inference. So all inference, demonstration as well as causal inference, traces a relation whose necessity is "spread" by the mind from itself onto its subject matter. This is no retraction on Hume's part of his earlier claims that "knowledge" of a priori relations of ideas, arrived at by intuition or demonstration, is different from what we get by experience-tested "proofs." But deductive reason's authority, its ability to *require* us to reach a particular conclusion from given premises, is assimilated to that of experience-based proofs and probabilities.

What is it that Hume believes does give authority to some habits of thought and some social customs; what is it that converts them into normative rules? My answer to this question, elaborated elsewhere,[4] is "surviving the test of reflection," where reflection has its narrow as well as its wider meaning. Not merely must we be able to keep up the custom or habit in question after we have thought long and hard about its nature, its sources, its costs, and its consequences; we must also be able to turn the habit in question on itself and find that it can "bear its own survey" (T. 620). The most authoritative survey is that of the "whole mind" of which the operation being examined will usually be merely one among others. All the operations of "the understanding"—namely, memory, demonstration, causal inference, and the use of the "fictions" of the identity of physical and mental continuants (bodies only interruptedly observed; minds, in the first-person case, observed to show a more thoroughgoing "variation" than the concept of identity is deemed strictly to tolerate)— are eventually tested by Hume by a survey that it takes the passions, including society-dependent passions, to administer. Epistemology in the usual narrow sense (and metaphysics with it) becomes subject to the test of moral and cultural reflection. The questions become, "Would we perish and go to ruin if we broke this habit? Do we prefer people to have this habit of mind, and how important do we, on reflection, judge it that they have it?" What ultimately get delegitimatized are such modes of thought or extensions of some mode of thought beyond some limited domain, as are found "neither unavoidable to mankind, nor necessary, or as much as useful in the conduct of life" (T. 225). The approved habits are seen to be useful or agreeable, or both, either to their possessors, or to their fellows, or to both (Section IV of Part III of Book Three of the *Treatise*). They are habits that "bear their own survey," the survey of "the party of human-kind" who have such habits and who are concerned for the well-being of mankind.

I said that Hume shifts the source of epistemic authority from deductive reason, where the rationalists had divined it, to reflection. But of course the rationalists, and in particular G.W.F. Leibniz, had themselves given great importance to reflection in its strict sense, so it would be more accurate to say that Hume generalizes the reflective operation so that it becomes an open question whether reason is what is to be paired with reflection or whether other human psychic capacities have a better claim than deductive reason to being reflective faculties, ones capable of being turned on themselves without incoherence or self-condemnation. Both Locke and Leibniz had spoken in one breath of "reason and reflection" as what gives human persons their self-perceived special status. After Hume, the natural pairing becomes "passion and reflection," or "the moral sentiment and reflection." If Christine Korsgaard is right about Immanuel Kant,[5] he inherits a Humean pairing of morality with successful reflec-tion, albeit with a reversion to the rationalists' conviction that reason alone, not informed sentiment, is the source of our moral capacities, both of judgment and of living in accordance with our judgments.

Hume takes passions to be intrinsically reflective, cases of a "return upon the soul" of remembered experience of good and of evil, so that the fuller reflexivity of the moral sentiment is a development of a "return upon the soul" that every ordinary passion involves. Desire for a repetition of a past pleasure, for example, depends upon the revival in memory not merely of the thought "I enjoyed that," but of the "lively" wish for the pleasure's continuation, a wish often experienced simultaneously with the original pleasure. Desire the passion, as distinct from original instinctive appetite (which in any case soon gets mixed with and altered by the fruits of experience), is a memory-mediated will to repeat a familiar pleasure, a known good. Desires for repetition of pleasures are for minimally reflection-tested pleasures, ones whose goodness returns on the soul, ones not merely good at the time but good in retrospect, desire-generating at a later date. Ordinary experience-informed desire (the "direct" passion) is already an "impression of reflection," and its reflective success is developed and tested more stringently when it becomes the moral wish for the repetition of the special pleasure that one has got from contemplating, say, a good-humored character from a moral point of view. It becomes the wish that the character trait itself be not just an enduring one in this person but repeated in other persons, particularly in young persons whose characters are still malleable. So "reflection," that hitherto uncontested borrowing by the rationalists from the realm of sense, now gets reappropriated by an "empiricist."

To some extent it is John Locke who initiates this return of borrowed goods. Sense is reflective when "inner sense" reflects on sensation and on how we process our ideas of sense. "Ideas of reflection" are cases of sense returned on sense and on the operation whereby complex ideas of sense are constructed. Locke does not tell us enough about the "reflection" that he thinks is essential to moral responsibility and personhood, but it surely includes the primitive "return on the soul" that is involved in Humean-informed desire for repetition of familiar pleasures and includes some version of moral judgment. Locke officially takes this latter to be the ability to discern and apply a divine law, and there is no overtly reflective ingredient in his account of it.[6] He might have made recognition of divine law a reflexive turn of the human capacity for legislation, a legislation for legislators, a metalaw; but such proto-Kantian thoughts[7] are not, as far as I am aware, to be found in Locke's version of moral judgment. So although there is in Locke a doctrine of reflection that reappropriates the concept for psychic operations that are distinct from "reason," there is not a worked-out application of the concept to moral judgment. That was left for Hume (and even he leaves his readers quite a bit of the working out to do for themselves).

Now why would sensible people—in particular, sensible women—have any sympathy for this perennially popular view that authority, epistemic or moral, is ultimately a matter of having survived the challenge of reflective survey? Having become aware that Aristotle favored it ("thought thinking itself"), and that a motley crew of dead and living white males since him have also favored it, should we not just turn our backs rather than give it another hearing? I myself have raised the question[8] of whether it is not simply a fancy intellectualized version of narcissism, even in its empiricist naturalized version. I think this charge may be fair against reflection in its individualist variants (why should whatever I want to want, or love to love, be a "hypergood" rather than a particularly stubborn and self-reinforcing craving?). But when we ask "Why should we regard what we collectively, with as much information as we can get, prefer to prefer as our values?" a fair answer seems to be "What else could they be?" We have no resources other than our own evaluations and can do no more to revise lower-level evaluations than to repeat our evaluative operations at ever higher, more informed, and more reflective levels. So until a better account of values is offered, we may have no other choice than to discover our own values by collective reflection, starting from the base of our several (and collective) less-reflective desires, preferences, loves, and loyalties.

A view like Kant's makes a halfhearted gesture toward recognizing the relevance of the question "What do we will to will?" Kant's own preferred question is "What can I will that we all will?" But unless my metawilling is responsive to and corrected by what my fellows will to will, we will merely risk proliferating, at the metalevel, the discord and troublesome self-will that drove us in the first place to take a step away from the simple "What do I want?" No coordination is to be expected, except by good luck or preestablished harmony, if each buttoned-up Kantian works out his application of the categorical imperative on his own in his private study. And Kantians do disagree about the content of the moral law. As is pretty much granted, even by those sympathetic to Kant's moral philosophy, the Kantian tests underdetermine a moral guide capable of providing any sort of coordination between actual moral agents. Kant raises individualism to a higher level. It is high-minded individualism, but one that should be left with an unchanged guilty conscience about its failure to facilitate cooperation and coordination. Its ground for guilt remains the recalcitrant self-will that it was designed to moralize and transform. As long as the contrast between duties to self and duties to others is kept sharp—so that self-respect entails the goal of self-perfection, while respect for others is

paired with an obligatory regard for their happiness, not their perfection—then reasoning together can have none except formal common
goals. As long as the difference between autonomy and heteronomy,
between obeying "self alone" and obeying "others" (the same others
whose happiness is my duty?), is left unmediated by any recognition that
"I" of necessity include my reflective passions and a concern for others'
agreement with me, autonomy will be in danger of deteriorating into
pretend-sovereignty over compliant subjects. As long as the realm of ends
lacks any procedures for shared decision making, as long as it is a "Reich,"
not a cooperative, then the Kantian gestures toward the need to bring
some consideration of "all" into our moral and evaluative reflection and
decision making will remain token and incomplete. Reflection that starts
from guilty self-will seems, in Kant, to get us only as far as a higher version
of self-opinionated moralistic self-will.

But is not this Kantian case one that shows how undiscriminating the
test of reflection is? If the result that Kant endorses really is a product of
genuine reflection,[9] then must we not conclude that we get as many
different reflective "higher" values as we have differing lower level
psychologies first generating the salient maxims, that is, those that get
tested? Will not the guilt-haunted loner always get as his reflective
outcome autonomy and his right to his private space, along with his vague
dreams of an ideal realm of ends, preferably with himself playing the
role of Jean-Jacques Rousseau's "legislator" while his fellow ends-in-
themselves merely cast their privately arrived-at votes for or against
measures on an agenda that they have had no hand in setting? Will not
the sympathetic sociable Humean, naturally influenced by others' views
and preferences (but a little worried about the dangers of conformism and
vaguely aware of the need of gadflies), reliably get as her reflective
outcome not individual autonomy but rule by "the party of humankind,"
a party with vague plans to safeguard freedom of the press, to protect
peaceable dissenters, and to encourage a few cautious experiments in
thinking and living? Will not the puritan automatically reaffirm puritan
distastes and ambivalences, while the epicurean equally reliably gives
normative endorsement to the way of life of *l'homme moyen sensuel*? Must
we conclude: *Chacqun á son goûte réfléchi*?

Whether or not reliance on reflection will eliminate disagreements, it
surely does *not* give blanket endorsement to whatever is tested. The
Christian's humility, for example, can scarcely be thought to pass the test
of reflection, to be something that is a virtue because it can take itself as

its object. Incoherence does befall some attempts to turn an attitude of mind on itself, to make itself its own intentional object. The much-discussed problems that beset Kant's attempted demonstrations that some sort of contradiction results when a maxim such as, "If life becomes intolerable, arrange to end it," is tested by his version of reflection (if that is indeed what his tests amount to) concern the selection of the salient maxim, as well as the relationship between the universalization move and the reflexive turn. Such problems are real, on any version of "normativity as reflexivity." They are, however, more easily solvable on Hume's version of the authoritative reflection—namely, reflection by "the whole mind" rather than merely by a "sovereign reason" claiming to be its "highest" component.

Humean reflection is by the whole membership of the "party of humankind" listening to and influenced by each other's judgments. It is different from Kantian reflection by isolated individuals, let alone by ones who, in their moral judgments, follow Kant in endorsing a method of public decision making that gives no weight or very reduced weight to the opinions of the "weaker sex" and all the lower orders, such as servants and the unpropertied. (Hume, of course, is not too much better in his political endorsements. His ideal commonwealth, however, does not explicitly exclude women from voting or standing for office, and it has an income qualification for suffrage rather than a straight property qualification.[10]) "Am I willing for others to imitate my example?" is a relevant question if the goal is to detect exceptions that one might be tempted to make in one's own favor from some rule that one expects others to follow. It is less relevant for the attempt to find out what rule one *can* actually expect that others will follow and that they in turn can expect one to follow. To find that out, one must be willing to listen and discover what sort of example others are setting or prepared to set.

As I think is recognized in Hume's account of "convention" and in his characterization of the moral point of view as building on informed sympathy, there is no substitute for listening to others' views.[11] To get from "I will . . ." to "we will . . . ," or even to "I, as one of us, will . . . ," I must first listen to and understand the rest of us. Trying to imagine the other's viewpoint is no substitute for hearing it expressed, and even when all viewpoints are heard, there is still a difficult step to be taken before anyone is in a position to act or speak as "one of us." It is not so easy to act as a member of a realm of ends, especially when there is no agreement about the constitution of that realm. Simply to assume that what I can will others to do to me, they also can and do will me to do to them, without verifying that assumption case by case, is to arrogate to oneself the right to decide for others. It is to assume the pretensions of the patriarch. As, in Kant's version of an ideal commonwealth, women and servants have to rely on propertied men to look after their interests (indeed, to say what those interests are), so all Kantian persons, in their moral decision making, are licensed by Kant's tests to treat all others as virtual women[12] or virtual servants, as ones whose happiness is to be aimed at by other moral agents who are confident they know where that happiness lies. Moral decision making, for Kant, is responsible patriarchal decision making, made without any actual consultation even with the other would-be patriarchs.[13]

On the Humean alternative, norms—including norms for knowledge acquisition—are social in their genesis as well as in their intended scope. Mutual influence and mutual criticism as the background to self-critical independence of mind are fostered, not feared as threats to thinking for oneself. In his blueprint for an "ideal commonwealth,"[14] Hume includes elaborate procedures for debate at several levels and for the prolonged consideration of measures that, though failing initially to get a majority vote of elected representatives, had obtained substantial support. There are procedures for appeal and a special court composed of defeated candidates for senator who received more than one-third of the votes who may propose laws, inspect public accounts, and bring to the senate accusations against officials. The intricacy of the procedures for giving continued voice even to defeated candidates, the extensive provisions for debate at all levels, the division and balance of powers, are all constructive suggestions from Hume concerning how disagreeing individuals with some conflicting interests and some differences of perception of shared interests may still constitute a "realm." A realm must be constituted before its citizens can act as members of that realm. "The Idea of a Perfect Commonwealth" and other essays[15] give flesh to the rather skeletal account Hume had given in his moral philosophy proper (if that phrase is not out of place) of "the party of humankind" and how it might organize itself.

Hume's early formal account is, in several respects, more like that of Rousseau's version of the general will than is Kant's (which is more often said to show agreement with Rousseau). From the Humean moral point of view, one must have grounds to expect that other moral judges will concur with one's judgment, one must judge only on matters of general interpersonal concern (repeatable character traits, on Hume's version of this concern), and one must have freed one's mind as best one can of the canker of religious prejudice. It is not clear that Kant really recognizes any of these constraints (His religious toleration is, like Locke's, limited to other theists, if not just to other Christian sects.) He may think that because reason is supposed to be the same in everyone, we have a priori reason to expect that we will agree. But this a priori faith comes to grief in the plain facts of the disagreement of equally rational people, especially when each person's reasoning is not submitted to her fellow reasoners for criticism. Hume, unlike Rousseau and Kant, takes the grounds on which we expect others' agreement to be our *knowledge* of their views and our sympathy with their viewpoints. Mutual influence is seen as healthy and normal. "A good natur'd man finds himself in an instant of the same humour as his company" (T. 317), and some degree of good nature is a virtue.

It is not only mood and humor but also opinion that are contagious in our species. There are "men of the greatest judgment and understanding who find it very difficult to follow their own reason or inclination, in opposition to that of their friends and daily companions" (T. 316). This psychological fact about us does not make conformism a virtue, nor does it make independence of mind an impossibility. Hume himself clearly managed to follow his own reason and inclination in opposition to that of the majority of his Presbyterian friends and companions. Freedom of thought and speech is the value invoked in the quotation from Tacitus on the title page of the *Treatise*. But Hume also believed that every person needs the reaction of fellow persons in order to test and verify privately arrived-at judgments and verdicts. The difficulty of holding on to a view when one meets not merely some dissent but also contradiction "on all sides" (T. 264), even after one has made the case for one's views, is not merely psychological—it is epistemological. The chances that one is right and everyone else is wrong are about as great as that the one who testifies to having witnessed a miracle speaks the truth. Hume's epistemology, by the end of Book One of the *Treatise*, is like the moral epistemology he goes on to articulate, fallibilist and cooperative.

This social epistemology, launched by the end of the *Treatise*, is only slightly advanced in the *Enquiry Concerning Human Understanding*, despite the promising emphasis in its first section on the fact that "man is a sociable, no less than a reasonable being" (E. 8) and the hope expressed there that philosophy, "if carefully cultivated by several, must gradually diffuse itself throughout the whole society" (E. 10). Section X, "Of Miracles," does outline a collective procedure of evidence collection and of verification, both of laws of nature and of particular persons' or groups' reliability as witnesses. This fits with what the long footnote to Section IX, "Of the Reason of Animals," had recognized to be a source of superiority in reasoning—namely, "enlargement" of experience by information sharing (E. 107, note, point 9).

Because the *Enquiry Concerning Human Understanding* ends stuck in the book-burning mood that was merely a passing splenetic moment in the *Treatise* (T. 269), its presentation of Hume's "new turn" in philosophy is deliberately limited and partial. If it really is the case that our philosophical science should "be human, and such as has a direct reference to action and society" (E. 7), then any enquiry into the human understanding that is not part of an inquiry into human activity in society will necessarily be too "abstract." It is when Hume begins writing essays, intended for a fairly wide reading public, rather than writing inquiries, intended, perhaps (as M. A. Stewart has suggested is the case with the *Enquiry Concerning Human Understanding*) to get the author of a chair of philosophy in Edinburgh (a *very* ill-judged means, as it turned out, to what, with the wisdom of hindsight, we can say was an unwisely chosen end), that his social action–oriented epistemology gets its best expression.

In "The Rise and Progress of the Arts and Sciences," Hume attempts to "display his ingenuity in assigning causes," the causes for what, by his own account, it is very difficult to assign causes for—namely, the flourishing of learning in some societies but not others. His question is not, as in the *Enquiry Concerning Human Understanding*, "What is it for anyone to know anything?" but rather a development of the question of the footnote to Section IX of that work: "Why do some know more than others?" What is more, the question now becomes not one about differences between one truth-seeker and another, but one about differences between different human *populations* of truth-seekers. The theses that Hume defends, with some but not enough empirical supporting material, are that "the blessings of a free government" are needed if the arts and sciences are to arise; that commerce between neighboring independent states is favorable to the improvement of learning; that once the arts and sciences have advanced, they may be "transplanted" from free states into others; that republics are the best as "nurseries" of the sciences, whereas civilized monarchies are the best "nurseries" of the arts; that in states where learning has arisen and flourished, there is an eventual natural decline to be expected, so that, as the centuries pass, such learning tends to migrate from country to country.

This "natural history" of learning may strike us as underconfirmed by the historical evidence that Hume cites. His last thesis—that "the arts and sciences, like some plants, require fresh soil"—seems overinfluenced by his agricultural or horticultural metaphor of political societies as "nurseries" and "soils" for learning. But what is striking about the whole essay is the new turn given to epistemology. That any individual's or any group's chances of accumulating a store of truths depends, in the first instance, on the authority structure of the society in which such persons live was a fairly revolutionary bit of epistemology, one that anticipates later moves in this direction by Georg Hegel, Karl Marx, Michael Foucault, Robert Brandom,[16] and Lorraine Code[17] (to name a few probably inadvertent Hume followers). As Hume writes in "The Rise and Progress of the Arts and Sciences," "To expect, therefore, that the arts and sciences should take their first rise in a monarchy is to expect a contra-diction" (Es. 117). If a people are treated as slaves of their absolute ruler, "it is impossible they can ever aspire to any refinements of taste or reason" (Es. 117). "Here, then are the advantages of free states. Though a republic should be barbarous, it necessarily, by an infallible operation, gives rise to Law, even before mankind have made any considerable advance in the other sciences. From law arises security; from security curiosity; from curiosity knowledge" (Es. 118).[18] According to Hume's reformed active and social theory of knowledge, the first important human knowledge is that of jurisprudence.[19]

Hume takes the link between the structure of political authority and the prospects for epistemic progress seriously. "I have sometimes been inclined to think, that interruptions in the periods of learning, were they not attended with such a destruction of ancient books and records of history, would be rather favourable to the arts and sciences, by breaking the progress of authority, and dethroning the tyrannical usurpers over human reason. In this particular, they have the same influence, as interruptions in political governments and societies" (Es. 123).[20] This spirited defense of freedom of thought, these attacks on "blind deference," put even John Stuart Mill's On Liberty in the shade. Hume's linking of freedom, authority, and deference in thought with political freedom, authority, and deference is not just a speculative causal thesis; it is at the same time a transformation of the epistemological notions. The norms of thinking are no more clearly separable from the norms of human interaction than the "exchange" and "commerce" of ideas is a totally different sort of commerce from that to which Hume devotes a later essay, "Of Commerce." Mill's "marketplace of ideas" is a more competition-oriented successor to Hume's earlier discussion of intellectual exchange, including such exchange across national boundaries. If Hume gives us an early capitalist social epistemology, Mill gives a high capitalist version. The value of a theory such as Newton's, for example, is seen to be determined after "the severest scrutiny," a scrutiny made "not by his own countrymen, but by foreignors" (Es. 121). Emulation among scholars of different nations is a bit like international competition in free trade—it settles the value of any one person's or any one research team's "product." Critical scrutiny—both from competitors and from the "consumer" of the scholar's work—is, Hume argues, an essential accompaniment to freedom of thought in the rise and progress of the sciences.

In "Of Commerce" and "Of Refinement in the Arts," Hume cements the connections he had made between political, commercial, and industrial life on the one hand and intellectual life on the other. "The same age which produces great philosophers and politicians, renowned generals and poets, usually abounds with skilful weavers and ship-carpenters" (Es. 270). Hume is not saying that philosophy must guide the weavers' hands—the connection is, if anything, the opposite one: "Industry and refinement in the mechanical arts . . . commonly produce some refinements in the liberal" (Es. 270). Progress in these different aspects of a culture is mutually enhancing. The cooperation and coordination needed in the mechanical arts are also needed in the liberal arts. Their flourishing makes people more sociable, Hume argues. Once people are "enriched with science, and possessed of a fund of conversation," they will not be content to live in rural isolation; instead, they "flock into cities, love to receive and communicate knowledge, shew their wit or their breeding; their taste in conversation or living, in clothes or furniture" (Es. 271). Their tempers become refined, and they "must feel an increase of humanity, from the very habit of conversing together and contributing to each other's pleasure and entertainment. Thus, *industry, knowledge and humanity* are linked by an indissoluble chain" (Es. 271; emphasis on original).

I have quoted liberally from these essays, because I think that they develop and give detail to the *Treatise*'s and the *Enquiry*'s claim that "man is a sociable, no less than a reasonable being" (E. 8). They have been insufficiently appreciated by the readers of Hume's first, more "abstruse" works.[21] The *Enquiry Concerning the Principles of Morals*, in the fourth appendix ("Of Some Verbal Disputes"), followed the *Treatise* in assimilating "wisdom and knowledge" to the virtues. It also disputed whether there are any virtues that are not "*social* virtues" (E. 313). But it took the *Essays* (and the *History of England*) to enrich these social-cum-intellectual virtues into political, cultural, commercial, industrial, and cosmopolitan ones. Later essays such as "Of Money" give us yet more "thick" epistemology; in particular, they advance some interesting theses about the social need and point of representations and measures of value. Money is found to be "nothing but a representation of labour and commodities, and serves only as a method of rating and estimating them" (Es. 285). But the invention of money, like the invention of contract (secured exchange of future goods), can transform a society from an "uncultivated" one into a "cultivated" one. Hume's essays on economics are about cultural epistemology as well as about economics and add to what he had already done in that area in his earlier essays.

One last point needs to be added to complete my sketch of a case for seeing Hume as a "women's epistemologist." A fairly central part of Hume's characterization of the difference between a cultivated society, in which knowledge can advance, and a "barbaric" society, in which no such advance can be expected, concerns the position of women in such societies. Hume, from his experience of the contributions to culture and to conversation of the Scotswomen and the Frenchwomen he knew, offers his nonsolemn verdict that "mixt companies, without the fair sex, are the most insipid entertainment in the world, and destitute of gaiety and politeness, as much as of sense and reason. Nothing can keep them from excessive dulness but hard drinking."[22] Segregation of the sexes in social and work contexts is seen as a sign of a "rough" and "barbaric" society, whereas a social mixing of the sexes is a step toward civilization and the ending of tyranny. Hume sees all tyrannies as interconnected—the tyranny of husbands over wives, which is discussed in "Of Polygamy and Divorces," "Of Moral Prejudices," and "Of Marriage," is likened to the tyranny of absolute monarchs over subjects, which is discussed in his political essays. Neither of these tyrannies is independent of the threat of "tyrannical usurpers over human reason." Some of Hume's more apparently condescending remarks about woman's special role as a "polisher" and "refiner" of rougher and more "boisterous" male energies are distasteful to late-twentieth-century feminists. But we should not fail to appreciate the radically antipatriarchal stand that inspires them and that Hume takes throughout his philosophy. He clearly believes that men and women typically have *different* contributions to make to "industry, knowledge and humanity." What he calls the "Judgment of Females" (Es. 537) is valued as a needed corrective to that of males, as if the judgment of males is the natural place to start. But wherever we start, Hume's main message is that we all need to work together, to check each other's judgments and scrutinize each other's works, if barbarism is to be held at bay. We reflective women and men need, Hume argues, "a League, offensive and defensive, against our common Enemies, against the Enemies of Reason and Beauty, People of dull Heads and cold Hearts" (Es. 536). Such a league still has plenty of work to do.

One of the league's main tasks is to continue Hume's attempts to exhibit the links between dullness of head and coldness of heart and between "Reason and Beauty." I have followed the early Hume in using the word *reason* in a fairly narrow sense, thereby limiting its scope to what can be established by Cartesian (or Kantian) reason. Hume uses the word *reason* in shifting senses, and by the time he wrote his essays he was not willing to give the term to the rationalists; instead, he used it in a broad sense in which it no longer gets contrasted either with imagination or with passion, so it can be paired with a sense of beauty without strain. The human version of the "reason of animals," taken in Book One of the *Treatise* to include our deductive and inductive thought moves, gets further animated in Book Two when it becomes "the love of truth." In Book Three and in later writings, it comes to include also our capacity to coordinate our speaking and our actions with the speech and action of our fellows, to coordinate moral and aesthetic judgments as well as factual and mathematical ones. Hume in the end transforms the concept of reason.[23] From being a quasi-divine faculty and something that we share with God, it becomes a natural capacity and one that we essentially share with those who learn from experience in the way we do, sharing expressive body language, sharing or able to share a language, sharing or able to share our sentiments, sharing or able to share intellectual, moral and aesthetic standards, and sharing or aspiring to share in the setting of those standards.

Notes

1. See Lorraine Code, *Epistemic Responsibility* (Hanover: University Press of New England, 1987), and *What Can She Know? Feminist Theory and the Construction of Knowledge* (Ithaca: Cornell University Press, 1991).

2. David Hume, *A Treatise of Human Nature* (hereafter T.), ed. L. A. Selby-Bigge and P. H. Nidditch (Oxford: Clarendon Press, 1975); *Enquiry Concerning Human Understanding* (hereafter E.), ed. L. A. Selby-Bigge and P. H. Nidditch (Oxford: Clarendon Press, 1978); *Essays: Moral, Political, and Literary* (hereafter Es.), ed. Eugene F. Miller (Indianapolis: Liberty Classics, 1985). The page numbers given refer to these editions.

3. I have written about this in "Hume on Women's Complexion," *The Science of Man in the Scottish Enlightenment*, ed. Peter Jones (Edinburgh: Edinburgh University Press, 1990), and alluded to it in "Hume's Account of Social Artifices—Its Origins and Originality," *Ethics* 98 (July 1988): 757–78.

4. In Baier, *A Progress of Sentiments* (Cambridge: Harvard University Press, 1991), especially chaps. 4 and 12.

5. See Christine Korsgaard, "Normativity as Reflexivity." Talk given to the Sixteenth Hume Society Meeting, Lancaster, England, 1989.

6. See Ruth Mattern, "Moral Science and the Concept of Persons in Locke," *Philosophical Review* (January 1980): 24–25.

7. Or we could also say Aristotelian, or proto-Hegelian, or proto-Brandomian. See Robert Brandom's "Freedom and Constraint by Norms," *American Philosophical Quarterly* (April 1977): 187–96.

8. "Reply to Korsgaard," Sixteenth Hume Society Conference, Lancaster, 1989.

9. Suggesting this interpretation is the formulation of the Categorical Imperative given in the *Groundwork*: "Handle nach Maximen, die sich selbst zugleich as allgemeine Naturgesetze zum Gegenstande haben Können." Similar formulations in the second *Critique* also suggest this interpretation.

10. See "The Idea of a Perfect Commonwealth." Although a minimum income is the qualification for voting, only freeholders can stand for election.

11. See Code, *What Can She Know?* chap. 7, for a discussion of the need to listen to how aggrieved social groups actually present their situations in order to be capable of properly informed sympathy with them. There she takes issue with the belief, "that epistemologists need only to understand propositional observationally derived knowledge, and all the rest will follow" (269).

12. Calling someone a virtual woman will be an insult in the mouth of a patriarch, a compliment in more enlightened contexts.

13. I am consciously presenting an unsympathetic reading of Kant's views in the knowledge that other contributors to *A Mind of One's Own* will present more sympathetic readings and in the confidence that their views will balance mine, so that justice can be done.

14. Hume, "Idea of a Perfect Commonwealth."

15. See "Of the Rise and Progress of the Arts and Sciences," "Of Polygamy and Divorces," "Of Refinement in the Arts," "Of Some Remarkable Customs," "Of Moral Prejudices," and "Of Suicide."

16. Robert Brandom, unpublished manuscript, 1991.

17. Code, *Epistemic Responsibility* and *What Can She Know?*

18. The need for "security" before curiosity or the love of truth can flourish, and the need for a climate of trust to give modern scientists security, is explored by John Hartwig in "The Role of Trust in Knowledge," *Journal of Philosophy* 87 (December 1991): 693–708.

19. In his *History of England*, Hume develops this theme, especially when he describes the civilizing effect of the rediscovery, in 1130, of Justinian's *Pandects*. "It is easy to see what advantages Europe must have reaped by its inheritance at once from the antients so complete an art, which was itself so necessary to all other arts" (chap. 23).

20. This passage should give pause to those who want to dub Hume a conservative in politics.

21. A significant recent exception to this generalization is John W. Danford, *David Hume and the Problem of Reason* (New Haven: Yale University Press, 1990), esp. chap. 7. See also his essay "Hume's History and the Parameters of Economic Development," in *Liberty in Hume's History of England*, ed.

Nicholas Capaldi and Donald W. Livingston (Dordrecht/Boston/London: Kluwer Academic Publishers, 1990), 155–94.

22. Hume, *Essays*, 626. This passage, originally of "Of the Rise and Progress of the Arts and Sciences," was omitted from later editions.

23. I develop this claim in "A Progress of Sentiments, chap. 12.

This title is intended to make this paper a companion to my "Hume, the Women's Moral Theorist?" *Women and Moral Theory*, ed. Eva Feder Kittay and Diana T. Meyers (Totowa, N.J.: Rowman and Littlefield, 1987).

2

Hume on the Passion for Truth

Genevieve Lloyd

The Wholeness of the Mind

In her paper "Hume: The Reflective Women's Epistemologist?" Annette Baier has persuasively argued that Hume has contributed to the history of Western philosophy a transformation of reason that can be fruitfully appropriated to the concerns of contemporary feminist philosophy.[1] And in her earlier book, A Progress of the Sentiments, she has presented Hume as offering "an investigation of the whole mind by the whole mind."[2] In Hume's transformation of reason, she suggests, passions, imagination, and intellect converge in a new thought style—sociable rather than reclusive; self-reflective rather than abstract. In this essay I want to explore further Hume's version of the wholeness of the mind, with special reference to his treatment of the love of truth epitomized in philosophical thought.

The disinterested love of truth is, at first sight, an anomaly for Hume; for his version of reason lacks any inherent motivating force. For the rationalists of the previous century, reason had a driving force of its own that impelled it toward truth. For Descartes that force resided in a rational will, distinct from the understanding. For Spinoza it resided in the dynamic, conative nature of the understanding; in the lack of a separate faculty of will, he identified the mind's essence with its striving for ever more adequate ideas. For Hume in contrast reason is, notoriously, inert— "the slave of the passions."

The commitment to intellectual inquiry associated with seventeenth-century rationalism was strongly emotional. But the love of truth was not, for either Descartes or Spinoza, a passion. On Descartes's account, in *The Passions of the Soul*, there are intellectual joys produced in the soul by the soul itself, rather than through the movement of the bodily "animal spirits" that produce the passions, and these are superior to the passions that may superficially resemble them.[3] Descartes acknowledges that the passion of wonder may play a role in disposing us to seek scientific knowledge. But he advises us to free ourselves as much as possible from this passion, making good its absence through "that special state of reflection and attention which our will can always impose upon our understanding when we judge the matter before us to be worth serious consideration."[4]

It is important not to overstate the rationalists' distrust of the passions. In the concluding section of the *Passions of the Soul*, Descartes insists that a life devoid of passion would be an impoverished life. Although the soul can have "pleasures of its own" those common to soul and body depend entirely on the passions; and it is "those persons whom the passions can move most deeply" that are capable of enjoying "the sweetest pleasures of this life."[5] Although the ideal philosopher may devote his life to the pursuit of the rarified intellectual joys associated with mind alone, real philosophers spend the bulk of their lives in activities appropriate to unions of mind and body.[6] And Spinoza is even more insistent that the wise are enriched by sensuous pleasures—refreshed and restored "with pleasant food and drink, with scents, with the beauty of green plants, with decoration, music, sports, the theater," so that the capabilities of the whole body may find reflection in minds "capable of understanding many things."[7]

Baier rightly emphasizes the turn enacted in Hume's philosophy from "a one-sided reliance on intellect and its methods" to an attempt to use in philosophy "*all* the capacities of the human mind: memory, passion and sentiment as well as a chastened intellect."[8] But it is a turn that was made possible by pushing further elements that were ambivalently present in seventeenth-century rationalism. There is, nonetheless, something that is distinctive in Hume's version of the intellectual life; and it is precisely what makes it initially difficult for him to offer a coherent account of philosophical pursuits: they are now motivated entirely by passion. The challenge for Hume is to provide an analysis of the motivational structure of the search for truth that will give content to this motivating force of passion. In meeting that challenge he also offers a redefinition of the epitome of disinterested inquiry—the traditional figure of the philosopher.

There are in the Western philosophical tradition moments where intellect, imagination, and emotion cease to be polarized, coming into a unified structure. Plato's account in the *Phaedrus* of the soul's "growing wings" in response to beauty and Spinoza's imaginative fictions surrounding the ideal of the intellectual love of God are such moments. Hume's reconstruction of the love of truth as arising from passion is another. By reclaiming those moments, and trying to understand the structure of those unities, feminist philosophers can gain insight into the polarizations of the mind that prevail in our own contemporary ways of knowing and strengthen their insights into how these polarizations might change. In Hume's version of "wholeness" of mind, passions, imagination, and intellect enter a new unity; and the structure of that unity opens up new possibilities for rethinking the ideals of an intellectual life.

In this essay, then, I want to explore Hume's distinctive version of the wholeness of the mind and its implications for philosophical practice. My focus will be on the interconnections between intellect, emotion, and imagination, as they emerge in Hume's concluding sections to each of the three books of the *Treatise*; and on his treatment of some parallel themes in a cluster of essays in which he explores the varieties of intellectual character and the figure of the philosopher associated with them—essays titled "The Epicurean," "The Stoic," "The Platonist," and "The Sceptic." What makes Hume's transformation of reason in the *Treatise* so instructive is that he does not simply affirm an ideal of wholeness of mind. He shows how the integration of passions, imagination, and intellect is achieved in a unifying structure; and, in the essays, he enacts that unity for us in an intellectual practice that can provide a model for our contemporary efforts to "re-read the canon."

The ideal of a life nourished on the disinterested love of truth seems at first sight difficult to reconcile with Hume's transformation of the relations between reason and the passions. It is true that the traditional figure of the philosopher as a man in whom the power of reason prevails over that of the passions becomes for Hume an object of sardonic criticism. But with his integration of reason, imagination, and emotion, we get a new version of ancient ideals of the intellectual life as giving rise to a tranquillity centered on the love of wisdom. The relations between thought and the passions is a central theme throughout the *Treatise*, though one that can easily escape readers who take the main business of the work to have been completed at the end of Book I. The interconnections between the different books of the *Treatise* are particularly important in seeing the full import of Hume's reassessment of the love of truth. The concluding sections of each book focus on the integration between intellect, passion, and imagination. Together they yield a cumulative reflection on the ideal of an intellectual life—a succession of backward glances on the emerging naturalization of reason.

In the conclusion to Book I we see the motivating force of reason transformed into a mere "natural propensity" toward the pleasure of inquiry. But the contrasts between this "natural propensity" and the driving force that earlier philosophers had found within reason lack content until we are given, in the concluding sections of Book II, Hume's treatment of the love of truth as a passion. Here we are offered not only an account of the passion that motivates intellectual inquiry but also a subtle analysis of a unifying structure centered on Hume's description of "remote sympathy" as a passion that "goes no further than the imagination." Finally, in the concluding sections of Book III, Hume gives a fuller treatment of the crucial notion of sympathy on which that structure depends.

The Current of Nature

The conclusion to Book I of the *Treatise* is a richly metaphorical piece of writing. Metaphors of water play a crucial role: metaphors of oceans and shipwreck, of boundless immensities and forlorn, shore-bound rocks. The narrative persona is presented as in a "wretched condition,"[9] forced to choose between "perishing on the barren rock" or casting himself out on "the boundless ocean, which runs out into immensity." Solitariness and sociability are polarized in this imagery. The spatial contrast between the "barren rock" and the "boundless immensity" parallels an equally stark contrast between solitude and society. "Affrighted and confounded" in his forlorn solitude, in which he is placed by his philosophy, the narrator fancies himself at first "some strange uncouth monster," unable to "mingle and unite" in society, expelled from all human commerce, left utterly abandoned and disconsolate. Each side of the polarity is equally uncongenial. The desire to run into the crowd for shelter and warmth is balanced by a repellence to "mix with such deformity." Imagery of the storm brings together the two sets of oppositions: "I call upon others to join me, in order to make a company apart; but no-one will hearken to me. Every one keeps at a distance, and dreads that storm, which beats upon me from every side."

The narrator's predicament is partly the loss of the esteem of his intellectual peers. He is isolated from the sustaining comfort of intellectual sociability—"unsupported by the approbation of others." But there is a deeper dimension to this solitariness. Intellectual enquiry has entered a new and disturbing relationship with the goal of truth. The change arises from a problem that initially looks familiar: the criteria for truth. Can he be sure that, in leaving all established opinions, he is following truth? "[A]nd by what criteria shall I distinguish her, even if fortune shou'd at last guide me on her foot-steps?" The seventeenth-century rationalists had also addressed this issue. Descartes's response had been to insist on the will's inability to withhold assent in the presence of clear and distinct ideas. Spinoza's was to dismiss the problem by repudiating the distinction between will and understanding. Hume's response in contrast challenges a different gap—a gap, not between assent and understanding, but between truth and the propensity to assent. "After the most accurate and exact of my reasonings, I can give no reason why I shou'd assent to it; and feel nothing but a *strong* propensity to consider objects *strongly* in that view, under which they appear to me." The quality by which the mind "enlivens" some ideas beyond others has now nothing to do with reason. "The memory, senses, and understanding are, therefore, all of them founded on the imagination, or the vivacity of our ideas."

With this shift from reason to imagination, truth now seems to disappear into a mere "strong propensity" to assent; and assent itself seems to disappear into liveliness or vivacity. In aspiring to the knowledge of causes, the mind loops back on itself. The "connection, tie or energy" that the mind had sought outside itself is found to lie entirely within it. "Such a discovery not only cuts off all hope of ever attaining satisfaction, but even prevents our very wishes, since it appears, that when we say we desire to know the ultimate and operating principle, as something, which resides in the external object, we either contradict ourselves, or talk without a meaning." The challenge of distinguishing the true from the false becomes just the task of distinguishing "trivial suggestions" of the fancy from its "general and more establish'd properties."

Hume's narrator, famously, escapes from doubts about the viability of intellectual pursuits only because nature comes to the rescue. The recognition that our "strong propensities" are all we have, which initially seems to deprive us of even a coherent desire for knowledge, delivers the mind from its isolation. We trust those of our intellectual imaginings that are "easy and natural" and enter only with difficulty into those views of things that are more "remote." Hume's discussion here echoes themes from ancient Stoic thought, which had also been reworked by Descartes and Spinoza—themes of "cognitive impressions"; of "vividness"; of the conditions under which the mind should assent to "appearances." In these modern reworkings of old themes the concerns of late antiquity with how the mind can best attain tranquillity are interwoven with epistemological concerns. In Hume's version the stress is on the shift from reason to nature. What follows from the recognition that knowledge is the work of imagination rather than reason is not a "general maxim" that we *should* spurn all "refin'd or elaborate reasoning"—thus depriving us of all science and philosophy. The outcome is not a rationally founded principle but an acknowledgment of a natural process. We must "yield to the current of nature," in submitting to our senses and understanding; but it does not follow that we must strive against that current when it pulls us toward speculative thought. This is Hume's famous "careless philosophy." "Where reason is lively, and mixes itself with some propensity, it ought to be assented to. Where it does not, it never can have any title to operate upon us." The ideal of truth as an external goal of thought gives way to acquiescence in what is "satisfactory to the human mind."

Corresponding to this dissolution of the issue of the criteria of truth—the collapse of reason into nature—there is a transformation of attitude to the intellectual practices of truth-seeking. Never to be a "loser in point of pleasure" becomes the "origin" of Hume's philosophy; he will "no more be led a wandering into such dreary solitudes, and rough passages." The narrator loses the desire for truth under the pressure of the thought that there is nothing outside himself to be pursued. If truth is nothing more than a natural propensity to believe—a vividness of presence—the desire for intellectual pursuits evaporates. The desire for truth is initially thwarted by the turn to the self. But on reflection these natural propensities are seen to restore to us in a new form what we have lost. In giving up the boundless ocean of speculation, we are not left to perish on a rock barren of intellectual life. The mind now flows gently with the current.

The details of Hume's "careless philosophy" have been fully discussed in Annette Baier's *Progress of the Sentiments*.[10] What I want to stress here is that, although we are given in these concluding sections of Book I an account of the mind's "natural propensities" to intellectual inquiry as arising from imagination, we have not yet been given a full account of how these propensities operate. Hume has taken away the driving force that the rationalists attributed to reason and replaced it with a natural propensity to inquiry. Truth has of itself no magnetism to draw the mind to its pursuit. What had been reason's desire for an external truth is now absorbed into a propensity natural to mind itself. Despite the richness of the metaphors, that move may well seem an empty formal maneuver. The natural propensity seems to feed on itself; what sustains it remains mysterious. In the lack of some fuller account it may appear that Hume has simply found a new label for the motivating force that used to inhere in rationalist reason. What is missing from Hume's account awaits his treatment of the passions in Book II.

The Intellectual Hunt

It is the coming together of passion and imagination that provides the missing content of Hume's new naturalized version of intellectual life. He elaborates it in the chapter that parallels, in the structure of the whole work, the place of the one just discussed: the chapter on "curiosity or the love of truth" that concludes Book II.[11] Here Hume offers a subtle and ironic treatment of that "curious affection" that has been the source of all his inquiries.

Truth, Hume observes, is of two kinds—"the discovery of the proportions of ideas, consider'd as such" and "the conformity of our ideas of objects to their real existence." In neither case can the consideration of truth of itself explain our desire for it or our pleasure in it. The affection must be explained by other considerations. Hume's initial explanation is in terms of the process, the movement of the mind involved in truth-seeking—the "genius and capacity," employed in its invention and discovery.

Hume's juxtaposition of invention and discovery emphasizes the active, creative aspect of truth-seeking. It is the exercise of the mind that renders the search pleasant and agreeable. To be "merely informed" of truth yields "small entertainment." But this exercise of the mind demands that its attention be first fixed; and this in turn demands that the truth we discover must be of some importance. What follows is a shrewdly ironic analysis of the motivational structure of philosophical inquiry. Philosophers—whose behavior in general shows no "public spirit" or "concern for the interests of mankind"—have nonetheless "consum'd their time," "destroy'd their health," and "neglected their fortune" in the search of such truths as they "esteem'd important and useful to the world." Hume's analysis, despite the gentle irony of the illustration, is profound. The solution to the puzzle, he suggests, is to be found in the recognition of certain desires and inclinations that "go no farther than the imagination," and are rather the "faint shadows and images of passions, than any real affection."

Hume's explanation of the love of truth stresses the nexus between emotion and imagination; and here the passion of sympathy is crucial. These desires that "go no farther than the imagination"—the "faint shadows and images of the passions"—are instances of what Hume calls "remote sympathy." He illustrates the concept through an example in which imagination and emotion draw together. Think, he invites us, of the pleasure a man may take in the strengths and advantages of the fortifications of a city, for whose inhabitants he may have only indifference or even hatred. Such pleasure involves a "sympathy" with the inhabitants. To experience such pleasures we must be capable of an emotional identification with the recipients of the benefits of the design. But this sympathy does not take the form of love or even concern for them. The emotional identification involves also an exercise of imagination. We imagine ourselves in the position of others. But such imaginative shifts of perspective yield no pleasure unless we also empathize with their needs and concerns. Once the imaginative shift is withdrawn, the sympathy also will recede; for it rests on no bonds of community that preexist the assumed perspective. Nor is there any basis for continuing the emotional identification beyond the evaluation of the object that it makes possible.

The philosopher's appearance of "concern with the needs of human-kind"—to which he is in fact indifferent—is likewise, Hume suggests, a "remote sympathy." Just as the identification with the inhabitants allows the evaluation of the fortifications to proceed, so too the philosopher's imaginative identification with the needs of other human beings allows his attention to be fixed in the way requisite to allow the exercise of genius. This movement of mind is the true source of the philosopher's pleasure. The supposed social importance of the outcome serves only to get the mind into motion. But the momentum of the activity now extends the pleasure from the process to the outcome. "[B]y the natural course of the affections, we acquire a concern for the end itself, and are uneasy under any disappointment we meet with in the pursuit of it."

The analysis is reinforced through Hume's famous comparison of the pleasures of philosophy to those of hunting and gaming. The pleasure of hunting, he says, consists in the action of mind and body: "the motion, the attention, the difficulty, and the uncertainty." But to have any effect upon us these actions must be "attended with an idea of utility." A man may take pleasure in hunting partridges and pheasants, yet feel no satisfaction in shooting "useless" crows and magpies. "Here 'tis certain that the utility or importance of itself causes no real passion, but is only requisite to support the imagination." The same person may be uninterested in gaining greater profit in other ways, yet be "pleas'd to bring home half a dozen woodcocks or plovers, after having employ'd several hours in hunting after them." "To make the parallel betwixt hunting and philosophy more compleat, we may observe, that tho' in both cases the end of our action may in itself be despis'd, yet in the heat of the action we acquire such an attention to this end, that we are very uneasy under any disappointment, and are sorry when we either miss our game, or fall into any error in our reasoning."

Hume makes similar points about the passion for gaming. It affords, he says, a pleasure from the same principles as hunting and philosophy—a pleasure that does not arise from "interest" alone. For the same persons have no satisfaction when they play for nothing. "'Tis here, as in certain chymical preparations, where the mixture of two clear and transparent liquids, produces a third, which is opaque and colour'd."

Hume's analysis of the operations of the love of truth is meant to apply regardless of the subject matter of inquiry—to the study of mathematics, of morals and politics, as well as of philosophy. The point is not that some inquiries are such that we can only engage in them with the assistance of "remote sympathy," whereas others are intrinsically useful and hence need no such external stimulus to get the mind into motion. It is rather that the love of truth always derives from the movement of the mind, even where we feel obliged to recast the pleasure as deriving directly from the useful outcome of that movement. The love of truth is basically pleasure in a process—not satisfaction in the outcome—although, under the influence of the mind's activity, that pleasure may be extended to the product.

Hume has offered in these sections an analysis of the motivational structure of the intellectual life as a complex convergence of passion, reason, and imagination At the core of this structure is the mind's sheer delight in its own activity. But this intellectual joy cannot be explained by reference to reason alone. The point becomes clearer in Hume's consideration of a kind of curiosity that may at first sight appear to be a counterexample to his analysis, but that in fact serves to reinforce its general applicability. This is the more mundane curiosity instantiated by the "insatiable desire" some people have for knowing about their neighbors, although they are in no way "interested" in them. Here we rely on the testimony of others for our information, rather than on any exercise of the mind in "study or application" It may seem that such information-seeking does not involve the movement of mind that is at the core of intellectual inquiry. But on Hume's analysis this form of curiosity rests on a different aspect of the idea of mental movement: the inherent tendency of a motion already under way to continue of its own momentum unless something interferes with it. The mind, like physical objects in motion, tends to persist in what is familiar. "'Tis a quality of human nature, which is conspicuous on many occasions, and is common both to the mind and body, that too sudden and violent a change is unpleasant to us, and that however any objects may in themselves be indifferent, yet their alteration gives uneasiness." Even where we lack any genuine interest to know, an idea may have such force as to give us "an uneasiness in its instability and inconstancy." Familiarity can play a role similar to that provided by "remote sympathy."

Imagination, and the passions that "go no further" than it, are not needed where the closeness of the object suffices to fix our attention. So a stranger who at first lacks any interest in the history and adventures of his new neighbors comes, with the growth of familiarity over time, to acquire the same curiosity about them as the natives. Indeed there is, as

Hume goes on to show, an analogue of this role of familiarity in intellectual inquiry itself. The mind, once it is in motion, is uneasy in the face of any threatened disruption of that motion. Where the mind's attention is already fixed, its activity will proceed without the need for remote sympathy. Once the mind is engaged—when we are reading, say, the history of a nation—we may have an ardent desire for clarity about details, which recedes when the ideas of these events weaken. It is, again, the pleasures of intellectual activity itself that are central. That activity may be set going either by familiarity, or by the operations of remote sympathy; but once it is in process it proceeds under its own momentum.

The Fullness of Sympathy

The concluding section of Book III brings to a finale the treatment of the intellectual life we have tracked through the *Treatise*.[12] It is no surprise that Hume here returns to the topic of sympathy—now filled out with the intervening consideration of sociability and of morals. Sympathy, he now suggests, is the chief source of moral distinctions—a "very powerful principle in human nature," influencing our sense of beauty and our judgments of morals. Sympathy is involved in our approval of justice, which rests on a tendency toward a public good that is indifferent to us "except so far as sympathy interests us in it."

Sympathy and sociability come together in this final conclusion. The approval that others can bestow on us feeds our pleasures, including our pleasure in intellectual pursuits. The approbation of others now makes the final link between the solitary abstract speculations on human nature, whose coldness had originally dispirited him, and Hume's version of sociable reason. The pursuit of knowledge is now confidently presented as a source of "a new lustre in the eyes of mankind." The narrator has come full circle from the aridity, isolation, and self-doubt of the conclusion to Book I. Abstract speculations concerning human nature now emerge as subservient to "practical morality" through their integration into social life and their ready submission to the approbation of others. The inquiring mind is at last a "whole" mind—a mind able to "bear its own survey."

Hume, as Baier stresses in her fine discussion of the transformation, in her *The Progress of the Sentiments*, has enlarged the conception of reason, making it sociable and passionate. And sympathy is once again crucial to the outcome. We have moved from a remote sympathy—which depends on, and goes no further than, the imagination—to a more robust, fully socialized form of sympathy. This newly integrated version of reason is meant to apply, as we have seen, to all forms of intellectual inquiry. But its contrasts with the more rationalist versions of reason emerge most clearly in relation to philosophical enquiry. In the remainder of this essay, I want to explore the implications of Hume's transformation of reason for philosophical practice.

Reading with Hume

We have now seen the distinctive structure of Hume's version of the love of truth: a subtle integration of intellect, passion, and imagination. What can we do with it? I want to suggest that Hume himself has shown how his reconstruction of reason can be put to work in an intellectual practice that draws on the resources of the whole mind. Hume's own intellectual practice is informed by the ideal of philosophy he articulates in the *Treatise*. We can see it at work in his essays "The Epicurean," "The Stoic," "The Platonist," and "The Sceptic," where he enters imaginatively into a variety of intellectual styles and character.[13]

There are common themes in these essays, revisited from different perspectives: the relations between art and nature; the role of the passions in human life; the limitations of the philosophers' version of reason; the sociability of virtue; death and immortality; human vulnerability to fortune; the multiplicity—and the unity—of human nature. In a footnote to the first essay, on the Epicurean, Hume explains that his intention in the essays is not so much to explain accurately the sentiments of ancient philosophical sects, but rather to identify the sentiments of "sects that naturally form themselves in the world" entertaining different ideas of human life and happiness; to each such group he will give the name of the philosophical sect to which it bears the greatest affinity.

Hume thus brings his reading of the ancient philosophers to bear on an engaged analysis of the varieties of intellectual character to be found in his own cultural environment. Each essay is written from the perspective of one such intellectual character; but there is in each an internal dialogue between different personae. Hume enters into the spirit of each style of thought, adapting his writing style to capture its emotional resonances.

The "Epicurean"

The voice of Hume's Epicurean is initially detached and judicious. But the style becomes steadily more lyrical, taking on something of the "native enthusiasm" it attributes to the poets. The writing is richly metaphorical. Art, we are told, is the "underworkman" to nature. "Art may make a suit of clothes, but nature must produce a man." From the Epicurean perspective it is the "severe philosophers" that represent the most extreme departure from nature—the most ridiculous of the "fruitless attempts of art." The philosophers seek to produce an "artificial happiness," in a futile attempt to make us be pleased by rules of reason and by reflection. "You pretend to make me happy, by reason and by rules of art. You must then create me anew by rules of art, for on my original frame and structure does my happiness depend." Happiness implies ease, contentment, repose, and pleasure, not the watchfulness, care, and fatigue associated with philosophy. The "frivolous discourse" of the "proud and ignorant sages" is set against a poetic style that emphasizes the ease and repose of nature. The essay itself takes on the language of the poets, enacting the transition from "rules" to "inspiration."

The second half of the essay is given over to a lyrical evocation of the god Pleasure. The critique is directed at the Stoic, whose voice will be heard in Hume's following essay. But there is already an accommodation between the different voices. Even for the Epicurean, pleasure is suspect in the absence of reflection. Pleasure's "bed of roses" does not offer a stable joy. The roses lose their hue; the fruit its flavor; the palate becomes sated with wine. Pleasure beckons virtue to her assistance. But this is virtue from the Epicurean perspective—sociable and convivial: "the gay, the frolic virtue," bringing troops of jovial friends to renew the feast. Philosophical ideals themselves undergo a transformation in this new virtue. "In our cheerful discourses, better than in the formal reasoning of the schools, is true wisdom to be found." Wisdom points out the road to pleasure; and nature beckons to the same "smooth and flowery path." Adapting Epicurus's own repudiation of the fear of death, Hume's Epicurean insists that "frail mortality" need not dampen our gayest hours. The very fragility of life should be an impetus to the enjoyment of the present rather than a denial of pleasure.

The "Stoic"

Hume's Stoic holds views of art and nature not fundamentally different in content from that of the Epicurean. But the style and emotional tenor are different. Both reach an accommodation of reason and nature. But the Stoic's starting point is the "sublime celestial spirit" of reason rather than the ease and repose of nature. The metaphors have a different mood and tone. For the Stoic, nature provides the "rude and unfinished" materials for the refinement of "active and intelligent industry." Reason raises us above the "brute state" of nature. Where the Epicurean invokes pleasure as the end of human activity, the Stoic invokes a noble happiness; where the Epicurean emphasizes "native enthusiasms," the Stoic emphasizes industry and application. But both insist that reason cannot flourish at the expense of nature.

The style of Hume's evocation, in the second essay, of the joys of active engagement are more restrained than the studied lushness of the previous essay; but they are no less poetic. The imagery for the mind's industrious activity draws on the same sources as the metaphors we have seen in the *Treatise*: the movement and activity of the hunt. Scorning the softer pleasures of the "bed of roses," the "hardy hunters" rise early from their "downy couches" and hasten to the forest, leaving behind "delicious fare," which they might get without effort, to seek more challenging prey. But it is the conjunction of motion and rest—of industry and pleasure—that is crucial to the joys of the hunter. "Having exerted in the chase every passion of the mind, and every member of his body, he then finds the charms of repose, and with joy compares his pleasures to those of his engaging labours." Just as "vigorous industry" gives pleasure to the pursuit even of the most worthless prey, it can render agreeable the cultivation of our minds, the moderating of our passions, the enlightening of our reason. The moral message is fundamentally the same as in the first essay: there is no happy repose to be found in beds of roses. Without exercise of the mind, pleasures become insipid and loathsome. Virtue, again, must draw its energy from sociability; the "social passions" purify and stabilize our joys.

The figure of the philosopher is once again an object of derision. But Hume's Stoic derides the philosopher not for his industry, but for his "philosophic indifference"; for his disdain of natural sociability—perched on a rock, breathing the serene air above human malice and fury. The Stoic has a different basis also for his acceptance of mortality. For Hume's Epicurean—true to the spirit of his ancient model—the thought of death is not a source of fear. The inevitability of death does not intrude on present pleasure; indeed it intensifies it. "[If] life be frail, if youth be transitory, we should well employ the present moment, and lose no part of so perishable an existence." Philosophical reflection releases us to "love and jollity." The Stoic's release from the fear of death comes in contrast from the consideration that death's dominion extends over only a part of him—that "in spite of death and time, the rage of the elements, and the endless vicissitude of human affairs, he is assured of an immortal fame among all the sons of men."

Both Epicurean and Stoic exemplify a unity of emotion and intellect. But the Epicurean attains to that unity by transforming feeling into thought. The transition is from self-indulgent, unreflective pleasure—through the experience of languor and insipidity—into socialized passion, transformed through reflection. For the Stoic the transition is from the other direction—from the lofty, arrogant heights of solitary reason into a resoluteness and steadfastness tempered by social passion.

The "Platonist"

The intellectual character of Hume's Stoic is oriented to the approbation of others—to the desire for "immortal fame." In his version of the Platonist—"the man of contemplation and philosophical devotion"— that figure of the philosopher is in turn subjected to ridicule for his self-centered concern with the recognition of his own virtue. "O philosopher! thy wisdom is vain, and thy virtue unprofitable. Thou seekest the ignorant applause of men, not the solid approbation of that Being, who, with one regard of his all-seeing eye, penetrates the universe." The voice of the narrator now confronts the pompous philosopher with a different ideal—of a perfection that proceeds from "the most perfect thought." In the Platonic articulation of the recurring theme of the relations between art and nature, the emphasis is now on the inwardness of thought. "Art copies only the outside of nature, leaving the inward and more admirable springs and principles as exceeding her imitation, as beyond her comprehension."

Beauty and virtue remain the source of the mind's greatest happiness. But this happiness now derives from having them as the most perfect objects of contemplation. The theme of mortality too takes on a new twist: the shortness of our lives—along with the narrowness of our faculties—limits the possibilities for contemplation. But if we employ those faculties worthily they will be "enlarged in another state of existence," rendering us "more suitable worshippers of our maker"—a task that can never be finished in time but will be "the business of eternity."

The "Skeptic"

Finally Hume turns to the intellectual character and style of the Skeptic. The style and emotional tenor of this persona approach more closely what we may expect of Hume himself. The stance of his Skeptic echoes his treatment in the *Treatise* of reason and nature, of the love of truth, and of the character of the philosopher. The philosopher's "infirmity," we are told in the opening sections, is an excessive concern with principles—the tendency to extend them beyond appropriate limits of application, "as if nature were as much bound in her operations as we are in our speculation." This tendency to generalization is especially evident in philosophical reflections on life and happiness. The philosopher makes over the whole of humanity in terms of his own governing passions. His own pursuits are always, in his account, the most engaging, the objects of his passion the most valuable, and the road that he pursues the only one that leads to happiness.

From the perspective of the Skeptic, the different styles of life and of character are not to be categorically preferred. Different kinds of life are agreeable in their turn and their "judicious mixture" contributes to rendering of all of them agreeable. The Skeptic's concern is with the passions from which conduct arises. What makes for difference in the quality of lives is just difference in the steadiness or constancy of the enjoyment of the objects of passion. "All the difference, therefore, between one man and another, with regard to life, consists either in the *passion* or in the *enjoyment*: and these differences are sufficient to produce the wide extremes of happiness and misery."

Within this framework, the "philosophical devotion" that was, for the Platonist, the key to the good life, becomes no more stable an object of enjoyment than the enthusiasm of the poet that was central for the Epicurean. Philosophical devotion is the "transitory effect of high spirits, great leisure, and a habit of study and contemplation." Its concern with abstract objects cannot long "actuate the mind." If philosophical devotion is to endure, it must find some way of engaging senses and imagination.

Returning to the now familiar illustration of hunting and gaming, Hume, in the persona of the Skeptic, comments that "the amusements that are most durable, have all a mixture of application and attention in them, such as gaming and hunting; and in general, business and action fill up all the great vacancies in human life." Industry is endorsed, as in the Stoic's version of the best life. But there is no longer a preference for one style of life over another. The focus shifts to the way in which the life is pursued; and there is no special privileging of the philosophical pursuits. The life of the philosopher, whatever form he chooses it to take, remains at the mercy of the "prodigious influence" that nature has even upon the "wise and thoughtful." The "empire of philosophy" extends over few; and even with regard to these her authority is weak and limited. "In a word, human life is more governed by fortune than by reason."

The Skeptic gives his own twist to the recurring theme of mortality: "While we are reasoning concerning life, life is gone; and death, though perhaps they receive him differently, yet treats alike the fool and the philosopher." And the "Skeptic has the final word on the theme of the relations between art and nature. It echoes both in its content, and in its irony, the counterpointed tensions of Hume's treatment of the philosophical life in the *Treatise*: "To reduce life to exact rule and method is commonly a painful, oft a fruitless occupation: and is it not also a proof. that we overvalue the prize for which we contend? Even to reason so carefully concerning it, and to fix with accuracy its just idea, would be overvaluing it, were it not that, to some tempers, this occupation is one of the most amusing in which life could possibly be employed." Hume's Skeptic, like the "careless philosopher" of the *Treatise*, refuses to be "the loser in point of pleasure" by refraining from intellectual activity. But in the version in the essay, the skeptical ideal is extended to encompass a general stance toward life—an ideal that resonates with themes from the ancient sources out of which Hume has constructed his four personae. Shall we, the Skeptic asks, engage in life with passion and anxiety? "It is not worthy of so much concern. Shall we be indifferent about what happens? We lose all the pleasure of the game by our phlegm and carelessness."

The succession of figures of the philosopher that Hume has constructed in this cluster of essays do not take the stage as independent personae, each with an individual independent voice. Each is constructed out of the dialectic that brings them all together. Hume plays them off against one another, allowing the ideals of each to be reformulated by the others. But what finally emerges out of the dialectic is the version of the philosopher that best fits his own intellectual style and temper. By reading ancient sources imaginatively and sympathetically—and by engaging equally imaginatively and sympathetically with the intellectual characters of his own time—Hume has imbued each persona with his own spirit. The essays offer us a distinctively Humean Epicurean, Stoic, and Platonist. But the final words—which resist the idea that anything can really be the final word—are left to the Humean Skeptic.

The Humean "Feminist Philosopher"?

I have tried to show how sympathy and imagination are at stake in Hume's own writing practice, and in his reconstructions of ancient philosophical ideals—how his analysis of the love of truth, and of the nature of philosophical enquiry, informs his own intellectual practice. What we can now learn from Hume is not just a range of interesting theses about reason, emotion, and imagination. We can also look to him as a source of insight into how unities of intellect, imagination, and emotion can be integrated into philosophical practice.

Annette Baier has suggested that Hume can be seen as "the reflective woman's epistemologist" and—in his response to the status of outsider, in relation to his own cultural and intellectual context—perhaps even as "an unwitting, virtual woman."[14] Doubtless her suggestion is to be taken as itself an exercise in irony, in the spirit of Hume. But there is nonetheless a serious point at stake: the exercise of re-reading the canon from a feminist perspective does not have to involve a stance of repudiation or castigation There can also be positive appropriations and sympathetic accommodations.

Contemporary feminist philosophy has much to gain from treating Hume as a source of positive insights into the intellectual styles and practices that prevail in our own cultural context. His philosophy can point the way to ideals of intellectual character that are more hospitable to female presence than those associated with stark oppositions between reason, imagination, and emotion; between nature and art, including philosophy. However, rather than casting Hume—even ironically—as an honorary woman, I prefer to find in him a mind well aware of its own maleness, as part of a more general awareness of the contingencies and restraints of the position from which he spoke and wrote—a perspective from which he engages generously with what is different from himself.

The Humean "careless philosopher" delights in his capacity to en-gage—from a fullness of imagination and sympathy, which Hume himself refined—with what, in his own cultural context could be characterized as the preserve of women. Hume engages with the feminine and finds himself changed by that engagement, taking it up into a transformed version of reason. The capacity for such shifts and accommodations of intellectual perspectives and personae is the very core of Hume's essay writing. In his essay "Of Essay Writing,"[15] he identifies women with the "conversable world" that he has assimilated into his transformed version of reason—the world of reflective sociability; and he identifies himself, as essay writer, as "a kind of resident or ambassador" to that "conversable world." The symbolism of the feminine shifts, along with the understand-ing of reason, to which the feminine had traditionally been opposed. The identification is of course ironic; the whole essay is an exercise in the "gallantry and devotion" that its concluding sections gently mock. But the irony does not undermine the real accommodation that is enacted here. In transforming his ideals and intellectual practices in the direction of imaginative, emotionally rich sensibility, Hume is taking on what he understands as feminine, accommodating it into his own intellectual character and conceptually enriching it by thinking it through with an informed philosophical intelligence.

I have tried to show how Hume's re-reading of ancient philosophical sources—his own re-reading of his canon—transforms old ideals by his thinking them through in his own context and accommodating them to his own intellectual aspirations. Hume challenges those ancient ideals, transforming them through a fullness of engagement that draws on the resources of "the whole mind."

Feminist philosophers have much to learn from the intellectual practice defended in the *Treatise* and enacted in the essays. Hume re-read his canon in ways that allowed him to recast the intellectual ideals and practices of his own time—including a recasting of the figure of the philosopher. Hume in effect shows us how we might now re-read Hume, along with the rest of our canon. We can read him in the spirit of intellectual generosity and tough-minded, good-humored irony that was his own contribution to the formation of intellectual style and character—appropriating and accommodating his philosophy to the challenges of our own cultural context. Reading in the spirit of Hume can allow feminists to reinsert themselves into the philosophical tradition, rather than bemoaning its limitations from the margins. In our attempts to articulate a viable ideal of a wholeness of mind, beyond the old polarities of reason and its opposites, we can learn much from the irony, the wit, and the wisdom of David Hume.

Notes

1. Annette Baier, "Hume: The Reflective Women's Epistemologist?" in Louise Antony and Charlotte Witt, eds., *A Mind of One's Own: Feminist Essays on Reason and Objectivity* (Boulder: Westview, 1993), 35–48.
2. Annette C. Baier, *A Progress of the Sentiments: Reflections on Hume's "Treatise"* (Cambridge: Harvard University Press, 1994), 2.
3. René Descartes, "The Passions of the Soul," in *The Philosophical Writings of Descartes*, vol. 1, ed. John Cottingham, Robert Stoothoff, and Dugald Murdoch, Pt. II, Sec. 147 (Cambridge: Cambridge University Press, 1984), 381.
4. Descartes, "Passions of the Soul," Pt. II, Sec. 76, 355.
5. Descartes, "Passions of the Soul," Pt. III, Sec. 212, 404.
6. See Descartes's letter to Princess Elizabeth, 28 June 1643, in *The Philosophical Writings of Descartes*, ed. John Cottingham, Robert Stoothoff, Dugald Murdoch, and Anthony Kenny, vol. 3 (Cambridge: Cambridge University Press, 1991), 226–29.
7. Benedict de Spinoza, *Ethics*, Pt. IV, Scholium to Proposition 45, in *The Collected Works of Spinoza*, ed. Edwin Curley (Princeton: Princeton University Press, 1985), 572.
8. Baier, *Progress of the Sentiments*, 1.
9. Quotations are from Hume's *Treatise of Human Nature* [1739], ed. L. A. Selby-Bigge (Oxford: Oxford University Press, 1960), Bk. I, Pt. IV, Sec. VII, 264–74.
10. See especially chaps. 1 and 12.
11. Quotations in this section are from Hume's *Treatise*, Bk. II, Pt. III, Sec. X, 448–54.

12. Quotations in this section are from Hume's *Treatise*, Bk. III, Pt. III, Sec. VI, 618–21.

13. Quotations in the next four sections are from Hume's *Essays, Moral, Political, and Literary* [1748] (Oxford: Oxford University Press, 1963).

14. Baier, "Hume: The Reflective Woman's Epistemologist?" 37.

15. Hume, *Essays, Moral, Political, and Literary*, 568–72.

3

Reconceptualizing Reasoning and Writing the Philosophical Canon

The Case of David Hume

Anne Jaap Jacobson

In this essay, I take a general feminist question about an ideal of philosophical practice to specific topics in Hume's texts. I consider Hume's treatment of three classic philosophical issues: the External World, Knowledge of the Unobserved, and the Nature of Necessity. In Hume's texts I locate a way of producing philosophy that does not accord with the ideal, and I connect his practice to recent work in cognitive science.

At least in recent Anglophone philosophical circles, good philosophy has been for many ideally a matter of disinterested intellects undertaking

I am very indebted to Rupert Read for his comments on the penultimate version of this essay. Among my less direct debts is that to the many participants of the enGendering Rationalities conference, organized by Nancy Tuana and held in March 1997, at the University of Oregon, from whom I learned a great deal.

the logical investigation of abstract concepts. This ideal of a pure reason radically affects the goals, and so the practice, of philosophy. Thus logical argumentation is very widely considered to be essential to philosophical methodology, and consistency a sine qua non of the acceptable work.

Many feminist philosophers have recently questioned this ideal.[1] These theorists sometimes argue that having such goals produces a discipline that proceeds in opposition to much of what is traditionally thought of as the domain of women; namely, the body, the emotions, imagination, and, more generally, the highly nonabstract material of human life. Not only is such a discipline unlikely to be genuinely disinterested, but also the results are at least in part harmful for philosophy, and include both the distortion of many important issues and the neglect of others.

The questioning of the ideal certainly does not incorporate a recommendation that anything goes. Neither need it be part of constructing a supposedly feminine way of thinking, which leaves a dichotomy of reason and emotion in place and merely reverses what gets privileged. Rather, it is a call to reenvision the human mind. Such a call is made more motivating by the possibility that the historically familiar notion of a pure reason is a fiction; if it is such, we should suspect that it is held in place in large part by the erroneous belief on the part of some that they have it.

In this essay, I am going to look at several aspects of the feminist questioning. The central question I address is whether feminists who question the ideal are thereby placing themselves outside the tradition of philosophy. The difficulty that women have had in getting a voice within the tradition may be due in no small part to an identification of women with the irrational or the nonrational. Hence, feminist questioners of the purely rational may well be thought to participate ultimately in the silencing of women. Further, if philosophy is the abstract and rational, then those who reject the abstract and rational may seem to reject philosophy itself.

In this regard, I will argue that the picture of philosophy as the logical pursuit of consistent answers misleads us in at least one major case, that of David Hume. Hume, I shall argue, at times even explicitly rejects the goal of arriving at consistent answers to the questions addressed. On the account I shall give, it is wrong to ask what Hume really thought, if the answer to that question is supposed to supply the consistent answers to the important questions raised.

There are two more general concerns, however, that motivate this essay. The first is about the extent to which our conceptions of ourselves are infected with artificial bifurcations drawn between a misconceived reason and the equally misconceived emotions. There seems little doubt that our culture does generally possess a notion of reason that has it sharply opposed to the emotional. The resulting conceptions of ourselves are being questioned by researchers quite unconnected to feminist philosophical questionings, and we will look at some of this work in the section that follows.

A second concern is with the effects, sometimes political, of philosophical practice. Actual practice *fails* to match self-image; few philosophical works are revealed as even close to the ideal when subjected to the critical eye of a philosophical audience. Consequently, there are largely unaddressed political questions about how a voice in philosophy is acquired or allowed to continue.

Even if the notion of pure reason is merely an ideal, might not some people approximate it more closely than others? A recent theorist, Louis Sass, has been exploring the idea that a kind of affectless hyperrationality characterizes both full schizophrenia and a kind of schizoid creativity that one finds sometimes among, for example, mathematicians and philosophers.[2] It may be that those experiencing a psychic disintegration that seemingly isolates thought from emotion can produce work we can value. Certainly, for Sass we need this picture of creativity at least in addition to the perhaps more familiar one of the genius swept away by emotion. Even if we agree with Sass, however, it does not follow that the conception of reason we are discussing is correctly used to describe the schizoid personality. The fact that someone behaves in greatly exaggerated accordance with a cultural bifurcation of reason and emotion does not legitimate the bifurcation, either as an explanation of how that individual does behave or as a description of how we ought to behave in order to achieve some results. In addition, in this context the ideal of philosophy seems particularly questionable. The understanding attainable by the schizoid personality is very partial and often very distorted. If Sass is right, then we need some way to integrate the sometimes good results of schizoid creativity without insisting that everyone engaged in philosophy simulate the schizoid personality.

Before we turn to Hume, we will consider some contemporary questioning of the logical pursuit of the abstract truth. We will see that the feminist questioners are now joined by a significant number of other kinds of investigators. Let me emphasize that the aim need not be to replace the traditional ideal of pure reason with another and more romantic ideal of the emotionally swept-away genius. Rather, we can try to rethink the elements of the bifurcation, and not merely to reverse the accompanying valorization.

When we turn to Hume's philosophy, we will consider two major instances in his work in which the goal of consistent abstract inquiry is disregarded. We will also look at one of the several ways in which meaning is unstable in Hume's texts, a distinctly severe fault on the model of philosophy being discussed. Hume's texts clearly fail to manifest at least one condition of the ideal of a pure reason.

I have spoken of Anglophone philosophy's ideal self-image in terms of three things: disinterestedness, logical argumentation and abstract concepts. We give courses on the abstract nature of truth, beauty, goodness, meaning, the mind, knowledge, and so on. We take ourselves as able to pronounce on these matters without gender, race, class, or more general cultural bias or interest. We invoke, often enough as proof of our disinterestedness, a kind of logical rigor that rejects what cannot be proven true, and that takes inconsistency to be invariably a grave fault. In this essay, I will focus on the issue of consistency in Hume's philosophy., It would be a shame, however, not to read Hume as also far from disinterested and far from engaged in purely abstract pursuits. Hume had a mission, as perhaps we all really do. Because they are not always praiseworthy, it is a risky policy to pretend that such missions do not exist.

Assaults on the Ideal of the Pure Reason

The assaults on the ideal we will consider in this section come principally from researchers in cognitive science.[3] Cognitive science is an interdisciplinary area of research. Members of cognitive science centers may include people working in computer science, psychology, biology, engineering, optometry, neuroscience, philosophy, business schools, and more. One attack on the conception of pure reason invoked in the model of philosophy we have been discussing is by Antonio Damasio, a neuroscientist:[4]

> I do not know when I became convinced that the traditional views on the nature of rationality could not be correct. I had been

advised early in life that sound decisions came from a cool head, that emotions and reason did not mix any more than oil and water. I had grown up accustomed to thinking that the mechanism of reason existed in a separate province of the mind, where emotion should not be allowed to intrude, and when I thought of the brain behind that mind, I envisioned separate neural systems for reason and emotion. . . .

I began writing this book to propose that reason may not be as pure as most of us think it is or wish it were, that emotions and feelings may not be intruders in the bastion of reason at all: they may be enmeshed in its networks, for worse and for better. The strategies of human reason probably did not develop, in either evolution or any single individual, without the guiding force of the mechanisms of biological regulation, of which emotion and feeling are notable expressions.

Another assault on the privileging of abstract reasoning is given in Mark Turner's *The Literary Mind*.[5] Turner claims:

There is one transcendent story of the mind that has appeared many times in many avatars. In its essential lines, it claims that there are certain basic, sober, and literal things the mind does; that imaginative and literary acts are parasitic, secondary, peripheral, exotic, or deviant. . . . On this logic, since imaginative and literary acts are peripheral and exotic, they can be safely ignored [by neuroscience] while, as serious scientists, we investigate the basics.

This story, which is itself just an imaginative story. . . .

For Turner, the human mind is ineliminably literary and imaginative. The abstract and logical cannot inhabit successfully a fully independent sphere.

Turner's work draws in part on that by Mark Johnson, and a very recent work by this third thinker—*Moral Imagination*—furthers the attack on the value of abstract reasoning.[6] It does so in two importantly different ways. First of all, it challenges the idea that good moral reasoning can be characterized as making deductions from general moral principles. Rather, for Johnson:

My central thesis is that human beings are fundamentally *imaginative* moral animals. This is a provocative and potentially disruptive thesis, for, if we take seriously the imaginative dimensions of human understanding and reasoning, we will discover that certain basic assumptions of our shared Western conception of morality are highly problematic. . . .

We will see that this traditional picture of morality as rule-following presupposes a view of concepts and reason that has been shown by empirical studies in the cognitive sciences to be false.

Like Turner, Johnson is arguing that human reasoning is ineliminably imaginative. Second, Johnson's work goes even farther and argues that our reason does not really have the topics that the standard conception of philosophy has it having. That is, concepts such as that of moral goodness do not connote an essence for philosophy to investigate. Rather, such a concept is prototypical in structure. A standard example of a prototypical concept is "game." Prototypical concepts do not connote a set of necessary and sufficient conditions for their application. Thus, there is no set of features that all games possess. Instead, in acquiring a prototypical concert, one grasps central and paradigmatic examples of the concept, but deduction calculation alone does not tell one how to extend it to other instances. Rather, decisions about new cases involve our making imaginative extensions.

The writers we have seen align themselves against the idea that human reason is the sort of logical device that is assumed to operate in producing philosophy as standardly conceived. Stephen Stich has also written against a kind of privileging of reason and rational argumentation. At least in *The Fragmentation of Reason*, Stich is prepared to deny that logical argumentation confers any epistemic prize on its products.[7] Because that book, like Stich's other work, purports to be very rigorously argued, it is hard to believe that he really thinks rigorous arguments confer no epistemic benefits. However, that it does not is definitely what he asserts.

It is not my aim to endorse the above complicated and many-faceted views.[8] However, I do see them as providing us with some feminist-independent motivation for taking seriously the idea that a common opposition of reason and emotion is quite questionable. Those who take feminist questioning of pure reason to threaten women's position in the academy need to know that other areas are proving hospitable to such questioning.

It must also be said that the discussions in cognitive science often reveal the sorts of problems that feminists have worked to enable us to see. For example, Turner's work on the metaphoric conceptual structures we acquire as infants is radically and unrealistically unsocial. The infant's important experiences on which Turner focuses are highly selective and have as their basis what are arguably the typically male experiences of crawling (away from the mother) and putting things into things. Lorraine Code has argued recently that Johnson neglects the problem of the limits of our imaginative extensions when we are confronted with the other.[9] Damasio, at the end of his book, falls back into the dichotomizing between pure and applied reasoning and thus signals his failure to reexamine our conception of human reasoning completely.

Finally, if it is right to see as highly patriarchal Freud's insistence that the therapist has much better access to the patient's mind than the patient does,[10] then Stich's work may also need to be counted as such. For Stich's work is very much caught up in the idea that the philosopher may well be on the way to discovering that all our beliefs about our minds are false. Somewhat similarly, Hume is quite cheerfully prepared to say at least sometimes that, given his theory of ideas, the beliefs of ordinary people about the world outside their minds are largely false. In the hands of some, theories of ideas are particularly prone, it seems, to imply great revisions in our ordinary beliefs. This is a situation that would reward feminist investigation.

It should be noted that in drawing on recent literature in cognitive science, I am employing resources that are very congenial to Hume's philosophy. This is so for two reasons. First of all, Hume's science of human nature is at least a precursor of today's cognitive science. The theory of imagistic thinking that is found in Damasio's work, for example, is very like Hume's. Second, Hume is himself officially not at all a fan of the fruits of pure reason and logical argumentation. Not only does he incorporate an attack on pure reason as by itself essentially skeptical, but he further provides positive notions of natural beliefs and natural belief-forming mechanisms that are distinctly privileged. As he says:

> [A]s this operation of the mind, by which we infer like effects from like causes, and vice versa, is so essential to the subsistence of all human creatures, it is not probable, that it could be trusted to the fallacious deductions of our reason, which is slow in its operations;

appears not, in any degree, during the first years of infancy; and at best is, in every age and period of human life, extremely liable to error and mistake. It is more conformable to the ordinary wisdom of nature to secure so necessary an act of the mind, by some instinct or mechanical tendency, which may be infallible in its operations, may discover itself at the first appearance of life and thought, and may be independent of all the laboured deductions of the understanding. As nature has taught us the use of our limbs, without giving us the knowledge of the muscles and nerves, by which they are actuated; so has she implanted in us an instinct, which carries forward the thought in a correspondent course to that which she has established among external objects.[11]

Of course, it is nature as woman who rescues us from the impoverished pure reason. One could see Hume's invocation here as prefiguring the feminist questioning of the rational idealization we are discussing.

Feminist questioning of the commitment of philosophy to abstract reasoning tends to be part of a larger questioning of modernist or Cartesian elements in philosophy and other theoretical thought. Poststructuralist/ anti-Cartesian writers, some feminist theoreticians, and some cognitive scientists have overlapping views. The project of transcendent inquiry associated with Descartes and arguably part of the standard conception of philosophy is being thoroughly questioned.

Turning to Hume

If one values more than a logical reasoning in our thought, how might that affect one's views about text production and even one's own text producing? It seems quite clear that little or nothing about consistency in texts follows directly. Any adequate theory of the mind has at least to be compatible with the fact that human beings can often enough follow rules in a logically consistent fashion. However, if we think that an ideal of philosophy rests on a faulty conception of human nature, we do need to think rather harder about the picture of the production of philosophy as the production of logical arguments in support of the one (right) answer. Are we really capable of finding a final right answer to the important questions of philosophy? Perhaps we should wonder about whether there is one right answer.

I think that precisely what Hume did was to raise such questions often implicitly, and sometimes explicitly. For example, on the topic of religion and morals, Hume says:

> The whole is a riddle, an aenigma, an inexplicable mystery. Doubt, uncertainty, suspence of judgment appear the only result of our most accurate scrutiny, concerning this subject. But such is the frailty of human reason, and such the irresistible contagion of opinion, that even this deliberate doubt could scarcely be upheld; did we not enlarge our view, and opposing one species of superstition to another, set them a quarrelling; while we ourselves, during their fury and contention, happily make our escape into the calm, though obscure, regions of philosophy.[12]

Note that it is "our accurate scrutiny" that is so unsuccessful. The contrast with philosophy is one that we would see between philosophical reflection on religion and, say, theories of truth; accurate scrutiny is philosophy. The presented picture is far from that of the philosopher with an optimism about arriving at the one true answer. Similarly, on personal identity, Hume famously says:

> In short, there are two principles, *which I cannot render consistent; nor is it in my power to renounce either of them* [my emphasis], viz. that *all our distinct perceptions are distinct existences,* and *that the mind never perceives any real connexion among distinct existences* [Hume's emphases]. . . . For my part, I must plead the privilege of a sceptic and confess, that this difficulty is too hard for my understanding. I pretend not, however, to pronounce it absolutely insuperable. Others, perhaps, or myself, upon more mature reflection, may discover some hypothesis, that will reconcile those contradictions.[13]

These comments from Hume are certainly not those of someone who sees himself as presenting the one true solution to the problem he raises.

In what follows I am going to argue that, with regard to some topics Hume discusses and some texts of his, there is no correct answer to the question, What does Hume really think is the true answer? The texts resist providing us with an answer in a way that does not seem completely accidental. In addition, there are ample grounds for the attribution to Hume of each of two inconsistent answers. If good philosophy consists in rational argumentation for one true and consistent answer (or in trying to produce it), then Hume is often not doing good philosophy. However, if he is a good philosopher, then philosophy is not always rational argumentation (or attempts at rational argumentation) for the one consistent and right answer. In either case, one of the greatest figures in Anglophone philosophy does not fit that tradition's self-image.

The discussion will provide us with material for two important conclusions: First of all, a feminist questioning of the role of abstract reasoning in providing the ideals of philosophy is *not* a rejection of everything in the philosophical tradition. Secondly, Hume may be right in suggesting that the human mind is not suited to the pursuit of the one consistent and true conclusion on the important questions of philosophy.

Hume's Theory of Ideas

It is very hard to think about Hume's texts without having at hand some of his theory of ideas. Hume's presentation of the theory of ideas provides terminology central in his philosophy. Often judged to be highly problematic, the theory of ideas is, nonetheless, deeply embedded in the rest of his philosophy. Further, it is a very important piece of theorizing. For better or for worse, Hume's theory is a paradigm case of the Representational Theory of Mind, which is so prominent in our contemporary philosophy of mind.

It is useful to separate the Representational Theory of Mind from a Representational Theory of Perception. A Representational Theory of Mind is a theory about what mind states are; typically, it says that mind states consist in states of a part of ourselves that have at least semantic content. A Representational Theory of Perception is basically about evidence for perceptual statements such as "I see a tree." On this second theory, our evidence is provided by internal states. A traditional reading of Hume has seen him as endorsing the theory of perception, with a view to drawing a skeptical conclusion from it. Few Hume scholars today would make this attribution, not least because Hume presents the theory as a highly problematic invention of philosophers.

Hume's theory of ideas is at the center of an unified account of (outer) sensation, feeling, and thought. The theory is, to use Hume's term, one of perceptions. There are two kinds of perception: impressions and ideas. Impressions are sensory events, either of the outer senses or of the inner senses. The outer senses give us impressions of sight, touch, smell, and so on. The impressions from the inner senses are emotions and passions. For Hume, impressions are very vivid and forceful. Ideas are copies of the impressions, and they are less vivid and forceful. We have ideas when we remember or imagine or think in some more general way. For Hume, the contents of the mind are officially just these two kinds of perception.

Impressions and ideas can be simple or complex. The complex ones can be thought of as having simple parts that can be recombined to produce novel ideas. However, since simple ideas are all copies of impressions, simple ideas themselves are never completely novel. Complex ideas can be the result of rearranging simple ideas from different sources, but simple ideas themselves have to be derived from impressions.

It is a significant fact about Hume's texts that the account I have just given is very controversial, even though it is little more than a summary of the introductory sections of his *Treatise* and first *Enquiry*. What has created controversy is a general view about the connection between Hume's theory of ideas and skepticism. Critics from Thomas Reid to Antony Flew have seen Hume as severely and implausibly skeptical and have blamed the theory of ideas for the skepticism.[14] More recently, commentators such as John Wright and Annette Baier have accepted that the theory of ideas has skeptical implications and have maintained that it was not intended by Hume to be the centerpiece of his philosophy.[15] According to these critics, Hume radically modified or even rejected his theory of ideas.

I am going to present an approach to Hume's texts that is different from both of the sorts just mentioned. My interpretation places the theory of ideas in a foundational position in Hume's philosophy, but it rejects the notion that Hume unequivocally accepts the skeptical implications of the theory. In doing so, I take Hume at his word when he says: "There is no question of importance, whose decision is not comprised in the science of man; and there is none, which can be decided with any certainty, before we become acquainted with that science. In pretending, therefore, to explain the principles of human nature, we in effect propose a complete system of the sciences, built on a foundation almost entirely new, and the only one upon which they can stand with any security" (*Treatise*, xvi). It is not plausible, I think, to maintain that Hume began building the foundations with a theory he then rejected.

A World External and Independent

Hume characterizes our belief in the world outside our minds as a belief in a world that is external and independent of our minds. If we ask whether Hume believes that there is such a world, the obvious answer seems to be that he does. In addition to all the many instances when Hume presents himself as writing about such a world, there is support for the nonskeptical interpretation in the fact that Hume himself says that we cannot doubt whether there are material objects; all we can do is inquire into the causes of our belief.[16]

Nonetheless, Hume's discussions of the causes of our belief lead him to some very negative observations. The succinct form of the discussion, that in the first *Enquiry*, concludes: "Thus the first philosophical objection to the . . . opinion of external existence consists in this, that such an opinion, if rested on natural instinct, is contrary to reason, and if referred to reason, is contrary to natural instinct, and at the same time carries no rational evidence with it, to convince an impartial enquirer" (*Enquiry*, 155). Before we can understand the import of this remark, we need to review briefly what is behind Hume's saying it.

The belief in external existence when rested on natural instinct is the belief held by the vulgar. The vulgar are all of us, at one time or another.[17] In part the vulgar believe that they simply see and hear and feel objects. So characterized, the vulgar's view appears to be a kind of direct realism, where a direct realism says that our knowledge of the external world is not based on inferences or deductions from some evidence itself of a different nature. Hume seems to address a vulgar direct realism in the following: "But this universal and primary opinion of all men is soon destroyed by the slightest philosophy, which teaches us, that nothing can ever be present to the mind but an image or perception. . . . The table, which we see, seems to diminish, as we remove farther from it: but the real table, which exists independent of us, suffers no alteration; it was, therefore, nothing but its image, which was present to the mind. These are the obvious dictates of reason" (*Enquiry*, 152). Thus "the opinion of external existence consists in this, that such an opinion, if rested on natural instinct, is contrary to reason." That is, reason distinguishes between the object and the image and tells us that the image alone is present to the mind. Thus reason contradicts the deliverances of natural instinct.

The other view of external existence, the one "referred to reason," is, then, just the one that distinguishes between perceptions in the mind and objects in the external world, with the additional claim that the latter causes the former. It is this view that "is contrary to natural instinct, and at the same time carries no rational evidence with it, to convince an impartial enquirer." The view is contrary to natural instinct because natural instinct leads us to the vulgar view. Further, no one would accept the philosophical view without having held the vulgar view, for the philosophical view is entirely unsupported by evidence. This is so because, given the philosophical view, all we have present to the mind are images, and nothing enables us to reach around the images and secure evidence for the causal hypothesis that there is an external world causing the images.

The philosophical view is in fact in a worse position than simply having no evidence. It occurs in a context that blocks reviving it with a relaxed or naturalistic account of evidence. To see this, suppose, then, that we attempt to resuscitate the philosophical view by substituting a naturalized epistemology for the demand for evidence that Hume thinks wrecks the philosophers' view.[18] The idea here might be that we look at how we naturally form beliefs, and that we take the products of natural and reliable belief-producing mechanisms to be items of knowledge if they are true. The problem is that since our quest is for an account of what Hume thinks, we need to note that for Hume natural belief-forming mechanisms most certainly do not lead us to form the philosophical belief. Rather, natural belief-forming processes lead us to the vulgar view.

Can we then say that it is the natural view that is produced by reliable belief-forming processes that enable us to know, for example, that there is a table before us? Does a nonskeptical Hume simply hold the beliefs of the vulgar? The problem with this reading is that it ignores what Hume says is the *content* of our belief when we believe in "an external and independent world." That is, it looks as though for Hume our belief is really a belief about our perceptions. This is so as long as we speak with the vulgar, which we do, Hume tells us, most of the time; what we are talking about are not external objects but, rather, our perceptions. As a consequence, the instinctual belief-forming mechanisms of the vulgar are anything but reliable. As Hume says, "[W]hen men follow this blind and powerful instinct of nature, they always suppose the very images, presented by the senses, to be the external objects" (*Treatise*, 151). Thus, "[N]o man, who reflects, ever doubted, that the existences, which we consider, when we say, *this house* and *that tree*, are nothing but perceptions in the mind" (*Treatise*, 152).

Thus Hume has a semantic thesis that yields an uncomfortable account of what the vulgar mean when they talk. The vulgar are really talking about their perceptions, and they believe, utterly falsely, that their perceptions are external items. If we take Hume's theory of ideas at all seriously, we have to see this semantic thesis as deeply embedded in his philosophy. As Hume says, "['T]is impossible for us so much as to conceive or form an idea of any thing specifically different from ideas and impressions. . . . Let us chace our imagination to the heavens, or to the utmost limits of the universe; we never really advance a step beyond our selves, nor can conceive any kind of existence, but those perceptions, which have appear'd in that narrow compass" (*Treatise*, 68–69). Further, "The farthest we can go towards a conception of external objects, when suppos'd *specifically* different from our perceptions, is to form a relative idea of them, without pretending to comprehend the related objects. Generally speaking we do not suppose them specifically different; but only attribute to them different relations, connexions and durations" (*Treatise*, 68). (Hume has almost no use for the phrase "relative idea"; its occurrence here suggests that he is saying that if we think of them as specifically different, we are at most able to conceive of them as a variable in a relation. As he appears to put it elsewhere in the *Treatise*, we could "conceive an external object merely as a relation without a relative," 241.)

What is it to conceive of external objects as specifically the same as our perceptions? Thinking of an external object as being of the same species as our perceptions and as merely having different relations, connections, and durations from those that our perceptions in fact have yields the false views of the vulgar. The only alternative, the relative idea of the cause, whatever it is, of our perceptions, will simply get us at best the philosophers' thesis. However, we are now in a position to see a further and worse problem with the philosophers' view than that it is unverifiable. The philosophers' view fails to engage any of our ordinary beliefs about an external world, since our ordinary beliefs are not about some cause of our perceptions. Our ordinary beliefs are about our perceptions.

The philosophers' double-existence view is, in the words of the *Treatise*, "monstrous" (215). The belief in an external and independent world is, then, either the false belief of the vulgar or a grotesque invention.

If Hume really thinks that all our ordinary statements that appear to be about a world genuinely exterior and independent are in fact false or irrational statements about our perceptions, then it is very questionable whether we can correctly characterize him as believing in what we believe is an external and independent world. Indeed, he himself says:

> I began this subject with premising that we ought to have an implicit faith in our senses, and that this would be the conclusion I should draw from the whole of my reasoning. But to be ingenuous, I feel myself at present of a quite contrary sentiment, and am more inclined to repose no faith at all in my senses, or rather imagination, than to place in it such an implicit confidence. I cannot conceive how such trivial qualities of the fancy, conducted by such false suppositions, can ever lead to any solid and rational system. . . . It is a gross illusion to suppose that our resembling perceptions are numerically the same; and it is this illusion which leads us into the opinion that these perceptions are uninterrupted, and are still existent, even when they are not present to the senses. This is the case with our popular system. And as to our philosophical one, it is liable to the same difficulties; and is, over and above, loaded with this absurdity, that it at once denies and establishes the vulgar supposition. (*Treatise*, 217)

But if he does not, how can we account for the host of statements like the following: "I have seen *Paris*; but shall I affirm I can form such an idea of that city, as will perfectly represent all its streets and houses in their real and just proportions?" (*Treatise*, 3). Surely, Hume does not regard it as a largely false statement about perceptions that he has absurdly labeled "Paris" and "streets."

Let us state the problem clearly. On the one hand, there are many passages in Hume in which he appears to speak unhesitantly about what we know to be an exterior and independent world. However, he also offers us an interpretation of what these statements mean, and on this interpretation, many, and perhaps all, of his statements are false or the irrational products of a monstrous system.

There is a clear sense in which Hume is inconsistent. He asserts as true and unproblematic statements that he also says are false or irrational. Further, were we to let his later judgment be dominant, then he cannot be possessed of the evidence he claims to be possessed of as he develops his theory of ideas, discusses other philosophers, addresses his readers, and so on. This is so because his evidence draws on experiences of things external to his mind. His evidence, as it is presented, goes beyond his perceptions.

One reaction to the material of the texts just exhibited would be to take it to be superficial or incomplete and misleading, and to search for a way to make Hume consistent. The view of Hume as developing a consistent response to all the problems he addresses has led to the perception of him as either a tricky skeptic or an ironic but true believer. Seen as a tricky skeptic, Hume disguises the full impact of the skepticism until he has us lulled into acceptance of its very origins. Seen as an ironic true believer, Hume never really considers skepticism, but positions it in his text as the cost of rationalism.

The approach I recommend is different. This approach gives up the idea that Hume gives us—or aims to give us—a consistent response to all the problems he addresses. To say this is not to say that Hume is simply uttering things at random with no regard for coherence. There are ways to see the text as more complicated, instructive and interesting than that. For example, Book I of the *Treatise* could be seen as a reversal of Descartes's *Meditations*, one that starts with sciences of the mind and external world and ends up with insoluble skepticism problems that we can at best ignore. A reversal of the *Meditations* does, however, have a serious problem with inconsistency. It is one thing to start with propositions you regard as problematic and to vindicate them. It is quite another to start one's theory with propositions that seem not to need vindication and to draw from them negative conclusions about whether one can have any knowledge in the area being investigated, including one's starting propositions.

Early in this section I distinguished between a Representational Theory of Mind and a Representational Theory of Perception. The latter has usually been judged to be inherently skeptical. Does what we have seen above show that the former is also? Some writers have suggested that it is so committed.[19] However, on the account given above, the source of the skepticism is a particular semantic theory that is certainly not an essential feature of a Representational Theory of Mind.

Causation and Our Knowledge of the Unobserved

Another skepticism comes in at the end of the *Enquiry*, on page 159. The passage is worth careful study:

> The sceptic . . . had better keep within his proper sphere, and display those *philosophical* objections, which arise from more pro-found researches. Here [the sceptic] seems to have ample matter of triumph; while he justly insists, that all our evidence for any matter of fact, which lies beyond the testimony of sense or memory, is derived entirely from the relation of cause and effect; that we have no other idea of this relation than that of two objects which have been frequently conjoined together; that we have no argument to convince us, that objects, which have, in our expe-rience, been frequently conjoined, will likewise, in other in-stances, be conjoined in the same manner; and that nothing leads us to this inference but custom or a certain instinct of our nature; which it is indeed difficult to resist, but which, like other instincts, may be fallacious and deceitful. While the sceptic insists upon these topics, he shows his force, or rather, indeed, his own and our weakness; and seems, for the time at least, to destroy all assurance and conviction.

From the point of view of our discussion in this section, the two most important features of this passage are (1) its presentation of skepticism and (2) its claim that our idea of cause and effect is only "that of two objects which have been frequently conjoined together." In our discussion of the former, we will see once again ways in which Hume's treatment of a skepticism is inconsistent. In looking at the latter, we will see another kind of instability in the texts. This new instability is an instability in meanings.

Skepticism

The passage is concerned with a kind of skepticism. The skepticism is about our matter-of-fact-knowledge of what "lies beyond the testimony of sense or memory." To understand what the doubt is about, consider an example: Many people, when they are eating lunch, have beds in which they sleep but that they are not observing as they eat lunch. Almost everyone has a firm belief about where their bed is as they are eating lunch, even though they are not then observing the bed. If Hume as *historically understood* is right, no one of them *knows* where it is. The beliefs one has that fall under the scope of this doubt include all the factual things one has not observed or is not observing—the bed at this moment, dust under unobserved beds, what is now under one's skin, the whole of the future, most of the past and present, and so on. For many readers, this doubt *is* "Hume's Problem."

The grounds for the skepticism, Hume tells us, are just. Further, the skeptic seems able to destroy all assurance and conviction, Hume says. The area in which the skeptic is concerned is one, moreover, in which seeming is very close to being. At least typically, if one seems to find an argument convincing and destructive of one's former beliefs, one is at least very close to not having the beliefs. "I seem to have lost all faith in P" and "I no longer believe that P" are at least quite close. Hence, Hume appears to tell us that the skeptic has a powerful argument based on just grounds. Furthermore, the grounds are ones that Hume created. The material in the skeptic's hands is the material of the fourth, fifth, and seventh sections of the *Enquiry*. Hume's readers are clearly supposed to detect a similarity between the skeptic's voice and Hume's.

Hume's attack on this skepticism does not aim to place its truth in question. Rather, in the next paragraph he says, "The chief and most confounding objection to *excessive* skepticism [is] that no durable good can ever result from it; while it remains in its full force and vigour" (159). We indeed live in a "whimsical condition" and "must act and reason and believe; though [we] are not able, by [our] most diligent enquiry, . . . to remove the objections to [these operations]." We may not be able to live as skeptics, but the skeptic certainly appears to have won the truth game. At the very minimum, no one has bested the skeptic at it.

It is nature, not philosophy, that can save us from skepticism. We have to live with the fact that enlightening theories like the theory of ideas, at least as Hume saw it, have unpalatable consequences to which we get committed. Fortunately, the commitment is easily forgotten when nature holds sway.

We have seen two areas of Hume's philosophy where he supports a skepticism that puts into question his own beliefs and practices of belief formation. To say this is not to say that Hume is a skeptic, for that reading follows only upon an insistence on consistency. We will now look at another way in which Hume's texts belie the consistency that the official self-image of philosophy demands.

Constant Conjunctions and Inconstant Meanings

Hume's use of some terms contains a radical and systematic ambiguity. This is particularly true of the terms surrounding his discussion of causation and our beliefs about the unobserved. We can see one aspect of this with his use of "constantly conjoined" and similar phrases such as "always conjoined."

Though the view has recently become controversial, Hume has traditionally been thought to hold a regularity theory of causation. According to such a theory, the statement that a caused b implies that there are event types A and B such that events of type A are constantly conjoined with events of type B, and a is an A and b is a B. "Constantly conjoined" is understood in these discussions as "conjoined throughout all space and time."

A careful reading of the texts shows that this understanding of "constant conjunction" in Hume's texts, and the implied understanding of causation as a *philosophical* relation, is highly problematic. We will consider this issue by starting with the Treatise. It is true that in his early investigation of the notion of cause, Hume says the following: "Thus in advancing we have insensibly discover'd a new relation betwixt cause and effect. . . . This relation is their CONSTANT CONJUNCTION. Contiguity and succession are not sufficient to make us pronounce any two objects to be cause and effect, unless we perceive, that these two relations are preserv'd in several instances" (*Treatise*, 87). However, Hume's explanation of the addition is not the unrestricted "constantly conjoined throughout all space and time. Rather, he says: "This new-discover'd relation of a constant conjunction seems to advance us but very little in our way. For it implies no more than this, that like objects *have always been plac'd* in like relations of contiguity and succession" (*Treatise*, 88; my italics). Thus constant conjunction is "constant conjunction so far," and this explicitly restricted reading occurs throughout Book I of the *Treatise*.[20] For example, Hume says:

[T]he idea of cause and effect is deriv'd from *experience*, which informs us, that such particular objects, *in all past instances* [second emphasis mine], have been constantly conjoin'd with each other. (*Treatise*, 88–90)

[A]ll kinds of reasoning from causes or effects are founded on two particulars, *viz.* the constant conjunction of any two objects *in all past experience* [second emphasis mine] and the resemblance of a present object to any one of them. (*Treatise*, 142)

(See also *Treatise*, 87, lines 17–19; 92; 102; and 128. A similar point can be made for "always conjoined" on 93, lines 25–28; and 115. In addition, see "union . . . in all past instances," 166. Finally, note 164–65 where "their constant conjunction" refers back to "the several instances . . . of the conjunction of resembling causes and effect" and in discussed of "the several resembling instances.")

There are many other contexts in which "constant conjunction" must be understood as implicitly qualified. For example, in a passage where what is or has been observed is always deductively insufficient for nontrivial truths about the unobserved, Hume says: "We must in every case have observ'd the same impression in past instances and have found it to be constantly conjoin'd with some other impression" (*Treatise*, 88). (See also *Treatise*, 88, lines 22–24; 90, lines 20–23; 93, lines 30–32; 102; 125; 139; 170; and 171, lines 8–11. Note, in addition, the use of "experienc'd union," 166, and that of "experienc'd conjunction," 172.)

What, then, are we to say of causation as a philosophical relation, causation as constant conjunction? Here is the passage in which causality as a philosophical relation is first referred to: "Thus tho' causation be a *philosophical* relation, as implying contiguity, succession, and constant conjunction, yet 'tis only so far as it is a *natural* relation, and produces an union among our ideas, that we are able to reason upon it or draw any inference from it" (*Treatise*, 94). The unavoidable implication is that "constantly conjoined" in the passage immediately above does not imply "constantly conjoined throughout all space and time." Were it to be so understood, there would be no bar to reasoning upon it, and drawing an inference about the unobserved from it.

Hume famously gives two definitions of causation, and causation as a philosophical relation is causation according to the first definition. That the material of the first definition is temporally restricted is even more explicitly stated in Hume's *Enquiry*.[21] Here the first definition is "[W]e may define a cause to be an object, followed by another, and where all the objects similar to the first are followed by objects similar to the second" (76). Hume makes two important statements about this definition. First he says that "*where, if the first object had not been, the second never had existed*" is merely "other words" for this first definition (76). Second, he says that the following give us an application of the definition: "We say, for instance, that the vibration of this string is the cause of this particular sound. But what do we mean by that affirmation? We either mean *that this vibration is followed by this sound, and that all similar vibrations have been followed by similar sounds* . . ." (77). It is important to notice that in this last passage, we have an application of the first definition that is restricted to the past. The fact that Hume gives us this restricted statement strongly suggests that we should understand the first definition itself as implicitly so restricted.

If we do this, we can understand the "other words" as providing us with a conditional that is merely tensed. Suppose, for instance, I know that A and B were always conjoined. As an example, suppose Alice and Andrew had always traveled together. I may not know whether Alice had ever gone to Alaska, but want nonetheless to insist that *if she had not gone, neither had he*. There is nothing counterfactual about this conditional, and so neither need there be with Hume's.

The past-tense reading of the "other words" does not make the conditional equivalent to the first definition. The first definition correlates As with Bs; the conditional correlates not-As with not-Bs, a quite different matter. If we put them together, we have As and Bs as necessary and sufficient conditions of one another. Such an addition is much more modest than an implicit journey into possible worlds with a counterfactual conditional.

The material we have seen so far strongly suggests that if Humean causal statements say, "As are always followed by Bs," this means that As are so far followed by Bs. We are given this interpretation in Hume's comments on the first definition. However, there are two other ways of understanding such statements that Hume specifies.

The philosophers described in the section following the two definitions passage (Sec. VIII) believe if that an *a* causes a *b*, then As and Bs are constantly conjoined without temporal qualification. Accordingly, such philosophers also believe there is some difference that accounts for any occurrence of an A without a B, and so an apparent breakdown merely informs us that we need to refine our notions of A and B. Apparent breakdowns simply tell us we have not correctly described the relevant As and Bs. "[P]hilosophers form a maxim that the connexion between all causes and effects is equally necessary, and that its seeming uncertainty in some instances proceeds from the secret opposition of contrary causes" (*Enquiry*, 87).

There appears to be a third account of the generality implied by "cause" that is discussed in the first *Enquiry*. This is the reading of the vulgar that Hume reports and discusses in Section VIII. Hume tells us that unlike philosophers, the vulgar just allow that sometimes things do not work. For the vulgar, "As cause Bs" says something about what is beyond the experiences we have had, but it does not say that inexplicable breakdowns never occur. "The vulgar, who take things according to their first appearance, attribute the uncertainty of events to such an uncertainty in the causes as makes the latter often fail of their usual influence; though they meet with no impediment in their operation" (*Enquiry*, 86).

Given this proliferation of ways to understand "always conjoined," how we are to read Hume's causal statements? For example, are Hume's principles of association to be considered as merely about the past? The better answer here is in the negative. Hume has compared his principles of association with the laws of planetary motion (in Sec. I), which certainly are not restricted to the past in any standard interpretation. (If the entailments on Hume's understanding of these laws are only past- and present-tense, he needs to tell us.) Further, in the final sentence of Section III, Hume invites us to consider fresh examples, to show that what he is saying is correct. If what he was saying was temporally restricted, fresh examples would be beside the point. So, clearly, he takes what he is saying as unqualified as to time, or at least much more unqualified than "so far" would make it. The temporal restriction of the first definition has yet to appear.

There seem, then, to be three understandings of "always conjoined": (1) The unqualified constant conjunction probably used by Hume at times in his construction of a science of the mind (e.g., Sec. III) and employed by philosophers (e.g., as reported in Sec. VIII), (2) Hume in Section VII with the first definition, and (3) the vulgar's usage.

There is a parallel problem with Hume's second definition. That is, there are correspondingly three different ways to read the necessity it explicates. (I have discussed this issue at length elsewhere.)[22] The semantic variety clearly is no accident.

Conclusion

In this essay, I have been discussing Hume as an example of the tradition who so obviously fails to meet our ideal that his doing so appears intentional. Feminist questioners of philosophy's ideal, at least that which I attribute to Anglophone philosophy, do not, then, place themselves outside of the tradition in the sense of recommending a way of doing philosophy that the members of the canon eschewed. Rather, Hume himself appears to anticipate to some extent feminist thought on this issue, and he does so in a way that affects his texts.

If the more general point that the pure reason of philosophy is a fiction is correct, then we should expect that many texts in the canon are very faulty when compared to the ideal. If this is so, then we need to ask what purpose is served by reading out such errors in the texts, and attempting to transform a philosopher's thought into a single, consistent and well-argued position. Further, we should at least investigate the possibility that the inconsistency is playing a more essential role in philosophy than we may want to think.

There are two further issues with which we will close. First of all, there is a remaining problem regarding the texts on which I have focused. Hume's employment of inconsistency and ambiguity is systematic and quite clearly intentional. Is there some one true account of its role in the texts? Should we seek a final correct and constructive account of Hume's texts?

As a methodological point, we should resist searching for "the" true answer to the question of what is really going on in the texts. Indeed, I doubt that there is one overall correct constructive interpretation. To some extent we can see the text as dialogic.[23] There are clearly systematic ways in which different voices are present in the texts.[24] It would, however, be a mistake to assume that arguments will succeed in identifying some final winner, either among the voices in the texts or among the interpretators of the texts. To say this is not to rule out that there may well be losers.

The second is a feminist issue implicit in much of what has been said above. The issue is that of pedagogy. At least in my experience, many philosophy classrooms are positively hostile to anything other than fairly rigorous logical argumentation. To the extent that this is so, we may be silencing very valuable voices and thoughts. Teaching students in accordance with an ideal that may be rooted in serious misconceptions about human nature, and that is approximated by a disabling pathology, reflects a questionable pedagogy.

Notes

1. It would be wrong to think that there is a single feminist view on this question. See, for example, Phyllis A. Rooney, "Recent Work in Feminist Discussions of Reason," *American Philosophical Quarterly* 31, no. 1 (1994): 1–21; Ruddick, Sara, "New Feminist Work on Knowledge, Reason and Objectivity," *Hypatia* 8, no. 4 (1993): 140–49; Linda Alcoff, ed., *The Crisis of Reason in Feminist Epistemologies* (New York: Routledge, 1993); Lorraine Code, *What Can She Know? Feminist Theory and the Construction of Knowledge* (Ithaca: Cornell University Press, 1991); Genevieve Lloyd, The Man of Reason: *"Male" and "Female" in Western Philosophy* (Methuen, 1984; 2d ed., Routledge, 1993).

2. See Louis A. Sass, *The Paradoxes of Delusion: Wittgenstein, Schreber, and the Schizophrenic Mind* (Ithaca: Cornell University Press, 1993). The work on creativity and philosophy that I am discussing is largely developed in unpublished manuscripts.

3. I am concerned here with general questions about how to conceptualize human reasoning. Hence, I will not address the range of related and interesting issues about whether human beings systematically violate normative rules of reasoning. For an interesting discussion of these issues, see Edward Stein, *Without Good Reason: The Rationality Debate in Philosophy and Cognitive Science* (Oxford: Clarendon Press, 1996).

4. Antonio R. Damasio, *Descartes' Error: Emotion, Reason, and the Human Brain* (New York: Avon Books, 1995), xi–xii.

5. Mark Turner, *The Literary Mind* (Oxford: Oxford University Press, 1996), 113.

6. See Mark Johnson, *Moral Imagination: Implications of Cognitive Science for Ethics* (Chicago: University of Chicago Press, 1993), 1.

7. Stephen P. Stich, *The Fragmentation of Reason* (Cambridge: MIT Press, 1990).

8. See, for example, my reservations in my review of Stich in *Canadian Philosophical Reviews* 11 (1991): 362–65.

9. In unpublished talks at recent conferences in Eugene, Oregon, and Toronto.

10. Richard Webster, *Why Freud Was Wrong: Sin, Science, and Psychoanalysis* (New York: HarperCollins, 1995); see, for example, 511–26.

11. *An Enquiry Concerning Human Understanding and an Enquiry Concerning the Principles of Morals*, ed. L. A. Selby-Bigge; 3d ed., rev. P. H. Nidditch (Oxford: Oxford University Press, 1975), 55.

12. *The Natural History of Religion*, from David Hume, *Philosophical Works*, ed. Thomas Hill Green and Thomas Hodge Grose, 4 vols. (Scientia Verlag Aalen, 1964), 4:363.

13. *Treatise of Human Nature*, ed. L. A. Selby-Bigge; 2d ed., rev. P. H. Nidditch (Oxford: Oxford University Press: 1978), 636.

14. Thomas Reid, *Inquiry and Essays*, ed. R. E. Beanblossom and K, Lehrer (Indianapolis: Hackett, 1983); and Antony Flew, *David Hume: Philosopher of Moral Science* (Oxford: Basil Blackwell, 1986).

15. John P. Wright, "Hume's Rejection of the Theory of Ideas," *History of Philosophy Quarterly* 8 (April 1991): 149–62; "Hume's Academic Scepticism: A Reappraisal of His Philosophy of Human Understanding," *Canadian Journal of Philosophy* (Spring 1986): 407–35; *The Sceptical Realism of David Hume* (Minneapolis: University of Minnesota Press, 1983); and Annette Baier, A *Progress of Sentiments: Reflections on Hume's "Treatise"* (Cambridge: Harvard University Press, 1991).

16. *Treatise*, Bk. 1, Pt. IV, Sec. II, 187.

17. *Treatise*, Bk. I, Pt. IV, Sec. II, 205.

18. *Treatise*, 214.

19. Peter Dlugos, "Yolton and Rorty on the Veil of Ideas in Locke," *History of Philosophy Quarterly* 13, no. 3 (1996): 317–29.

20. This general feature of the text is noted for the first time in my "Does Hume Hold a Regularity Theory of Causality," in *History of Philosophy Quarterly* 1, no. 1 (1985): 75–91. Wade Robison, in "Hume's Causal Scepticism," in G. P. Novice, ed., *David Hume: Bicentenary Papers* (Edinburgh: University Press, 1977), notes that the restriction occurs on *Treatise*, 87–88, and at least twice elsewhere. Don Garrett, *Cognition and Commitment in Hume's Philosophy* (Oxford: Oxford University Press, 1997), wrongly takes this article of Robinson's and his other article, "One Consequence of Hume's Nominalism" in *Hume Studies* 8 (November 1982): 102–18, to make the general point. Indeed, the latter article, in controversially maintaining that Hume holds that the extension of general terms is limited to the perceived, makes a mystery of Hume's use of tensed qualifications. On Robison's reading, Hume's extensive qualifications are in fact redundant.

21. The temporal restriction argues a skepticism implicit in the passage. I describe the skepticism, and the argument on which it is based, in "The Problem of Induction: What Is Hume's Argument?" *Pacific Philosophical Quarterly* 68, nos. 3–4 (1987): 265–84.

22. In Rupert Read and Kenneth Richman, eds., *The New Hume*, forthcoming from Routledge.

23. I have explored this interpretation in unpublished papers presented at conferences. See also Donald W. Livingston, *Philosophical Melancholy and Delirium: Hume's Pathology of Philosophy* (Chicago: University of Chicago Press, 1998).

24. I explore this issue in my essay in *The New Hume*. Baier, *A Progress of Sentiments*, makes interesting use of these voices. My disagreement with her is principally over whether one can discern a clear "Hume's one position" in the texts. I am arguing that one cannot.

4

The Metaphorics of Hume's Gendered Skepticism

Aaron A. Smuts

In "Of Scepticism with Regard to the Senses" (*Treatise*, Bk. I, Sec. IV, Pt. II) David Hume begins by saying that he will attempt to trace the causes of our belief in a mind-independent world, "a belief we must take for granted in all our reasonings" (187). Yet the causes arrived at—namely, natural inclination or imagination—are presented as so untrustworthy as to cast doubt on the credibility of the inescapable belief itself. However, in the *Enquiry Concerning Human Understanding*, Hume presents a radically different evaluation of natural inclination, in which Nature is seen as a trustworthy, guiding Supreme Mother. The present inquiry will employ rhetorical analyses to explain why Hume has (or rhetorically uses)

I would like to sincerely thank Professor Anne Jaap Jacobson for her insightful comments, much needed encouragement, and the opportunity to pursue this topic.

this change of heart, why Nature earns a disparaging evaluation within "Scepticism," and the significance of these metaphors to formulations of his arguments.[1]

In *The Man of Reason* Genevieve Lloyd argues that in the discourse of Western philosophy, reason has been formulated as masculine through an exclusion of Nature, which became associated with the feminine.[2] Her work serves as the impetus of this examination of the rhetorical effects of Hume's metaphors. In "Scepticism" Hume's use of gendered metaphors has three obvious rhetorical purposes: (1) Dead, widely understood metaphors appear as obvious truths to the reader, who supplies past knowledge and understanding, making acceptable their personifying function; (2) metaphors dramatize to entice and entertain the (assumed-to-be-male) reader; and (3) metaphors add a shock value to the final conclusions, through dramatic and uncomfortable associations. Thus, metaphors make points stronger, easier to formulate, and more memorable, all of which aid in the primary goal of rhetoric, which is to "transform the way in which the audience receive[s]" the argument.[3] But these three purposes underplay the potent and latent affects that metaphors can have on their audience and the crucial roles they play in these mostly argumentative texts. It is through a fourth functional purpose that the rhetorical force of Hume's metaphors becomes evident. That is, his metaphors serve as "weapons designed to win adherents and destroy enemies."[4] As we shall see, Hume's use of a feminized notion of Imagination (or Nature), while equating woman with seductress, destroys the credibility of Imagination throughout the text. This has the unexpected result of winning Hume over to the side of "her" detractors. The principal effect of the analysis below will be to show that Hume's use of gendered metaphors and gendered "faculties" (Reasoning as male; Imagination as female) in scenarios of loss and deception has the rhetorical effect of slandering Imagination and emasculating reason, and, hence, making our assumed relation to any external world unacceptable for Hume.

I. Methodological Justification

Since rhetorical analyses of philosophical texts are rarely performed in Anglo-American, analytic philosophy, and as such may seem strange to many philosophers, a methodological justification may be warranted.

Richard Lanham discusses the split between rhetoric and philosophy that dates back at least to the conflict between Plato and the Sophists.[5] For Plato philosophy was characterized by dialectic, the means for searching for timeless truth, rather than by rhetoric. Disparaged, rhetoric was (and still is) perceived as skillful lying; hence, metaphor as a rhetorical trope was to be expelled from the realm of pure and correct thought associated with logic. Rhetoric took on the associations of common thinking, and logic that of philosophical thinking, and the hierarchical binary opposition[6] logic/rhetoric was established (Lanham, 153–55). Such an opposition takes logic to be the pure and foundational pole that must be kept free of the contaminating pole of rhetoric. The resulting binary opposition—related to those such as literal/metaphorical, Philosophy/literature, Reason/Nature, active/passive, and masculine/feminine—has provided the impetus for one species of rhetorical analysis, a seek-and-destroy (or deny) method characterized by a move toward formalized discourse upholding the left side of all these binaries. This can be seen in the virtual absence of metaphor from philosophical discourse, and the inattention paid to those present in canonical texts.

Antithetical to this traditional privileging of the left (in this case logical) pole of the opposition is the theoretical movement deconstruction, which, in some forms, seeks to either blur the distinction or to strategically privilege the disparaged pole (in this case the rhetorical). Samuel Wheeler describes deconstruction, and its relation to such oppositions as a technique "in the history of philosophy of arguing that neither pure case of a dichotomy makes sense": "The condition for a dichotomy to function foundationally is that the pure cases of the sides be coherently describable. A deconstructive argument shows that each of the pure cases in fact presupposes the other half of the dichotomy. Ontologically speaking, the allegedly pure cases of one side must in fact contain the other. So both sides of the dichotomy are in fact impure, and the foundational project cannot succeed" ("Wittgenstein as Conservative Deconstructor," 242–43).[7]

In this sense, deconstruction shares the dissolution-of-dualisms approach, antiessentialism, and antifoundationalism with Classical American and Neo-Pragmatism. In "Nineteenth-Century Idealism and Twentieth-Century Textualism" (or quasi-deconstruction), Richard Rorty argues that "we should best understand the role of textualism within our culture if we see it as an attempt to think through a thorough-going pragmatism, a thorough-going abandonment of the notion of discovering the truth which is common to theology and science" (150–51). Rorty identifies two senses of "deconstruction": In the wide sense it names a large movement characterized by a "sudden infusion of Nietzschean and Heideggerian ideas into the English speaking world" mostly through the writings of Jacques Derrida ("Deconstruction," 167).[8]

In the second, narrow sense it refers to a critical technique adopted by Paul de Man, his followers, and colleagues that seeks to show how the "accidental" features of a text subvert and betray its "essential" meaning. Gayatri Spivak explains this method with specific reference to metaphor in her preface to *Of Grammatology*:

> If in the process of deciphering a text in the traditional way we come across a word that seems to harbor an unresolvable contradiction, and by virtue of being one word is made sometimes to work in one way and sometimes in another and is thus made to point away from the absence of a unified meaning, we shall catch that word. If a metaphor seems to suppress its implications, we shall catch at that metaphor. We shall follow its adventures through the text and see the text coming undone as a structure of concealment, revealing its self-transgression, its undecidability.[9]

This critical technique offers a second impetus for rhetorical analysis: to demonstrate the inability to control and produce a self-sustaining coherent meaning, in order to critically evaluate attempts to formulate foundational discourse. Also, such rhetorical analyses may help identify normative, hierarchical relations (such as masculine over feminine) and associations (such as reasoning with masculinity) that were previously ignored.

In the traditional view, metaphor should be avoided, for it is not a proper mode of philosophical discourse, and if used it is seen as an embellishment that could be replaced by a literal equal. This is what Max Black calls the substitution view of metaphor, where they are seen as economic aids and as a species of *catachresis*—the use of words to "remedy a gap in the vocabulary."[10] And if not shortcuts, they are to be glossed as stylistic decoration meant for the pleasure of the reader (34). A similar view of metaphor, the comparison view, was set out by Aristotle in the *Poetics*: "Metaphor consists in giving the thing a name that belongs to something else" (quoted in Black, *Models and Metaphors*, 36).

Recently these traditional theories of metaphor have been substantially reevaluated, leading Mark Johnson to assert that we are now in a period of Metaphormania characterized by a blooming, budding array of opinions.[11] Though a rhetorical analysis of a philosophical text can proceed from an unrefined conception of metaphor or one such as Nelson Goodman's (metaphor as the transference of a scheme onto a new realm), the notion elaborated by Richard Rorty and Donald Davidson will be most helpful here because of its emphasis on the active involvement and assimilation required by the reader.[12] Roughly, they hold that metaphors are essential to intellectual progress; lack meaning and cognitive content until they have been incorporated into one's common usage, thereby becoming reasons for belief; and, require a person to engage the metaphor, thereby reweaving one's beliefs around the unfamiliar noise until it dies and is given a literal meaning. James Guetti argues that Rorty and Davidson preserve some of Max Black's insight "that both terms of a metaphor are affected by their conjunction, that our reading of each is shaped by the presence of the other—the 'interaction.'"[13] Hence, an analysis of a metaphor from the eighteenth century can demonstrate the attempts at constructing and solidifying novel meanings, or in this case, gender roles and stereotypes. Wayne C. Booth emphasizes the importance of raising to consciousness and evaluating widespread metaphors: "To understand a metaphor is by its very nature to *decide* whether to join the metaphorist or reject [her or] him, and that is simultaneously to decide either to be shaped in the shape [her or] his metaphor requires or to resist. The only question is whether to attempt reasoned critical discourse about such judgments" ("Metaphor as Rhetoric," 63). An analysis of a dead metaphor can locate a pernicious element of the web of belief and justification, and bringing these dead metaphors back to the level of awareness may be the first step in assuring their final passage into a vanquished, nullified state. I hope to further the task of the evaluative exorcist; however, it must be acknowledged that some of the living dead cannot be killed.[14]

The analysis of symbols and metaphors from our past offers a third reason to perform rhetorical analyses on philosophic texts: to think critically about the latent functions and formulations of some of our most central notions. Feminist textual analyses can strategically adopt a deandrocentricized version of the stance Richard Rorty outlines in "Philosophy as a Kind of Writing" in order to bring to consciousness the gendered formulations of theories and concepts, such as imagination and reason.[15] By identifying the patriarchal cultural and historical location of the writing of philosophy we may, in turn, better understand the broader influence of philosophy on culture.

In "Feminism, Ideology, and Deconstruction" Rorty acknowledges the gendered development of the philosophical tradition: "Derrida's most original and important contribution to philosophy is his weaving together of Freud and Heidegger, his association of 'ontological difference' with gender difference. This weaving together enables us to see for the first time the connection between the philosophers' quest for purity, the view that women are somehow impure, the subordination of women, and 'virile homosexuality'" (103 n. 10). The first two of these connections roughly and partially describe the project Genevieve Lloyd has undertaken in *The Man of Reason*. In the introduction to the second edition, she argues that the maleness of reason "belongs to the operation of symbols" and "the metaphor of maleness is deeply embedded in the philosophical articulations and ideas of reason" (vii). As I intend to do for Hume, Lloyd, if she were to rewrite her book, would make more prominent the "metaphorical aspects of the male-female distinction as it occurs in philosophy texts" (vii). The metaphor of maleness "had been constitutive of ways of thinking of reason which have deep repercussions in ways of thinking of ourselves as male or female. Metaphorical though it may be, maleness has been no mere embellishment of reason" (vii). Lloyd thinks more needs to be done in considering the interaction of the symbolic in the social construction of gender. By considering the social effects and context, the study of the "History of Philosophy can be a form of cultural critique," and can, at least, promote a more complete understanding (109).

II. Summary of Hume's Argument

A summary of Hume's "Scepticism with Regard to the Senses" may prove beneficial in showing the centrality of the Imagination throughout the text. Hume's said purpose is to ask, "[W]hat causes induce us to believe in the existence of body? But 'tis vain to ask, Whether there be body or not? That is a point we must take for granted in all our reasonings" (187). So rather than solely looking for an epistemological justification, he is attempting to give a reasoned account of the formation of this belief. Instead of beginning as an epistemological skeptic (as he seemingly ends) he could be thought of as an ur-evolutionary epistemologist or, perhaps strainingly, as a pragmatist antiepistemologist who puts aside Cartesian doubt.

Hume sets out to decide whether the senses, reason, or Imagination causes the belief in the existence of continued and distinct (external and independent) body. First, he argues that the workings of the senses "do not, nor is it possible they shou'd deceive us," for they cannot give the notion of something distinct from themselves because they only convey to us a single perception and can give nothing beyond an impression (192). Hume also rejects the view that reason gives us the belief in continued and distinct body, for the vulgar notion of the continued and distinct perception is problematized by reflection, which shows perceptions to be dependent on the perceiver. Also, for reasons similar to Hume's account of causation, when object and perception are distinguished it is impossible to reason from one to the other. In addition, there is no access to the nonperceived object.

So, it is the Imagination (or "Nature") that is in charge of forming the belief in the external world. Classifying perceptions, the Imagination allows for the grouping of primary and secondary qualities, distinguishing them from internal perceptions such as pain: "the difference betwixt them is found neither on perception nor on reason, but on the imagination" (192). Constancy and coherence in perception allow the imagination to give "assurance of the continu'd and distinct existence of a body" (193). Imagination goes beyond sensory evidence and supposes a continued existence, for a central maxim of Hume's is that the imagination "is apt to continue even when its object fails it" (198). For Hume, the mind detects coherence among some senses, which is amplified by supposing the perceptions as continuing to exist. The mind stays on this train of thought looking for coherence among the objects of perception, which is amplified by uniformity, which in turn is enhanced by supposing a continued existence of perceptions, which in return maximizes coherence. Coherence combined with constancy of perception allows the Imagination to produce the notion of the continued existence of body to combine and connect our memories of past sensation, which leads to the concept of their distinct existence.

To justify this explanation of how the notion of the continued and distinct existence of body arises in the vulgar, Hume shows how imagination plays an essential role. The imagination is apt to confuse one idea for another if they are sufficiently similar, so it is natural for the mind to mistake one perception for another, leading to the idea of identity. "The imagination is seduc'd into such an opinion only by means of the resemblance of certain perceptions" (209). For the "vulgar" (everyone most of the time) who think of perceptions and objects as one, the imagination makes smooth the succession of related perceptions/objects by filling in the gaps, so that "thought slides along the succession with equal facility, as if it consider'd only one object" (204). The imagination also unites broken perceptions while positing one body, producing the "fiction of a continued existence." In addition, present perceptions are combined by the imagination with those in the memory to produce the belief in the continued existence of bodies. This leads necessarily to the notion of their distinct existence (200–210).

However "natural" the propensity by which it is arrived at, the vulgar assumption of the unity of perceptions and objects is easily dismissed and replaced by a notion of the dependency of perceptions on one's sense organs. Thus, contrary to the expectations with which Hume started, the belief that results from natural causes becomes problematized. Pushing on one's eye produces two images but we do not assign both existences; thus the dependency becomes evident. Philosophers distinguish between perceptions that are interrupted and perishing and objects which are uninterrupted and have a continued existence: this philosopher's notion is the double-existence view. Hume argues that one must have already held the vulgar notion of continued existence in order to retain it in regard to bodies in the notion of the double existence. The imagination would not produce this unfounded double notion, in this form, on its own. The concept's formation is influenced by reason, which does not allow the vulgar conflation of perception and object, and by the reluctance of the imagination to discard the notion of continued existence. This philosopher's notion has no primary recommendation from reason or from the imagination, for all one has access to are perceptions, making it impossible to observe a conjunction between objects and perceptions, hence precluding any evidence for the double existence.

Hence, Hume doubts the capacity of reason and ends up partially subverting the traditional hierarchy that places reason above Nature in privilege and prestige. That is to say, the production of the belief we must all take for granted is primarily the responsibility of the Imagination and not reason. As we have seen, reason fails to produce the belief in external objects, and in the hands of the philosophers the belief is complicated into an unsupported double-existence view. Now that we have demonstrated the centrality of the operations of the imagination in Hume's theory of ideas and in his account of the origin of our belief in the external world, we can move on to examine the forms Hume gives the imagination and reason.

III. The Metaphorical Identities of Imagination and Reason

Given the importance of the imagination in "Scepticism," the underlying gendered metaphors appearing near the end of the section warrant analysis. These crucial metaphors contribute to the formulation, expression, and dynamics of nature, reason, and imagination throughout. The gender metaphorics Hume employs in discussing reason and imagination/ nature are complex in their associations and multiple in their differentiations.

As we shall see more clearly, there are several inconsistently drawn characters in "Scepticism." Some are distinct but others are more schizophrenic, with multiple identities. Hume aligns "calm and profound reflection" and "study'd reflection" with the good male philosopher's reasoning. The male practice of "reasoning" is here to be distinguished from the faculty of "reason." The good philosopher can use more than strictly logical reasoning, since he can reason causally, which requires a form of agreeable imagination. Imagination on her good days helps us reason causally, and is sometimes praised as keeping us alive by producing the belief in the continued and independent existence of bodies. However, Imagination has her bad days as well. When out of control and acting like a harlot, Imagination interferes with the good philosopher's studied reflections. The bad philosopher, though reason contests, gives into the bad Imagination, and the result is the fiction of the double existence. It also appears that when the bad philosopher's "study'd reflection" is disturbed by the bad Imagination, he becomes a spectator of and later involved in an affair between two women—Reason and Imagination.

The principal metaphor in "Scepticism" is the equation of Nature with woman. As we shall see, Hume's metaphors form several equivalences, such as woman with nature, nature with imagination, imagination with woman, woman with seductress (sometimes savior), woman with fancy, and fancy with folly. Imagination takes the place of Nature and a gendered metaphor is set up around the revised dichotomy reason/imagination, where imagination is a feminine variable with both a good and a bad persona, whereas reason when personified is a feminine constant and an actor influencing and manipulated by the masculine philosopher. Reasoning becomes a male domain that is guided by and guides reason, which for Hume is a weaker force than Imagination: "Nature is always too strong for principle" (*Enquiry*, 191). The principal "woman," imagination, is given only the two elaborations of seducer and savior, the former being the most prevalent in "Scepticism," the latter in the *Enquiry*.

As we will see, there are interesting and important comparisons to be made between the *Treatise* and the *Enquiry*. A cross-textual comparison of the metaphors of reason and Nature will make apparent the particular importance of the Nature-as-seductress metaphor in the *Treatise* section "Scepticism." By ascribing Imagination to the role of seductress, Hume makes all that the imagination contributes throughout the section become suspect.

In addition, how Hume accounts for the origin of the theory of the double existence involves a manipulation of gendered metaphors where there is struggle between opposing genders: woman-nature-imagination-vulgar versus man-philosopher-reasoning. He writes that the dependency of our perceptions should give rise to the conclusion that there is no continued existence; instead, the object is said to exist while the perceptions are interrupted. Hume explains:

> There is a great difference betwixt such opinions as we form after a calm and profound reflection and such as we embrace by a kind of instinct or natural impulse, on account of their stableness and conformity to the mind. If these opinions become contrary, 'tis not difficult to foresee which of them will have the advantage. As long as our attention is bent upon the subject, the philosophical and study'd principle may prevail; but *the moment we relax our thoughts, nature will display herself, and draw us back to our former opinion. Nay she has sometimes such an influence, that she can stop our progress, even in the midst of our most profound reflections*, and keep us from running on with the consequences of any philosophical opinion. Thus tho' we clearly perceive the dependence and interruption of our perceptions, we stop short in our career, and never upon that account reject the notion of an independent and

continu'd existence. That opinion has such deep root in the imagination it is impossible to eradicate it. (214; emphasis mine)

The skeptical conclusion is prohibited or, rather, for Hume the skeptic is lured away from *his* (the reader and any possible philosopher are suggested as male) conclusion by the wiles of a negatively feminized Nature, and progress is halted.

Rather than saying metaphorically what could be said literally, Hume offers notions of reason and nature and the roles they play as explicitly gendered. Hume perpetuates the formulation of a feminized "Nature" that must be overcome by the reasoner, supporting Lloyd's point that "philosophy has defined ideals of 'reason' through the exclusion of the feminine" (*Man of Reason*, 106). When "woman" is associated with nature, the "calm and profound reflection" contrasted with "natural impulse" and nature, referred to as "she," is essentially a male/female or masculine/feminine distinction (sex and gender being conflated). The gender contrast is again drawn on the next page between "our natural and obvious principles" and "our study'd reflections" (215). That this is a gender distinction is further evidenced by Hume's repeated references to the philosopher and reader as male:

> *He* must assent to the principle concerning the existence of body, though *he* cannot pretend by any arguments to maintain its veracity. Nature has not left this to his choice. (187; emphasis mine)

> Whatever may be *the reader's* opinion at the present moment, that an hour hence he will be persuaded there is both an external and internal world. (218; emphasis mine)

> When *he* awakes from *his* dream, *he* will be the first to join in the laugh against *himself*. (*Enquiry*, 191; emphasis mine)

The objection that Hume meant "he or she" when using "he" is generally weak and specifically faulty given the particular sexually suggestive metaphors and Hume's obvious ability to see the importance of specifying gender in these heavily gendered contexts.

Nature/Imagination is ascribed the stereotypical trappings of the deceptive woman who uses sexual ploys to lead virtuous men astray. When "Nature" is said to "display herself" as if exposing herself or flaunting her "charms" in a sexual lure, Hume's characterization of woman is as seductress/temptress/leader-astray found frequently in Western culture (e.g., in Genesis). He metaphorically applies this to imagination by way of nature.

The eighteenth-century and present-day reader can readily understand this metaphorical comparison. The interactive associations of seductress as Nature and Nature as seductress would require little work or input on the part of the reader, for Hume is tapping into a cultural reservoir containing the dead metaphors of "Mother Nature" and Nature-as-woman that act as preestablished links, ready for his further elaboration. The nature-as-woman metaphor manifests itself in a particular sense of limit that was seen frequently in scientific investigation of that time: nature like a woman can only be penetrated so far, and as with all women (as the classic cliché goes) no man can fully understand her.

There is other evidence suggesting that Hume sees manipulative features as defining women, for in the *Enquiry Concerning the Principles of Morals* he explains that "such are the insinuation, address, and charms of their fair companions, that women are commonly able to break the confederacy, and share with the other sex the rights and privileges of society" (191). Also, in "Scepticism" Hume continues to use the word "deceive" (190, 192, 202), saying it is not fit to describe the functioning of the senses or of reason, but does characterize the imagination, the only insidiously metaphorized notion of the three. So when the woman's deceptive diversion prevents the philosopher from making "progress," "she" becomes and acts through another of the negative stereotypes played by concepts personified by women.

In this section we have seen some of the basic metaphorical identities that imagination and reason take, noted the multiple identities of reason, and differentiated between "reasoning" and "reason." We can now investigate the differences between the metaphors of the *Enquiry* and the *Treatise*.

IV. Comparison of the *Enquiry* and the *Treatise*

Like the section "Scepticism" in the *Treatise*, Section XII, Part I of the *Enquiry* ends on a note of hopelessness. However, in Section XII, Part II of the Enquiry the inability to keep from believing in the continued and distinct existence of bodies is quite fortunate, for "all human life must perish, were his [skeptical] principles universally and steadily to prevail" (191). What must be noted about the *Enquiry* is that it contains a completely different metaphorics from that of "Scepticism": Nature is a virtuous woman that keeps the men out of trouble—an "Angel in the House."[16] Hume is much more comfortable with feminine Nature in such a role than in the seductress mode found in "Scepticism," and this makes all the difference in the way in which he, supposedly, evaluates the text and formulates his conclusions.

The *Enquiry*'s metaphors deserve further analysis to make more apparent the contradistinction with "Scepticism" and to explore their repercussions. In Section XII, Part II of the *Enquiry*, Hume uses Nature (Imagination) as a sort of "Angel in the House" stereotype, which keeps philosophers from falling into skeptical danger: again, if skepticism became accepted "all human life must perish . . . [a]ll discourse, all action would immediately cease," but not to worry, for "Nature is always too strong for principle" (191). Nature here refers to natural dispositions and principles like those associated with feminine Nature in "Scepticism": when skeptical principles are "put in opposition to the more powerful principles of our nature, they vanish like smoke" (159). Nature is both more powerful and more highly privileged than Reason in the *Enquiry*.

In the last section of Book I of the *Treatise*, Hume gives a much weaker evaluation of the benefits of nature than he does in the *Enquiry*. He celebrates nature: "Since reason is incapable of dispelling these clouds, nature herself suffices to that purpose, and cures me of this philosophical melancholy and delirium" (*Treatise*, 269). Yet, the praise is tempered and partially retracted when he characterizes those who follow nature and enjoy the pleasures of life as indolent (269). Imagination is also criticized: "Nothing is more dangerous to reason than flights of the imagination, and nothing has been the occasion of more mistakes among philosophers. Men of bright fancies may in this respect be compar'd to those angels, whom the scriptures represents as covering their eyes with their wings" (267). Hence, the *Treatise* ends with an evaluation of Nature with reservations somewhat similar, but, perhaps, less harsh than that of the earlier section "Scepticism."

In sharp contradistinction to the *Treatise* are the metaphors of Nature throughout the *Enquiry*. As discussed above, Section XII, Part II contains a laudatory evaluation of Nature as a mothering figure that protects philosophers from excessive skepticism. Of greater importance is Section V, where nature takes on the function of a benevolent god or a Supreme Mother holding a Leibnizian preestablished harmony in place:

> Here, then, is a kind of pre-established harmony between the course of nature and the succession of our ideas; and though the powers and forces, by which the former is governed, be wholly unknown to us; yet our thoughts and conceptions have still, we find, gone on in the same train with the other works of nature . . . As nature has taught us the use of our limbs, without giving us the knowledge of the muscles and nerves, by which they are actuated; so has she implanted in us a kind of instinct, which carries forward the thought in a correspondent course to that which she has established among external objects; though we are ignorant of those powers and forces, on which this regular course and succession of objects totally depends (96–97).

This apotheosis of Mother Nature, far from the seductress metaphor of the *Treatise*, is the highest evaluation Hume gives of the role of nature.[17]

We have seen the pronounced distinctions between the metaphors of Nature as Supreme Mother in the *Enquiry* and as seductress in the *Treatise*. Now we can analyze the importance of these metaphors in Hume's texts.

V. The Extent and Effects of the Gender of Imagination and Reason

The sexual-symbolic dynamics involved in Hume's account of the production of the double-existence view demonstrate, as we shall see, how embedded gender is in all of the terms and concepts. Hume appeals to gendered interaction to explain the conflict between reason and imagination:

> In order to set ourselves at ease in this particular, we contrive a new hypothesis, which seems to comprehend both these principles of reason and the imagination. This hypothesis is the philosophi-

cal one of the double existence of perceptions and objects; which pleases *our reason*, in allowing, that our dependent perceptions are interrupted and different; and at the same time is agreeable to the imagination, in attributing a continu'd existence to something else, which we call *objects*. This philosophical system, therefore, is the *monstrous offspring* of two principles, which are contrary to each other, which are both at once embraced by the mind, and which are unable to mutually destroy each other. (*Treatise*, Bk. I, Sec. IV, Pt. II, 215; emphasis mine)

Feminine here, reason is attended to by the seminal mind of the philosopher. The product of a double copulation is the double-existence hypothesis, "the monstrous offspring of two principles, which are contrary to each other, which are both at once embraced by the mind" (215). So, the conceptual-carnal embrace between the two contrary (good and bad) "faculties" produces a doubly existing offspring confusingly composed of part of each of its progenitors.

Here, Hume's metaphor is that of a masculine mind that tries to use feminine reason as a lover. This may seem like a curious counterexample to Lloyd's thesis that reason is masculine, but reasoning is still a province occupied by men: she is "our reason." The masculine philosopher is doubly confronted by two feminine characters who are struggling to win the mind's favor, thus placing the masculine philosopher/mind as an arbitrator and a lover of both: "Nature is obstinate, and will not quit the field, however strongly attacked by reason; and at the same time reason is so clear to the point, that there is no possibility of disguising her. Not being able to reconcile these two enemies, we endeavor to set ourselves at ease as much as possible, by successively granting to each whatever it demands, and by feigning a double existence, where each may find something, that has all the conditions it desires" (215). Perhaps the "monstrous offspring" is this problematic tripartite relationship (ménage á trois), or the offspring of that relationship—the double-existence view. The philosopher is not a detached spectator, rather he is an active participant in the affair between two women whom he embraces, who compete for his favor, and both of whose "demands" and "desires" he must satisfy. Hume suggests that the double-existence view is popular because the similarities between the vulgar and philosophic positions allow for an easy interchange between them in case "we [need to] humor our reason for a moment, when it [or she] becomes troublesome and solicitous" (216).

Consequently, when the masculine philosopher does not give into the whims of reason, he remains with the vulgar in assuming perceptions and objects identical. The philosophers who have given in to reason's demands and humor her are suggestively said to, "immediately upon leaving their closets, mingle with the rest of mankind in those exploded opinions" of the vulgar.

Here again the feminine figure or principle plays a seductive/obstructive role preventing the masculine philosopher from formulating any "high" principles. So the double-existence view is thrice disparaged, for not only does it lack evidential support, it is also associated with the credulous imagination and emasculated reason. Even though reason shows that what we call objects are dependent perceptions, it is too weak to make imagination abandon the notion of continued existence, presented as deceptive in its partial role in producing fictions, and emasculated in its failure to move far beyond the vulgar. The feminine nature and imagination must be overcome by reason, but when this proves impossible, it becomes tragic for Hume.

Reason is again feminized and emasculated in Section XII, Part II of the *Enquiry* where "Nature" is portrayed as more powerful and beneficial. In reference to puzzles such as Zeno's paradoxes, Hume says that "Reason here seems to be thrown into a kind of amazement and suspense . . . she is so dazzled and confounded" (188). This shows that Hume's emasculation of reason through feminization and descriptions of powerlessness is common in both texts where nature is seen as a more powerful contender.[18] Since this emasculation is a constant in both texts, which otherwise result in contradictory evaluations by Hume, it points to the changing metaphorical descriptions of imagination as an independent, and crucial, variable.

Hume's manipulation of gendered metaphors produces a rhetorical effect by metaphorical force, and the force of his metaphors and their effects on the concepts of reason and imagination occurring earlier in the text is not realized until the end. His rhetorical strategy emphasizes the principle role that imagination plays in one's belief of the external world and how, even though it conflicts with reason, it is too strong for one to be able to drop the notion of continued existence: "nature is always too strong for principle" (*Enquiry*, 160). So in a sense, Hume, for different reasons, is arguing the pragmatic point Peirce made in "What Pragmatism Is," wherein philosophical doubt is dismissed as having "nothing to do with any serious business," and it is asserted that "what you cannot in the least help believing is not, justly speaking, wrong belief . . . for you it is the absolute truth."[19] But for Hume skeptical doubt about representational perception is serious business, according to his theory of ideas and his notions of reason, imagination, and nature. In part, the felt significance of his subversion of the dichotomy reason/nature (or more precisely philosopher/nature) is seemingly due to his own gendered metaphorical application. Hume finds it difficult to relinquish the position of power and superiority enjoyed by the masculine philosopher to feminine nature in her bad incarnation.

Directly following the most heavily metaphorical passages where the gendered struggle is most evident, he says that he no longer feels comfortable resting his confidences on the imagination, here a harlot. Taking the traditional interpretation of Hume as a total skeptic, the metaphors and his apparent shift could be part of a rhetorical strategy to discredit the reliability of the mechanism accounting for the belief in body, in an attempt to emphasize a skeptical conclusion. Regardless of his initial purpose, which seems far from a skeptical one, Hume ends up saying that he does not see how reliance on the feminine imagination can "lead to any solid rational system," for woman is soft and hollow while man is firm and solid (Treatise, 217). But the calm and reflective (masculine) philosopher can only stay firm for a brief time in the presence of such a bad woman, who will, after a short struggle, cause him to become soft again. Uncomfortable with the described fate, he states that following the guidance of the character he describes as a bad woman is to follow "illusion" (217).

VI. Conclusion and Significance

Through his metaphorics, Hume reinforces and helps create oppositions between reasoning, reason, and nature, for metaphors help create similarities by pushing us to look for and create them. He alters the standard masculine/feminine conflict between reason and nature. As reason is emasculated and nature is slandered, the conflict becomes one between two women, observed by a male philosopher who fails to maintain the critical distance required for studied reflection. Nature is further associated with the feminine and reasoning or studied reflection with masculinity through the masculine mind. The behavior characteristics and

social options are further ingrained and limited. Reason, though emasculated, becomes more the province of males and maleness more reasonable;
Nature becomes more feminine as the feminine becomes more natural. In
a process of reflexive and interacting formulations, these associations are
made. "What has happened has not been a simple exclusion of women,
but a constitution of femininity through exclusion" (Lloyd, *Man of
Reason*, 106).

Taking Black's interactionist view, we can see that both sides are
effected and affect the understanding of the metaphor. On a Davidsonian
account one must savor the metaphor, carry it around for a while, look for
similarities it suggests, and try it out. Then when it becomes accepted and
one has adjusted one's web of belief around the anomalous noise, it
becomes literalized, ascribed a meaning, and dies off into a literal or
dormant state. Thus, it becomes ingrained into one's patterns of justification and belief after repeated use or standardization. Some of Hume's
elementary metaphors may have been so familiar in the eighteenth
century that they fell stillborn, already literalized at the moment of
conception, from the press. Through his perpetuation and preservation of
dead metaphors Hume becomes what Wayne C. Booth calls a metamor-
tician. Yet, Hume is not merely confirming an already existent sexism,
rather he is involved in the continual reproduction of cultural symbols,
myths, associations, and values that are re-gen(d)erated through use.

Hume subverts the dichotomy reason/nature only to the extent that it
is partially reversed, not eliminated. Nature is said to be stronger than
reason since it cannot be bullied away, it plays a crucial role in the belief
in the external world, and it has seductive power over the philosopher
and his study'd reflection. Yet in the *Treatise*, the power of nature/
imagination does not earn as agreeable an evaluation as that of study'd
reflection and the use of reason by the reasoning male philosopher. The
contrast between reason and nature is not subverted, but reinforced. This
is evidenced in that reason is still valued more highly than nature, reason
shows an error in imagination's notion of the independence of perception,
and the reasoning philosopher must exclude female nature from his calm
reflection when she is bad. Rationality is still in a struggle to assert its
masculinity against the feminine nature. The resulting power of nature
over reason in the hierarchy is not happily accepted by Hume, who plays
upon eighteenth-century fears and stereotypes of the ubiquitous, irrational woman. The point made by Peirce is echoed forbodingly by Hume in
this section when he says, "[W]hatever be the reader's opinion at this

present moment, that an hour hence he will be persuaded there is both an external and an internal world" (218). The male philosopher will, sure enough, give into the alluring powers of that feminine seductress nature/ imagination, and after falling into illusion he will eventually accept imagination's belief in the continued existence of bodies. The "fiction" of the double existence is not a sole product of a good, natural propensity, rather it results from the interactions of an emasculated "reason" and a harlot-like imagination.[20]

Hume only finds it unacceptable to relinquish the position of power and privilege enjoyed by the "masculine" philosopher to "feminine" nature when "she" is in the seductress role. His reflection upon this section—"I began this section with premising, that we ought to have an implicit faith in our senses, and that this wou'd be the conclusion, I shou'd draw from the whole of my reasoning. But to be most ingenuous, I feel myself *at present* of a quite contrary sentiment, and am more inclin'd to repose no faith at all in my senses, or rather imagination, than to place it in such implicit confidence"—is a result of the effectiveness and boomer-anging effect of his own metaphors (217). I hope to have shown, unlike the result of a deconstructive reading, that Hume's own metaphors have played an essential role in supporting his conclusion. But paradoxically, Hume's rhetoric is too effective (in, supposedly, his own perception), so much so that he concludes that his initial purpose has been subverted. So the "incidental" or "marginal" features of the text have had a pervasive effect on the status of earlier discussions on the role of the imagination, resulting in a degradation of these processes. Hume acknowledges this and undermines his initial purpose by constructing a more skeptical text through the uncontrollable rhetorical force of the nature-as-seductress metaphor. Hume's metaphorical weapon backfires.

In recognizing the unacknowledged metaphorical subtext we can see how Hume's gendered dramas reflect his society's androcentricism. Be-yond being a sociological mirror, these metaphors help re-create that culture through repetition and modification. In addition, and fundamen-tal to the purpose of this paper, the rhetorical dimensions of Hume's texts are intimately connected with his philosophical conclusions through the metaphorically gendered concepts. Regardless of whether Hume's original intent was subverted by his own rhetoric, his presentation that this has occurred highlights the significance of the contrasting metaphorics of the passages for the history of philosophy.

Notes

1. Throughout, I will be referencing these editions of Hume's texts: An Enquiry Concerning Human Understanding [1748], ed. Anthony Flew (La Salle: Open Court, 1988); and A Treatise on Human Nature [1739] (New York: Oxford University Press, 1978).

2. Genevieve Lloyd, The Man of Reason: "Male" and "Female" in Western Philosophy, 2d ed. (Minneapolis: University of Minnesota Press, 1993).

3. Arthur C. Danto, The Transfiguration of the Commonplace (Cambridge: Harvard University Press, 1981), 166.

4. Wayne C. Booth, "Metaphor as Rhetoric: The Problem of Evaluation," in Sheldon Sacks, ed., On Metaphor (Chicago: University of Chicago Press, 1979), 57.

5. Richard A. Lanham, A Handlist of Rhetorical Terms, 2d ed. (Berkeley and Los Angeles: University of California Press, 1991). Alternately, Stanley Fish, in "Rhetoric," in Frank Lentricchia and Thomas McLaughin, eds., Critical Terms for Literary Study, 2d ed. (Chicago: University of Chicago Press, 1995), discusses Cicero's view of rhetoric as advertising of the truth, where rhetoric is seen as an aid in glossing the truth to make it more widely acceptable.

6. The attention paid to binary oppositions stems from Ferdinand de Saussure's protophonemic principle, now comparable to meaning holism, where the meaning of a sign or a concept is in its difference from all other signs and concepts: "In the language itself, there are only differences" (Course in General Linguistics, trans. Roy Harris (La Salle: Open Court, 1986), 118). This was elaborated by Roman Jakobson in his "theory of the distinctive features of phonology," where all structural distinctions are seen as binary oppositions. Levi-Strauss applied the theory of polar opposites and the method of structural analysis onto culture. The poststructural movement adopts the meaning through difference principle but attacks the stability of binaries. Terry Eagleton explains that in order to "demonstrate how one term of an antithesis secretly inheres within another . . . Deconstruction tries to show how such oppositions, in order to hold themselves in place, are sometimes betrayed into inverting or collapsing themselves" (Literary Theory, 2d. ed. [Minneapolis: University of Minnesota Press, 1996]).

7. Samuel C. Wheeler III has written several helpful essays on deconstruction and its similarity to some recent analytic philosophical theories of language. See "Metaphor According to Davidson and de Man," in Reed Way Dasenbrock, ed., Redrawing the Lines (Minneapolis: University of Minnesota Press, 1989); "Indeterminacy of French Interpretation: Derrida and Davidson," in Ernest LePore, ed., Truth and Interpretation: Perspectives on the Philosophy of Donald Davidson (Oxford: Blackwell, 1986); "Wittgenstein as Conservative Deconstuctor," New Literary History 19, no. 2 (1988): 239–58.

8. Richard Rorty, "Nineteenth-Century Idealism and Twentieth-Century Textualism," in Consequences of Pragmatism (Minneapolis: University of Minnesota Press, 1982). "Deconstruction," in The Cambridge History of Literary Criticism, vol. 8 (New York: Cambridge University Press, 1995).

9. Gayatri Chakravorty Spivak, translator's preface to Jacques Derrida, Of Grammatology (Baltimore: Johns Hopkins University Press, 1976), lxxv.

10. Max Black, Models and Metaphors (Ithaca: Cornell University Press, 1962), 31–32.

11. There are many other competing theories of metaphor. Derrida, in "White Mythology: Metaphor in the Text of Philosophy," in Margins of Philosophy, trans. Alan Bass (Chicago: University of Chicago Press, 1982), suggests that all discourse and meaning are essentially metaphorical, and Paul de Man, in Allegories of Reading (New Haven: Yale University Press, 1979), sees all predication as metaphorical. Donald Davidson, at another extreme, argues in "What Metaphors Mean," Critical Inquiry 5 (Autumn 1978): 31–47, that metaphors have no meaning and lack cognitive content. George Lakoff and Mark Johnson argue in The Metaphors We Live By (Chicago: University of Chicago Press, 1980) that metaphors are ubiquitous and structure one's entire gestalt. Nelson Goodman's scheme/content theory of metaphor and Max Black's interaction view posit metaphors as possessing

meaning and cognitive content and as essential to intellectual progress (Goodman's *Languages of Art* [Indianapolis: Hackett, 1976] and "Metaphor as Moonlighting," in *Reconstructions in Philosophy* [Indianapolis: Hackett, 1988]; and Max Black's *Models and Metaphors* [Ithaca: Cornell University Press, 1962]). And W. V. Quine sees the literalization of metaphor as the process of scientific theory formulation, on the model of jungle clearing ("Postscript on Metaphor," *Critical Inquiry* 5 [Autumn 1978]: 161–62).

12. Davidson, "What Metaphors Mean," Richard Rorty, "Philosophy as Science, as Metaphor, and as Politics," in *Essays on Heidegger and Others: Philosophical Papers*, vol. 2 (New York: Cambridge University Press, 1995); and "Unfamiliar Noises: Hesse and Davidson on Metaphor," in *Objectivity, Relativism, and Truth: Philosophical Papers*, vol. 1 (New York: Cambridge University Press, 1994).

13. James Guetti, *Wittgenstein and the Grammar of Literary Experience* (Athens: University of Georgia Press, 1993), 187 n. 3.

14. However, the possibility must be addressed that the concepts and the metaphors that helped create them might be so intermeshed that like Siamese twins, neither can be removed without threatening the other's existence. Lloyd is confident that "philosophers can take seriously feminist dissatisfaction with the maleness of Reason without repudiating either Reason or Philosophy" (*The Man of Reason*, 109). But Christine Di Stefano wonders if Lloyd has not been too optimistic. She asks: "Has she perhaps underestimated the implications of her own analysis? What is 'Reason' or 'Philosophy' stripped of its androcentric content and associations, which, as Lloyd has demonstrated is ubiquitous throughout the history of Western philosophic discourse? Can these terms even be thought without the residues of that content?" ("Dilemmas of Difference: Feminism, Modernity, and Postmodernity," in Linda J. Nicholson, ed., *Feminism/Postmodernism* [New York: Routledge, 1990], 72).

15. Richard Rorty, "Philosophy as a Kind of Writing: An Essay on Derrida," in *Consequences of Pragmatism*.

In "Revealing Gendered Texts," *Philosophy and Literature* 15 (1991): 40–58, Cynthia Freeland exposes the androcentricism in Rorty's writings, and in conclusion, she suggests that it still might be a valuable technique to approach philosophy as just another type of writing for one type of analysis, namely, to examine the interrelations of gender and philosophical concepts.

16. Here Lloyd's discussion of Rousseau's view of nature becomes relevant:

> Nature is both the model and the source of an unspoiled simplicity and spontaneity which will break the bonds of distorting convention and artificiality . . . Nature thus becomes for Rousseau [and for Hume in the *Enquiry*] a model for, and a source of, moral regenera-tion . . . Reason should be held in check by closeness to nature . . . This dual location of Nature creates new possibilities for women as a symbol. Female closeness to Nature enables women to function as moral exemplar . . . But it is men who make Rousseau's journey from corrupted Reason to Nature [and men, for Hume, who proceed from the vulgar to the philosopher's study'd reflection and back, and from natural inclination to skepticism and back]. It is they who enact the full Drama of Rousseau's transformation . . . Rousseau's women never really make the journey; for them, unlike men, closeness to Nature is a natural state, not an achievement of Reason. (*Man of Reason*, 62–64)

17. The ease of the Mother Nature or Angel in the House metaphor's substitutability for the seductress metaphor limits women to two main positions in the barrage of metaphorical applications: Madonnas and Magdalenes. This highlights the danger of appealing to certain forms of essentialism (celebrating and describing the supposedly specifically innate characteristics of women) that can, at times, lead one to stumble into oppressive forms of discourse with limited, unappealing options—for example, the doctrine of the separate spheres. Such attempts resuscitate the Angel in the House, thus perpetuating the struggle that Virginia Woolf describes: "It was she that used to come between me and

my paper when I was writing reviews. It was she who bothered me and wasted my time and so tormented me that I at last killed her . . . Had I not killed her she would have killed me" ("Professions for Women," in M. H. Abrams, ed., *The Norton Anthology of English Literature*, 6th ed., vol. 2 [New York: Norton, 1993], 1987–88).

18. Of course the most obvious example of the ineffectiveness of reason is stated in the now clichéd phrase "Reason is and ought only to be the slave of the passions, and can never pretend to any other office than to serve and obey them" (*Treatise*, 415).

19. Charles Sanders Peirce, "What Pragmatism Is," in *Pragmatism: The Classic Writings*, ed. H. S. Thayer (Indianapolis: Hackett, 1982), 101–23; quotes are from 107, 109.

20. Hume discusses another "fiction" in "Scepticism," "the fiction of a continu'd existence" (205). Given the negative form the imagination takes later in this section (a harlot), any of its workings throughout are viewed as problematic. Within the gendered dynamic of this section, the "fiction of a continu'd existence" is not the product of a beneficial natural tendency.

5

Hume and the Reality of Value

Jacqueline Taylor

> How then did it work out, all this? How did one judge people, think
> of them? How did one add up this and that and conclude that it
> was liking one felt, or disliking? And to those words, what meaning
> attached, after all?

When we first encounter Lily Briscoe, the character in Woolf's novel who
asks these questions, she has as much trouble affirming her own identity
as she does relating to others.[1] It is in the process of internalizing the
nurturing and creative qualities of Mrs. Ramsay, the maternal heroine of
the story, that Lily learns better to chart the complexities of her dependence on the thoughts and sentiments of others. By the novel's close, she
no longer feels the force of the voice (Charles Tansley's, the philosophical

Earlier versions of this essay were read at Bryn Mawr College, Tufts University, Wesleyan
University, and the 22nd International Hume Conference. Thanks to Thomas E. Hill, Jr., for his
constructive comments at the Hume conference. I've also profited from discussions with Anne Jaap
Jacobson, David Owen, and Christine Swanton. I am especially grateful to Elisabeth Young-Bruehl
for her encouragement.

protégé of Mr. Ramsay) that proclaims, "Women can't paint, women can't write," and instead finds a way to affirm her own fragile ambitions. As important as putting brush to canvas is the way in which Lily works out her own answer to the question: "What is the meaning of life? . . . The great revelation had never come. The great revelation perhaps never did come. Instead there were little daily miracles, illuminations, matches struck unexpectedly in the dark; here was one. . . . Mrs. Ramsay bringing them together . . . Mrs. Ramsay making of the moment something permanent . . . this was of the nature of a revelation. In the midst of chaos there was shape; this eternal passing and flowing (she looked at the clouds going and the leaves shaking) was struck into stability."[2] Woolf emphasizes in this passage how life's meaning manifests itself for many of us in the modern age: not through our apprehension of eternal, immutable laws, but rather because we discover that our engagement in certain forms of social activity and communication can impart a "shape" and "stability" to our lives.

My aim in this essay is to try to draw out the way in which David Hume gives philosophical expression to Woolf's insight that we find meaning in the activities and evaluations that our sociality makes it possible and necessary for us to share. Hume gave us one of the best and most wide-ranging philosophical treatments of the emotions, including our moral sentiments, yet this fundamental component of his science of human nature remains one of "the most neglected" (T 273).[3] Feminist concerns with moral development, with how we learn about our feelings and about appropriate expressions of them, find a resonance in Hume's work. I believe that his philosophy can help us to reinterpret our current views of the relation between the emotions, self-understanding, and value, and so can help to advance the ends of feminist philosophy. I first present an argument for how I think we should read Hume in light of one recent ethical debate concerning the status and source of value. In the conclusion of the essay, I will illustrate the resourcefulness of the Humean view as it relates to feminist concerns by considering how the inclusion of women as authorities in aesthetic discourse (women can not only paint but can also judge and write about painting) helps us better to understand the relations between the different aspects of our value discourse.

I. Positivism's appropriation of Hume's philosophy earlier in this century has left a lasting impression, one that makes it difficult to appreciate the significance of his philosophy, if one does not read his works with care, for feminism. Beginning with the publication of A. J. Ayer's *Language, Truth, and Logic* in 1936, Hume's empiricism has been regarded as an important forerunner of positivism and its ethical accompaniment, emotivism. More recently, Hume's moral philosophy has been linked with more sophisticated forms of noncognitivism that have tried to address the shortcomings of emotivism by showing how the norm-governance of our expressive attitudes renders them "quasi-objectivized."[4]

The sort of noncognitivism with which Hume is typically associated distinguishes between fact and value and denies the reality of moral facts.[5] When we respond to some person or situation in terms expressive of morality (e.g., "his statement was praiseworthy" or "we all admired her courage"), our evaluative judgment does not depend on our first perceiving specifically moral features in the person or situation. The person's morality will not be one of her features apparent to us in the way that her size, shape, coloring, nationality, stubbornness, or pride are. Rather, we have a felt emotional or attitudinal response, typically to some perceived feature of the person. For example, we feel pleasure upon witnessing her courage, and then because we regard whatever gives us pleasure as good, we project the notion of goodness onto that feature of the person, in this case her courage, that stimulated the pleasure in the first place. In this way we "judge" that courage is good, or a virtue.

Our affective response is quite distinct from the perception of facts or objective features. Moral judgments derive from our felt responses or are expressive of them, and do not purport to state facts about moral qualities perceivable in the object or action itself. Properly speaking, such judgments are expressive of subjective feelings, and do not state objective moral facts. Typically, the contemporary noncognitivist distinguishes the descriptive function of language from the expressive one. Factual language is the kind of discourse taken to include sentences with a truth status, and used to describe what is perceived out there in the world. Evaluative language, on the other hand, does not communicate truth or falsehood, but rather expresses attitudes, which are neither true nor false. For the purpose of this essay, I will contrast this noncognitivist view with a view I will call moral realism; the latter view holds that value predicates can be made out to represent objective and cognizable features of the world.

Sabina Lovibond argues that contemporary noncognitivism rests on the same sort of metaphysical view to which the seventeenth- and eighteenth-century empiricists (she makes reference to Hobbes, Locke, and Hume) subscribed. By focusing here on her account of the similarities between empiricism and noncognitivism, we can draw into the foreground issues about the roles of reason and sentiment, and the status of fact and value, that underlie the contemporary debate concerning language and meaning. Lovibond argues that the contemporary distinction between fact and value perpetuates the reason-sentiment distinction that dominated modern British empiricism. She characterizes empiricism as holding that (1) thought is prior to language, and language is conceived as a medium for communicating thought; (2) the content of our thought and our inferences about how things really stand in the world derive from our immediate sense perceptions, for example, Humean impressions; so that (3) we understand 'the fabric of the world' or reality to be comprised only of what we perceive through the senses and can denote by the terms of the experimental sciences.[6] On this view, we reason from or about the date provided by fundamental sense impressions and thus employ an essentially passive mode of judgment in forming beliefs about the real world. Our capacity as reasoners contrasts with our capacity as evaluators. When we evaluate or assess the worth of persons or things, we employ affective propensities that contribute in no way to our knowledge of how things are. According to Hume, for example, we are, through our faculty of taste, "gilding and staining all natural objects" with the colors of our internal feelings "and raising in a manner a new creation" (E 294). The evaluative judgments we make about art or morality simply express those feelings and attitudes engendered in us when we encounter certain qualities in objects, persons, or actions. We can use empirical methods to establish the existence of the natural qualities that stimulate our affective responses, but neither our feelings and attitudes nor our expression of them evidence apprehension of some *further* moral or aesthetic quality. Our role as judges of value therefore renders us active and creative, since through our passionate responses we confer value on a world that is otherwise "morally or spiritually dead."[7]

The realist critique of noncognitivism centers on the untenability of the bifurcation of fact and value. Making the existence of values depend entirely upon our affective states, instead of allowing that they are real, perceivable features of the world suggests, according to John McDowell, that the noncognitivist assumes some ontologically prior objective conception of reality onto which moral and aesthetic attitudes are projected. The noncognitivist must posit "authentic" features that are really there, that we cognitively apprehend and can describe, and to which our subjective evaluations correspond.[8] But the positing of such authentic features masks "the desire for a security which is actually quite illusory" (since reality must continue to present itself to us in readily classifiable ways), and is an attempt to escape the "vertigo" that threatens to befall us should we attend too closely to the free-floating nature of our evaluative attitudes.[9] If values derive ultimately from our subjective affective states, then they lack a grounding in external reality. David Wiggins argues that noncognitivism fails because it holds that our affective propensities are the source of value even though they are neither themselves percipient nor determinant of perception; the doctrine thus "treats the objects of psychological states as unequal partners or derivative elements in the conceptual structure of values and states and their objects."[10] The affective part of our mental life seems to get "logically isolated" from that part that concerns factual beliefs and is governed by external reality, and this split poses a problem in terms of guaranteeing the link between authentic features of the world and the evaluative attitudes that we project onto them.[11] Lovibond identifies a more radical noncognitivist, R. M. Hare is her example, who asserts openly that our attitudes are entirely unconstrained by any facts or reality. This more radical noncognitivist argues that people should be free to make commitments as they please and to make their own decisions about where they stand on moral issues.[12] But having the freedom to choose as we please places our moral sentiments beyond the reach of rational appraisal or correction, and suggests that any affective state could arbitrarily light upon any object.[13]

Moreover, the realist argues that regarding value as a mere projection of emotions or attitudes fails to accommodate the phenomenology of our moral experience. Wiggins asks whether we actually do think of our affective propensities as introducing value into the world, and how they could do so in any meaningful way if they are "psychological states conceived in independence of what they are directed to."[14] He argues that we try to find meaning in our activities and goals through an appeal to objective reasons. For when we act deliberately, we often see ourselves as making a choice on the basis of what we take to be good reasons, and for some end that we regard as better than other things that we could have chosen. It is only at the cost of neglecting what the internal processes of deliberation and evaluation are like that the noncognitivist can regard value as a mere projection of affective states. We are not content for value to be merely of a relative nature, contingent on the desires we happen to have. And we do not think that the worth of our ends and activities is constituted solely by those desires and is independent of (more) objective considerations. As Lovibond points out, if our desires and evaluative attitudes, simply as such, engender the only value there is, then we have "no objectively valid reason" for preferring one thing over another.[15]

Removing moral value from the realm of reality means that there are no moral facts of the matter. But if each of us is simply free to favor whatever we choose, how do we explain the obvious importance that moral and aesthetic values have in our lives? We think morality has an important role, for example, in regulating conduct and attitudes; our capacity to govern ourselves in accordance with norms enables us to have expectations of one another, and to assign responsibility, praise, and blame. But if no facts can constrain or govern our evaluations (in a nonarbitrary way), and there are no rationally justified standards to which our evaluations should conform (and so no way rationally to appraise our sentiments or attitudes), then the noncognitivist has difficulty explaining the fact that we make moral mistakes and think in terms of moral improvement. Morality turns out simply to reflect the attitudes we happen to have, rather than providing us with *standards for* the attitudes we in fact ought to have.

Lovibond's feminist concerns add a further, *ethical* dimension of criticism. She charges that both empiricism and noncognitivism reflect a traditional view of society that sets up dichotomies such as public/private, reason/sentiment, and masculine/feminine. In giving priority to reason over sentiment and in associating attributes of rationality with masculinity and those of moral sensitivity with femininity, both philosophies end up devaluing value in a way that does not bode well for humanism and moral progress. The feminine attributes of sentiment and sensitivity get relegated to the private realm rather than being part of the public 'real world', and serve, like the "bourgeois wife," merely as "trimming round the edge of the serviceable, fact-stating fabric of language proper."[16] Thus, despite the alleged neutrality of metaethical theories, Lovibond's criticism reveals how both ethical and metaethical theories may at their worst reflect and perpetuate 'ruling illusions'.

In contrast, realism offers us a picture of morality that emphasizes the perceptual and sensitive aspects of our affective propensities. John Mc-Dowell, for example, has suggested that our affective propensities are themselves percipient, and that, analogously to our physical senses, they provide us with more information about the world (in this case, moral facts) by "expanding our sensitivity to how things are."[17] Wiggins concurs with McDowell: moral features of the world are "lit up" by our human perspective.[18] The idea that we use our moral sensibility to illumine what is already there stands in contrast to the projectivist "gilding and stain-ing," which *adds to* what is there. The realist rejects the fact/value distinction, and with it the idea that our factual beliefs have a rational justification that our evaluations lack, and that the former describe entities with a superior ontological status in contrast to those expressed by our moral sentiments. The realist thus rejects the idea that there are two distinct kinds of speech act, description and expression, accompanied by two sorts of meaning, cognitive and emotive. At the same time, this sort of realist is careful to avoid the idea that there is a world that is "externally characterizable," apart from all human perspectives.[19] The aim instead is to present an account of objectivity that satisfies the demand we make for the kind of valid reasons that render our choices worthwhile and mean-ingful.

Such an account of objectivity is achieved through appeal to the notion of consensus. By consensus, we establish how we are to 'go on' in a way that can impart objective or impersonal validity to our moral judgments, in the sense that the meaning of moral judgments can transcend the individual's own particular perspective. With respect to morality, the realist focuses on what Bernard Williams has called "thick" concepts, various character traits construed as virtues and vices that are highly specific in their application, rather than on the more abstract, "thin" value concepts such as goodness and rightness.[20] To gain credibil-ity with the other members of society, each individual participating in the social practices employing these value concepts must learn how to use the rules governing their application. By giving primacy to thick concepts, the realist can argue that we need a properly cultivated moral sensibility in order to have *cognitive* access to moral properties, since such access depends on the individual's being experienced in how to use the rules governing the application of moral concepts (which will necessitate her being able to 'see' a situation for what it is). The realist's hypothesis is precisely that these rules "are not invented by the individual, and cannot be overturned by him."[21] The noncognitivist idea that moral evaluations or judgments simply express contingent and freely formed commitments denies the realist conception of morality that holds that the individual must learn the rules that constitute the possibility of having a shared moral sensibility. For the realist, there are moral facts there to be perceived (but only by way of a properly cultivated moral sensibility that depends on consensual practices) such that we are not free to prefer or commit ourselves to whatever we please.

II. One can easily point to passages in Hume's texts that seem to support the noncognitivist interpretation of his moral philosophy. In his essay "The Sceptic," he writes, "[T]here is nothing, in itself, valuable or despicable, desirable or hateful, beautiful or deformed" (Es 162). Rather, "beauty and worth are merely of a relative nature, and consist in an agreeable sentiment, produced by an object in a particular mind, according to the peculiar structure and constitution of that mind" (Es 163). And in "Of the Standard of Taste," Hume describes a view clearly echoing the radical noncognitivist view that we saw Lovibond associating with Hare:

> All sentiment is right; because sentiment has a reference to nothing beyond itself, and is always real, wherever a man is conscious of it. But all determinations of the understanding are not right; because they have a reference to something beyond themselves, to wit, real matter of fact. . . . Among a thousand different opinions which different men may entertain of the same subject, there is one, and but one, that is just and true; . . . On the contrary, a thousand different sentiments, excited by the same object, are all right: Because no sentiment represents what is really in the object. . . . Beauty is no quality in things themselves: It exists merely in the mind which contemplates them; and each mind perceives a different beauty. One person may even perceive deformity, where another is sensible of beauty, and every individual ought to acquiesce in his own sentiment, without pretending to regulate those of others. (Es 230)

Here, beauty is in the eye of the beholder, and each beholder ought to be free to decide what he sees. If, through our taste, we gild and stain natural objects, and raise "in a manner a new creation," then we are the creators of beauty who confer value on an objective world that is in itself morally indifferent (Enq 294).

Hume argues, however, that common sense opposes the view that "all sentiment is right," and he explicitly rejects what we have here identified as radical noncognitivism (Es 230). He claims that "it is natural for us to seek a standard of taste" that transcends and regulates the momentary sentiments of our own individual perspective, a way either to reconcile our sentiments, or at least to confirm one sentiment and condemn its opposite (Es 229). Whether as deliberators or evaluators, or as sympathizers with our friends, kin, colleagues, and fellow citizens, we want a way to determine what is right, especially when our judgments conflict with those of others or with our own previous judgments. Indeed, our moral sentiments have a special authority to regulate our passions and actions (T 457). But if, for example, both comic and moral value have their source in our "original" and "unrepresentative" psychological states, what lends a superior authority to our moral judgments (T 415)? Why on occasion, for instance, might my sense of morality stand as a corrective to your sense of what's funny?

While he appeals occasionally to an analogy between moral qualities and sensible qualities, Hume approaches the issue of moral authority primarily by comparing different orders of beauty, the various 'species' of natural, artistic, and moral beauty.[22] All kinds of beauty are associated with a feeling of pleasure in the spectator. The peculiar pleasure produced in the possessor or spectator is "the distinguishing character of beauty, and forms the difference between it and deformity, whose natural tendency is to produce uneasiness" (T 299). Natural, artistic, and moral beauty "cannot be defin'd," and all are "discern'd only by a taste or sensation" (T 299). We can also identify the qualities in objects or persons that produce the pleasant feeling in the spectator. The natural beauty of persons and other animals, for example, is of "such an order and construction of parts as . . . is fitted to give a pleasure and satisfaction to the soul" (T 299). Similarly, with artistic beauty, "there are certain qualities in objects, which are fitted by nature to produce" aesthetic pleasure or pain in creatures with our affective makeup (Es 235). Such qualities are productive of pleasure, and typically are not perceived as beautiful independently of our experiencing a pleasurable sentiment. Hume argues that all kinds of beauty depend on our having some knowledge of the objects to which we are responding. For example, of the natural beauty of a geometric shape, he says that "it is on the proportion, relation, and position of parts, that all natural beauty depends" (E 291). Indeed, "in all decisions of taste or external beauty, all the relations are beforehand obvious to the eye; and we thence proceed to feel a sentiment of complacency or disgust, according to the nature of the object, and disposition of our organs" (E 291).

When considered as qualities of persons, all kinds of beauty share one other feature, their tendency to produce pride in the person who possesses them, and love or esteem in those contemplating the beautiful people. As spectators, our sympathy with the pleasure that the quality under review affords the possessor leads us to feel admiration or approval for the person. Hume defines virtue as "a quality of the mind agreeable to or approved of by every one who considers or contemplates it" (E 261 n). Similarly, since we find useful and agreeable qualities of the body, as well as creative qualities such as 'genius' or eloquence, we ascribe both natural and aesthetic beauty to persons. Any quality that makes us beautiful or deformed in mind or body contributes to our sense of identity, shapes our assessment of our own worth, and forms one of the characteristics whereby others evaluate us.

Notice that in the passages I have cited, it is unclear whether we are to regard beauty as consisting in the feeling of pleasure we have, or whether the qualities that arouse in us the pleasant feeling comprise the beauty. Hume's statement that "pleasure and pain . . . are not only necessary attendants of beauty and deformity, but constitute their very essence," captures this seeming inconsistency (T 299). My contention in this section is that we can find in Hume's view not inconsistency, but the means to accommodate the realist's practical concerns about establishing authoritative standards that transcend the perspective of the individual, and providing mutually acceptable reasons that support as meaningful or worthwhile our preference of one thing or course of action over another. Simon Blackburn has suggested that whereas the realist holds that moral features of things are the parents of our sentiments (making perception logically prior to feeling), the Humean sees moral features as the children of our sentiments.[23] I see Hume's view as a more integrative one than Blackburn suggests, with moral features and sentiments as reciprocal and mutually guiding concepts. To offer a general statement about value, we could say that Hume relativizes the partnership between the evaluating agent and the object evaluated according to the importance for us of the object. Sometimes, as in the case of the physical beauty of persons, we may place more emphasis on the affective propensities of the person; at other times, we may think the object 'demands' a certain response. But in order to see how different kinds of evaluation function for us, we must first examine how we decide on the importance of what is evaluated.[24]

In the case of physical beauty, Hume argues that we associate having a certain physical appearance with pleasure or utility for the possessor; thus we imagine that the "order and construction" of someone's bodily parts, as well as his bodily strength and accomplishments, are useful to the person, enabling him to live a more pleasant life. We admire animals according to the features that allow them to live successfully as members of their species: "that shape, which produces strength, is beautiful in one animal; and that which is a sign of agility in another" (T 299). Hume's exemplar of human beauty is the male who possesses "broad shoulders, a lank belly, firm joints, taper legs," for these are the signs of "force and vigor" (E 244). Whatever about a person's physical appearance indicates health, strength, dexterity, fertility, or potency is the object of our approbation. We take the taper leg to be a sign of good physical condition, and the youthful face or body to be a sign of fertility; and because both physical fitness and fertility are useful, we admire these bodily indicators of them.

But not all of our evaluations of the physical attractiveness of persons are based on utility. We also tend to think of others as beautiful because of the "primary constitution of our nature" (T 299). Here Hume might mean, for example, that we are biologically adapted to find appealing the young of our own and most other animal species, and this leads us to feel protective towards them. He elsewhere suggests that we naturally feel uneasy around and disapprove of those who are deformed, diseased, or evidence dire poverty (see T 350, 362).[25] Finding another beautiful is sometimes linked to our sexual nature, and Hume claims that "the most common species of love" arises first from physical beauty, before developing with time into a concern for the well-being of the beloved (T 395). We may also find ourselves fancying others "more beautiful than ordinary" because of our lust or concern for them (T 395). Our evaluation of others as attractive may simply be capricious. The "passionate lover," for example, extols the divine beauty of his mistress, whereas to a different man, she "appears a mere mortal being, and is beheld with the utmost indifference" (Es 162).

Certainly, Hume draws attention to the way in which our outward appearance forms an important dimension of our sense of our own identity and self-worth. Physical beauty is a source of pride and admiration and can stimulate feelings of care and concern. But his account of our admiration of physical beauty also emphasizes the relatively unreflective nature of our responses. Sometimes they arise from natural drives or mere caprice. Empirical studies confirm a tendency on our part to arrive at our judgments of physical beauty and draw conclusions from them in this unreflective way: apparently, we tend to think of good-looking people as more intelligent, more successful, healthier, happier, and even morally better than less attractive people.[26] Even when we are judging according to standards set by utility, our response is often mistaken.[27] Moreover, there is something frivolous, "weak and imperfect," about some of our standards, such as those established in contests to evaluate the natural beauty of people (T 631). Beauty may not be as useful or effective as we imagine. The beautiful person is not necessarily happier, smarter, healthier, or morally better than anyone else, and our judgments may often be unreflective, if not mistaken, governed by social custom or caprice. In general, species of natural beauty (including the physical beauty of persons) tend "on their first appearance, [to] command our affection and approbation; and where they fail of this effect, it is impossible for any reasoning to redress their influence" (E 173). In the case of the assessment of physical beauty, we privilege the first-person perspective because our experience of doing so shows that differences between individuals' appraisals or mistaken appraisals tend not to prove costly

As in the case of natural beauty and deformity, our own and others' assessments of qualities that make us morally beautiful or deformed contribute significantly to our sense of identity and of self-worth. But in our moral appraisals, we expect more agreement; and even in order to converse about moral matters, we expect someone to "depart from his private and particular situation," and to "choose a point of view, common to him with others" (E 272). And whereas we allow for a wide margin of error in our assessment of physical beauty, our moral evaluations require that we "employ much reasoning, in order to feel the proper sentiment; and a false relish may frequently be corrected by argument and reflection" (E 173). Our appraisal of moral beauty "demands the assistance of our intellectual faculties" if the beauty is to have "a suitable influence on the human mind"; we must make "nice distinctions" and "distant compari- sons," draw "just conclusions," examine "complicated relations," and fix and ascertain the "general facts" (E 173). After reason shows us what the object is and its likely influence on our misery or happiness, it "makes us feel from the whole a new sentiment of blame or approbation" (E 294). One might think that here, in the case of moral value, McDowell's charge against noncognitivism applies to Hume. The object of rational judgment seems to have an ontological status that the object of evaluation lacks, and we are able to reach agreement in our moral judgments because the projected affective responses we associate with moral evaluation correspond to 'authentic features' of the world about which we have formed antecedent factual judgments.

Although Hume does argue that our moral sentiments depend on beliefs or factual judgments, this is not a one-way dependency of subjective affective states on judgments about an objectively knowable world. Practical reason governs our evaluations and choices, and to do so successfully, it requires theoretical knowledge of the world and the persons who inhabit it with us. In turn, the social institutions we create as practical agents influence our scientific practices and our views about how much and what kind of knowledge we need.[28] Human nature is "compos'd of two principal parts, which are requisite in all its actions, the affections and understanding"; without the balance afforded by the mutual direction of each 'part', their separate operations may be merely "blind motions" (T 493). The moral philosopher's task includes learning about the maladies, malfunctions, and health of the human mind.

Making sense of our passions and sentiments, in terms of understanding what we are feeling and why, and whether it is appropriate to feel as we do, requires that we attend to the influences on them, their causes and effects, and their objects. We saw that Wiggins charged noncognitivism with treating the objects of our desires and evaluative responses as unequal partners, since the view presumes that no objective goodness or value exists. I think we can, with Wiggins, reject the view that each individual subject sets his own standard for the value for all things, and still accept that to some extent our passions do serve to make us projectors of value. The way in which value figures in our lives is complicated. Value is neither straightforwardly perceived as an objective feature of things, nor does it result simply from the projection of passion, unconstrained by the features of things. Hume defines the moral sentiments along with our other passions as "secondary" impressions, or impressions of "reflexion," because they depend on prior sensations or ideas or memories of pleasure or pain (T 275). Our passions are in a sense modifications of pleasure and pain, and their diversification into more cognitively informed perceptions with more complex causal origins requires their temporal dependence on some antecedent perception of pleasure or pain. But the content of our passions does not derive from the antecedent perception in the way that the content of ideas represents "in all their parts" those ideas' antecedent impressions (T 96). It is this fact to which Hume draws our attention when he claims that passions are not copies or representatives of their antecedent perceptions, but are rather "original facts or realities, compleat in themselves" (T 458). The 'compleatness' of any passion thus need not imply that it stands independently, insulated from the influence of belief, imagination, or other passions.

Our passions and sentiments are influenced by imaginative propensities, our capacity to sympathize with others, as well as by the reasonings, reflection, and argument that contribute to our understanding of what a particular object is. While there may be individual variation such that you do not find pleasant the same things that I do, we do not (usually) make things good or pleasant simply by desiring or praising them. The imagination, that aspect of the mind that associates our ideas and feelings together in various, often habit-forming ways, can exert its own influence over our affections. Feelings and likings can become habits, and we may desire and evaluate something simply from the force of custom, rather than because we think the thing is good (T 419). We may take pleasure in doing something because we have done it a sufficient number of times to be good at it or to appreciate its value; repetition "produces a facility" of acting, and no doubt of liking or hating too (T 422–24). Objects or activities that are forbidden may seem more lovely or tempting so that we desire them more, as the security with which we can attain something may diminish our desire for it (or as our familiarity with something others may find to have a real value breeds in us a contempt for it) (T 421–22). We may be inclined to view favorably or desire objects that suit our way of life, even when we could choose something that seems better but is foreign to us (T 426). Our sympathy with the opinions of others, especially when these are eloquently expressed, affects our own opinions, appraisals, and desires (T 427). Here, then, Hume draws attention to how factors such as habit, an object's attainability, its suitability to our current circumstances, or the opinions of others can all influence what we see when we contemplate an object and may lead us to project a value onto the thing that others fail to find there. Although I cannot work out the details here, I believe that these neglected sections of Book II of the *Treatise*, when read in conjunction with the Book I account of corrective general rules and the Book III account of the emergence of norms, give us a valuable key to how we form our habits of projecting value and distinguish between those habits we can reflectively endorse and those that lead to insupportable internal or social conflicts.[29]

Hume also emphasizes the role that our sympathy with social forces plays in determining what we will find desirable or worthwhile. In "The Sceptic," he writes that "the prodigious effects of education may convince us, that the mind is not altogether stubborn and inflexible, but will admit of many alterations from its original make and structure" (Es 170). What we value or prefer is not fixed; and a variety of influences, such as family, form of government, as well as education, can change our preferences. Since "the human mind is of a very imitative nature," a change in what we value may often result from our sympathizing with the opinions and preferences of others (Es 202). And our reliance on others, for example, on their teaching us to use language, and initiating us into local tradition, ritual, and practice, is essential to our learning both the nature of our own feelings and how to express them:

> If a person full grown, and of the same nature with ourselves, were on a sudden transported into our world, he wou'd be very much embarrass'd with every object, and wou'd not readily find what degree of love or hatred, pride or humility, or any other passion he ought to attribute to it. The passions are often vary'd by very inconsiderable principles; and these do not always play with a perfect regularity, especially on the first trial. But as custom and practice have brought to light all these principles, and have settled the just value of every thing; this must certainly contribute to the easy production of the passions, and guide us, by means of general establish'd maxims, in the proportions we ought to ob-serve in preferring one object to another. (T 294)

Despite the variability of preferences that different social institutions produce, our need to live in relatively close proximity with one another, along with our own desire for stability and uniformity, will result in coalescent and overlapping sympathies so that we formulate, rely on, and appeal to some "general rules" with respect to what we find valuable.

Of course, individuals experience differently the process of socializa-tion. We each have our own place in a family structure, and families differ from one another in terms of their traditions, values, and commitments. Some of us reject our family's values whereas others of us replicate them. And while people may share or attribute to others a "common or national character," the individuals of nations still retain their "personal" charac-ter (Es 203). What remains constant is our need to find in others a sounding board for our passions and beliefs. Sympathy is a "force" so powerful that "we can form no wish, which has not a reference to society," and none of our passions would be able to motivate us "were we to abstract entirely from the thoughts and sentiments of others" (T 363). When he says that "the minds of men are mirrors to one another," Hume points out that he does not mean merely that we share a similar structure of affections and preferences; in addition, others must affirm the objects of our preferences if we are to retain confidence in our powers to assess worth and value: "the secondary satisfaction" arising from the sympathetic affirmation of others "becomes one of the principal recommendations of riches [for example], and is the chief reason, why we either desire them for ourselves, or esteem them in others" (T 365). We require this same sort of mirroring for our assessment of moral as well as nonmoral goods; in the second *Enquiry*, Hume writes that his moral system displays "the force of many sympathies," and that in order to "bear our own survey" we have "to prop our tottering judgment" of our character "on the correspondent approbation of mankind" (E 276, T 620).

Our sense of morality depends on our exercising a more "extensive sympathy," and sympathy in turn depends on belief (T 586). Our beliefs about what something is and its likely influence on us are "almost absolutely requisite to the exciting our passions," including our sympathetic responses to others (T 120). Our capacity to predict, anticipate, and remember which objects are likely to bring us pleasure or pain enables us to pursue or avoid a certain course of action. Since "nothing can be more real, or concern us more, than our own sentiments of pleasure and uneasiness," it is crucial that we determine where mistakes are costly, and in such cases, that we learn to judge accurately the causes of our sentiments, their appropriate objects, and their consequences, including their effects on the emotions of others (T 469). It is through our experience of living in society with one another that our socially informed practical understanding helps us to see that "morality is a subject that interests us above all others" (T 455).

Annette Baier has argued that Hume gives us an epistemology that is "subject to the test of moral and cultural reflection," and in which epistemic norms "are social in their genesis as well as in their intended scope."[30] Hume's principle of judgment, or belief, constitutes a system of "reality" that "peoples the world, and brings us acquainted with such existences, as by their removal in time and place, lie beyond the reach of the senses and memory" (T 108). He follows this sentence with a discussion of our reliance on human testimony, including autobiographical and historical records. His remark that belief 'peoples the world' is particularly apt, given the contribution that the arguments and opinions of others make to our own set of convictions. As belief projects our minds beyond what we immediately sense and remember, sympathy enables us to take up and respond to the opinions, concerns, and passions of the persons in our belief-extended world. Hume notes that we have a tendency to "embrace the opinions of others" when they concern ourselves; we do so "both from sympathy, which renders all their sentiments intimately present to us; and from reasoning, which makes us regard their judgment, as a kind of argument for what they affirm. These two principles of authority and sympathy influence almost all our opinions" (T 320–21). Thus, belief and sympathy must work in tandem even in the cases where someone tries to convince us of some fact or conclusion or presents us with reasons for believing one thing rather than another. We first infer by various external signs that someone is presenting an argument. Then sympathy, in making us susceptible to the person's opinions and emotions, gains a hearing for them, enabling judgment to determine which arguments, pleadings, reasonings, and so forth are convincing so that we might respond appropriately. Hume indicates that, in order to accommodate the multiplicity of perspectives of those who purport to report the past, observe with us the present, or predict the future, and to assess the varying degrees of influence these have on us, our epistemology must reflect our sympathetic as well as our imaginative propensities.

There is no difference, on the Humean view, in the metaphysical status of the objects of belief and those of our moral sentiments. Neither our system of belief nor that of values is 'externally characterizable', nor can we take the objects of either system to exist independently of our perspective in a way that matters to us. As David Falk has pointed out, Hume does make judgments of fact and judgments of merit "logically distinct," and we discover what has moral significance for us through our felt responses to the previously ascertained facts.[31] But this view is not equivalent to the noncognitivist one about the free expression of attitudes: belief and emotion are not 'logically isolated' from one another. Moral beauty has a 'suitable influence' on the mind only when all of the known circumstances are laid before us. The process by which we fix on characters as the proper objects of our sentiments is a social one, requiring correction and reflection, and a shift in our beliefs about what things are beneficial and harmful. With respect to their varying authority, the difference between our responses to kinds of beauty is brought out by attending to the extent and validity of the prior knowledge that we expect people to have. We get from Hume a detailed account of how we must subject our evaluative responses to a sufficient reflective scrutiny if they are to count as moral judgments with which we can expect others to concur.

III. The standard of taste, with respect to the various beauties of objects and persons, rests in the judging subject. When our faculty of taste is in "a sound state" it will not fail to feel the influence of the "qualities" (e.g., of character) that are calculated to please or displease, whereas any "defective" condition can "throw a false light on the objects, or hinder the true from conveying to the imagination the proper sentiment and perception" (Es 234). One worry expressed by Wiggins concerned the implications of viewing our psychological states, conceived of as such, and independently of the real objects that have elicited a response in us, as the sole source of value. If the objects that satisfy our desires or elicit our approval have no intrinsic value, then the value we, by virtue of our feelings, invest them with is essentially arbitrary and contingent. I find in Hume's account of value a convincing explanation for why absolute arbitrariness is a problem for most of us in the first place. He shows that the problem with *mere* projection of our own propensities, (e.g., the kind of unreflective, merely customary, or capricious projections we looked at above), is that in the case of moral value such judgments tend to lead to conflict and can undermine our own interests. We extend our sympathetic responses in mutually acceptable ways once we find our judgments conflicting with those of others, and so learn how to establish standards for correction. As we form more general and shared evaluative perspectives, and adjust our sentiments in light of these, we can acquire common interests and construct a view of the public good.

Moral appraisal differs from our appraisal of physical beauty (although see the conclusion below) in that the former requires regulation if we are to avoid destructive conflict and self-contradiction. The way that the understanding and feeling must work together illustrates the *emergent* normativity of moral and aesthetic judgment (the notion that there is a right or wrong taste, that it can be in a sound or defective state) and the dependence of moral authority on our need to resolve the conflicts that our passionate and imaginative propensities generate.[32] The rules concerning the objects to which we should direct our moral sentiments are not fixed a priori (in any way that we can apprehend). But they are fixed to some extent by our nature, as we discover through the observation and experience of our sentiments and responses (although on any particular occasion our feelings may not conform to our sentiment-based standards).

Hume's account of justice details the progress we make, both as individuals and as members of political groupings, from our natural, "uncultivated" ideas of virtue and vice to a more cultivated sense of morality based on "extensive sympathy" (T 488, 586).[33] Our uncultivated ideas really are "obscure and confused" sentiments, based on the 'narrower' passions of self-interest and limited generosity, and that lead us to praise or blame inconsistently the same character trait depending on whether the consequences of the particular actions it leads to benefit or harm us (Es 237). Once we begin to acknowledge the fundamentally social character of our needs, we are in a position to recognize our mutually inconsistent judgments, and can move toward more "exact and nice" ideas of virtue and vice, and a mutually acceptable sense of morality (Es 237). The unreflective operation of natural sympathy, facilitated (like the blind, unregulated custom that Hume considers in Book I of the *Treatise*) by various resemblances between ourselves and those with whom we sympathize, as well as by the contiguity that gives us a special interest in the case at hand, or the vividness of our perception of others' situations, produces responses that contradict our previous ones and that conflict with the responses of others. Particularly in the cases that we designate as moral or political we find that remaining in situations of mutual partiality produces a destructive "opposition of passions, and . . . of actions" (T 487). The establishment of rules of justice redirects our sympathy so that we acquire a concern for all those who participate in the convention. In sympathizing more widely with the interests of society, we move from arbitrarily assigning value to vivid results or consequences (which we assess in terms of our own benefit or harm), to identifying character traits as the fixed objects of our evaluations (the importance of justice in engendering social stability explains why "the [more cultivated] sense of moral good and evil follows upon justice and injustice" [T 499; see also T 533]).

This more extensive sympathy enables us to "fix on some steady and general points of view," to "arrive at a more stable judgment of things," and agree on "some general unalterable standard" that we employ in our evaluations of individual agents (T 581–82, 603). With respect to the moral perspective, "general rules" enable us to make our sympathetic responses sufficiently extensive in the way required for our sentiments of praise and blame to count as moral evaluations. In cases where we are considering two instances of the same character trait, general rules correct for the different appearances produced because one of the characters is contiguous and the other remote. The rules enable us to extend our sympathy to the agent's own "narrow circle" so that we adopt the perspective of those "who have any commerce with the person we consider," and from which we disinterestedly assess the effects of her character (T 602, 583). As Hume says, prejudice is contrary to good taste as well as sound judgment (Es 240). Whether our views are entrenched through a too narrow familiarity with only our own way of doing things, or perverted by interest, appropriate judgment requires that we depart from our own "particular and momentary situation" (T 587).

In other cases, general rules produce a "species of probability" that allows us to complete imaginatively the causal connection between a virtuous motive and its usual effect (T 585). Here the "delicacy" of extensive sympathy or aesthetic taste that produces our felt responses to the properly efficacious qualities depends on the understanding, with its rules by which to judge of causes and effects. Sometimes, reconstructing and sympathizing with the whole of the agent's circle may not by itself be sufficient to result in a proper moral evaluation, since the members may themselves respond only to actual consequences—harms or benefits— rather than to the agent's character. To avoid this sort of consequentialist error, the judge must herself be experienced in comparing the *tendencies* of character traits, so that she can project herself beyond the agent's actual circle to consider how the members *ought* to respond.

In both sorts of case, general rules extend our sympathy, either by projecting us beyond our own present situation to consider a distant character, or by enabling us to sympathize with the usual tendencies of character traits rather than with the actual observed consequences. Because the general principle of praise and blame is formed in abstraction from our particular situation, and according to principles that steady and stabilize our responses, the "general calm determination of the passions, founded on some distant view or reflexion" provides the kind of authority that overrides our (sometimes more intense) immediate feelings (T 583).

IV. I intended my brief overview of how Hume accounts for the emergence of our methods of correction and improvement to highlight the difference between our relatively unreflective natural response to physical beauty and our reflective and regulated response to moral beauty. Let me pause here to take stock of the similarities between the Humean position and the realist one.

1. The object of moral evaluations is character and character traits. We take up the general point of view in part to reach agreement about the merit of characters (T 581). Thus, value judgments for the Humean do make fundamental the virtues and thicker ethical concepts. How we assign praise and blame or determine that a trait is virtuous or vicious is rule governed. These rules emerge in our social practices, as we draw them "from established models, and from the observation of what pleases or displeases," and learning how to use them properly takes experience (Es 235). The "true judges" must evidence "strong sense, united to delicate sentiment, improved by practice, perfected by comparison, and cleared of all prejudice" (Es 241).

2. The idea that the verdict of the true judge establishes the standard of moral or aesthetic correctness has affinities with the realist notion of "semantic depth."[34] A relatively inexperienced judge may have learned how to apply the rules in some contexts, but not all. The sentiments of the learner may be confused, and his taste unable to distinguish "the particular character of each excellency," so that some features of the moral situation may transcend his awareness and thus be misjudged from his particular perspective (Es 237). The "delicate sympathy" that yields "more exact and nice" sentiments is something we must learn, and indicates that we have sufficient practice in applying the rules (Es 237).

3. Morality does not simply reflect the attitudes we happen to have. There are standards for our moral attitudes, even though their basis lies in our sentiments and attitudes. Hume's account of the transformation of our "uncultivated nature" and of the reflexive nature of our sentiments gives more substance to Blackburn's claim that we can use our evaluations to improve our evaluations (T 488).[35] Although the standard lies in the evaluating subject rather than the object, it is used to appraise objects. Our commitments are not simply free, unconstrained by facts or by standards of correctness. Something is virtuous if it is appraised as such by a "true judge."

What Baier describes as the 'fit' between our mental projection of causal necessity (which makes it possible for Hume to give an account of warranted belief) and uniformly occurring features of the external world that stimulate the projection in the first place would seem to hold similarly between projected values and, in the moral case, those features of persons' characters that stimulate our approval and blame.[36] The process by which we fix on characters as the proper objects of our moral sentiments is a social one, requiring mutual correction, individual and shared reflection, and self-awareness. While it is true that on the Humean view it is only because we have the sort of affective structure that we do that we identify things as having value, it is also true that this structure is highly educable and that our moral sentiments are initially uncultivated, alighting on unsuitable objects and requiring the guidance of reason insofar as it leads us to acquire a new concern for the public good that we would not otherwise have. This notion of the public good is to some extent constructed from our common interest; in turn it shapes our individual sense of value. Because the human mind "will admit of many alterations from its original make and structure," and we adjust our affections in light of a better understanding of society, I see no reason to ascribe authority to sentiments conceived without knowledge of their causal histories, tendencies, and ends, and their socially determined "just bounds" (Es 170, T 293).

V. In "Standard of Taste," Hume says that the same object may taste either sweet or bitter depending on the disposition of the organ. He maintains, however, that while our 'organ' of moral taste may be in either a sound or a defective state, only the sound state can afford a "true standard of taste and sentiment" (Es 234). Let me link the idea that we can recognize sound and defective states to the realist's notion that objectivity is grounded in consensus. Lovibond, for example, argues that our sharing a common perceptual structure, such that we all see objects as colored in more or less the same way, makes it possible for us to agree on the use of color-predicates, and so to discourse objectively about colors.[37] Her point is that the agreement about the use of color-predicates makes our talk objective, and that we do not need to appeal to some more ultimate foundation. And for the realist, consensus provides a necessary and sufficient condition for the notion of moral objectivity as well as objectivity about secondary property judgments.

Blackburn has argued that although we may easily admit consensus with respect to judgments of secondary qualities, the case is quite different with respect to moral judgments. If we all, in a relatively healthy state, taste lemons as sour, then that is *what it is* for them to be sour. But if we all experience some moral situation in the same way, recognize it as relevantly similar to some previous situation that we judged as good, and so judge the present case as good as well, it does not follow that our agreement that it is good in fact makes it good. We could all agree, and yet all be wrong; and the correct assessment of the case at hand could still exist.[38] One important difference between secondary-quality judgments and moral judgments is that sight (and seeing things as colored) is a natural capacity that we do not acquire by frequent seeing. We already had the sense when we exercised it, and did not get it by exercising it. But both virtue and the ability to judge virtue are acquired; we become virtuous by doing virtuous actions, and we become judges of virtue by gaining experience in appraising characters and conduct. (It is of course arguable that secondary-quality judgments also admit of refinement and are to some extent the product of education and cultural norms. If we take that view and also agree with Hume that our moral sensibility results from the cultivation of some of our natural affective propensities, then moral judgments and secondary-quality judgments may be comparable in more interesting ways.)

It will not do in the case of virtue simply to appeal to a common perceptual structure. For the problem is precisely that we do not agree on what situations or characters are pleasing or painful, and so morally fine or vicious. According to Hume, we may find within a given community an almost universal agreement on moral vocabulary. Everyone agrees that the courageous agent is an estimable character. But we either disagree about whether we should attribute the quality to some particular agent, or dispute what courage actually is. Although our judgments of virtue and vice do depend on our sharing a common structure of sentiments (we apply moral epithets in virtue of feeling the appropriate sentiment, or the sentiment we would feel were we suitably disposed), our moral taste must exhibit progress beyond our initially uncultivated and 'narrower' responses.

We want agreement, then, not only on the meaning of our moral vocabulary, but on how it is to be used. In order to ascribe moral concepts appropriately, we should be 'true judges'; we should have sufficient practice, possess good sense and a delicate sympathy, and be free of all prejudice. Although "the principles of taste be universal," and we may all in principle be capable of cultivating the proper moral sensibility, it can still be the case that "the taste of all individuals is not upon an equal footing" (Es 241–42). If someone lacks the "delicacy of temper" needed to feel the sentiments associated with virtue, then "he must be ignorant of the beauty," and he must have recourse to "the durable admiration" of better judges (Es 166, 233). While there may be consensus on what qualities a moral judge should have, the true standard for general and particular moral judgments is established by the "joint verdict" of true judges who meet the criteria establishing the "sound state" of our faculty of taste (Es 241). Earlier we had seen the realist arguing that a properly developed moral sensibility depends on learning how to use the rules governing the application of moral concepts. If the realist makes agreement on the use of these rules (rather than simply the shared sensibility or shared vocabulary) the criterion for moral objectivity, then this aspect of the dispute (cognitive vs. projective, objective vs. intersubjective) between the realist and the Humean may be little more than a verbal one.[39]

Nevertheless, for the Humean, the superior taste and the true judgment can exist even where no consensus supports them. Hume makes this point with his example of *Don Quixote*, in which Sancho's kinsmen claimed to find the taste of leather and iron in the wine. The villagers ridiculed the kinsmen, but after emptying the hogshead of wine, an iron key attached to a leathern thong was found. We cannot always prove the superiority of taste, and cannot always silence the bad critic and the "pretended judges" (Es 235–36). But even if we never methodize our rules or never explicitly acknowledge an excellent model, the different degrees of taste would still have existed and "the judgment of one man been preferable to that of another" (Es 236). The consequentialist error that I discussed in Section III shows that the true judgment may exist even if no one holds it. Biases of either the imagination or the affections may lead us to sympathize entirely with an agent's narrow circle even though all the members are mistaken. We can therefore agree with Blackburn that even though the Humean account is a projectivist one, it is possible that the correct judgment or the correct way to act exists even if none of us can see our way to it.

Finally, we can see how the sympathetic, reflective stance we can take that makes possible extended social perspectives and generates new concerns and higher-level sentiments speaks to Wiggins's concern about the meaning of life. Value is not constituted by our desires or evaluative responses *simply as such*. The reflective affirmation of others, particularly of those whom we regard as morally admirable, of something that we value, increases our sense of its worth and can make our choices and actions seem more purposeful. Wiggins notes that rather than looking for one source of value, we should pay attention to "the set of concerns" that a man has, that is, to the sort of "categorical desires" discussed by Bernard Williams.[40] We see that Hume emphasizes how the influences of our social context make our concerns and projects depend on shared meanings and give a social cast even to our most individual interests.

VI. In "Standard of Taste," Hume notes that aesthetic judgment is less universal than moral judgment: in aesthetic matters we may find a "diversity" that is "entirely blameless" and no standard for reconciling the contrary sentiments (Es 244). He gives two instances of such blameless diversity:

1. You like comedy and I like tragedy: we both recognize an excellent comedy and an excellent tragedy when we see one, but differ over which we find most preferable.

2. The different ages of men: whereas the younger man likes Ovid, the older one prefers Tacitus. We tolerate these "innocent" differences, says Hume, and only a "want of humanity and of decency" will diminish our esteem for the author (Es 246).

We might ask why it is that the young man prefers Ovid. Since the passions of the younger man are "warm," the reason is surely that Ovid gives us lusty tales, full of sex and violence, love and passion. These works were intended for a male audience, and were read (no doubt voraciously) by schoolboys and studied for their use of rhetoric by law students; during the Middle Ages, aspiring clerics learned their Latin through reading Ovid. Women are not the intended audience. How, then, does Ovid portray women? In his *Metamorphoses* there are fifty tales of rape in fifteen books, and in the *Fasti*, there are ten tales of rape in six books.[41] Over and over again in these tales, women are described as more being more beautiful and more tempting by virtue of their fear when pursued or confronted by their rapists.

Denying women the opportunity to develop and exercise their talents as artists and critics and diminishing the significance of their response to artistic works has allowed male artists and audiences to be the guardians of culture and to turn women into cultural as well as sexual property. Andrea Dworkin has noted that "pornography is not a genre of expression separate and different from the rest of life; it is a genre of expression fully in harmony with any culture in which it flourishes. . . . [It] functions to perpetuate male supremacy and crimes of violence against women because it conditions, trains, educates, and inspires men to despise women, to use women, to hurt women."[42] Our society is becoming increasingly sensitive to the point Dworkin makes. So when such depictions of women are found in work that otherwise has literary merit, how are we to balance our appraisal of the work's aesthetic value with our moral appraisal of it?

I have argued here that the criteria for establishing a sound state of the taste of the judge are more or less rigorous depending on what is being appraised.[43] In the case of physical beauty, where conflict is less likely to result from differences in taste, we tend to allow for flexibility and to privilege the first-person perspective. In contrast, our moral standards are more important to us, because our disagreements are more destructive and self-defeating for us, so we need there to find a more widely shared standpoint. Morality emerges, however, as a dimension of our community practices, and we develop and employ our moral sensibility to identify or resolve certain conflicts and to publicize the significance of certain expectations and choices. Moral judgments do not straightforwardly trump value judgments (sometimes, for example, your view about what's funny in a situation might stand as a corrective to my misdirected sense of morality), and there are no metaphysical boundaries between kinds of value. A work of art need not depict morality in order to have aesthetic value. A game need not be educational in order to provide fun for those playing it. But the endorsement or celebration of inhumanity in the work does diminish our esteem for the author of it. Likewise, we need to provide correctives to the attitudes of those who consume pornographic works in the name of freedom or fun, especially when they do so at the cost of the women who are depicted or who suffer from the attitudes engendered in the consumers.[44] Deciding which value judgments may be defeasible by others is best done by including the perspectives of all who are affected by the endorsement of the values at issue.

One might worry that by appealing to the verdict of true judges for what counts as an appropriate sentiment of praise or blame, we abandon the responsibility or privilege of judging for ourselves; could not those who wish to exclude women use unscrupulously the true-judges strategy? A point Hume makes that I noted earlier should allay this worry. Whether someone has the character of a true judge is a matter of fact. Establishing that fact is not done merely on the say-so of the purported judge. It takes our arguments and the contributions of our different, including our sexed, perspectives. Hume argues that we should admit as many perspectives as possible, for "envy and jealousy have too much place in a narrow circle," and "a familiar acquaintance" with someone may "diminish the applause" or the admiration owed to her performance or judgment (Es 233). Extending this view, Luce Irigaray has suggested that we should attempt "to progress toward a culture of the sexed subject," and include sexed perspectives as a way of creating "a future that is *more* rather than *less* cultured than the past or present, a future in which symbolic exchanges will be more free, more just, and more developed than at present."[45] Because Hume's method for establishing standards of value is relatively open ended, it allows for the important moral shifts we must make as we learn more about ourselves and about the members of our own and other communities.

A Humean feminist approach to finding endorsements of inhumanity in canonical works need not advocate throwing Ovid out of the canon (or abolishing the canon).[46] I take Hume's observation of the change of taste from the younger to the older man to show his awareness of what we now refer to as developmental psychology. The young man, afraid of the strength of his own desire, projects his fear onto the object of his lust. Training his literary attention so that he learns to distinguish between the aesthetic aspects of the work and those features that appeal to his 'warmer' passions will help to refine his moral and aesthetic taste, and to diminish the grosser passions, such as the lust that when combined with fear becomes a desire to violate others. The older, more experienced man perhaps naturally prefers to read Tacitus, because this author, in his account of Germany, commends the Germanic men for honoring their women and protecting them from harm, and both sexes generally for honoring the sanctity of marriage and family.[47] Including women as full participants in our cultural practices enhances our sensitivity to what makes a work aesthetically pleasing. We can in this way gain a shared perspective on how the depictions of women as objects for violation and as more beautiful when terrified detract from the beauty of the work and lessen our admiration for the author.[48] While physical appearance is a "convenient" way of making distinctions among people, false standards of beauty may easily become tools of oppression (E 248). Thus, even in the case of our appraisals of natural beauty, we can establish "just bounds," recognized by those whose "internal sentiments are more regulated by the personal characters" of men and women, rather than by our unreflective propensities or "the accidental and capricious favours of fortune" (T 293, E 248).

Notes

1. Virginia Woolf, To the Lighthouse (New York: Harcourt Brace Javanovich), 40.

2. Woolf, To the Lighthouse, 240–41.

3. In this essay, I refer to the following works by David Hume: A Treatise of Human Nature, ed. L. A. Selby-Bigge and P. H. Nidditch (Oxford: Clarendon Press, 1978), 295. References in the text will be given parenthetically as T. Enquiries Concerning Human Understanding and Concerning the Principles of Morals, ed. L. A. Selby-Bigge and P. H. Nidditch (Oxford: Clarendon Press, 1975), references to be given parenthetically as E. Essays: Moral, Political, and Literary, ed. Eugene F. Miller (Indianapolis: Liberty Classics, 1985), references to be given parenthetically as Es.

4. Simon Blackburn's version of projectivism has perhaps the strongest connections to Hume. I take the term "quasi-objectivized" from the discussion of noncognitivism in Stephen Darwall, Alan Gibbard, and Peter Railton, "Toward *Fin de siècle* Ethics: Some Trends," *Philosophical Review* 101 (January 1992): 115–89.

5. Let me stress that I think it important to compare Hume's views with the different sides of this contemporary debate both because philosophers continue to label views that never were Hume's as "Humean," and because Hume's actual views contain resources for advancing beyond the metatheoretical debate, and effectively analyzing institutions and practices. Hume and his contemporaries were engaged in a different debate over the reality of value; my interest here is not with the historical Hume but with the direction in which Hume's views, properly understood, push moral philosophy.

6. Sabina Lovibond, *Realism and Imagination in Ethics* (Minneapolis: University of Minnesota Press, 1983), 17–23.

7. Lovibond, *Realism and Imagination*, 22.

8. John McDowell, "Noncognitivism and Rule-Following," in Steven Holtzman and Christopher Leich, eds. *Wittgenstein: To Follow a Rule* (London: Routledge and Kegan Paul, 1981), 145.

9. McDowell, "Noncognitivism," 145, 149.

10. David Wiggins, "Truth, Invention, and the Meaning of Life," in *Needs, Values, Truth: Essays in the Philosophy of Value* (Oxford: Basis Blackwell, 1987), 106.

11. Lovibond, *Realism and Imagination*, 9.

12. Lovibond, *Realism and Imagination*, 1–2.

13. See Wiggins, "Truth," 105.

14. Wiggins, "Truth," 97.

15. Lovibond, *Realism and Imagination*, 9.

16. Lovibond, *Realism and Imagination*, 96. She remarks further that when C. L. Stevenson wrote of the "wedding of descriptive and emotive meaning" in *Ethics and Language* (1944), we have "no need to ask . . . which of the parties is wearing the long white dress" (96).

17 McDowell, "Noncognivitism," 143.

18. Wiggins, "Truth," 137.

19. McDowell, "Noncognivism," 157.

20. Bernard Williams, *Ethics and the Limits of Philosophy* (Cambridge: Harvard University Press, 1985), chap. 7 and 8.

21. Lovibond, *Realism and Imagination*, 16.

22. He remarks that just as sensible qualities lie in our senses, beauty and virtue lie in our sentiments, not in the objects. However, "this doctrine . . . takes off not more from the reality of the latter qualities, than from that of the former, nor need it give any umbrage to critics or moralists. Though colours were allowed to lie only in the eye, would dyers or painters ever be less regarded or esteemed?" Since this "supposed" discovery concerning sensible qualities "makes no alteration on action and conduct; why should a like discovery in moral philosophy make any alteration?" (Es 166 n). Moreover, Hume thinks that like judgments concerning primary qualities, moral judgments are susceptible to the distortions of nearness and remoteness in time and of place, and the methods of correction are the same for both sorts of judgment; see, e.g., T 582, 603, 632.

23. Simon Blackburn, "Rule-Following and Moral Realism," in Holtzman and Leich, *Wittgenstein: To Follow a Rule*, 165.

24. At one point, Hume suggests that we distinguish between our evaluations through introspection, since the different satisfactions associated with various gastronomic, aesthetic, and moral pleasures keep "our sentiments concerning them from being confounded" so that we ascribe robustness to wine and virtue only to characters (T 472). He might mean here that the difference between kinds of pleasure is phenomenological, one we measure by the intensity of feeling; and our perception of moral beauty and deformity can be among our most strongly felt pleasures and pains: we find "no spectacle so fair and beautiful as a noble and generous action; nor any which gives us more

abhorrence than one that is cruel and treacherous" (T 470). But although Hume refers to the "force," "energy" and "authority" of moral and artistic beauty, his critical views on theology and teleology preclude him from holding the position of his predecessor Shaftesbury, namely, that moral pleasure has a "superior charm" because our judgment of virtue is guided by the "pre-sensations" or "anticipation" implanted in us by the Divine Mind (Es 232–33); see Anthony Ashley Cooper, third earl of Shaftesbury, "An Inquiry concerning Virtue and Merit," in *Characteristicks*, vol. 2 (n.p., 1727), 103. While the intense satisfaction of moral pleasure could figure in an explanation of why we view something with favor or why our moral sentiment compels us to action, it does not suffice to explain how the favor is *merited* or why moral judgments should by virtue of their authority *override* other considerations. Hume's references to the causes of our sentiments in the passage at T 472 suggest that he has in mind a better argument, one that I try to develop below.

25. Although he notes too that "there is something extraordinary, and seemingly unaccountable in the operation of our passions, when we consider the fortune and situation of others . . . [and] particular views and incidents [of deformity, disease, or poverty] may," depending on the circumstances, sometimes raise the passion of pity (E 248 n). Part of Hume's project, and mine, is to draw attention to the complexities involved in providing an account of where it is ethically appropriate to adjust our natural attitudes.

26. See, e.g., Linda K. Jackson, *Physical Appearance and Gender* (Albany: SUNY Press, 1992).

27. And even when we are not mistaken, we need to pay attention to the effect of custom and local practices on standards of utility; see, e.g., E 249 and T 293–94.

28. One question Hume takes up in his essay, "Of the Standard of Taste," is why we admit a standard of truth in science but not in morality and aesthetics. He answers that we can only support this view "in speculation"; but in practice, scientific theories are constantly exploded, and are subject to chance, fashion, and social forces, while we all still agree on the aesthetic importance of Shakespeare and Cicero (Es 242). In the *Essays* in general, Hume devotes much attention to the significance of social forces in our advancement of knowledge; the importance of justice in making shared and general perspectives possible applies to progress in knowledge as well as in morality, as this statement from "Of the Rise and Progress of the Arts and Sciences" shows: "From law arises security: From security curiosity: And from curiosity knowledge. The latter steps of this progress may be more accidental; but the former are altogether necessary" (Es 118). For more on the social character of Hume's epistemology, see Annette Baier, "Hume, the Reflective Women's Epistemologist," in *Moral Prejudices: Essays on Ethics* (Cambridge: Harvard University Press, 1994).

29. We see anticipation of Hume's task in Vico's "new science": "because of the deplorable obscurity of causes and almost infinite variety of effects" of human institutions such as language, customs, and practices, "philosophy has had almost a horror of treating" of them; see *The New Science of Giambattista Vico* (Ithaca: Cornell University Press, 1968), 6. Jane McIntyre, in "Character: A Humean Account," *History of Philosophy Quarterly* 7 (1990), and Annette Baier, in A *Progress of Sentiments: Reflections on Hume's "Treatise"* (Cambridge: Harvard University Press, 1991), chapter 7, both show how Hume's treatment of the passions in *Treatise*, Book II, Part III is relevant to his account of character.

30. Baier, "Hume, the Reflective Women's Epistemologist," 82, 87.

31. W. D. Falk, "Hume on Practical Reason," in *Ought, Reasons, and Morality* (Ithaca: Cornell University Press, 1986), 144–45.

32. At T 547 n, Hume writes, "In what sense we can talk either of a *right* or a *wrong* taste in morals, eloquence, or beauty, shall be consider'd afterwards." His essay "Of the Standard of Taste" is his fullest consideration of this issue.

33. I show in a more detailed way how our cultivated sense of morality depends on the conventions of justice in "Justice and the Foundation of Social Morality in Hume's *Treatise*," forthcoming in *Hume Studies*.

34. See Mark Platts, *Ways of Meaning* (London: Routledge and Kegal Paul, 1979), 261; and Lovibond's discussion in *Realism and Imagination*, 31–36 and 71–72.

35. Blackburn, "Rule-Following and Moral Realism," 175–76.

36. Baier, *A Progress of Sentiments*, 93.

37. Lovibond, *Realism and Imagination*, 39, 72.

38. Blackburn, "Rule-Following and Moral Realism," 174–75.

39. In "Values as Response-Dependent Concepts" (unpublished), Carla Bagnoli suggests that the realist can profitably use Bernard Williams's notion of convergence. The idea is that there is a shared sensibility that evaluators ought to cultivate, and convergence results, not merely as agreement in judgment, but as a form of agreement about appropriate responses. This brings the realist position into closer alignment with Hume's.

40. Wiggins, "Truth," 136. Williams introduces categorical desires in "Persons, Character and Morality"; see *Moral Luck* (Cambridge: Cambridge University Press, 1981), 11.

41. My source is Amy Richlin, "Reading Ovid's Rapes," in Richlin, ed., *Pornography and Representation in Greece and Rome* (Oxford: Oxford University Press, 1992).

42. Andrea Dworkin, "Pornography and Grief," in *Letters from a War Zone: Writings 1976–1989* (New York: E. P. Dutton, 1989), 22–3.

43. We admit "the principle of the natural equality of tastes" only "on some occasions, where the objects seem near an equality" (Es 231).

44. As Andrea Dworkin says with respect to women and pornography: "Your nightmare is someone else's freedom and someone else's fun"; see "Pornography is a Civil Rights Issue," in *Letters from a War Zone*, 280.

45. Luce Irigaray, *Je, tu, nous: Toward a Culture of Difference*, trans. Alison Martin (New York: Routledge, 1993), 58.

46. "Art will have to go," as Susan Kappeler says in *The Pornography of Representation* (Minneapolis: University of Minnesota Press, 1986), 221, expressing perhaps the most radical solution.

47. See Tacitus, "Germany and Its Tribes," in *Complete Works of Tacitus*, trans. Alfred John Church and William Jackson Brodribb, ed. Moses Hadas (New York: Random House, 1942), especially ¶¶ 1–20. Hume refers specifically to this work in his "Populousness of Ancient Nations," in *Essays*.

48. Significantly, in the Middle Ages, Christine de Pisan was already recasting Ovid's tales to illustrate the real virtues of women; see, for example, Christine de Pizan's *Letter of Othea to Hector*, trans. Jane Chance (Newburyport, Mass.: Focus Information Group, 1990).

6

"Mr. Hobbes Could Have Said No More"

Joyce L. Jenkins and Robert Shaver

Were there a species of creatures intermingled with men, which, though rational, were possessed of such inferior strength, both of body and mind, that they were incapable of all resistance, and could never, upon the highest provocation, make us feel the effects of their resentment; the necessary consequence, I think, is that we should be bound by the laws of humanity to give gentle usage to these creatures, but should not, properly speaking, lie under any restraint of justice with regard to them, nor could they possess any right or property, exclusive of such arbitrary lords. . . . [A]s no inconvenience ever results from the exercise of power, so firmly established in nature, the restraints of justice and property, being totally *useless*, would never have place in so unequal a confederacy.[1]

This passage has not proven popular. Balfour objects that Hume "seems to have lost sight of the interest of others and to have reduced the rule of justice to the standard of self-interest alone."[2] Reid comments that "though, in other places, Mr. Hume founds his obligation of justice upon its utility to *ourselves* or to *others*, it is here founded solely upon utility to *ourselves*. For surely to be treated with justice would be highly useful to the defenceless species he here supposes to exist. . . . Mr. Hobbes could have said no more."[3] Contemporary critics cite this passage to show that Hume favors "justice as mutual advantage" over "justice as impartiality,"

We wish to thank Anne Jaap Jacobson, Sigrun Svavarsdottir, and members of audiences at the University of Manitoba; the twenty-first International Hume Conference, Rome, June 1994; and the 1995 Central Division Meetings of the APA for helpful comments.

or "justice as reciprocity" over "subject-centred justice."[4] They then attack their Hobbesian target.[5]

In section I, we argue against the Hobbesian interpretation of the passage. Hume prefers humanity to justice on broadly utilitarian grounds. In section II, we argue that Hume's recommendation of humanity remains open to criticisms of the sort raised by John Stuart Mill in *The Subjection of Women*.

Three clarifications are needed.

First, when Hume writes of "justice" here, he refers to property. Thus to prefer humanity to justice is to prefer humanity to the introduction of property rights.

Second, the controversial passage speaks of two groups, one inferior to the other. Hume specifies a test for inferiority: members of the inferior group are incapable of resistance and cannot make their resentment felt. Animals are the one group that Hume clearly endorses as inferior (when compared to humans). But some animals are capable of resistance and can make their resentment felt: sharks and tigers kill humans; our dog makes his resentment felt by his sad, guilt-producing expression as we leave him at the kennel. Further problems afflict some of Hume's less clearly endorsed examples: he sees some women as inferior to men, without noting that some men are equally inferior to other men (and some women). We propose to avoid careful explication of Hume's test. Instead, we shall take as given the groupings into stronger and weaker that Hume offers, and consider what Hume recommends.

Third, the Hobbesian and broadly utilitarian interpretations must be distinguished. Both make normative claims about when justice ought to be introduced. On the Hobbesian interpretation, Hume makes it a necessary condition on the introduction of justice that some parties gain from it and that none lose. On the broadly utilitarian interpretation, Hume imposes the weaker necessary condition that the total well-being of all concerned be increased. The issue between these interpretations is best seen by considering a case where the introduction of justice brings about an increase in total well-being at the expense of one of the parties. Here the broadly utilitarian interpretation can endorse the introduction, while the Hobbesian interpretation must oppose it.[6]

I

Balfour, Reid, and others take the controversial passage to support the Hobbesian interpretation. Justice should not be introduced, because doing so would not profit both parties. In particular, it would not profit the superior party.

One might avoid the Hobbesian interpretation by supposing, with Thomas Pogge, that "Hume does not make a *normative* point about *any*, but a *factual* point about *natural*, inequality of powers." Hume is making a point about the origins of justice—a point with no normative upshot, and so no relevance to a Hobbesian theory of justice.[7] Hume opens the section on justice by claiming to show that "public utility is the *sole* origin of justice, and that reflections on the beneficial consequences of this virtue are the *sole* foundation of its merit" (E2 183). And he introduces the inferior-creatures passage by writing that "[t]he more we vary our views of human life . . . the more shall we be convinced, that the origin here assigned for the virtue of justice is real and satisfactory" (E2 190). This suggests that the *Enquiry* follows the *Treatise*, where Hume gives, and sharply separates, an explanation of the origin of justice and an explanation of our approval (T 484, 498–500). It also suggests that the inferior-creatures passage is part of the explanation of origins.

Assessing this interpretation is difficult. In the *Enquiry*, Hume does not carefully distinguish between the explanation of approval and the explanation of origins, nor, within the origins account, between an explanation of the conception and of the institutional existence of justice. At still other times, he seems to be explaining the motivating power of justice.[8] For example, given abundance or extensive benevolence, justice "would never once have been dreamed of," or would never have "been thought of" (E2 184, 185). The "very notion" would be "banished" in the golden age (E2 189). The rules of justice "owe their origin and existence" to utility (E2 188, 190). In extreme scarcity, justice would "give place to the stronger motives of necessity and self-preservation" (E2 186). Other passages imply an explanation of approval. It is the "merit" or "moral obligation" of justice that is linked with usefulness (E2 183, 188). In the scarcity case, the point is that we do not take acting out of self-preservation to be a "crime" or "criminal" (E2, 186, 187). The explanandum is why justice has a "place in the catalogue of virtues" rather than being "suspended" or "an idle ceremonial" (E2 184; 185, 186, 187, 188, 190; 184).

Despite this confusion, we think Hume's main project, in both the inferior-creatures passage and the section as a whole, is to explain our approvals. This reading is demanded by the context. Hume describes his method:

> [W]e shall consider every attribute of the mind, which renders a man an object either of esteem and affection, or of hatred and contempt. . . . The only object of reasoning is to discover the circumstances on both sides, which are common to these qualities; to observe that particular in which the estimable qualities agree on the one hand, and the blameable on the other; and thence to reach the foundation of ethics, and find those universal principles, from which all censure or approbation is ultimately derived. (E2 173–74)

The method requires listing traits that we approve and disapprove of, and then finding what the approved traits have in common and what the disapproved traits have in common. In Section II, on benevolence, Hume notes that we approve of benevolence. He then explains our approval, in part, by noting our belief that benevolence is useful. In Section III, on justice, we expect Hume to note that we approve of justice and then explain our approval by noting our belief that it is useful. This is what we find, though the case is more complex than with benevolence, since justice is not always approved of; Hume argues that, in these cases, it is not useful either. When Hume reflects on Section III, it is this explanation of approval that he stresses (E2 204, 212). Overall, he is engaged in discovering the "foundation of moral praise," or in the "explication of . . . applause," "esteem," "praise or censure," or "approbation" (E2 284, 276, 277, 289). Considering the origins of a virtue is relevant only insofar as it helps explain approval.

On this interpretation, the *Treatise* and *Enquiry* differ, but need not disagree. In the *Treatise*, Hume begins by explaining the "*original motive to the* establishment *of justice*" (T 499). The explanation has two parts. First, he notes that society is in the interest of each agent and that justice is needed to preserve society (T 484–89, 493–95, 497). Second, he argues that the benefits accruing to everyone from one's justice do not explain why one is just. The benefit the agent derives provides a better explanation (T 490, 492, 494–96). Hume then explains our "moral approbation" of justice by noting that injustice "displeases us; because we consider it as prejudicial to human society, and pernicious to every one that approaches the person guilty of it" (T 500, 499). We "partake of their uneasiness by *sympathy*" (T 499). He introduces this discussion of approval by saying that "[t]his question will not detain us long after the principles, which we have already establish'd" (T 498). The reason is that, in the first part of the explanation of the original motive, he has argued that justice is needed to avoid "the solitary and forlorn condition" (T 492). The second part of the explanation of the original motive is not needed—the part that relies on the benefits accruing to the agent and that concludes that "*self-interest is the original motive*" (T 499).

In the *Enquiry*, Hume mixes the explanation of origins with the explanation of approval. Sometimes he moves directly from settling the "true origin" of justice to "determin[ing] what degree of esteem or moral approbation may result from reflections on public interest and utility" (E2 203). The explanation of the origin seems to explain the approval. There is no explicit reference to self-interest as the original motive. This suggests that the references to origins in the *Enquiry* are intended to refer only to that part of the origins story in the *Treatise* that was relevant to explaining our approval, namely the connection between justice and society. Hume probably still considered self-interest as the original motive, but the project of the *Enquiry* makes discussion of this superfluous.

Say, then, that the inferior-creatures passage makes a point about our approvals. Perhaps, for Hobbesian reasons, people approve of justice only where it is mutually advantageous. No normative conclusions about Hume's theory need follow, for Hume himself need not endorse the common approvals. This way of avoiding the Hobbesian interpretation, however, is unlikely. Hume writes that "we should be bound by the laws of humanity to give gentle usage to these creatures, but should not, properly speaking, lie under any restraint of justice with regard to them" (E2 190). This looks like a contrast between two sorts of bounds, one of which is morally endorsed and one of which is not. He concludes that justice is "totally *useless*" in this case, after exclaiming "what praise is implied in the simple epithet *useful*! What reproach in the contrary!" (E2 190, 179). "By rendering justice totally *useless*, you thereby . . . suspend its obligation upon mankind" (E2 188). Similarly, in the other "circumstances of justice," Hume is not morally indifferent to whether justice should hold when the circumstances fail. For example, where there is abundance, justice "being totally useless . . . could never possibly have place in the catalogue of virtues" (E2 184). More generally, Hume takes our approvals to indicate what is really virtuous and vicious. The Hobbesian interpretation cannot be evaded by claiming that Hume has purely explanatory intentions.

It does not follow that the Hobbesian interpretation succeeds. For there is reason to think that Hume would reject its claim that justice ought to be introduced only where it is mutually advantageous.

Hume notes that we approve of virtuous acts performed "in very distant ages and remote countries" and where we "never so much as enquire in what age and country the person lived" (E2 215–16; 218, 219, 230, 273, 274, T 499). We approve of qualities useful to their possessors, such as discretion and riches, without considering whether we gain anything from them (E2 234, 243–44, 246). We even approve of virtuous acts performed "by an adversary," although the consequences of the virtuous act "may be acknowledged prejudicial to our particular interest" (E2 216; also 217, 218, 219, T 582–83). In all these cases, our approvals outstrip our self-love. Hume concludes that our approvals are explained by a "fellow-feeling with others" and that this fellow feeling is "one great source of moral distinctions" (E2 219 n, 218).[9] Given this, it would be surprising were Hume to say that mutual advantage is needed for justice to be properly endorsed. That we might, for example, be hurt by treating animals better should not prevent us from approving of better treatment of animals, given that our approvals are not tied to our self-love in other cases.

(This is not conclusive evidence against the Hobbesian interpretation. One might reject self-love as the explanation of our approvals yet still require mutual advantage. One might, for example, reject hurting one party for the sake of others because doing so seems unjust. One might be appalled even when one's self-love is unaffected by the redistribution. It is unlikely, however, that *Hume* would give this as a reason for requiring mutual advantage; he is, after all, trying to explain our moral sentiments on grounds of fellow feeling. We ally self-love and mutual advantage, then, because self-love seems the more likely Humean rationale for requiring mutual advantage—if Hume *were* requiring mutual advantage. Self-love explains why one might prefer mutual advantage to total well-being as a condition on the introduction of justice in cases, such as that of humans and animals, where we would be hurt by introducing justice.)

The oddity of insisting on mutual advantage as necessary for introducing justice can be seen in another way. Reid is surprised that, in the inferior-creatures passage, Hume seems to found justice on its usefulness to ourselves rather than others. Reid is right to be puzzled: when Hume reflects on his overall project, he supposes that justice is approved (even "solely") because of its usefulness to others (E2 277; 269, 280–82).[10] If so, the textually preferable interpretation will take him to be arguing that, because justice is not useful to others, it ought not to be introduced.

Hume writes that, when inferior creatures are intermingled with superior ones, it is a "necessary consequence" that the inferior be given "gentle usage" (E2 190). The point seems to be that humanity, rather than justice, is approved here.[11] Elsewhere, when considering relations between un-equals, Hume consistently notes the importance of virtues such as "Generosity, Humanity, Affability, and Charity," but not justice (MS 546; also AS 132–33, PA 383–86, 397).

Hume's preference for humanity requires defense. He must also explain why humanity does not dictate simply giving property to the inferior creatures. The controversial passage does not reply to either query: it states only that humanity rather than justice applies between superior and inferior. We suggest that Hume is thinking of justice as precisely that virtue that sometimes stands in the way of humanity. Elsewhere, Hume stresses its "inflexible" nature and blindness to "the characters, situations, and connexions of the person concerned, or any particular consequences which may result." With justice, "it is impossible . . . to prevent all particular hardships, or make beneficial consequences result from every individual case" (E2 305).[12] Justice requires that "a profligate debauchee," who "wou'd rather receive harm than benefit from large possessions," be given those possessions anyway (T 482). Justice "put[s] into the hands of the vicious the means of harming both themselves and others" (T 579; also T 532, E2 305). In these cases, Hume holds that long-term humanity is served by permitting people to "combine;" any arrangement other than justice would not suffice to keep the combination together (E2 307, T 532). But no such arrangement is necessary in the case of inferior creatures. When our dog reduces his bone to a stump he can easily swallow, or picks up a razor blade on the street, we do not suppose that we should leave him with it, on the ground that this is humane in the long run because it is needed to maintain the combination of canine and human. In order for humans to combine with inferior creatures, justice is not needed, since the inferior creatures cannot tear apart the combina-tion should they dislike what we do. This is not a Hobbesian thought: the point is not that justice is misplaced because it fails to advantage both parties, but rather that nothing so insensitive to the particularities of the case as justice is needed for the parties to combine. Suppose our dog continued to swallow stumpy bones and razor blades, but gained sufficient strength to become our equal. In this case, we could not so easily help him by taking the bone, since he could resist. Justice might well enter, to prevent endless fighting—but it would enter as second best.[13] It would be better for our dog were we able to give and take the bone as circumstances dictate. It is this freedom to decide on a case-by-case basis that separates humanity from justice.

So far, the defense of Hume's preference for humanity has proceeded by our arguing that the superior may be able to help the inferior more by means other than rigidly respecting property rights. This is especially true in the case Hume considers, where superior and inferior are "intermingled." Suppose Stronger (S) and Weaker (W) begin with equal and legitimate holdings. S soon improves his holdings, so that in any competition for customers between S and W, S wins. In time, W is broke. Humean justice does nothing to help W, but humanity would—by, for example, giving aid to W, or by putting restrictions on the ways in which S might employ W.

Here one might object that other theories of justice could help W—particularly those giving a prominent role to fairness. Hume sees the suggestion: he briefly countenances such theories of justice, and he sometimes treats "equity" as a natural virtue of fairness, distinct from property-respecting and promise-keeping (T 502, E2 193–94; T 411, 513 n. 1, 538, 578, OG 40, PA 384, FP 33, OE 102, E1 145, E2 186, 187).[14] He does not, however, develop the point, since he thinks considerations of utility rule out these theories, and that humanity can perform their tasks. More generally, the objection can be left aside, because the aim is to explain Hume's preference for humanity over what *he* considers the best theory of justice.

There is a further worry. Hume's method requires that he report our approvals. In the section on justice, he explains our approvals by correlating them with usefulness. For example, we do not approve of property in a world of abundance; the reason is that property would have no use (E2 183–84). This suggests that the inferior-creatures passage is intended as a report of our approval: we do not approve of justice between greatly unequal parties. But here Hume is open to an obvious objection: Reid, Balfour, and many others *do* approve of justice between greatly unequal parties.[15] As Don Hubin writes, "If adherence to rules of justice is productive of human well-being when we are all roughly equal in our abilities, it can only be *more* important for this end when some are able to totally dominate others."[16]

Now, this is an objection to both the Hobbesian interpretation and our interpretation. But our interpretation has an advantage. On it, Hume thinks that we do not approve of justice here because we think some other virtue is preferable. In effect, Hume could say to Reid: "Do you really believe that we should bar ourselves from helping those inferior to us? Don't you think, on the contrary, that, say, property rights given to animals or children should be infringed when they might hurt themselves?" This reply to the objection may not always succeed. But on the Hobbesian interpretation, Hume does not have recourse even to it. For on the Hobbesian interpretation, the proper explanation for our failure to approve of justice between greatly unequal parties is that justice does not benefit both parties. It is unlikely that Reid, or others who initially approve of justice here, would be at all tempted to revise their approval by *this* explanation.[17]

II

Hume considers three possible inferior creatures: animals, Native Americans, and women. He finds animals inferior. In the case of Native Americans, "[t]he great superiority of civilized Europeans . . . tempted us to imagine ourselves on the same footing with regard to them" (E2 191). Hume does not say whether the Europeans are correct. In the case of women,

> the female sex are reduced to like slavery, and are rendered incapable of all property, in opposition to their lordly masters. But though the males, when united, have in all countries bodily force sufficient to maintain this severe tyranny, yet such are the insinuation, address, and charms of their fair companions, that women are commonly able to break the confederacy, and share with the other sex in all the rights and privileges of society. (E2 191)

Reid comments, "If this be sound morals, Mr. Hume's Theory of Justice may be true."[18]

On our interpretation, Hume's morals should not be seen as unsound because Hobbesian. Nonetheless, they may be unsound on other, broadly utilitarian, grounds of the sort Hume favors and Mill brings to bear on the treatment of women.

Hume's apparent view excludes women from the set of weaker creatures. Women can, he says, use their charms and insinuations to make their resentment felt. Presumably they may also use what Mill calls the "shrewish sanction."[19] However, elsewhere Hume suggests that women are significantly weaker than men.

> As nature has given *man* the superiority above *woman*, by endowing him with greater strength both of mind and body; it is his part to alleviate that superiority, as much as possible, by the generosity of his behavior. . . . Barbarous nations display this superiority, by reducing their females to the most abject slavery; by confining them, by beating them, by selling them, by killing them. But the male sex, among a polite people, discover their authority in a more generous, though not a less evident manner; by civility, by respect, by complaisance, and, in a word, gallantry. (AS 133)

The passage closely parallels Hume's *Enquiry* discussion of the position of the weaker creatures. Of them he says that "[o]ur intercourse . . . could not be called society, which supposes a degree of equality; but absolute command on the one side; and servile obedience on the other. Whatever we covet, they must instantly resign: Our permission is the only tenure, by which they hold their possessions: Our compassion and kindness the only check, by which they curb our lawless will" (E2 190). Weaker creatures must rely on compassion, not justice, and women must rely on gallantry, not justice.[20]

The *Enquiry* discussion notes that women are "commonly" able to break the confederacy, so it seems that one should conclude that they are not weaker, whereas "Of the Rise and Progress of the Arts and Sciences" asserts the reverse. "Of Polygamy and Divorces" adds to the confusion. "[I]t may be urged with better reason, that this sovereignty of the male is a real usurpation, and destroys that nearness of rank, not to say equality, which nature has established between the sexes. We are, by nature, their lovers, their friends, their patrons: Would we willingly exchange such endearing appellations, for the barbarous title of master and tyrant?" (PD 184). Now, it might be thought that the implication is that women are men's natural equals. On that reading, women require gallantry and are generally inferior in body and mind only because of social conditioning.[21] However, we think that this interpretation is ultimately indefensible. Hume recommends that women study history rather than a more demanding discipline such as philosophy on the grounds that it is the occupation "best suited both to their sex and education" (SH 563). Women are barred from the severer studies "by the tenderness of their complexion, and the weakness of their education" (SH 565). Women's education alone does not explain the bar. The sex, or complexion, of women are additional reasons. If Hume thought that women's weaker minds were the result of situation rather than nature, there would be no purpose in adding the point about their sex. Again, in "Of the Immortality of the Soul" Hume repeats his view about women's inferiority. "On the theory of the soul's mortality, the inferiority of women's capacity is easily accounted for: their domestic life requires no higher faculties either of mind or body" (IS 593).[22] Moreover, the one passage in which Hume seems to imply that women are men's equals is ambiguous. He says that polygamy destroys that "nearness of rank, not to say equality" between the sexes. One can read this as suggesting that women are in fact equal, or as suggesting that polygamy destroys nearness of rank, but not equality, since the sexes are unequal. Because Hume adds that male tyranny destroys the status of men as women's patrons, the second reading is much more plausible. Men are to guide women, as in the gallantry passage, not to tyrannize over them.

Suppose we are wrong: Hume thinks that women are weaker because of their social situation, not because of their nature. One might think that, if so, justice is owed them. But there is no evidence that Hume would draw this conclusion. He still recommends that women should be treated gallantly, compassionately, and with humanity. Nowhere do we find Hume saying that laws, education, and the situation of women should change to reflect a natural equality.

So we conclude that Hume's considered view is probably that women are in general naturally weaker in mind and body though there are exceptions to the average case.[23] Hence, he is committed to the view that at least many women are among the weaker creatures whom we should treat humanely rather than justly.

Annette Baier has said of Hume's position on women that he "saw that change would come only when the oppressed felt resentment, and used what power they have to make the oppressors feel the effects of their resentment. He saw very clearly both the causes of women's social inferiority, and what could alter that." Moreover, Hume is described as more realistic than Mill, "who naively seemed to have thought that male moral tracts urging men to share power and privileges with women would effect any change."[24] We shall examine the cogency of these claims, and we shall argue that Mill saw much more clearly than Hume both the necessity of justice for women and the difficulties that they face in obtaining it.

In contrast to Hume's ambivalence, Mill has no doubt that justice is both useful for women and superior to humanity, or "chivalry."

> Chivalry . . . only encouraged a few to do right in preference to wrong, by the direction it gave to the instruments of praise and admiration. But the real dependence of morality must always be upon its penal sanctions—its power to deter from evil. The security of society cannot rest on merely rendering honour to right, a motive so comparatively weak in all but a few, and which on very many does not operate at all. Modern society is able to repress wrong through all departments of life, by a fit exertion of the superior strength which civilization has given it, and thus to render the existence of the weaker members of society tolerable to them, without reliance on the chivalrous feelings of those who are in a position to tyrannize. The beauties and graces of the chivalrous character are still what they were, but the rights of the weak, and the general comfort of human life, now rest on a far surer and steadier support; or rather they do so in every relation of life except the conjugal. (SBJ 328–29)

Although chivalry may be nice, it is unreliable at best, and so justice is preferable.

Now, if we are right that Hume recommends humanity, not because it is the best the weaker creatures can expect, but because they are better off, on his view, if accorded humanity rather than justice, Hume is vulnerable to Mill's objection that even if *ideally* humanity is best, in the real world people cannot be relied upon to be humane. Cases in which rights are not protected produce the worst abuses. If one party is weaker than the other, the proper solution is not to leave the weaker at the stronger's mercy. If women are weaker than men, they need protection, not platitudes about the necessity of gallant behavior.

> Whether the institution to be defended is slavery, political absolutism, or the absolutism of the head of a family, we are always expected to judge of it from its best instances; and we are presented with pictures of loving exercise of authority on one side, loving submission to it on the other—superior wisdom ordering all things for the greatest good of the dependents, and surrounded by their smiles and benedictions. All this would be very much to the purpose if anyone pretended that there are no such things as good men. Who doubts that there may be great goodness, and great happiness, and great affection, under the absolute government of a good man? Meanwhile, laws and institutions require to be adapted, not to good men, but to bad. (SBJ 287)

Mill's position here is reminiscent of Hubin's objection that we approve of justice even more in situations where some are able totally to dominate others. We considered that Hume might respond that all would approve of a denial of property rights to a dog eating a razor blade. To settle the question of who is right, we would have to calculate which course is likely to be more harmful. Are the abuses that attend dominance worse than the misfires of general rules of justice that may not be appropriate in particular cases? It depends both on the degree of abuse likely to be seen in the dominant party and on the degree of rationality achievable by the weaker creatures. In the case of women at least, it is utterly implausible to suppose that they are so irrational that their mishandling of their own affairs would outweigh the abuses that they suffer under a patriarchal system.

Hume might respond that humanity can be enforced by law. Humane behavior, if not humane sentiments, could be enforced to prevent abuses. However, this response is not open to Hume, because he thinks it is the business of government to enforce the rules of justice, not of humanity (e.g., OG 37).

Hume might also respond that Mill is right that we need to formulate laws under the assumption that people will act badly, but wrong that this rule applies to the intimate relations between men and women. It is, he says, "a just political maxim, *that every man must be supposed to be a knave*. Though at the same time, it appears somewhat strange, that a maxim should be true in *politics*, which is false *in fact*. But to satisfy us on this head, we may consider, that men are generally more honest in their private than in their public capacity" (IP 42–43). The implication is that we need not assume that men are knaves in their private capacity. However, the empirical evidence shows that this is false. Mill speaks of the many men who are inspired by the dependence of their wives "not with a generous forbearance, and a point of honour to behave well to one whose lot in life is trusted entirely to their kindness, but on the contrary with a notion that the law has delivered her to them as their thing, to be used at their pleasure, and that they are not expected to practise the consideration towards her which is required of them towards everybody else" (SBJ 287). The assumption that men are private knaves is also justified. Hume wishes that in marriage "every thing was carried on with perfect equality, as between two equal members of the same body" (LM 560). He cannot, however, expect to rely on the generous forbearance of men to achieve this result.

There are other reasons for thinking that the case for humanity should not apply to women. First, one can plausibly argue that it is society's exclusion of women from the rules of justice that makes justice inapplicable to them. As Mill puts it,

> in the case of women, a hot house and stove cultivation has always been carried on. . . . Then because certain products of the general vital force sprout luxuriantly and reach a great development in this heated atmosphere . . . while other shoots . . . which are left outside in the wintry air, with ice purposely heaped around them, have a stunted growth . . . men . . . indolently believe that the tree grows of itself in the way they have made it grow, and that it would die if one half of it were not kept in a vapour bath and the other half in the snow. (SBJ 276–77)

Mill's point here is general, but we can apply it to Hume's position on property rights. Men deny women property rights. Women thus develop no skills at handling property. Men then reason that because women are incapable of handling property, they should be denied property rights. Our dog's inability to interact with us as an equal is not the result of our denial of his property rights. If it were, the case for paternalistic humanity toward him would be as unpalatable as it is for women.

Second, Hume's preference for humanity over justice is blind to some of the valuable by-products for humans of having control over their own property. Mill's view is that "after the primary necessities of food and raiment, freedom is the first and strongest want of human nature" (SBJ 336). One might think that this is exaggerated; humans can be fairly happy without being free to order their own affairs. But it is certainly true that self-esteem is an important ingredient in human life, and it is hard to have self-esteem while others have control, even if humane control, over one's life.

Third, Mill suggests that justice is needed to encourage humanity.

> [T]he almost unlimited power which present social institutions give to the man over at least one human being—the one with whom he resides . . . seeks out and evokes the latent germs of selfishness in the remotest corners of his nature—fans its faintest sparks and smouldering embers—offers to him a licence for the indulgence of those points of his original character which in all other relations he would have found it necessary to repress and conceal, and the repression of which would in time have become a second nature. (SBJ 289)

Mill's idea is that since justice forces one to pay attention to the interests of others, it becomes one's second nature to do so. Justice increases humanity.

Fourth, Hume points out that general rules of justice are clumsy, so that humanity is preferable because it is sensitive to particular cases. Mill responds that excluding individuals from justice is just as clumsy.

> [I]t is [now] felt to be an overstepping of the proper bounds of authority to fix beforehand, on some general presumption that certain persons are not fit to do certain things. . . . Even if it be well grounded in a majority of cases . . . there will be a minority of exceptional cases in which it does not hold: and in those it is both an injustice to the individuals, and a detriment to society, to place barriers in the way of their using their faculties. . . . In the cases . . . in which the unfitness is real, the ordinary motives of human conduct will on the whole suffice to prevent the incompetent person from making, or from persisting in the attempt. (SBJ 274)

Again, Mill's point here is general, but it can be applied to the exclusion of women from owning property. There are many women who are capable of managing their own property. It is a detriment to prevent them. Those who are not fit will self-interestedly allow their men to manage their property for them. The misfires attached to applying rules of justice are equally attached to suspending the rules.

Even if we are wrong in what we have argued, and Hume thinks that women have the power to procure justice for themselves, on any reading, Hume shows a lack of awareness of women's historical inability to make their resentment felt against those who would tyrannize over them. Mill has a much more acute sense of the difficulties that women face in making their resentment felt either by using their charms and insinuations, or by confederating. "Charms" only work well on men who are anyway disposed to treating women well, so they work only when they are not necessary. And the effectiveness of charms is ephemeral.[25] "Mere feminine blandishments, though of great effect in individual instances, have very little effect in modifying the general tendencies of the situation; for their power only lasts while the woman is young and attractive, often only while her charm is new, and not dimmed by familiarity; and on many men they have not much influence at any time" (SBJ 289). Mill also emphasizes the difficulties that women face in confederating to shift power. Confederation is more difficult for women than for other oppressed groups because women are emotionally attached to their men, whereas slaves and serfs are not usually emotionally attached to their masters. Moreover, each woman has her own private master (SBJ 268). Mill thus provides a possible explanation of why the subjection of women has been more durable than other forms of oppression, and of why women were not able to confederate and rebel. Compare Hume's fanciful Scythian women, who got together and gouged out their husbands' eyes so that the women could rule (LM 559). Hume might be taken as suggesting to women that they have the power to confederate. Mill shows why given women's psychological and material situation they had no such power. And Mill's position is supported by recent claims that women have, by and large, an ethic of care. Those who care most about sentiment-based personal attachments may be the people who are most incapacitated when it comes to demanding abstract justice for themselves.[26]

Mill sees more than Hume. We close with two possible explanations.

First, Hume's method starts from our approvals. The results of the method tend, unsurprisingly, to be conservative. They need not be: Hume rejects the monk's approvals, as based on "the delusive glosses of super-stition and false religion" (E2 270). But where religion is less directly concerned—in the case of women's chastity or property, for example—Hume is not so alert to other delusive glosses. Perhaps Hume might plead, in his defense, that religion provided sufficient delusions to keep him occupied.

Second, Hume is not a utilitarian, and in particular is not keen on maximizing. This may make him attractive to those who find utilitarian-ism too demanding. But it also makes him content with suboptimal outcomes, and, here, content with an *objectionably* suboptimal outcome. This—rather than an unexpected concession to Hobbes—may best explain why Hume is satisfied where Mill is not. It is perhaps no coincidence that another leading utilitarian, Henry Sidgwick, was instru-mental in women's admittance into Cambridge.[27]

Notes

1. David Hume, *An Enquiry Concerning the Principles of Morals*, in *Enquiries*, ed. L. A. Selby-Bigge and P. H. Nidditch (Oxford: Oxford University Press, 1975), 191–92 (henceforth E2). E1 = *An Enquiry Concerning Human Understanding*, in *Enquiries*; T = *A Treatise of Human Nature*, ed. Selby-Bigge and Nidditch (Oxford: Oxford University Press, 1978); D = "A Dialogue," in *Enquiries*; AS = "Of the Rise and Progress of the Arts and Sciences," PA = "Of the Populousness of Ancient Nations," MS = "Of the Middle Station of Life," OG = "Of the Origin of Government," FP = "Of the First Principles of Government," PD = "Of Polygamy and Divorces," SH = "Of the Study of History," IS = "Of the Immortality of the Soul," OE = "Of Eloquence," IP = "Of the Independency of Parliament," LM = "Of Love and Marriage," all in *Essays*, ed. Eugene F. Miller (Indianapolis: Liberty, 1985).

2. James Balfour, *A Dilineation of the Nature and Obligation of Morality, with Reflexions upon Mr. Hume's Book, intitled, An Inquiry concerning the Principles of Morals* (Edinburgh, 1753), 46. See also 49–54, 57, 73.

3. Thomas Reid, *Essays on the Active Powers of the Human Mind*, in *Philosophical Works*, vol. 2 (Hildesheim: Georg Olms Verlag, 1967), 660.

4. Brian Barry, *Theories of Justice*, vol. 1 (Berkeley and Los Angeles: University of California Press, 1989), 161–62; Allen Buchanan, "Justice as Reciprocity Versus Subject-Centred Justice," *Philosophy and Public Affairs* 19 (1990): 227–52, 227.

5. One exception should be noted. David Gauthier offers the best statement of the Hobbesian interpretation, but approves of Hume's position. Although Gauthier's interpretation has been attacked, few critics have met his reading of this passage, on which the interpretation turns. Annette Baier, for example, agrees that Hume demands mutual rather than total advantage. See Gauthier, "David Hume, Contractarian," *Philosophical Review* 89 (1979): 3–38, 19–21, and Baier, *A Progress of Sentiments: Reflections on Hume's "Treatise"* (Cambridge: Harvard University Press, 1991), 243, 250.

6. For a somewhat different statement of these rival interpretations, see Gauthier, "David Hume,"

10–11. The "broadly utilitarian" interpretation differs from a strict utilitarian position by not requiring that well-being be maximized.

7. Thomas Pogge, review of *Theories of Justice*, by Brian Barry, *Journal of Philosophy* 87 (1990): 375–84, 380–82. A similar reading is canvassed by Don Hubin, "The Scope of Justice," *Philosophy and Public Affairs* 9 (1979): 3–24, 9–16. Pogge offers this as part of a larger interpretation, which takes Hume to be explaining rather than justifying moral practices. We find the larger interpretation mistaken, but it remains possible that Pogge is right about this passage. See Robert Shaver, "Hume's Moral Theory?" *History of Philosophy Quarterly* 12 (1995): 317–31.

8. For these possibilities, see Hubin, "The Scope of Justice," 9–16.

9. Hume often refers to this explanatory "fellow-feeling with human happiness or misery," this "concern for others," as "humanity" (E2 260, 231; 226, 230, 231, 235, 272, 273, 274, 276, 286). Here we reserve "humanity" for the particular virtue—on a par with justice, courage, and the like—of which our fellow feeling approves.

10. At E2 238, Hume notes that "[h]onesty, fidelity, truth" are also praised because they are useful to their possessor, but he sees this as derivative from their usefulness to others.

11. Hobbesian interpreters often ignore this. One, Christopher W. Morris, conveniently deletes, without ellipsis, the claim that "we should be bound by the laws of humanity" in his quotation of the passage ("Moral Standing and Rational-Choice Contractarianism," in Peter Vallentyne, ed., *Contractarianism and Rational Choice* [Cambridge: Cambridge University Press, 1991], 87 n. 30). Other interpreters consider humanity, but cannot make much of it. Jonathan Harrison asks, "[W]hat turns . . . behaviour . . . from being just to being merely humane?" He suggests that perhaps justice requires that all parties concerned be able to enforce the rules. But as he notes, the point cannot be simply that rules of justice must be enforceable, since the superior creatures could enforce rules against themselves. This leaves the requirement that all must be able to enforce the rules unexplained (*Hume's Theory of Justice* [Oxford: Clarendon Press, 1981] 273–74). Hubin suggests that "[p]erhaps Hume would say that . . . the institutions are not institutions of *justice* but of *benevolence*." He worries, however, that "this misses the point. An institution is not generally categorized in virtue of the motives people have for compliance but in virtue of the justification for the rules which define the institution" (Hubin, "The Scope of Justice," 15).

12. Thus Barry notes, in contrasting humanity and justice, that "the crucial characteristic of justice is that the obligation to make the transfers required by it does not depend upon the use made of them by the recipient." See "Humanity and Justice in Global Perspective," in J. R. Pennock and J. W. Chapman, eds., *Nomos XXIV: Ethics, Economics, and the Law* (New York: New York University Press, 1982), 248.

13. We ignore Hume's claim that animals are "incapable of . . . property," since the *Enquiry* passage turns on power rather than on limitations on what can be conceived (T 326).

14. See Baier, *Progress of Sentiments*, 260–61, and Reid, *Essays*, 660.

15. Barry and Gauthier may seem to avoid this objection by taking Hume to make a point about the origins rather than approval of justice (Barry, *Theories*, 163, 174; Gauthier, "David Hume," 17–19). However, Barry treats "justice as mutual advantage" as a rival to a normative impartial-observer theory, and Gauthier insists that the contractarianism he ascribes to Hume is normative (Barry, *Theories*, 146–52, 163–65, 175; Gauthier, "David Hume," 3, 6, 13). Here the explanations separate: Barry is interested in mutual-advantage theories that might be inspired by Hume; Gauthier perhaps thinks that displaying mutual advantage is in itself normative. In the latter case, the problem is that this fails to show that *Hume* thinks mutual advantage justifies.

16. Hubin, "The Scope of Justice," 18.

17. Even those who tried to justify European dispossession of Native Americans—to cite one of Hume's putative inferior creatures—did not resort to considerations of mutual advantage (E2 191). Sepulveda, for example, argued that the natives could be dispossessed because, as a community, they committed "crimes against nature." Everyone, before and after Hobbes, wanted to avoid the "might

makes right" position. Hobbes himself is not so Hobbesian about the dispossession: colonists "are not to exterminate those they find there," but rather convert them to space-saving agriculture. See Thomas Hobbes, *Leviathan* (Harmondsworth: Penguin, 1968), 387. For Sepulveda and the Spanish debate, see Anthony Pagden, "Dispossessing the Barbarian: The Language of Spanish Thomism and the Debate over the Property Rights of the American Indians," in Pagden, ed., *The Languages of Political Theory in Early-Modern Europe* (Cambridge: Cambridge University Press, 1987), 79–98.

18. Reid, *Essays*, 660.

19. John Stuart Mill, "The Subjection of Women," in *The Collected Works of John Stuart Mill*, vol. 21 (Toronto: University of Toronto Press, 1984), 289 (henceforth SBJ).

20. In light of this, it may be that Hume was not being merely whimsical when he describes France as a nation that "gravely exalts those, whom nature has subjected to them. . . . The women, though without virtue, are their masters and sovereigns" (D 332).

21. See Annette C. Baier, "Hume on Women's Complexion," in Peter Jones, ed., *The Science of Man in the Scottish Enlightenment* (Edinburgh: Edinburgh University Press, 1989), 33–53.

22. Baier suggests that Hume is teasing the silly religious. It is conceivable that he is joking, but not plausible, given his many other statements of the same view (Baier, "Women's Complexion," 41).

23. This is further supported by Hume's claim at T 309: the general rule is that a father is superior to a mother though it may happen that "the mother shou'd be possest of a superior spirit and genius." He also notes that women are often content to take fools for mates, so that they "might govern with less controul" (LM 559).

24. Baier, "Women's Complexion," 45.

25. Hume is also aware of the temporary nature of effective charms. In his tale of the Scythian women, he relates that those wives who initially refuse to blind their husbands became "obliged, as their youth and beauty decayed, to imitate the example of their sisters" (LM 559). It seems that women must become weaker creatures once they lose their charms.

26. Even feminists who now argue that care is a more central moral concept than justice agree with Mill that justice is sorely needed in traditionally private institutions such as the family. See, for example, Virginia Held, "The Meshing of Care and Justice," *Hypatia* 10 (1995): 128–32.

7

Compassion as a Virtue in Hume

Christine Swanton

The suffering of others infects us, pity is an infection.
—Nietzsche, *Will to Power*

An accident which happens to another offends us: it would make us aware of our impotence, and perhaps of our cowardice, if we did not go to assist him. We repel this kind of pain and offence and requite it through an act of pity; it may contain a subtle self-defence or even a piece of revenge.
—Nietzsche, *Daybreak*

An "altruistic" morality—a morality in which self-interest wilts away—remains a bad sign in all circumstances.
—Nietzsche, *Twilight of the Idols*, "Skirmishes of an Untimely Man"

I

It may seem perverse to begin an essay on Hume with quotations from Nietzsche, and particularly so in an essay for a collection titled *Feminist Interpretations of David Hume*.

However, the comparison with Nietzsche is instructive. In showing that Hume has answers to the difficulties Nietzsche poses for the status of compassion or pity as a virtue, one shows that Hume has much to offer a normative ethical viewpoint that has become salient in the feminine ethics of care. A discussion of the Humean account of the altruistic

I am indebted to Marcia Baron, Rosalind Hursthouse, and Jacqueline Taylor for helpful comments on an earlier draft, and to Anne Jacobson for her helpful editorial suggestions.

virtues, and of difficulties in that account, has relevance to an ethics of care in at least three ways.

First, Nel Noddings's ethics of care invites the charge that self-interest—indeed the self—"wilts away" in 'engrossment,' an essential feature of caring on her view.[1] According to Noddings, engrossment is a condition of receptivity, contrasted with what she terms 'projection' where one analyses the condition of others, and then attempts to "put oneself in their shoes." In a state of engrossment, "I receive the other into myself, and I see and feel with the other, I become a duality."[2] It is a condition where "I have been invaded by this other." The other "fills the firmament" and "I do not ask myself whether what I am feeling is correct in some way." As we shall see, however, Hume's psychology shows how sympathy has self-protective aspects that render Humean sympathy less vulnerable than Noddings's engrossment to the charge of loss of sense of self.

Second, the accusation that "pity is an infection" because it involves the sympathetic transmission of others' pains, is one to which Noddings's engrossment is also subject. However, as we shall see, the Humean account of virtue-status has robust consequentialist elements, which allow for criticism of traits that have bad effects on the agent.

Third, Noddings's caring is highly particularistic, and as such seems in tension with a more generalized benevolence understood as a concern for overall good.[3] Hume's pluralistic account of the altruistic virtues, however, makes room for both particularistic caring, which gives expression to the 'original instinct' of, for example, kindness to children and parental love, and general benevolence, which gives expression to the original instinct of benevolence. This point is important. It is a distortion of Hume's thought on the altruistic virtues to represent him as a precursor of utilitarian thought by emphasizing the 'weak' sentiment of general benevolence, as *opposed* to an ethics of care or a pluralistic virtue ethics that combines a range of altruistic virtues, such as generalized benevolence, particularized caring, love, pity, gratitude, and friendship. The gratitude that a mother may feel to her obstetrician or midwife after a difficult birth may be overwhelming, and in Hume's terms "violent." Pity too, can be a particularly strong emotion, and Hume is sensitive to the moral significance of proximity, particularity, and personal engagement.

The Humean account of the altruistic virtues has much to offer a "feminine ethics" of care. In this essay, however, I wish to concentrate on one main issue. I wish to show how Hume himself could answer the kinds of problems Nietzsche poses for an understanding of compassion as a virtue. To this end, I concentrate on two problems raised by Hume's employment of two psychological principles, those of sympathy and comparison.

The first problem, illustrated by the first quotation from Nietzsche, is generated by the principle of sympathy. Hume's recognition of the problem is remarkably evocative of Nietzsche: "Pity is an uneasiness . . . arising from the misery of others, pity should naturally as in all other cases, produce hatred."[4] He claims that, though "there is always a mixture of love or tenderness with pity . . . it must be confessed that this mixture seems at first sight to be contradictory to my system" (T 381). The problem lies in the fact that the transmission of emotion and feeling via the mechanism of sympathy causes 'uneasiness' when receptive to the plight of another. In that sense, as Nietzsche puts it, "pity is an infection."

The second problem, illustrated by the second quotation, is generated by the principle of comparison, according to which, for Hume, a more lively idea of our own happiness can be caused by witnessing the misery of another. Compassion arouses in the compassionate not only sorrow for others' misery but also pleasure from the contemplation of their own more fortunate circumstances. For Nietzsche, this pleasure makes pity an ignoble motive. It involves a consciousness of our own vulnerability, a consciousness that at once makes us feel superior, because not currently suffering like the one pitied, but also angry at our vulnerability. Hence for Nietzsche, pity expresses narcissism, cowardice, and a subtle form of revenge.

In order to understand the precise nature of these difficulties in Hume's system, we need first to set the stage by outlining Hume's theory of virtue. This is done in the following section. In section III, I discuss the problem arising from the principle of sympathy, and in section IV, that arising from the principle of comparison.

II

According to Hume, what makes a 'mental quality' a virtuous one resides basically in the passions, namely pleasure and pain: "[T]he chief spring or activating principle of the human mind is pleasure and pain" (T 574).

Virtues and vices are those qualities of mind that, respectively, excite in the observer, and in certain circumstances, certain kinds of pleasure or pain: specifically those pleasures or pains that in turn arouse the indirect passions of, respectively, pride and love, humility or hatred: "[E]very quality in ourselves or others which causes pleasure always causes pride or love; as every one, that produces uneasiness excites humility or hatred. It follows that these two particulars are to be considered as equivalent with regard to our mental qualities, virtues and the power of producing love or pride, vice and the power of producing humility or hatred" (T 575). The traits that *in fact* have the power to cause pleasure, those that we are pleased with and approve of because they "present us with the lively idea of pleasure" are those having "a tendency to the good of mankind" (T 580).

Traits tending to the "good of mankind" come in four types: those that are "immediately agreeable" to their possessors or to others, or are "useful" to their possessors or to others (T 590–91). Hume's view of *what* kinds of traits arouse pleasure is based on his views of human nature. Just as the various virtues of benevolence (those that are useful to others) arouse pleasure, on account of the original instinct of benevolence, so does "love of life" (T 417) explain our approbation of virtues useful and agreeable to ourselves. In this sense, Hume emphasizes, our sentiments are uniform: "The notion of morals implies some sentiment common to all mankind, which recommends the same object to general approbation, and makes every man, or most men, agree in the same opinion or decision concerning it. It also implies some sentiment, so universal and comprehensive as to extend to all mankind" (*Enquiries* § 221). Persons "unaffected with the images of human happiness or misery" cannot operate with our notions of vice and virtue (*Enquiries* § 183).

Nonetheless, uniformity exists only at the most general level. First, as Hume recognizes, there can be considerable controversy concerning the tendencies of traits. Second, as Hume arrestingly points out in "A Dialogue," the tendencies of traits can differ quite markedly in different social contexts. Not only do "men differ in their judgement about the usefulness of any habit or action," but "[s]ometimes also the peculiar circumstances of things render one moral quality more useful than others and give it a peculiar preference."[5] Finally, and interestingly, Hume claims a third source of difference: "Different customs have also some influences as well as different utilities; and by giving an early bias to the mind, may produce a superior propensity, either to the useful or the agreeable qualities; to those which regard self, or those which extend to society.

These four sources of moral sentiment still subsist; but particular accidents may, at one time, make any one of them flow with greater abundance than at another."[6] None of these explanations for our differences of judgment are incompatible with the uniformity assumption: that we ("most men") approve of those traits that we take to have tendencies for the good of humankind.

In general then, for Hume, a virtue is a trait of character that is "immediately agreeable" or "useful" to its possessor or others, (T 590–91) because, he believes, these are the kinds of traits that we are pleased with and approve of. Since we approve of them because we believe them to have "a tendency to the good of mankind," we would withdraw our approval if we should discover our views about tendencies to be mistaken. Hume makes it clear that true belief plays a crucial role in the appropriate formation of moral sentiment: we need to know the "tendency" of traits if we are to know if they are *worthy* of moral esteem: "One principal foundation of moral praise being supposed to lie in the usefulness of any quality or action, it is evident that *reason* must enter for a considerable share in all decisions of this kind; since nothing but that faculty can instruct us in the tendency of qualities and actions, and point out their beneficial consequences to society and to their possessor. In many cases this is an affair liable to great controversy" (*Enquiries* App. I, § 234).

In order that the controversy be lessened, and to ensure the proper operation of reason, judgments about the tendencies of traits must be made from the "steady" and "general" point of view (T 581–82). Moral judgments are moral sentiments of approbation or disapprobation experienced by a person who is acquainted with the beneficial or deleterious tendencies of traits, but as in all putatively reliable judgments concerning matters of fact, we must correct for distortions of perspective when making judgments about tendencies. When moral judgments are being made, we must correct for distortions occasioned by the varying degree of proximity (on various dimensions) of those appraised to ourselves. Consequently, in judging a trait, we must judge its influence not on us, but on those who "have an intercourse with" (T 582) the person judged, and on the possessor of the trait him or herself (T 583).

In summary then, a virtue in a person is a mental quality that we approve of as a causal consequence of its producing a certain kind of pleasure in us once we have taken the general point of view in the "contemplation" or "survey" of that quality. The causal mechanism is sympathy; the kind of pleasure is that kind that produces pride or love in the beholder of the virtuous qualities.

We are now in a position to see more clearly the problems posed above for understanding compassion as a virtue in Hume's system. Let us now examine the first of these problems.

III

The first problem has two aspects. First, how is compassion possible on Hume's system? And second, how can it be a virtue?

Compassion at first sight seems impossible because, as Hume notes, the sympathetic transmission of the misery of another would be expected to cause hatred of the person producing such disagreeable effects on one (T 381). Furthermore, the indirect passions of pride, love, hatred, and humility reinforce desire for or aversion to objects producing those passions: "These indirect passions, being always agreeable or uneasy, give in their turn additional force to the direct passions, and increase our desire and aversion to the object" (T 439). Given that hatred reinforces pain, and pain gives rise to aversion that involves "separation" from the objects causing those pains, it is at first sight a mystery that the communication of others' pains via the mechanism of sympathy does not result in us avoiding the objects that are suffering.

Hume resolves the problem in a quite complex way. First he notes that pity is not a "pure sensation . . . without any direction or tendency to action" (T 382). It is not just the having of a pain resultant upon the sight of another's pain. What causes the pains transmitted not to be connected with the hatred of another, is the connection between pity and benevolence. Given that I take an empathetic interest in a person's misery, I can take a pleasure at its mitigation. Our happiness or misery at the happiness or misery of another person is mediated by the nature of our interest in that person, and that in turn determines the "bent or tendency" of a passion. Hence, as Hume says at T.381, "One impression may be related to another, not only when their sensations are resembling . . . but also when their impulses or directions are similar and correspondent. This cannot take place with regard to pride and humility; because these are only pure sensations." Hume describes the relationship between the passions of aversion and those of benevolence thus: "When the present misery of another has any strong influence upon me, the vivacity of the conception is not confin'd merely to its immediate object, but diffuses its influence over all the related ideas, and gives me a lively notion of all the circumstances of that person . . . By means of this lively notion I am interested in them; take part with them; and feel a sympathetic motion in my breast" (T 386).

What Hume is saying here is that while the operation of the imagination causes the sympathetic transference of another's pain, this transference awakens ideas that bring the general circumstances of the sufferer vividly before one so that one takes an *interest* in him or her. Thereby is aroused an empathetic concern. As benevolence, the desire for the happiness of those loved, is an original passion *awakened* by the *force* of the communicated sentiment of his pain, we are able to feel that "tenderness and love" that constitutes pity. Hume concludes: "A strong impression when communicated, gives a double tendency of the passions; which is related to benevolence and love by a similarity of direction; however painful the first impression might have been" (T 387). Thus does Hume resolve the apparent "contradiction" that threatens his system. Since there is "always a mixture of love or tenderness with pity," pity involves the desire to "unite" as opposed to a desire to "separate" from the object suffering.

The reason that pity is not a mere "infection" then is described by Hume's analysis of the process of empathy, which involves a rejection of a purely phenomenological account of the passions.[7] By contrast, Nietzsche's neglect of empathetic processes in his attack on pity as a virtue allows him to see virtuous altruistic motivation only as a kind of powerful and energetic "overflowing" of feelings and motives of "superabundance," where one gives from motives of having more than enough for oneself, rather than from a recognition of another's neediness. There is a curious neglect of the "pull" aspect of morality—the aspect that leads to response to vulnerability.[8] Hume's account of the altruistic virtues is centrally based on responsiveness to vulnerability, and therefore has far more in common with feminine ethics of care than any Nietzschean account of altruism.

We have seen how pity is possible on Hume's system. Now we must consider how it can be that compassion is a virtue.

Hume's resolution of the problem of the putative impossibility of pity apparently sends him from the frying pan into the fire. This new problem concerns the *extensiveness* of the passion of pity. According to Hume, pity is "a concern for . . . others . . . without any friendship . . . to oc-casion this concern . . . We pity even strangers, and such as are per-fectly indifferent to us" (T 365). Though the desire for the happiness of those we love, as "an original instinct planted in our nature," is a highly partial desire for the happiness of friends and near and dear, the more extensive love involved in pity for strangers is made possible by the operations of "secondary principles" of thought or imagination: "But if we examine these affections of pity . . . we shall find them to be secondary ones, arising from original affections, which are varied by some particular turn of thought or imagination" (T 369).

Now if pity is to be as extensive as Hume suggests, through the operation of the imagination, then the problem posed by the sympathetic transmission of others' pains and sufferings delivers a particularly nasty sting flamboyantly expressed by Nietzsche: "Pity *increases* the amount of suffering in the world: . . . Suppose it was dominant even for a single day mankind would immediately perish of it."[9] Exaggerated though it is, this assertion dramatically points up the problem faced by Hume. Granted a wide-ranging receptivity due to a love of even strangers, and granted that as a feature of that love, "counterfeit" though it is (T 368), we are peculiarly receptive to the communication of others' pains via the mechanism of sympathy, how can it be that pity as Hume understands it is not an extremely debilitating state?

The problem has two aspects. Would not the mechanism of sympathy make pity debilitating in two ways: emotional transmission means that we take on the pains of the world, and the process of empathy results in a degree of altruism that would be destructive to our personal projects and loves, and ultimately to ourselves? Hume's psychology of the process of empathy extricates him, however, from the first aspect of the problem. Sympathetic transmission is weakened as the objects whose sentiments are communicated become more remote: "Sympathy, we shall allow, is much fainter than our concern for ourselves, and sympathy with persons remote from us much fainter than that with persons near and contiguous" (*Enquiries* § 186).

The second aspect of the problem is dealt with by Hume's recognition of the fact that witnessing others' pains does not always result in empathy. When the communicated impression of pain is sufficiently lacking in force or vivacity, the imagination is not kick-started into operation in such a way as to call forth benevolence. "If I diminish the vivacity of the first conception, I diminish that of the related ideas; as pipes can convey no more water than what arises at the fountain . . . If it be another's misery, which is presented in this feeble manner, I receive it by communication, and am affected with all the passions related to it: But as I am not so much interested as to concern myself in his good fortune, as well as his bad, I never feel the extensive sympathy, nor the passions related to it" (T 386). Indeed, where the impression of pain communicated is slight, the uneasiness so caused may occasion contempt: "A certain degree of poverty produces contempt; but a degree beyond causes compassion and good will" (T 387). At the other extreme, a highly forceful impression of a pain may prevent the engagement of the imagination: "Thus we find, that tho' everyone, but especially women, are apt to contract a kindness for criminals, who go to the scaffold, and readily imagine them to be uncommonly handsome and well-shap'd; yet one, who is present at the cruel execution of the rack, feels no such tender emotions; but is in a manner overcome with horror, and has no leisure to temper this uneasy sensation by any opposite sympathy" (T 388). Thus Hume adverts to two protective devices against excessive empathy. The sympathetic communication of misery, if sufficiently faint, will generate no empathy and if sufficiently forceful will generate such overload that benevolence cannot operate.

It seems then that Hume possesses the psychological weaponry necessary to blunt the full force of Nietzsche's attack on pity. The baneful effects of the mechanism of sympathy in transmitting pain and causing empathy are attenuated in a variety of ways. However, given that sympathy allows us to disapprove of traits "immediately disagreeable" to the possessors of those traits, the problem of understanding compassion as a virtue has not disappeared. The operation of empathy described above presupposes the prior communication of pain, and Hume offers us no criterion for weighing the mixed effects of mental qualities in our assessment of them as virtues or vices. Of course, it is open to Hume to have us esteem only the compassion of those relatively inured to the suffering of others: the compassion, for example, of experienced doctors, psychiatrists, and aid workers. In fact, however, we often seem to admire the compassion of those who suffer in being compassionate, and who force themselves to succour the needy despite their squeamishness.

The resolution of this difficulty raises the interesting and controversial issue of the relation between virtue and pain or pleasure in being virtuous. To what extent, and in what circumstances, does "disagreeability to self" in exercising compassion display either a want of virtue or heightened virtue? And if it displays a want of virtue, should the agent in a somewhat Nietzschean manner regard her compassion as a *vice*, and stop *behaving* compassionately, or should she regard her state as merely one of incontinence or self-control? In the latter case, should she strive (perhaps heroically) to get rid of the disagreeable aspects?

The general difficulty raised in the first of these questions is addressed by Philippa Foot. As she claims in her *Virtues and Vices*, "[W]e both are and are not inclined to think that the harder a man finds it to act virtuously the more virtue he shows if he does act well."[10] Foot and Rosalind Hursthouse[11] resolve the problem by addressing the issue of what causes the difficulty in acting well: only if the difficulty is indicative of faulty values is there a want of virtue. If a person's compassion is "overclouded by sorrows of his own" (to use Kant's example, which Hursthouse discusses), the difficulties in the way of compassion do not reflect badly on his values, and there is no want of virtue. Unfortunately however, "reflecting badly on one's values" is not a notion easy to apply. One's espoused values may not be the same as one's lived values. Consider a depressive who often finds it difficult to take pleasure in things that she knows she would and should find pleasurable or not unpleasurable were she not depressed, and in whom sadness and sorrow is easily aroused. Say acts of compassion always arouse sorrow in her. Could not her being "overclouded by sorrow" (yet again) be a character failure, even some kind of mental disorder? On a Humean picture of virtue, such compassion could be seen as a vice because disagreeable to self. But Hume has the following problems. First, are not *some* states of disagreeability to self appropriate? Is not difficulty in being compassionate, occasioned by grief causing one to be overclouded by sorrow, appropriate? Is it not the case too, that difficulties in being compassionate, occasioned by squeamishness caused by the sympathetic transmission of pain, might also be appropriate in various contexts? Second, is not the *inappropriateness* of some states of disagreeability to self while one is acting putatively virtuously indicative not of vice but of continence or self-control?

Consider the following case: The sight of his ill grandmother awakens in a youth, aged twenty, considerable uneasiness. Although he pities her in Hume's sense, the uneasiness that her condition arouses makes him avoid seeing her on his own. When he is with others of the family, he will visit, since his uneasiness is less, or he is more distracted from it. However, these visits are relatively seldom, since he has commitments independent of those of the rest of the family. Nonetheless not all of these commitments are very pressing.

The issue is this. What could Hume say about the status of the youth's compassion as a virtue in the youth, given that it is so disagreeable to himself? Could Hume say that the youth's passions of uneasiness should be corrected by his acquiring a belief that they are *inappropriate* to their object? Could he say that they are of a force and vivacity that is unfitting and unseemly, and that, at present, he lacks the virtue of compassion but at best displays mere self-control or continence?

It might be thought in general that the problem of status of a trait as a virtue is resolved in the Humean system, if he had a robust sense of fittingness of passions. If one could correct one's passions of unease by moral education, would not the problem of the status of compassion as a virtue be solved? The disagreeable tendencies would be extirpated, since inappropriate passions of unease simply would not exist in the virtuous agent. In assessing the tendencies of traits on this view, we do not take people's passions as given. Rather, we would unequivocally understand compassion as a virtue on the assumption that, when inappropriate passions are corrected by moral education, we find that compassion has on the whole agreeable and useful tendencies for humankind. Hume does recognize that the "prejudices of education" (T 295) and custom will determine appropriateness of passions: "The passions are often vary'd by very inconsiderable principles. . . . But as custom and practice have brought to light all these principles, and have settled the just value of everything; this must certainly contribute to the easy production of the passions, and guide us, by means of general established maxims, in the proportions we ought to observe in preferring one object to another" (T 294).

The passions of the oversensitive youth may be deemed out of proportion, because custom and experience have taught us what we can reasonably expect of people in the amelioration of traits tending to the bad of humankind, in various respects. Such expectation is governed by a sense of what is "usual" and "common" in human nature; Hume rejects a sense of "appropriateness" that presupposes an overly demanding conception of virtue. We are to recognize, for example, that we are selfish to a degree: "We make allowance for a certain degree of selfishness in men; because we know it to be inseparable from human nature, and inherent in our frame and constitution" (T 583). How much allowance is to be made for natural selfishness in our account of virtue is, however, not specified, or even perhaps specifiable. Much selfishness can be eliminated in a climate where selfishness is vilified, but it is unclear how far this educative process should go. Though Hume's system does not allow for a highly determinate or a priori specification of appropriateness, his emphasis on the "usual" and the "common" allows him to strike a balance between conceptions of virtue that assume a heroic level of correction of passions in the interests of producing character traits of maximal utility/agreeableness to (appropriate combinations) of self/other, and those that assume relatively uncorrected passions. On a view that assumes a heroic level of correction, compassion would unequivocally be a virtue, given that all such disagreeable passions as the following are eliminated: unease at the sight of suffering, shame on receipt of well-motivated assistance, resentment at personal vulnerability occasioned by the sight of another in distress, glee at being able to display one's superiority and relative lack of vulnerability to someone in worse shape than oneself, glee that is subtly transmitted to the other, and so on. On a view that assumed no correction, the status of compassion as a virtue would be far more doubtful: Nietzsche may well be right. On Hume's rather more balanced picture, we do assume correction of the passions, but we must also bear in mind what is "common" or "usual" in human beings, constituted as we are in fact constituted.

We can now see that Hume does have some resources for dealing with the difficulties posed by the disagreeable aspects of compassion. If the sensitivities of the youth described above were "unusual," and their correction were possible without excessive cost, then the agencies of moral training could legitimately undertake the task of correction. On the other hand, we should not demand more than is consistent with our common nature. The object of my compassion who has no eyes may need an eye, but does that mean I should give him one of mine? If we were differently constituted, and found such levels of altruism quite natural, we might regard such action virtuous. As it is, given that we are creatures of naturally selfish or rather self-protective tendencies, we should not expect compassion of that nature, and would regard its manifestation as a likely symptom of self-destructiveness. Hume's demand to recognize what is "usual" in human nature (see T 483–84, 488) is not a recipe for complacency: rather, he recognizes that there are aspects of our nature that are deeply ingrained, and we ignore or thwart them at our peril. If a degree of selfishness in our makeup is not recognized, we may turn our children into adults who display inward forms of aggression that will make them sour, self-hating, or masochistic.

Finally, to the objection that Hume has no objective criterion for weighing the contributions made by disagreeability/agreeability to self/other; utility/disutility to self/other in the assessment of traits as virtues, Hume might reply that he is perfectly comfortable with the idea that there is no such criterion that would allow for determinate answers to the problem of weighing. As he says in "A Dialogue" in the passage cited above, "custom" gives an "early bias to the mind" in such weighings, and assuming the general point of view is adopted, such "accidents" of custom are not a concern.[12]

IV

We turn now to the second of the problems outlined in section I—that of the ignobility of the pleasure excited by the comparison between one's own state and the misery of the object of compassion.

A putatively unadmirable aspect of compassion that is targeted by Nietzsche is that we are "thinking very strongly of ourselves" when we pity another. This disagreeable insight is already in Hume, who is quite blunt on this issue: "The misery of another gives us a more lively idea of our happiness, and his happiness of our misery. The former, therefore, produces delight; and the latter uneasiness" (T 375). This observation is a corollary of a second psychological principle contrasted to that of sympathy: that of comparison. Hume illustrates it thus: "Suppose I am now in safety at land, and would willingly reap some pleasure from this consideration. I must think on the miserable condition of those who are at sea in a storm, and must endeavour to render this idea as strong and lively as possible, in order to make me more sensible of my happiness" (T 594). For Hume, though, this awareness of one's happiness as one contemplates the misery of another is not invariable: "Suppose the ship to be driven so near me, that I can perceive distinctly the horror, painted on the countenance of the seamen and passengers, hear their lamentable cries, see the dearest friends give their last adieu, or embrace with a resolution to perish in each others arms: No man has so savage a heart as to reap any pleasure from such a spectacle, or withstand the motions of the tenderest compassion and sympathy" (T 594).

For Nietzsche, the fact that in pity we are thinking so strongly of ourselves unless our passions are swamped in this way, is a mark of its being a "virtue" of the weak, as opposed to the strong, who do not need to get a sense of their happiness from the contemplation of the lesser fortunes of others. Rather, their happiness is constituted by *their* powerful strivings, creativity, and vitality.

Now if Nietzsche were correct about the deeper motivations of compassion, would Hume's account of virtue preclude him from addressing the problem this poses for the status of such compassion as a virtue? The ideas of a virtue being an admirable trait, and of a virtue being a trait constituted by the pleasure arising from a general survey of that trait, seem to lead to different views of what are virtues.

One way of resolving this difficulty is to reject an interpretation of Hume according to which a virtue is understood in terms of its power to produce pleasurable consequences. Rather, one might insist that, contrary to certain appearances, traits are judged virtuous inasmuch as they are judged admirable. This is the view of Marie A. Martin,[13] who claims that for Hume the natural virtues have intrinsic (aretaic) value as human excellences.

Martin is correct to reject the view of Hume as "some sort of proto-utilitarian" (whether of the trait or the act variety). Nonetheless, though Hume is no utilitarian, what makes a disposition a virtue for Hume is its power to arouse certain kinds of pleasure in the beholder. It can have this power, even though it is generally disutile. No matter how admirable from some objective point of view, if a generally disutile trait did not arouse pleasure by virtue of, for example, its "dazzling" qualities, or its ability to "seize the heart" by its "noble elevation" or "engaging tenderness" it could not be a virtue. (*Enquiries*, § 208). And the reason that "excessive bravery" and "resolute inflexibility" are approved is that we take pleasure in "splendour and greatness of appearance" (*Enquiries*, § 208; see also T 601). Indeed, the basis of virtue-status in the power of traits to arouse pleasure allows Hume to accept as virtues not only disutile traits, but also traits that are both disutile and (arguably) unadmirable.

Since I do not reject an interpretation of Hume according to which a virtue is a mental quality having a power to produce pleasurable consequences, it seems that the problem of ignoble pleasure is not resolved. However, we must recall the part played by rational belief in that derivation of pleasure. In the "general survey" of a trait's effects, we need to adopt a corrected sympathy. The same applies to the assessment of the operations of the principle of comparison. According to Hume, the psychological principle of comparison, like that of uncorrected sympathy, can result in distortions militating against the adoption of a "general point of view": "So little are men governed by reason in their sentiments and opinions, that they always judge more of objects by comparison than from their intrinsic worth and value" (T 372). In the case of perception, the phenomenon is readily apparent: we may judge an average-sized man short when he is standing beside a tall one. However, on what basis would Hume suggest that we should correct for our happiness in witnessing the sufferings of others when assessing this aspect of compassion? Presumably, this would be done on the basis of a belief that such happiness has no intrinsic worth, but is some kind of distortion. Beliefs about the psychological nature of such pleasure could lead to the view that it is some kind of distortion.

Consider now someone who surveys the mental quality of compassion. This person is well aware of the phenomenon of narcissism. She does not just rest with the psychological principle of comparison, she goes further in understanding certain manifestations of that principle as narcissistic. When she applies the term "narcissistic" to the pitying person's relief and joy at her *own* fortunate position resulting from the witnessing of misery in *others*, she is filled with a sense of distaste. Inasmuch as she sees compassion as *expressing* deplorable human motivation, she is pained, for she sees the joy occasioned by the sight of others' misery as a defective joy. Similarly, if we see the splendor of military glory, "resolute inflexibility," and excessive courage as tarnished, we will not be "elevated" by the contemplation of it. If the joy at the misery of others caused by comparison is also seen as "tarnished," a defect, then it, too, will cause distaste. This distaste might well lead to our regarding it as a vice despite the longer-term utility of the trait. To use Hume's language, the contemplation of such a trait may be "immediately disagreeable," and compassion "contaminated" by ignoble pleasure at others' suffering may, on Hume's view, be regarded as a vice.

V

In this essay, I have shown that compassion is a problematic virtue for Hume, but that his theory of virtue offers interesting resources for resolving those problems. These resources suggest that a Humean philosophy of benevolence or indeed an ethics of care need not be as vulnerable to criticism as might be imagined. Many of the qualities that Nietzsche attributed to pity were anticipated by Hume. Hume recognized the "infectious" nature of pity and the potential for the "unease" it creates to arouse hatred of those suffering. He is also aware that in witnessing the misery of others, we are made more sensible of our own vulnerabilities and of our gladness that we are not similarly afflicted. Hence, in witnessing the misery of others we are made more aware of our own happiness.

Hume resolves the first problem by a sophisticated account of empathy—an account that also solves the problem of the potentially debilitating effects of large-scale altruism. The way in which Hume describes the operations of the imagination in the mechanism of sympathy displays the self-protective tendencies of those mechanisms. Hume's recognition of the fact that the sympathetic transmission of pain need not be productive of empathy, let alone "engrossment" in Noddings's sense, is a useful adjunct to an ethics of caring. Such an ethics has been criticized for its apparently overly demanding nature, but the self-protective aspects of the mechanism of sympathy, described by Hume, suggests ways in which an ethics of care can avoid that criticism. Furthermore, Hume's emphasis on what is "common" or "usual" in human nature tempers any tendencies to an overly demanding ethics of benevolence or caring. In general it seems clear from Hume's discussion of the "good and the benevolent" that the exemplars of the benevolent do not standardly go forth into miserable conditions in order to minimize the suffering of humanity. The *motive* of compassion is not a dominant motive in the benevolent. The benevolent person is one who is "serviceable and useful within his sphere" (T 602), but there is no suggestion that his "sphere" should be chosen in such a way that relief of misery is dominant as an object of benevolence, let alone maximized. Indeed Hume's description of the humane, beneficent man emphasizes, first, "pious attachment" and "duteous care" to parents; second, good parenting, and ties of friendship; and finally, not just charity, but also a desire to improve the intellectual and moral caliber of those in his sphere. (*Enquiries*, § 141). And in T.606 the qualities of the benevolent person are cited as those that make him "a safe companion, an easy friend, a gentle master, an agreeable husband, or an indulgent father."

The second aspect of compassion discussed renders its status as a virtue problematic because of its ignobility. But Hume's philosophy of virtue is not based on ideas of nobility or admirability that might be exemplified by a Nietzschean hero. For Hume, a trait is not a virtue simply because it is expressive of noble motives. Its nobility must be of the kind that can arouse pleasure informed by rational belief, in "normal" "usual" human beings. If our knowledge of the real motivations of compassionate behavior causes distaste, then it is open to Hume to decry the trait as a vice.

Hume's emphasis on the rationality constraints on our judgements of virtue is of importance in combating the apparently antirational aspects of an ethics of care, and other approaches to ethics where emotions and "natural" virtue are paramount. The feelings of pleasure arising from judgments of longer-term utilities but also arising from the contemplation of immediate agreeableness to possessors of traits, must be undistorted. They must be based on adopting the general point of view. The operations of both comparison and sympathy are to be corrected from that point of view. Accordingly, we must assess the objective nature of motives of caring, benevolence, and compassion, in order to see if the pleasure produced is defective in some way (for example, the immediate agree-ableness to the caring agent of caring actions may be narcissistic, may involve a needy desire to make the object of caring dependent on one, or may involve a lack of esteem or regard for one's own projects or advantage). Furthermore, we must also reason concerning the longer-term utilities of mental qualities. Only then is a pleasing sentiment of approbation in a motive or trait to be deemed rational. Contrast this approach with that of Noddings, illustrated by the following example: A mother gives her son permission to stay at home from school in order to do something they both consider worthwhile. To avoid the situation of her son getting detention, she writes a lying note saying that he was ill. Noddings states, "I may choose to lie regularly in order to meet my son as one-caring rather than as conforming to principle."[14] On a Humean picture, a motive of caring is arguably not virtuous if it is a trait having generally deleterious consequences. If such parental "caring" had tendencies to undermine the authority of the school, encourage truancy, and cause a child to grow up into someone who is self-centered and with a tendency to lie for his own convenience, it would be unlikely to be a virtue.

There is much to learn from Hume in the development of an ethics in which the virtues of benevolence, compassion, or caring are central.

Notes

1. Nel Noddings, *Caring: A Feminine Approach to Ethics and Moral Education* (Berkeley and Los Angeles: University of California Press, 1984).

2. Noddings, *Caring*, 30.

3. It should be noted, however, that Noddings denies that caring requires encounter in "Review Symposium: A Response," *Hypatia* 5 (1990): 120–26.

4. David Hume, *A Treatise of Human Nature*, ed. L. A. Selby-Bigge (Oxford: Clarendon Press, 1978), 381. Future references to this work will be abbreviated to "T" in the text, followed by a page number.

5. In *Enquiries Concerning Human Understanding and Concerning the Principles of Morals*, 3d ed. (Oxford: Clarendon Press, 1975), 336.

6. Ibid., 337–38.

7. I am grateful to Jacqueline Taylor for helpful comments on the phenomenon of what Hume calls "parallel direction."

8. Cf. Robert Nozick's distinction between pull and push views of morality in *Philosophical Explanations* (Cambridge: Harvard University Press, 1981), esp. 400 ff. According to "pull" considerations, values inhering in the objects of moral concern demand a response from moral agents. According to "push" views, values possessed by, espoused by, moral agents motivate those agents to exhibit moral responses.

9. *Daybreak: Thoughts on the Prejudices of Morality*, trans. R. J. Hollingdale (Cambridge University Press, 1982), 134.

10. In her *Virtues and Vices* (Oxford: Basil Blackwell, 1978), 1–18, 10. For an excellent discussion of this claim, and a defense of the view that Kant and Aristotle are not as far apart as one might think, see Rosalind Hursthouse, "Virtue Ethics and the Emotions," in Daniel Statman, ed., *Virtue Ethics: A Critical Reader* (Edinburgh: Edinburgh University Press, 1997), 99–117.

11. In Hursthouse, "Virtue Ethics."

12. For a very interesting discussion of Hume's somewhat pragmatist approach to the problem of weighing, and a defense of an anti-utilitarian reading of Hume according to which there is no commitment to the commensuration of consequences, see Geoffrey Sayre-McCord, "Hume and the Bauhaus Theory of Ethics," in Peter A. French, Theodore E. Uehling Jr. and Howard K. Wettstein, *Moral Concepts*, Midwest Studies in Philosophy, vol. 20 (1995), 280–98. As Sayre McCord puts it, "The Bauhausian can, at least in principle, rest comfortably with the discovery that moral commensuration is not always possible."

13. See Marie A. Martin, "Hume on Human Excellence," *Hume Studies* 18 (1992): 383–99.

14. Ibid., 57.

8

Sympathy, Empathy, and Obligation

A Feminist Rereading

Nancy J. Hirschmann

The concept of sympathy is not a major player in the world of political theory, which is generally more concerned with justice, freedom, or rights. David Hume, however, gave sympathy a central place in his political and moral theory. Sympathy serves as an axis for bringing together conflicting

Many thanks to Anne Jacobson for her extremely helpful comments and suggestions. The errors that remain, of course, are mine alone. In this essay, references to Hume's works will be made in the text, by the following abbreviations, to the following editions: (THN): *A Treatise of Human Nature*, ed. L. A. Selby-Bigg, 2d ed., rev. P. H. Nidditch (Oxford: Clarendon Press, 1978); (ECPM): *Enquiry Concerning the Principles of Morals*, in *Enquiries Concerning Human Understanding and Concerning the Principles of Morals*, ed. L. A. Selby-Bigg, 3d ed., rev. P. H. Nidditch (Oxford: Clarendon Press, 1975); (Es): *Essays: Moral, Political, and Literary* (Oxford: Oxford University Press, 1963); (H): *The History of England from the Invasion of Julius Caesar to the Revolution in 1688*, vols. 5 and 6, ed. W. B. Todd (New York: Liberty Classics).

parts of his theory, though it has been the focal point for a number of problems in Humean analysis as well.

This is particularly the case regarding political obligation. Hume is famous for his critique of consent theory; few have been able to improve on his scathing rejection of the social contract on both logical and historical grounds.[1] Instead, Hume grounds political society and our allegiance to it in the importance to human happiness of relationships and society; and he argues that the sympathy humans naturally feel for one another is a vital part of our political allegiance. In this, Hume is similar to some recent feminist theorists who have been severely critical of "abstract individualism" and who argue for a politics that reflects women's historical location in relationship.[2] Such theories develop an "ethic of care" and model of moral reasoning that give priority to issues of connection and responsibility, and derive at least in part from a notion that women have a greater propensity for empathy, whether by "nature or nurture."

The concept of empathy developed by these theorists can be seen as significantly similar to Humean sympathy. Yet the picture of politics that Hume develops is quite different from the participatory-democratic model that many feminists advocate. While "Hume's science of politics potentially has a dynamic effect" that points toward social democracy, several aspects of his theory—particularly his views on the right of resistance—lead the way toward conservative authoritarianism.[3] Key to this apparent ambivalence is a tension in Hume's theory between human sociability and individualism, and in this essay I will consider Hume's concept of sympathy as an important element in this tension. I will then explore whether and how a feminist recuperation of Humean sympathy can help resolve the tension, and thereby open up a more democratic potential in Hume.

Feminist Empathy and Connected Knowing

Several different strains of recent feminist theory develop a notion of empathy that may provide a useful link to Humean sympathy. The most obvious, explored by Annette Baier and others, involves the work of Carol Gilligan and her colleagues, who maintain that girls and women tend to think in terms of a "morality of care" that gives priority to relationships, connectedness, and responsibility, basing conflict resolution on communication and consensus, as opposed to a rights-based morality based on abstract principles, rules, and law.[4]

This care orientation derives from a conception of the self as intimately connected to others in a network of relationships, where one's identity and even one's own feelings are conceived in terms of others'.[5] Gilligan and Wiggins call this trait "co-feeling," which involves the "ability to *participate* in another's feelings (in their terms)": rather than projecting what I, with my history and context, would feel in your situation, I seek to share in what you are actually feeling by imagining that I have *your* history and context.[6]

Similarly, object relations psychoanalytic theory maintains that because women, and not men, have primary responsibility for the care and nurturance of young children, boys and girls develop different senses of themselves as gendered subjects, as well as different conceptions of their relation to the "object-world." Boys are culturally and psychically required to perceive the gendered self as separate and different from the mother, and thence from "others," whereas girls come to see the world as connected to, even continuous with, the self. As a result, Nancy Chodorow argues, girls have "a basis for 'empathy' built into their primary definition of self in a way that boys do not."[7]

For Chodorow as for Gilligan, empathy is not simply an emotion, however, but a way of perceiving and understanding the experiences of others, an epistemological framework for "knowing" the world. This notion is further developed by Belenky and colleagues' theory of "connected knowing." More common to women and girls according to their data, it involves an orientation toward relationship rather than rules, intersubjectivity rather than objectivity. It involves treating the known as a subject rather than object, and treating others on their own terms. The "connection" is not merely between knowers, but between knowers and the known; yet in the process, intimate relations with other knowers— and with their knowledge—becomes a central enterprise of human social life: "at the heart" of connected knowing "is the capacity for empathy. Since knowledge comes from experience, the only way [one] can hope to understand another person's ideas is to try to share the experience that has led the person to form the idea."[8] Thus connected knowers "learn through empathy," where empathy is described as "feeling with," as merging the self *with* the other, rather than imposing the self *on* the other. By contrast, "separate knowing" is an "adversarial form" that operates from premises of separation between knower and known. Its concept of objectivity, with its rule-governedness and mastery over the known—which is seen as an other opposed to the self—disjoins knowing and feeling; objectivity is equated with dispassion, a process that excludes the private concerns and feelings of both oneself and one's adversary.[9]

Experience-based "materialist" feminist theorists also view relationship as the basis for a feminist morality and epistemology. For instance, Sara Ruddick argues that the material activities of mothering produce an epistemological perspective called "maternal thinking," a major attribute of which involves attention to others' needs.[10] Patricia Hill Collins develops a similar "way of knowing" from African American women's experience, and suggests that the experiences of black "community othermothers" provide an even stronger foundation for an ethic of care because of the racial privilege in which white women's experiences of mothering occur.[11] Despite its essentialist undertones, and although the specifics of maternal practices in various cultures can differ significantly, caretaking is one of the major "jobs" that women have had throughout history; it thus can provide a historical, material basis for an ethic of care. Indeed, Nancy Hartsock argues that the material dimensions of women's caring labor—in child rearing, cleaning, and cooking—establish the ground for a "feminist standpoint" *epistemology*; they provide an experiential basis for seeing the world in concrete and contextual ways that place relationship at the center of one's epistemological framework.[12]

Reading connected knowing to suggest that experience has a material effect on one's intellectual and cognitive perceptions and emotional consciousness can address a potential problem with this literature, namely that the degree of connection can be exaggerated or romanticized. For instance, Chodorow defines the empathy that girls develop not simply as "experiencing another's needs or feelings as one's own" but also as *"thinking that one is so experiencing another's needs and feelings."*[13] That one sees oneself as so connected as to actually experience another's pain may be erroneous, even delusional; since we occupy separate bodies, I cannot literally have your experience. Indeed, Chodorow suggests that women's tendency to overidentify with the other and lose the self is the *pathology* of the "feminine" model.

But at the same time, such perceptions are often part of cultural definitions and expectations of women's empathy. The "pathology" is one that patriarchal cultures force on women and pass off as "normal." On this view, the "feminine" exaggeration of connection is no more pathological than the "masculine" exaggeration of separation between individuals, an exaggeration that similarly has come to be seen as normal in political philosophies of abstract individualism. Indeed, the notion of "experience" makes the feminist view *more* plausible; as the academic and popular literature on grief and trauma suggests, sharing particular experiences can help one to understand others more completely and deeply, to "share" in feelings that are more than simply "similar," but rather reverberate in the self's experience.[14] The "knowing" that comes from experience allows one not simply to project one's experience onto the other, but to hear the other's account in a more profound way. Accordingly, these feminists do not want to say that experiences are merely similar or "parallel"; the connection they posit is more profound and requires that one "set aside his or her own mental stance . . . and imagine having the different stance adopted by another person,"[15] or what Sandra Harding calls "reinventing ourselves as other."[16]

Humean Sympathy: Individualistic or Social?

Does Hume posit such connectedness? And is this feminist empathy comparable to Hume's sympathy? According to Hume, sympathy is "a very powerful principle in human nature" (THN 577), and is experienced or felt by humans in a three-stage process. First I observe others' experience: "When any affection is infus'd by sympathy, it is at first known only by its effects, and by those external signs in the countenance and conversation, which convey an idea of it" (THN 316). Second, such observation leads to inference about a state of mind; for instance, from observing someone who is shouting in anger, I infer that she is angry. Third, this idea is "enlivened" by the imagination, and "converted into an impression, and acquires such a degree of force and vivacity, as to become the very passion itself, and produce an equal emotion, as any original affection" (THN 316). Through sympathy, then, I feel what you feel: "The sentiments of others can never affect us, but by becoming, in some measure, our own" (THN 593).

The phrase "in some measure" is, of course, key. Hume can be read to suggest that we literally share a feeling; by observing you in pain, I feel the pain too, and would therefore seem to be feeling *your* pain. But another interpretation might be that I "imagine" what your pain is like by drawing on my own experiences. The notion of one's own experience is not overtly discussed by Hume in his account of sympathy, but I believe that it is at least implicit. Hume says that "resemblance" strengthens sympathy; while such resemblance often refers specifically to appearance, it seems logical that experience would be relevant as well. As Pall Ardall argues, "one can sympathize only with experiences one has had oneself";[17] if I have never experienced pain, for example, then observing you react to being burned cannot in itself be sufficient to cause me to feel that pain. My imagination could not be "enlivened" without *some* pain experience on which to draw; and indeed having burned myself in the exact same way would provide the strongest basis for a sympathetic reaction.

The relevance of experience to Humean sympathy is also implicit in the fact that, although we may feel sympathy "naturally"—that is, spontaneously and "antecedent to human conventions" (THN 542)—this feeling is still "artificial," namely, the product of reason or custom: "However instantaneous this change of the idea into an impression may be, it proceeds from certain views and reflections, which will not escape the strict scrutiny of a philosopher, tho' they may the person himself, who makes them" (THN 316). As Forbes points out, while the *process* of sympathetic reaction may be the same in all humans across cultures and historical periods, the *substance* of the reactions will differ according to the "views and reflections" that are strongly affected by one's experiences within a particular cultural environment.[18]

The notion of experience leads to a highly relational account of Humean sympathy that resonates with feminist empathy. The most obvious similarity concerns the closeness of the connection between others' feelings and one's own. Hume suggests that sympathy engenders the other's actual feeling in me, so that "there is no difference in principle between the thought of pain and real pain,"[19] simultaneously blurring categories such as "your" pain and "mine;" this echoes the idea found in co-feeling of imagining myself *as* the other and not merely imagining how I would feel in that other's situation. On this view, sympathy is not simply an emotion, but rather a way of understanding others and the world.[20]

At the same time, however, Hume is ambiguous in this matter, for his account of sympathy is also quite individualistic, and even mechanical: "As in strings equally wound up, the motion of one communicates itself to the rest; so all the affections readily pass from one person to another, and beget correspondent movements in every human creature" (THN 576). Thus, by being in the proximity of someone in pain, I too feel pain. But this simple awareness does not mean anything, morally or socially: it does not necessarily motivate me to do anything about the other person's discomfort.[21] For Hume, benevolence and sympathy are often at odds; while sympathy can result in benevolent action, it does not have to. Sympathy may create a predisposition or attitude toward particular kinds of action—"approval" and "disapproval"—but does not itself produce action; indeed, it would seem to be more of an "involuntary *reaction*."[22]

This disjunction of feeling and action is a considerable weakness, according to some critics, in undermining the social dimensions of Hume's political theory. Mercer maintains that Hume operates from "a Cartesian picture of emotional life" and that Hume's doctrine of sympathy is "unduly egocentric."[23] And Ardall notes that Hume's imagery of mirroring and echoing "shows how mechanically he thinks about the way in which emotions and opinions are transferred from one person to another."[24] Moreover, the procedural requirements of sympathy, wherein the feeling follows from the idea, and the idea depends on one's own sense impressions, suggest that sympathy may be self-referential and perhaps even somewhat solipsistic, rather than social and other-directed. "Our affections depend more upon ourselves, and the internal operations of the mind, than any other impression" (THN 319). Since "resemblance and contiguity" promote "sympathy in its full perfection," then "no person is ever prais'd by another for any quality, which wou'd not, if real, produce, of itself, a pride in the person possest of it" (THN 320). Here Hume suggests that we impose our own values and experiential framework in the sympathetic process; so perhaps we do *not* react to the other person's experience per se but to our perception of that experience, mediated by our own contexts.

This poses several difficulties for a feminist reading, the most important being the static and unitary understanding of the self that it suggests. For Hume, our ability to feel what another feels depends on our developing an idea of that feeling through observation. But each person is dependent on his or her own perceptions and experience. In Hume's view, the self seems to be fully formed prior to the sympathetic response, rather than being formed by and through it and the social relations giving rise to it. Our understanding of another's experiences and feelings would simply be projections of our own experiences and feelings onto the screen of their behavior, indeed, onto the screen of our *perceptions* of their behavior.

This suggests a problematic individualism. The experience of sympathy in Hume's account does not seem to alter me in any deep way; the self that feels sympathy does not seem to carry any lasting changes into the next sympathetic response, but returns to a neutral "default" self in between separate and discrete incidents of sympathetic reaction. By contrast, for the feminist account, the Humean process is inverted: rather than making feeling depend on inferring an idea, ideas of and knowledge about others are based (in part) on feeling. By locating feeling as part of knowledge's foundation rather than its product, feminist empathy posits humans as more intimately connected, and entering into the feelings of others has a deeply transformative potential; "through mutual stretching and shar- ing" of empathic relationships, connected knowers "seek and grow."[25] As a result, this kind of feminism maintains a historical view of humans, seeing people as developing through relationships, whereas Hume seems to operate from a more static "time-slice" conception; the feminist theorists cited here include an understanding of how males and females tend to *develop* their supposed orientation toward separateness or con- nectedness—through socially constructed social relations of reproduction and divisions of labor, as well as socialization norms of femininity and masculinity—but Hume lacks such a developmental conception. His static notion of the self would seem to conflict with the feminist understanding of empathy, which is relational not only in the sense of deep connection, but in the sense that the related self is dynamic, fluid, and responsive.

Of course, the reading of Hume as an individualist is not without difficulties, and is often tied to the view of Hume as a skeptic, which theorists such as Annette Baier have refuted.[26] Space does not permit me to explore the controversy over Hume's skepticism.[27] But while I agree with Baier that Hume is arguing that we need to broaden what we call knowledge, and that, somewhat in keeping with the feminists considered here, knowing takes place in many different ways that include the "sentiments," I do not think that he necessarily fully realized this. Though the "atomism" that critics such as Miller assert may be exaggerated,[28] knowledge is at least "individualistic" for Hume in that each person is dependent on his or her own perceptions. Such an epistemology could make knowledge of others and our relationships with them difficult. The fact that there are individualistic tendencies in Hume's epistemology does not make him a skeptic; but nor does abandoning the skeptical reading of Hume eliminate his individualism, much less bring us to feminism's connected knowing. As Forbes notes, "atomism and individualism . . .

are in fact there" in Hume's work; they must be acknowledged and their transformation explored.[29]

Thus rather than to deny the individualistic elements of Hume's theory, it is more helpful to recognize an important tension in Hume's work: between a social, even communal, ontological outline and a psychology that is problematically individualistic.[30] Although Hume locates individuals in societies and describes them as inescapably social, his static conception of those socially located individuals means that he must be logically compelled to a strong, perhaps even Hobbessian, individualism at important points in his work.

Hume argues that as isolated individuals, people cannot get what they want, because they are inadequate alone. "When every individual person labours apart and only for himself, his force is too small to execute any considerable work" leading to "inevitable ruin and misery" (THN 485). From sexual passion arise love relationships and then families, with parents feeling a natural affection for their offspring; but people do not "naturally" gather together in harmonious groups, for "our primary instincts lead us either to indulge ourselves in unlimited freedom, or to seek dominion over others" (Es 467). Nature "has determined us to judge as well as to breath and feel" (THN 183), however, and so humans can learn that cooperation with others may help them overcome their inadequacies: "It is by society alone he is able to supply his defects" (THN 485). Thus, as families teach people, particularly children, the material advantages of cooperation, people come to understand that acts of self-love and pursuit of "contiguous," or short-term, immediate interests can be ultimately destructive; they thus check their impulses, and form "friendships" of mutual utility.

People further see that they must submit to certain rules and authority to maintain society as the environment within which they can most easily pursue their individual interests, particularly the stable possession of property, the transference of property by consent, and fidelity, or the keeping of promises: given our individualism, scarce resources, and the counterproductive tendencies of warring over those resources, rules of justice make our interactions manageable and it is in our best interest to follow them. When society grows larger, however, the interest in promoting justice is "more remote; nor do men so readily perceive that disorder and confusion follow upon every breach of these rules, as in a more narrow and contracted society" (THN 499). Since the passions are governed by the imagination, and since contiguous interests, being more immediate, impress themselves more vividly on the imagination, the passions will give preference to contiguous interests over remote ones, as real interests are forsaken for the apparent (THN 535). Because interest can no longer guarantee allegiance, Hume says, something else must provide the base. This is where sympathy takes on its central political role, because sympathy facilitates our adoption of the "general point of view," which is necessary to understanding the remote interests (THN 581), especially about the importance of rules and the continuation of society in general. Rules that were thus originally created (in smaller societies) because of interest, now (in larger societies) begin to be approved by people out of sympathy that they naturally feel for others:

> [T]ho' in our own actions we may frequently lose sight of that interest, which we have in maintaining order, and may follow a lesser and more present interest, we never fail to observe the prejudice we receive, either mediately or immediately, from the injustice of others. . . . Nay when the injustice is so distant from us, as no way to affect our interest, it still displeases us; because we consider it as prejudicial to human society, and pernicious to everyone that approaches the person guilty of it. We partake of their uneasiness by *sympathy*. (THN 499)

Because we can see what injustice does to us, sympathy enables us to extend our conclusions about the "viciousness" of injustice to society at large. Sympathy enables us to feel for others, to extend the feelings we have about our personal experience to those others, and thence to approve of justice and disapprove of injustice.

The "sympathetic" foundation for social life is particularly important to political obligation. The ability to understand the need for justice might seem to preclude the need for government; and Hume admits that in small, "uncultivated" societies everyone can follow the rules of their own accord in order to secure harmony. But when societies grow larger, informal means of insuring cooperation become less stable and effective, and some impartial overseer is needed. As justice is necessary to society, government is necessary to justice. And just as sympathy causes us to approve of justice even when we are unable to see its relation to our interest, so does sympathy cause us to approve of government. As we adopt the general point of view, we begin to realize the complex interdependence of justice, property, and government as the "moral" dimensions of political obligation fully take root. The "natural" obligation of interest has lost its force, leaving only sympathetic approval of the artificial and conventional institutions of government.

Thus sympathy contains an odd mixture of strong individualism and strong sociability: if sympathy derives importantly from a self-referring tendency in each separate individual, it also locates such individuals in the context of social relationships. Sympathy translates self-reference into sociability by connecting our minds—or more accurately, our feelings and our inner lives—with those of others. And of course, in the process, it reveals our feelings and inner lives, including our "imaginings" and "beliefs," to be not *inferior* to knowledge, but *part of* it, as theorists such as Baier assert.

At the same time, however, Hume undercuts this sociability via a self-referential way of "knowing" sympathy. For instance, interest and sympathy are consecutive in determining the base for obligation, rather than concurrent; while "*self-interest is the original motive to the establishment of justice . . . a sympathy with public interest is the source of the moral approbation which attends that virtue* (THN 499–500). Hume says society is formed because of self-interest solely, and that sympathy enters as an important element in obligation only later, when society grows larger. But why do we not approve sympathetically from the start? Indeed, if sympathy is a natural sentiment, then it seems more likely that we would feel it in a small society, where there is more common ground for agreement on interests, and "resemblance and contiguity" (THN 320) are stronger.

This inconsistency points to the individualism that underlies Hume's otherwise social ontology and undercuts his sympathy. The fact that sympathy cannot on its own motivate people to act suggests that it is a deeply individualist psychological principle: my sympathetic feelings may be "natural," but they are locked inside me until some "trigger" happens to motivate me to act. This may be why government is needed, to bridge this gap between feeling (sympathy) and action; the fear of sanction could motivate people to *do* the things that sympathy *ought* to approve, and benevolence *ought* to tell them to do, namely obey the law and promote peace. Yet Hume is adamant that fear of sanction is not what makes people obey. Public opinion is extremely important to the authority of government (Es 29–30); and sympathy should logically be key to that opinion. It is as if sympathy comes to us through this self-referential process but then somehow gets translated into a highly social and relational set of emotions in the form of approval or disapproval, which form the basis for further knowledge about subsequent observations.

It may be such a tension that requires Hume to assert that humans are all the same, even guided, as Penelhum argues, by "instinct."[31] "The minds of all men are similar in their feelings and operations, nor can any one be activated by any affection of which all others are not, in some degree, susceptible" (THN 575–76). Such an assertion ironically supports the skeptical readings of Hume's epistemology: that is, skepticism seems to arise inevitably from individualism, from the notion that we are fundamentally separate. The assertion of sameness allows Hume to circumvent this: if we all can reliably be expected to feel the same approval or disapproval, then it does not matter if we are epistemologically separate, because the end result is the same as if we were epistemologically linked. In this view, Hume needs to assert people's sameness in order to circumvent his individualism and make plausible his assertion that people are ontologically social.

Feminist Frameworks and Humean Reconstruction

Can feminist empathy help resolve this tension? By eschewing individualist underpinnings, feminism wants to suggest that the connections between people are not quite natural but that they are nevertheless fundamental to humanity, much as Hume argues. However, the notion of "connected knowing" through shared experience may allow Hume to substantiate his claims of sameness; if knowledge is based on experience, and we share experiential frameworks, then our knowledge is the same. At the same time, it would allow him to acknowledge greater differences between people without fearing their destructive effects. A central aspect of feminist empathy is that difference does not bar relationship, but is necessary to it. The dynamic qualities of connected knowing, co-feeling, and empathy suggest that difference is a crucible for the formation of community. And this is in part because in connected *knowing*, empathy is epistemological, a notion that is less clearly and consistently true for Hume. Connected knowing is not simply a strategy that can be selectively utilized to connect otherwise separate individuals; it is a way of seeing the entire world that in turn *constructs and creates* people as fundamentally connected.

Although Hume's social ontology gestures toward connectedness, his individualism throws up repeated and persistent stumbling blocks to its realization. By redrawing the sympathizing "self," feminist empathy could address this. For instance, it would permit a stronger link between sympathy and interest, particularly within the context of obligation, which requires us to take the general point of view. According to Hume, people see that others have similar interests and desires, and sympathy transforms these ideas into impressions; but they are impressions of what people want, what is good for them, what is in their interest. Indeed, Hume holds that we must approve of something for ourselves before we can approve of it for others; this should not change if such approval is made from the general point of view. But this already suggests that the disjunction between sympathy and interest is mistaken, even from an individualist point of view.

Furthermore, feminist empathy highlights that sympathy at least partly enables people to form society in the first place; if children learn the benefits of cooperation because their parents feel a natural affection for them, then "interest" is not the sole origin of such cooperation, contrary to what Hume maintains. Aside from acquiring an understanding of the material benefits of cooperation, family life could reasonably be expected to encourage emotions and attachments to develop, thus introducing the notion of "moral" obligations and bonds at a much earlier stage in the social developmental process. While we originally form society out of self-interest, Hume also says that our interest in society is more than a "modification of self love" (ECPM 219), and involves a natural tendency toward the "principles of humanity" and a general "disinterested interest" in society. On this reading, Hume could be saying that our individual interests are transformed into a collective interest for a safe community. Hume says that "the interest of each individual is, in general, so closely connected with that of the community" (ECPM 218) that we approve of that which is useful for society in general, regardless of whether it serves our contiguous interests. We view the public interest as our own, but in a disinterested, not selfish sort of way. So we approve of it partly out of disinterested sympathy; that is, out of a feeling about what gives other people in general pleasure or pain. This could be what Hume means when he says we are obligated to that which we all approve of, the interests we can define by adopting the general point of view. Yet we are also always concerned with our own pleasure and pain, which is why we also—and *concurrently*—have a natural obligation to utility.

On this feminist rereading, sympathy would be *part* of the notions of utility and interest. Sympathy would not merely enter at the end of the reasoning process to make us feel bound to those things we objectively or rationally need; since it is a natural sentiment, it ought to be present from the beginning. Hume cannot logically separate interest from sympathy, for the former forms a basis for the latter; and there is no reason why it must substitute interest rather than coexist with it. If Hume admitted this, the basis for political obligation would not have to change; if we approved of something sympathetically (from a general point of view), our motivation to act upon that approval could be interest itself, rather than limited benevolence or fear of sanction. A recognition of the possibility of collective interests would help ease this problem; once people understood their common and collective interests, they would not necessarily lose sight of them just because society got larger. Indeed, society's growth might dictate a new set of needs or interests, but there is no reason to think that people will not be able to see what those are.

Reformulating the operation and role of sympathy would also help redress the conflict posed by Hume's view on the right of resistance. The authoritarian elements here again betray a fear of people's individualism and how this will inevitably decay into irreconcilable conflict. Given that "long possession" is the strongest basis for government (followed by "present possession"), Hume thinks that whatever government is in power will most likely provide for justice, and that we therefore ought to obey because it serves our interests. Although a government may be resisted if it violates the public interest of justice and security, he believes that this will only happen in cases of "grievous tyranny and oppression" (THN 554). The destruction of government leaves us without the formal mechanisms that guarantee the maintenance of the laws of justice and fidelity; and such a state of affairs makes pursuit of individual interests impossible. Resistance is thus "the last refuge in desparate cases" (Es 475).

Even modifying the government as we go along (as opposed to engaging in revolution) tends to destabilize government, which will inevitably lead to its destruction. Hume says that "government is useless without an exact obedience" (THN 554); and even an absolute government, "as it is as *natural* and *common* a government as any . . . must certainly occasion some obligation" because it provides order and security (THN 549). Though Hume does seem to support "republican" government and its attendant liberties (of the press and habeas corpus in particular), these are clearly "subordinated to a reverence for established government" (H 6:365–66). Indeed, such liberties are desirable only to the extent that they *promote* political order.[32]

Such a view would seem at odds with the democratic impetus of feminist theory.[33] Though Hume vacillates between republicanism in his "perfect commonwealth" and absolute monarchy as the only "civilized" government, he is clearly opposed to democracy, which he sees as "disorderly . . . unable to pursue a steady line of policy" and "liable to be bought by the rich" (H 5:295–96). In "The Idea of a Perfect Common-wealth," he supports a "well tempered democracy," but as Miller notes, "the tempering is very thorough," involving "the admission of the middle ranks of people to a small share of power in a government that remains predominantly autocratic in character."[34]

This conservatism is due in part to the individualism in his theory of sympathy. Hume admits that a government may *not* be serving the public interest and yet people may still *feel* obligated, out of a habit of obedience, for instance, or perhaps out of misplaced, or "uncorrected," sympathy, that is, uncorrected from the biases of contiguous interest and social relations. In such cases, we will feel ourselves obligated even though sympathy *should* lead us to perceive, if we take the general point of view, that we have no further obligations. Hume implies that in such cases, people can be mistaken in feeling obligated and in feeling sympathetic approval.

So should obligation be based on what citizens *do actually feel* about their government at a given point in time? Or should it be based on some objective "judgment" about what *we ought to feel* obligations to, as Miller suggests?[35] Hume's theory of society, with its notion of "corrected" sympathy, would seem to commit him to the latter, but his moral epistemology may make that impossible: if approval is based on our feelings, then what would be the basis on which we disapprove of the feelings that we have?[36] We would have to will a new feeling into existence, which Hume says we cannot do.

Hume again circumvents this by asserting that we all simply feel the right things. If that is true, then it does not practically matter whether obligations are based on actual feeling or on truths about how we should feel; for those two categories become coextensive. This is particularly so in political matters, where people behave with "a much greater unifor-mity" than in artistic taste or scientific development (Es 98). But this simply brings us full circle: if psychological and psychosocial mechanisms make us all pretty much the same, why will attempts to improve government not be successful rather than disastrous? If sympathy ensures that the remote interests we have in common prevail over the contiguous ones that divide us, why are we not obligated to pursue the *best* government, rather than simply accepting any merely useful one? The answer seems to lead back to individualism: though we may all know the same things, though we may all have the same interests, our individualism prevents us from knowing that we know that. The fact that Hume insists that rebellion is doomed suggests that popular participation and ongoing reform—which *should* be part of Hume's sympathy-laden theory of politics and political allegiance—are de-emphasized in favor of security and order, making Hume sound suspiciously like Hobbes.

Hume's use of sympathy to overcome his individualist tendencies and forge the social link is thus flawed by a certain circularity. A feminist rereading of Hume—or an appropriation that excises his individualism— could address these inadequacies. The feminist perspective of connectedness produces a conception of sympathy not as a natural emotion that simply waits for particular empirical incidents to trigger its expression, but rather as a social dynamic that develops in and through relationships, that changes us through its different expressions. Rather than focusing on one's own passions and feelings produced mechanically by a sympathetic reaction to observed behavior, connected knowing takes a more dynamic and interactive approach: just as "therapists learn to use their reactions to a client to help them understand the client,"[37] the sympathy that connected knowers engage in is an ongoing interpersonal process that creates and constructs both the social formations that individuals participate in, and the individuals that make up these social formations. In Humean terms, this connectedness should enable individuals to engage in *self-reflection about* their passions and sympathetic responses to learn more about what the observed person is feeling and experiencing. Observation, sympathy, and identity would be seen as interrelated and dynamic, as feelings and impressions alter our observations and interpretations, which in turn affect our impressions.

This would in turn give way to a more social-democratic notion of political society and political obligation. From a feminist perspective, rather than arguing that absolute obedience was necessary to safeguard society, Hume could have more consistently asserted that interest would motivate people to strive for improvement in the community's situation and to try to achieve a better form of government; and that sympathy would approve of such actions over passive tolerance of near tyranny. A society in which sympathy and interest were concurrent rather than consecutive, and in which sympathy existed at all stages in the social process, would create greater opportunities for democratic action, for continual revision and improvement of government. By combining sympathy and interest more closely, Hume could form a richer and more consistently social notion of obligation and political society. The ontological perspective of enmeshment in a social network leads to the moral conclusion that freedom—the central element in social contract theory, which Hume attacks—is, while important to the concept of a person, not necessarily the primary element. Obligation or allegiance would seem to be more important in maintaining the fabric of social relations, as Hume maintains.

However, from a feminist perspective of human connectedness, obligation needs to be considered in a very different light from what Hume suggests. The political point of feminist empathy is not simply to make us obey whatever government is in power, but to enter into different modes of assessing that government and our obedience to it. The centrality of sympathy to human community need not lead to a conservative enshrinement of the status quo; on the contrary, it requires a communal effort to improve the social and political situation for all. Connectedness requires inquiry and debate, not passive obedience; indeed, the latter is hardly compatible with Hume's ontological sociability, but is more in keeping with the abstract individualism of Hobbes. If human interaction always resulted in conflict, then it could occur only through the medium of the sovereign. But people as socially located as Hume asserts can do more than that, and indeed must, according to Hume's own description.

Thus a feminist rereading of sympathy can help Hume. But in turn, Hume can help feminists. The feminist literature on empathy is sometimes accused of lacking theoretical rigor; yet unless care is theorized more fully, it will continue to be misread and dismissed as an essentialist story about gender, instead of a political story about power.[38] As Baier has suggested in a different context,[39] feminist attention to Hume could help us remind our nonfeminist colleagues that the picture of morality and politics that the "different voice" portrays has a long historical tradition importantly developed by male theorists. It can reinforce the idea that the view of human nature put forth by liberal individualists, and which feminists reject, is the historical product of a particular cultural location of men of a particular race and class at the dawn of market capitalism.

Hume—or at least Hume revised along lines suggested here—could thus provide an intellectual "home" from which feminism can develop a vision of politics that is more grounded in the "malestream" canon of the history of Western political thought. Feminism's relationship to that canon has been predominantly critical, and rightly so. But even malestream philosophy and political theory was not written in a vacuum, but rather in a world populated, influenced, and worked on by women. So it is important to reclaim aspects of that thought that cohere with women's historical perspectives and experiences. Such reclamation can certainly enrich feminist critique of major figures. But it can also help us to reread the canon through the lens of women's presence, and not just our absence. In such a rereading lies a powerful tool for new kinds of feminist theory.

Notes

1. Hume asserts that consent has never been the basis for any actual government's legitimacy or authority, yet legitimate governments exist and people owe allegiance to them (THN 547). Hume particularly scorns the notion of residence as tacit consent, comparing arguments about nonimmigration to the situation of a shanghaied sailor (Es 462; THN 547). Consent theory is even more implausible on logical grounds; basing obligation on promise-keeping is circular, for promising is itself a convention created by humans to ensure security in social relations. Government performs similar functions necessary to society. Since promising and allegiance are distinct and equal, founding political obligation on promising is illogical (THN 544; Es 467–68). Indeed, the observance of fidelity "is to be considered as an effect of the institution of government, and not the obedience to government as an effect of the obligation of a promise" (THN 543).

2. For instance, Nancy C. M. Hartsock, Money, Sex, and Power: Towards a Feminist Historical Materialism (Boston: Northeastern University Press, 1984), Nancy J. Hirschmann, Rethinking Obligation: A Feminist Method for Political Theory (Ithaca: Cornell University Press, 1992), and Joan Tronto, Moral Boundaries: A Political Argument for an Ethic of Care (New York: Routledge, 1993).

3. David Miller, Philosophy and Ideology in Hume's Political Thought (Oxford: Clarendon Press, 1981), 144; see also Nicholas Phillipson, Hume (New York: St. Martin's Press, 1989).

4. Annette C. Baier, "Hume, The Women's Moral Theorist?" in Eva Feder Kittay and Diana T. Meyers, eds., Women and Moral Theory (Totowa, N.J.: Rowman and Littlefield, 1987); Carol Gilligan, In a Different Voice: Psychological Theory and Women's Development (Cambridge: Harvard University Press, 1982).

5. Nona Plessner Lyons, "Two Perspectives: On Self, Relationships, Morality," in Carol Gilligan et al., Mapping the Moral Domain (Cambridge: Harvard University Press, 1988). Although I read these psychological works as attributing gender difference to material experience, see Hirschmann, Rethinking Obligation, chap. 3, for a discussion of the essentialist potential in this literature.

6. Carol Gilligan and Grant Wiggins, "The Origins of Morality in Early Childhood Relationships," in Gilligan et al., Mapping the Moral Domain, 122.

7. Nancy Chodorow, The Reproduction of Mothering: Psychoanalysis and the Sociology of Gender (Berkeley and Los Angeles: University of California Press, 1978), 167.

8. Mary Field Belenky, Blythe McVicker Clinchy, Nancy Rule Goldberger, and Jill Mattuck Tarule, Women's Ways of Knowing: The Development of Self, Voice, and Mind (New York: Basic Books, 1986), 113.

9. Ibid., 115, 122, 106, 109.

10. Sarah Ruddick, *Maternal Thinking: Towards a Politics of Peace* (Boston: Beacon Press, 1989).

11. Patricia Hill Collins, *Black Feminist Thought: Knowledge, Consciousness, and the Politics of Empowerment* (Boston: Unwin-Hyman, 1990), 119, 129, 219.

12. Hartsock, *Money, Sex, and Power*.

13. Chodorow, *Reproduction of Mothering*, 167, emphasis added.

14. See for instance, Marylou Hughers, *Bereavement and Support: Healing in a Group Environment* (Washington, D.C.: Taylor and Francis, 1995); L. M. Tutty, B. A. Bidgood, and M. A. Rothery, "Support Groups for Battered Women—Research on Their Efficacy," *Journal of Family Violence* 8, no. 4 (1993): 325–43; Myra MacPherson, *Long Time Passing: Vietnam and the Haunted Generation* (New York: New American Library, 1984), esp. Pt. III, chap. 4, "The Vet Centers"; T. R. Williams, M. O'Sullivan, S. E. Snodgrass and N. Love, "Psychosocial Issues in Breast Cancer," *Postgraduate Medicine* 98, no. 4 (1995): 97–110.

15. Paul Harris, "The Work of the Imagination," in Andrew Whiten, ed., *Natural Theories of Mind: Evolution, Development, and Simulation of Everyday Mindreading* (Oxford: Basil Blackwell, 1991), 290. The similarities between connected knowing and the "simulation theory" of cognition are noteworthy but cannot be explored here; see other essays in Whiten's volume, plus Robert M. Gordon, "The Simulation Theory: Objections and Misconceptions," *Mind and Language* 7, nos. 1–2 (1992): 11–34.

16. Sandra Harding, *Whose Science? Whose Knowledge? Thinking from Women's Lives* (Ithaca: Cornell University Press, 1991), 268.

17. Pall S. Ardall, *Passion and Value in Hume's "Treatise,"* 2d ed. (Edinburgh: Edinburgh University Press 1989), 45. Elizabeth Radcliffe, in "Hume on Motivating Sentiments, the General Point of View, and the Inculcation of 'Morality,'" *Hume Studies* 20, no. 1 (1994): 37–58, notes "although Hume doesn't make it explicit, one effective way to extend our sympathies is to broaden our experience" (47).

18. Duncan Forbes, *Hume's Philosophical Politics* (Cambridge: Cambridge University Press 1975), 107–9.

19. Ardall, *Passion and Value*, 43.

20. Or as Ardall puts it, a "principle" not a "passion." Ibid., 42.

21. According to some such as Philip Mercer (*Sympathy and Ethics: A Study of the Relationship Between Sympathy and Morality with Special Reference to Hume's "Treatise"* [Oxford: Clarendon Press, 1972]) and Jonathan Harrison (*Hume's Theory of Justice* [Oxford: Clarendon Press, 1981]), if I am motivated to act, I do so to alleviate my own discomfort, the source of which is causing the other person's discomfort. Ardall rejects this "hedonistic" view, arguing that sympathy can provide a motive to act if I sympathize with a motive, or with a strong emotion such as anger (*Passion and Value*, 46). Also, while love and sympathy are distinct, sympathy can give way to love and will be stronger if I love the person with whom I sympathize (ibid., 66–67, 72–73). But see text accompanying n. 24 below.

22. Ardall, *Passion and Value*, 56, emphasis added.

23. Mercer, *Sympathy and Ethics*, 24, 44.

24. Ardall, *Passion and Value*, 46.

25. Belenky et al., *Women's Ways of Knowing*, 119.

26. Annette Baier, *A Progress of Sentiments: Reflections on Hume's "Treatise"* (Cambridge: Harvard University Press, 1991).

27. See Simon Blackburn, *Essays in Quasi-Realism* (New York: Oxford University Press, 1993); Anne Jaap Jacobson, "Inductive Scepticism and Experimental Reasoning in Moral Subjects in Hume's Philosophy," *Hume Studies* 15, no. 2 (1989): 325–38; John P. Wright, *The Sceptical Realism of David Hume* (Manchester: Manchester University Press, 1983).

28. Miller, *Philosophy and Ideology*, 22.

29. Forbes, *Hume's Philosophical Politics*, 103–4.

30. See Terence Penelhum, "Hume's Moral Psychology," in David Fate Norton, ed., *The Cambridge Companion to Hume* (Cambridge: Cambridge University Press, 1993).

31. Ibid., 124. See also THN 624, 471.

32. Miller, *Philosophy and Ideology*, 157.

33. Anne Phillips, *Engendering Democracy* (University Park: Pennsylvania State University Press, 1991); Carole Pateman, *The Disorder of Women: Democracy, Feminism, and Political Theory* (Stanford: Stanford University Press, 1989); Hirschmann, *Rethinking Obligation*.

34. Miller, *Philosophy and Ideology*, 153.

35. Ibid., 51.

36. John B. Stewart, *Opinion and Reform in Hume's Political Philosophy* (Princeton: Princeton University Press, 1992), 140.

37. Belenky et al., *Women's Ways of Knowing*, 123.

38. Tronto, *Moral Boundaries*.

39. Baier, "Hume, the Woman's Moral Theorist?"

9

Social (Re)Construction

A Humean Voice on Moral Education, Social Constructions, and Feminism

Susan A. Martinelli-Fernandez

The purpose of this essay is to demonstrate why feminists might be interested in reading the work of David Hume and how a Humean theory of moral education could bear successfully the scrutiny of a doubtful feminist eye surveying the appropriateness, applicability, and relevancy of a traditional moral theorist's work to women's lived experience. Further, our discussion will give us a potentially valuable way to judge the question of the role of rules in Hume's moral philosophy. I claim that Hume's theory is on an equal footing with those theories of moral development that are acceptable to feminists, for the illustrations given and instruction provided by this account are based upon our lives and the social and moral practices as we, in fact, live them. By recognizing the virtue of some aspects of Hume's theory and incorporating them into a collective feminist narrative about how our knowledge and attitudes about ourselves, others, and our world is derived, a truly inclusive feminist perspective, one that is neither abstract, imperialistic, nor independent from women's experiences, could be constructed.

Introduction

How are people morally and socially educated? One method is through our observing the conduct of individuals who are deemed by parents, friends, and institutions as paradigms of virtuous conduct. It is through such models of behavior and conduct that various concepts and conceptions of moral and social excellence are provided to us.[1] This is not merely an appeal to commonsense matters of fact; recent models of cognitive architecture suggest that human beings are much better at judging approximations to a paradigm than following rules.[2] Are such paradigms, however, based upon essentialist, a priori standards or environmentalist constructions of evaluation?

Roughly, essentialists see various aspects of human nature as inherent and universal. For example, an essentialist might suggest that we share a common nature as rational choosers. In contrast, environmentalists view human nature as constructed from the world and our experiences in it. According to this view, our basic beliefs about our and others' character, actions, and place in the world are dependent upon human experience and interactions in the past as well as in the present rather than a priori givens created in isolation from others. Following the lead of Carol Gilligan in her work on moral development and moral orientation, an environmentalist might argue that the experiences of the individual, and not some innate difference between women and men, are significant factors in the creation of the different voice, the care voice. Environmentalists emphasize differences, particularly gender. The emphasis here is not on an inherent difference between the sexes, since such an understanding of environmentalism would be no different from an essentialist position. Rather, environmentalism is best understood as placing difference in particular practices and politics. Thus, on this view, we are to recognize that many of our beliefs about ourselves and others that we commonly take for granted often serve social interests and tend to create and maintain inequities.

There are those feminists, radical and liberal, however, who see the importance of maintaining some essentialist account of human nature in order to ground rights and responsibilities. This view is part of an important debate that, in this work, I do not enter into directly. My use of these distinctions is restricted and will point to understanding two different ways in which to view human nature—essentialist, emphasizing inherent and universal standards of character, conduct, and actions; or environmentalist, emphasizing socially constructed concepts and conceptions of character, conduct, and actions. Environmentalist social constructions are derived from systems of classification that are recognized as human created; that is, they are taken from and informed by the world within which we find ourselves.[3]

I begin this inquiry by addressing two questions. One question invites us to determine whether Hume's theory should be classified as essentialist or environmentalist. The second question leads us from the conclusion that Hume's theory is, in general, environmentalist to a problem about environmentalist social constructions—although environmentalism avoids the problem of an a priori, ideal view of the world, we are still left with an existing description of the world embedded in a system of classification that may be filled with basic, unreflective assumptions and acceptance about what the world is like and who we should be. Consequently, why should we accept a theory of moral education that appeals to the use of examples of moral and social conduct that are constructed within a perspective that attempts to mold women and their conduct to preconceived expectations of a given social, political, and moral order?

It is the above question that motivates my investigation of examples as educational heuristics. I analyze the concept of a social construction and its various components, namely, content, structure, and method, offering a feminist interpretation and sketching a Humean response. First, I ask about the content of a construction; that is, what is it that some example recommends? I discuss examples of moral and social conduct that Hume provides in the *Enquiries Concerning Human Understanding and Concerning the Principles of Morals* within the context of a contemporary cognitive science view that attempts to get rid of rules as preferred educational heuristics and, instead, appeals to learning via paradigms of conduct. Second, I discuss the structure within which the content of social constructions arise. I examine whether a Humean theory of moral development can accommodate different perspectives and avoid privileging one standpoint or having us judge from some some ideal perspective, given Hume's view that there are certain features common to human psychology. In the final section, I argue that what is really at stake in feminist critiques of social constructions and, derivatively, in the desirability of including examples of behavior and conduct in theories of moral education, is the question of who may lay claim to the images that have informed the individual herself and the conceptions we have of ourselves.

Hume's Environmentalism

Hume offers a very complicated perspective of human nature, embedded deeply in the Enlightenment view that all men are created equal, without that equality being understood to hold for many members of humankind. In the introduction to A *Treatise of Human Nature*, we find passages suggesting that Hume might hold the view that there is something like one human nature. For example, he writes:

> Even Mathematics, Natural Philosophy, and Natural Religion, are in some measure dependent on the science of Man; since they lie under the cognizance of men, and are judged of by their powers and faculties. 'Tis impossible to tell what changes and improvements we might make in these sciences were we thoroughly acquainted with the extent and force of human understanding. (xv)

> Here then is the only expedient, from which we can hope for success in our philosophical researches, to leave the tedious lingering method, which we have hitherto followed, and instead of taking now and then a castle or village on the frontier, to march up directly to the capital or center of these sciences, to human nature itself; which being once masters of, we may every where else hope for an easy victory. (xvi)

Are we to think that passages such as the above are misleading? Or, might we recognize that the problem lies within the contradictions of the Enlightenment project itself and its understanding of human nature, equality, and the *querelle des femmes*?[4] Accepting the latter interpretation, we find that an essentialist view of one common human nature does not infect Hume's theory so thoroughly that an environmentalist will, or ought to, dismiss it. Further, we find that there are passages that support an explicitly environmentalist reading, for Hume's theory relies on the influence of cultural differences on human thought and activity. We see this in the essay "Of the Rise of the Arts and the Sciences," as well as in his other works. For example, in the introduction to A *Treatise of Human Nature*, Hume writes: "So true it is, that however other nations may rival us in poetry, and excel us in some other agreeable arts, the improvements in reason and philosophy can only be owing to a land of toleration and liberty" (xvii).

There is another equally pressing problem for a feminist interpretation of Hume. Even if models of conduct derived from Hume's theory and applied to a Humean account of moral development and education are not the result of or themselves essentialist constructions, such models, feminists might argue, are inappropriate, at best, or dangerous, at worst, for they necessarily rely upon our acting according to an already given description of the world that, according to Julia Penelope, "erodes our self-esteem, damages our self-images, and poisons our capacity for self-love."[5] Here we must again confront a problem about social constructions. We might understand this problem in two ways. First, we might think the question has to do with the particular kinds of concepts that are presented to us. This would be a question about the kind of models of behavior and conduct that are embedded in social constructions. We are asking, "What is the material or content of social constructions?" Second, we might think that the question of social constructions has to do with how such concepts and images are derived; that is, their origin. This way of thinking about social constructions can be broken down into two further considerations. One is to determine the structure within which the content of social constructions arise. The other is to determine the method by which this content is presented to us.

Content

Interpretation

Many social constructions contain images, that is, views, pictures, we have of our selves and others. The components of these images include concepts, ideals, and, often, implicit rules. Many concepts are seemingly descriptive, such as Mother/Father, Woman/Man. Our understanding of these terms, however, goes beyond mere description and recommends acceptable behavior and appropriate conduct, for they include attitudes we are to hold, values we are to embrace, and conduct we are to engage in, all of which are generally recognized, understood, and approved of by our society. For example, what comes to mind when we think "Mother?" Do we have in mind some general idea of a female who has a particular relation to specified others based on a biological connection? Or, is there more to it? Do we imagine a particular "Mother," perhaps a June Cleaver, a grand matriarch, or an overbearing, interfering empty-nester?

The concept of 'mother,' initially a descriptive concept, based on a particular kind of relationship between a female and her offspring, becomes an extended, filled-out evaluative conception of what a mother is supposed to feel and do. The components of this evaluative conception include a specific kind of recommended conduct such as nurturance and protection and a set of prescribed sentiments including love. From a biologically descriptive concept, we have arrived at a socially prescriptive ideal that itself is driven by and ultimately dictates a given set of attitudes, values, and conduct. Further, implicit rules of conduct that are meant to govern our actions are embedded in this ideal. For example, a mother is to place her children's welfare above her own.

From the toys we played with as children to the media images we see in print and on screen on a regular basis, there is an endless parade of how we can present, improve, change, and construct ourselves. These images, and the ideals and rules embedded in them, recommend and command, normatively, how we ought to present ourselves and, more insidiously, how we actually should be. This is at the heart of Sandra Bartky's discussion of a "social ontology," that is, the idea that our very conceptions of ourselves are based upon socially constructed concepts and sanctioned images by which we are held prisoner, at times, willingly.[6] How can there be, she asks, any true or real self-determination when the way that we view ourselves is externally imposed and socially manipulated?

It is not only these images of femininity that are socially constructed; so is every image that all of us, of every race, religious belief, gender, sexual preference, social class, and so on are bombarded with every day of our lives. How can I really be myself, when the "self" is a perspective from another's point of view, a socially constructed conglomerate of concepts, categories, and conceptions? Yet, can we really isolate ourselves and others from images and their influence? Maxine Harris, in *Down from the Pedestal*, suggests that we should appeal to different themes of living found at different time periods of our lives rather than to culturally imposed images of womanhood.[7] For example, rather than appealing to an image of some eternal young girl present in a role model of 'Mom and Dad's good girl,' one might offer the theme of learning to cooperate in an individual's familial relationships.

Should we find, as Harris suggests, a different use for the images that are present in our everyday life? Or do we reject any attempt at finding a role for such images? Are we rejecting images because many of them seem neither real nor realizable? Would we suggest that both the image and its components have been imposed externally upon us and, as such, are ones to be avoided? Are they to be rejected not merely because they are imposed externally, but because the perspective in which they arise is sexist? Further, if we are rejecting images, would we not have to reject theories of moral education that rely on learning by example, for examples contain images as well as function in the same way as images? Both have prescriptive exhortations, whose explicit purpose is to teach people how to conduct themselves.

Response: Examples, Role Models, and Ideals in Hume

Moral education is promoted, in part, by the example of others whom we consider virtuous. As children, we are encouraged to emulate the actions and take on the character traits of those whom our parents and other individuals and institutions participating in our formal and informal education believe to be paradigms of virtuous conduct. In this way, we are provided initially with our conceptions of virtue and standards of social and moral excellences.

Let me return to an earlier discussion in which I claimed that an appeal to the use of models of moral and social conduct in moral education does not rely merely on an appeal to commonsense matters of fact. Paul Churchland, in "The Neural Representation of the Social World," argues that moral disagreements are not about the veracity of moral rules; rather, they concern competing internal representations of knowledge, called prototypes, which serve as means by which individuals come to understand various matters, including environment, people, and actions. In general, prototypes are at the same sort of level as concepts. Those who espouse a prototype theory of concepts are concerned with how similar something is to a prototypical example of a concept, [F], rather than whether it satisfies a definition of (F).[8] I understand prototypes as representations and use that term to cover both internal representations in the mind or brain and more exterior representations such as those in literature.[9] When the theory is applied to moral education, prototypes serve as portraits of moral persons who exhibit various perceptual and behavioral skills.

Churchland believes that emphasizing prototypes and their purpose of making available very important cognitive skills rather than recommending the following of certain rules allows us to shift skeptical ethical debates from questions about why individuals should follow rules, which seem to yield no satisfactory answer for those who want to persuade the moral skeptic of the viability of moral discourse and activity, to a question of why people should develop certain kinds of skills. The answer to the latter question is "Because they are easily the most important skills you will ever learn."[10] This recommendation for approval based on the usefulness of some action or character to ourselves and others harkens to a distinctively Humean account of moral assessment. However, Churchland's effort to dismiss rule-based theories is problematic. The function of a rule and the evaluation of conduct are confused with the function of an example and the description of conduct. Further, there is no account of what makes the educational heuristics of prototypes and exemplars moral rather than merely competent or successful. Turning to Hume's theory, I construct an account of moral education by example that meets Churchland's challenge as well as an ethics of care concern of going beyond the following of rules. Further, this account of the educational heuristics of examples, unlike Churchland's, supplies a source of moral value. To support this claim, I discuss Hume's account of the sensible knave and the honest man in the second *Enquiry*. Specifically, I claim that rules have a role in Hume's theory, for they enable us to engage successfully in various activities and to achieve our goals; however, they are not sufficient in themselves to either initiate action or be the source of moral value.

Moral exemplars, following Churchland's analysis, are exterior representations of commendable conduct who serve as examples to others. An exemplar exhibits certain sorts of skills that, when abstracted from it, result in a nonexperiential internal representation of knowledge—a prototype. Such exemplars appear in philosophical writing, such as Cleanthes in David Hume's *Enquiry*. Cleanthes is approved of because of his usefulness and agreeableness to others and himself. He is successful in matters of business as well as social intercourse. There are rules in matters of commerce, such as rules of justice, and in matters of polite conversation, such as rules of good breeding, that he acknowledges, understands, and follows. Through Hume's discussion of Cleanthes, we learn that understanding and applying rules are skills that it is to people's benefit to learn and practice. Among these benefits is being approved of by others. Thus, the ability to recognize some activity as either useful or agreeable will be a skill that is, itself, important for individuals to learn so that they may successfully navigate throughout their lives.

Cleanthes is among several character(izations) of social and moral conduct in Section IX of the second *Enquiry*. He meets the "test of reasoning and inquiry" and is, himself, a role model for others. As such he is an exemplar, an existing person or named instantiation of commendable conduct who serves as an example to others. He exhibits conduct that is generally approved of by people who know him well and those who know him only by reputation. It is through this model that we learn about sources of moral approval, for it illustrates to us how we can earn praise and receive love when our conduct and actions are useful or agreeable to others, or both. In addition, we learn that we are to approve of others' actions and character when we find these to be useful or agreeable to ourselves as well as to others. Cleanthes is an educational heuristic, offering us a glimpse of skills that will serve us well in getting on in the world successfully and that are generally approved of. Hume himself writes, "A philosopher might select this character as a model of perfect virtue."[11] A question that arises is why Hume includes the caveat "might." Hume writes that following such a model may lead "to the amendment of men's lives, and their improvement in moral and social virtue;" however, such a result is not guaranteed. Perhaps, the suggestion is that Cleanthes is solely an object for judgment by others that we include in what Annette Baier terms 'interpersonal' practical deliberation?[12] Yet, does Cleanthes himself approve of his skills, talents, and virtues and his exercise of them independently of the opinion of others? As I will suggest at the end of this section, this will lead us to another feature of the problem of social constructions, the issue of perspective.

The next character presented in this section of the *Enquiry* is Virtue. Virtue is a prototype, an internal representation of the mind. It is a standard of conduct constructed by the mind through one's familiarity with individuals who exist or have existed that we may call ideal. It is not based upon essentialist views of a priori standards of conduct and actions. Rather, it is an environmentalist social construction, for we create it from the world and our experiences in that world. It is ultimately re-formed by our reflections upon both.[13] Virtue's initial 'qualities' are naturally beautiful to the eyes of the beholder and thus are attractives to engaging in moral conduct. Yet, there is a potential repulsive quality of Virtue, for she has a requirement: "The sole trouble which she demands, is that of just calculation, and a steady preference of the greater happiness." These attractive and repulsive qualities strongly suggest that Virtue's role, as an ideal of conduct, is beyond illustration and instruction—it is that of motivation, an attraction to moral conduct that is beautiful, demanding, and, at times, troublesome.[14] It is precisely this motivational quality that will help us to determine differences between the remaining two Humean characters, the sensible knave and the honest man, the latter of whom I will call the honest woman. By distinguishing between the sensible knave and the honest woman, along with their reasons for acting, we will see how to broaden the content of a prototype so that standards such as Virtue can be seen as present and operative. In this way, we will be able to produce an account of a *moral* ideal of character.

The sensible knave and the honest woman are prototypes that have been derived from the exemplar Cleanthes. Both exhibit some of Cleanthes's skills. They are internal representations of the mind that do not directly correspond to an existing exemplar or stereotype, although they are derived from one's acquaintance with such examples. They are, in effect, constructed by the mind in order to represent various features and skills of an exemplar.

The sensible knave is an individual who is well versed and knowledgeable in rules and regulations. In addition, she has a very robust sense of self-interest. She can see things from her own point of view as well as from that of others,' although she acts always with a view to her own particular interest(s). She understands fully the source and force of general and specific rules and knows when she can break them. Rules of justice, for example, would never be followed by the sensible knave because of any disinterest, for she is quite interested in their general and specific effects. Although she sees the importance of rules for some sort of social stability, her concern is, and her motive to actions will be, her own overriding advantage.

The attractive source of motivation for this individual is not the beauty of virtue—it is, rather, a fixed view to her own self-interest and advantage. Skills such as understanding and being able to apply rules are quite present and effective in this prototype. What is lacking, however, is precisely what is missing from Churchland's prototype—a moral standard that might also serve as a means of recognizing appropriate sources of motivation. The motivation of the sensible knave is purely self-interested and, at best, enlightened, for she will weigh the effects of her not following rules on the commonweal. While she knows who she is and what she wants, and will get it, she "has lost a considerable motive to virtue."[15]

The final character to be discussed is the honest woman. Like the sensible knave, this individual manifests a number of useful skills, such as understanding rules and regulations. In contrast to the knave, however, she "feels . . . reluctance to the thoughts of villainy or baseness when she thinks of breaking them for purely her own advantage."[16] Her motivational attractions are to the beauty of "natural necessities" and pleasures "of conversation, society, study, even health and the common beauties of nature, but above all the peaceful reflection on [her] own conduct."[17] Thus, the prototype of the honest woman includes the standard of Virtue, for she sees the attractiveness of moral activity. She is repelled by villainy and is attracted to 'doing the right thing.' This attraction is not merely 'natural,' for the honest woman's motivations are strengthened by her reflections on herself, her actions, and her conduct. Her perspective, like that of the sensible knave, is a view to her own interest and a recognition of and acting upon those skills that help one to interact successfully with others. However, the honest woman's interest is more appropriately called 'a proper self-concern.' Unlike the knave, the honest woman's interest includes conceptions of good which are common and shared, and not merely individualist. Her individual interest is not found in the attainment of those fleeting goods which the knave finds choiceworthy; rather, the honest woman's interest is attached to a concern for having "an inward peace of mind, consciousness of integrity, a satisfactory review of [her] own conduct."

As suggested earlier, a prototype encourages us to see the desirability of acquiring important skills; however, for it to be a *moral* ideal of character, the mere usefulness of some set of skills or adroitness at following a rule will not be enough for a distinctively moral commendation. We see this most strikingly in Hume's account of the sensible knave. This prototype embodies skills of understanding a rule and being very good at applying it; however, the rule will be followed in most instances only when it is beneficial to that entity. Something else, missing from Churchland's analysis of prototypes, must be present—that which makes such an example morally salient, and not merely practically desirable. We might argue, quite correctly, that part of the Humean story about morality concerns the general point of view, for it is from this perspective that our moral evaluations are made possible. When we can see beyond our own particular interests, including our natural partialities toward those whom we love, and take on this perspective, we will be able see the praiseworthiness of various motives, sentiments, characters, and actions. But this tells us nothing about the content of an ideal or prototype itself. Any example that is morally recommended must include a standard that serves as the basis of and perhaps an attractive to moral actions. For Hume, this standard is Virtue. By extending the account of prototypes to include such standards, we will have an account of a moral ideal of character.

Even if we are persuaded that exemplars and prototypes are effective ways of acquiring skills that contribute to a process of moral education, we are left, nonetheless, with the question of "Whose images are these?" This leads us to the second consideration of social constructions, their origin, and the question of "From what point of view/perspective are these heuristics derived?"

Structure

Interpretation

Are sex, gender, race, and class classifications essential, innately derived characteristics of individuals? Are they categories created by social, economic, and political forces that place individuals in particular positions within a given society and its structures? Or, are they both? For example, to be a 'woman' is not to merely function biologically as a female; it is to be classified as a member of a group subjected to norms and values that have been derived historically, socially, economically, and politically. In a 1982 interview with Margaret A. Simons, Simone de Beauvoir traces the origin of her idea for the Second Sex to a conversation with Jean-Paul Sartre. Sartre had suggested that any work in which she would write about herself needed to include a discussion of "What it is to be a woman."[18] This was not, however, the question with which de Beauvoir introduced the *Second Sex*—it was "What is a woman?" The latter questions the classification itself, while the former assumes that the classification is already valid. This shift of focus in questions supports de Beauvoir's assessment of the evolution of her work from studying "myths and different views of the world" to "understanding the reality" and appeals implicitly to the idea of social construction. She writes: "So I had to come back to reality, all of it, physiological, historical, etc. Then afterwards, I continued on my own on women's situation as I saw it."[19]

In response to these socially constructed classifications, scholarly concern in areas including feminism and cultural studies; in disciplines such as sociology, political science, literature, and philosophy; and in intellectual movements including phenomenology and postmodernism has extended beyond traditional debates about nature and nurture to include critiques of the systematized domination of traditionally under-represented groups who are the subjects of these classifications including women, people of color, lesbians, gays, as well as those who are disadvantaged economically, physically, or emotionally. Theoretical frameworks such as cultural materialism and poststructuralism have been taken up by feminist thinkers including bell hooks, Sandra Bartky, Judith Butler, Julia Kristeva, and Luce Irigaray.

What is at stake in these discussions is the question of how we are to understand the terms that we use to identify and describe ourselves and others. In addition, we must ask how our knowledge about ourselves, others, and the world around us is produced and validated. It is an important part of many feminist projects to determine what the underlying concerns and perspectives of thought, whether social, political, moral, religious, really are. One very interesting approach to setting forth a unique feminist framework is that of feminist standpoint theory.[20] Here we are presented with a distinctive feminist perspective from which social constructions and questions of essentialism, essence, and identity can be addressed. This perspective is based upon a feminist, gender-based analysis of knowledge calling for a feminist epistemology structured by women's work, "the real material activity of concrete human beings."[21]

Some might think that embedded in feminist standpoint theory is the view that there is only one particular way that women view the world, themselves, and others and it is from this view that women's beliefs, decisions, and actions are derived. Criticism of feminist standpoint theory falls roughly into two areas—one is essentialist. The problem expressed here is that the epistemological basis of 'women's work' of standpoint theory has an ontological foundation of 'Woman,' thus potentially reinforcing stereotypical views of womanhood. The other area of criticism is that of privileging only one dominant, all-encompassing feminist perspective and allowing one particular narrative to express the stories of many different women. Here we see one story about "Woman" and not the diverse stories of all women. Another way of understanding these criticisms is to return to de Beauvoir's attempt to formulate a response to the question of "What is a woman" and ask two further questions: Does standpoint theory really address the 'reality' of an historical context when social considerations of race, ethnicity, age, ableness, and class are not considered? Is its foundation essentialist, appealing ultimately to a common physiology as the essential common quality among women?

Thus we see that it is not only the images that are presented to women throughout their personal histories that are problematic; it is the perspective from which women are presented and ultimately view such images that is of equal concern. Unfortunately, it appears that even within a particular feminist structure, social constructions can be problematic. Thus, we are left both with the question of "Whose images are these" and our current question, "From what point of view?" These questions will be addressed, in the next section, by turning to Hume's evolutionary account of justice, including a discussion of the general point of view and why feminist theorists might want to include this feature of Hume's thought in constructing a feminist perspective.

Response

Departing from the Enlightenment Hobbesean story about justice, David Hume's account of the rise of justice focuses on an anthropological story about society's internal organization.[22] The virtue of this account is that it can be read as environmentalist, for Hume's narrative is about the evolution of communal ties and the search for stability and security that extends beyond one's immediate environment of family and friends. However, embedded in this account is an essentialist assumption, for the starting point of this evolutionary account is the attraction "betwixt the sexes" and an account of traditional family relationships.

If we turn to Hume's essay "Of Love and Marriage," we find that, although the feminist is well wary to claim Hume as a champion of gender neutrality in *this* instance, Hume is no friend to the misogynist. Hume argues that although there is a tension between women and men, it is the latter who bear the bulk of responsibility for this state of affairs. After retelling the story of Scythian women who were moved to the extreme measure of blinding men to ensure women's better treatment and freedom from slavery, Hume writes:

> But to be just, and to lay the blame more equally, I am afraid it is the fault of our sex, if the women be so fond of rule; and that if we did not abuse our authority, they would never think it worth while to dispute it. Tyrants, we know, produce rebels; and all history informs us, that rebels, when they prevail, are apt to become tyrants in their turn. For this reason I could wish there were no pretensions to authority on either side, but that every thing was carried on with perfect equality, as between two equal members of the same body.[23]

A reconstructive task for a feminist-sympathetic Humean account might be to jettison the familial evolutionary part of the story of the rise of justice and focus on other features of this account, such as natural partiality and the general point of view, a perspective that allows us to distance ourselves from our particular and unique points of view. It is from the general point of view that our moral evaluations are made possible, for when we can see beyond our own particular interests, including our natural partialities toward those whom we love, and take on this perspective, we will be able see the praiseworthiness of various motives, sentiments, characters, and actions. A question might arise, however: Would a feminist standpoint theorist reject such a Humean account in favor of an ethics of care which would not put as much value on the general point of view? Answering this question requires a more general discussion of the benefits of retaining various features of Hume's evolutionary account of the rise of justice. In this way, we will be able to see why feminist standpoint theorists as well as other feminists with different theoretical commitments might find a Humean account appealing.

There is a twofold benefit in retaining certain parts of Hume's evolutionary account of the rise of justice including the general point of view and a general account of basic features of individuals' original frame of mind such as natural partiality. First, these discussions show us how to correct for our own natural biases. For example: In tracing the origins of justice in *A Treatise of Human Nature*, Hume assumes certain features common to individuals' original frame of mind such as self-interest and partiality. He argues that partiality, expressed as a limited benevolence toward those close to us, is naturally approved of.[24] However, its natural and usual force is a threat to the continued existence of society and peaceful relations among its members if left unchecked. "['T]is certain," Hume writes, "that self-love, when it acts at its liberty, instead of engaging us to honest actions, is the source of all injustice and violence."[25] A solution to this problem is to redirect the natural and usual force of partiality. This solution depends upon the regulatory force of general rules and rules of justice, as well as the influence of education and experience, upon partiality itself, for only partiality can restrain itself.[26] Thus we see that the need for rules of justice arises, in part, because partiality must be redirected. They must smooth out, moderate, and stabilize the "natural and usual force" of partiality.[27] Ultimately, it is partiality that restrains itself. This solution suggests how we might address the problem that much of our knowledge and our beliefs have arisen within a patriarchal perspective, fraught with preexisting prejudices. By recognizing, for example, that the words we use to describe and identify ourselves and others arises out of this perspective, we can begin to reform our language, moving from one that is less male dominated to one that is more woman centered to, ultimately, a gender-neutral system of verbal communication.

A second benefit is that Hume's account demonstrates how we take on perspectives that are different from ours. In effect, we are pushing away our particular interests from ourselves and, thus, toward others as well as pulling in interests of those whom we have no reason to benefit. An account of how different perspectives are taken on relies on Hume's discussion of partiality and its connection to taking on the general point of view. Hume, in the *Treatise*, suggests a process by which partiality becomes regulated and interest becomes educated. This regulation is, in part, accomplished through stabilization of the possession of goods and partiality restraining itself once the rules of justice are in force. One has an interest in both restraining natural partiality and stabilizing the possession of goods, for it is to one's benefit to do so. And most people would reasonably expect a rational individual to have and exercise this interest. When restrained in this way, this kind of interest is enlightened self-interest. However, once stability of possession is secured, an individual's approval of justice as a virtue no longer rests on the usefulness of justice to herself to secure possession of external goods. Rather, approval rests on this individual's ability to see the usefulness and the pleasure to others of justice as a virtue that stabilizes her relations with others and promotes the good of all. She shares a sympathetic interest with fellow members of society in their overall pursuit of human good including personal talents as well as wealth. The final interest, constructed from the *Treatise*, is an interest of an individual in herself as a member of a community to secure a common good rather than as an individual in retaining a particular object. She sees herself as a member of a community not merely of interests but, in addition, a community of reciprocal concern, for the natural and usual force of partiality is redirected away from an immediate concern for the self and those she loves and toward a more general concern for others more remote from her immediate perspective. Thus, through the regulation of partiality this individual takes on more general points of view. Understanding the importance of this aspect of Hume's thought and incorporating it into feminist theory-making can lead us to acknowledging and correcting for the very specific and, at times, narrow, particular interests incorporated in our theories and practices that have excluded the interests of many women with a variety of experiences, needs, and desires.

If we can retain Hume's accounts of the general point of view and regulation of partiality, the problem of the structure within which the content of social constructions arises might be solvable, for we are now in a position to claim that there can be a shared, nonsexist structure within which social constructions arise. Further, this structure will be able to avoid the problem of privileging only one dominant, all-encompassing feminist perspective that is, as discussed previously, associated sometimes with feminist standpoint theory, for the different experiences of women and different kinds of oppression that diverse groups of women encounter will be included. It is only through an inclusive feminist point of view that is informed by and addresses race, class, sexual preference, ableness, and age as well as gender that we will begin to see and correct our own biases, which would otherwise remain hidden even to ourselves. This is only part of the story, however, about how we begin to take on a more inclusive feminist perspective as well as understand various features of social constructions and their connection to moral education. In addressing the question of the method by which the content of social constructions is presented to us, we will see how to complete a theory of moral development reconstructed from Hume's works that might be attractive to many feminists.

Method

Interpretation

In "Have We Got a Theory for You," Maria C. Lugones and Elizabeth V. Spelman offer a suggestion that can be used to create an account of women's experience that would not suffer from the kind of problem associated with feminist standpoint theory, that of privileging one particular perspective. They write: "It is one thing for both me and you to observe you and come up with our different accounts of what you are doing; it is quite another for me to observe myself and others much like me culturally and in other ways and to develop an account of myself and then use that account to give an account of you."[28] It is the first way that the authors recommend as an appropriate feminist method of inquiry that could avoid the dangers of a unified, hegemonic discourse of some ideal 'woman.'

By taking this suggestion and applying it to the issue of moral education, we see that, minimally, it is a negative recommendation setting limits for a feminist theory. Thus, we are going to dismiss any theory that requires one to count only oneself and one's particular views as the basis or standard of judgment. Positively, we might look for a theory that, although not excluding an individual's particular perspective, includes the perspectives of others in matters concerning theoretical constructions. By combining these two recommendations, we can begin to construct a more inclusive feminist method by which the content of social constructions is presented to us. Instead of appealing to one particular feminist perspective to address feminist issues, feminist theorists could appeal to another feminist perspective, one in which various perspectives are acknowledged as appropriate and viable means of inquiry. At the heart of this perspective is a polyphonic narrative[29] that is a dialogue between its creators, explicitly, and, implicitly, the subjects of the narrative, and the intended audience, with an ever vigilant eye on the following questions:

- Who is the audience of the proposed perspective?
- Who is doing the talking about this perspective?
- Who is being talked about in this perspective?

212 Feminist Interpretations of Hume

The construction of this perspective demands more than one theorist, for its hallmark is the inclusion of a variety of feminist positions and perspectives. Theorists begin their construction of this perspective with a discussion about how their project is being created. It would go something like this: "I talk. You listen. You talk. I listen. We both talk about what we have heard. In concert, we derive a mutually constructed account of our observations." It is through such a dialogue that theorists can guarantee that their theorizing and theory-building is neither abstract, imperialistic, nor independent from women's experiences. The construction of this inclusive feminist perspective is based upon a continuing dialogue between its creators, and not on an independent search for 'the truth.' Theorists form this perspective through an examination of their own particular theoretical commitment and their explicit relationship to one another as well as on their implicit relationship with those about whom they are writing and those to whom they are writing. It is through this method of theory-building, one that demonstrates our interdependence, that a respectful, dynamic, and inclusive feminist perspective is constructed.

Response

Hume's theory fares well in regard to the above concerns and recommendations. According to Hume, we do not view ourselves as autonomous personalities and, as such, independent actors and choosers, with moral decision-making processes that are free from any type of coercion, regardless of how gentle such force or how heartfelt some natural partiality may be. Further, we neither judge ourselves, others, and situations from some ideal standpoint that any individual in our situation could place herself nor follow principles that conform to the structure of or are derived from that standpoint.

Each one of us is a relational self on Hume's theory. This means that we view ourselves from a shared perspective, which, in some sense, is a mirror that allows us to see ourselves from our and others' points of view. There is no sense to be made of a self independent of or from others. We are participants in the creation of mutually held and applied rules, rules that are derived from the world that we experience and share with others. Our moral decision-making process, from this perspective, does not occur from or in an ideal or hypothetical perspective. It is, rather, a process that takes into account the particular concerns of others as well as ourselves.

Hence we find that we can re-read and re-construct the writings of David Hume in a way that is sympathetic to the suggestion of Lugones and Spelman and reflects a theoretical agreement with theorists such as Carol Gilligan and Nancy Chodorow: Human beings are relational selves. We come into the world as members of an existing community, a community with rules and expectations of people already in place. There is no such entity as an 'independent self.' D. W. Winicott, in *The Child, the Family, and the Outside World*, put the point this way: "There is no such thing as a baby. . . . A baby cannot exist alone, but is essentially a part of a relationship."[30] The attraction of Hume's theory is that the method by which we come to have a conception of self and become morally educated need not privilege one particular perspective, given that, according to Hume, we learn about the world, one another, and ourselves in concert with, and not in isolation from, one another.

Conclusion

The discussions that have been offered have addressed why Hume's theory should not be immediately dismissed and why parts of this theory, properly understood and at times re-constructed, could strengthen various feminist positions and help re-solve some feminist concerns. We find there is no inherent bias toward male-modeled or -sanctioned images in our re-constructed account of Humean examples. Further, we see that such examples of moral and social conduct can be given a different role to play in a story about how individuals are morally educated, by emphasizing various skills that are embedded in these examples.

Hume's account of the general point of view, including his discussion of certain kinds of tendencies present in people's original frames of mind, will be another part of a Humean story about moral education. Here, it is the inclusiveness of the general point of view that well serves a particularly feminist narrative. The questions of structure and method of social constructions are answered by our appeal to the general point of view. How helpful is this appeal, however, in supporting the initial claim that these two questions are distinct ways of addressing the origin of social constructions? We need to see that the question of the structure of social constructions is a matter of origin—this is a matter of where images, role models, exemplars, and prototypes come from. In contrast, the question of the method by which the content of social constructions is acquired is a matter of how we are presented with images, role models, exemplars, and so on. One might claim that there is a clear line of demarcation between method and structure, perhaps by invoking a Millikan/Anscombe-like distinction between representations that are descriptive and those that are prescriptive.[31] Thus, one could suggest that the structure of social constructions merely describes various models of conduct that are available to us and that the method of social construction is itself a recommendation, a prescription of appropriate models that ought to be followed. Accepting this solution, however, ignores the importance of asking independently what the method by which the content of social constructions is and results in our failing to see what is really at stake in feminist critiques of social constructions—the question of who may lay claim to various images that have informed the individual herself, by which she assesses her actions and her own conception of herself.

What is required for a complete Humean story about moral education is a notion of Hume as a reformer and not as a conservative in his account of morality. This account relies on Hume's discussion of how we come to regulate our actions and our character from a perspective that includes an individual's view of herself and is not thoroughly dependent upon the views of others. Too many people are willing to assess Hume's theory as merely a social theory of conduct. I believe that this view is wrong, for Hume offers prescriptions for right conduct that one learns and tests for oneself. Let me explain: At the conclusion of the second *Enquiry*, Hume suggests that the surest guarantee and support of virtue is through viewing ourselves through the eyes of sympathy with others.[32] These others are not only concrete others, they will be idealized and abstracted others that serve as educational heuristics derived from exemplars such as Cleanthes that result in prototypes such as the honest woman. Ultimately, it is one's own judgment that one will have to withstand. Successful interactions with others is surely an important component of Hume's theory; yet, so is the withstanding of one's own judgement. The contribution to feminist theory is found in this 'tension' in Hume—our conduct is informed by the world around us yet we will be our own judges of this conduct.

All theories must face a feminist challenge of social constructions and address the questions of "How do I really assess myself and my particular talents; is it from my or others' perspective? Can I really claim ownership of the actions, the character, and the self that I call mine?" These questions addressed from a Humean perspective will be based upon a prior question that is not "Who is it that I see?" with a debate cast between Hume's theory as either an agent- or spectator-based theory. The question will be "Whose is it that I see?" that is, "Whose actions, whose character, whose self do I see?" with responses, following Lugones and Spelman, in a voice of an all-inclusive feminist perspective, a polyphonic voice of "Mine," Yours," and "Ours."[33] It is this voice that will allow us to hear the voices and the stories of many women, ensuring that no woman's voice can be silenced and that no woman's story will be ignored. If we are persuaded that a polyphonic feminist narrative is valuable to creating a truly inclusive feminist perspective, then we will find that re-reading Hume, while not sufficient, is necessary to its construction.

Notes

1. Here, I have in mind John Rawls's distinction between concept and conception. The idea is roughly this: While various cultures and individuals share common concepts such as justice, the way that such a concept is filled out, that is, as a particular conception, will vary. See John Rawls, *A Theory of Justice* (Cambridge: Harvard University Press, 1971), 5.

2. Paul Churchland in "The Neural Representation of the Social World" suggests that such evidence could support a virtue ethics, perhaps such as Hume's, as opposed to a rule-based ethics (in *Mind and Morals*, ed. L. May, M. Friedman, and A. Clark [Cambridge: MIT Press, 1996]).

3. Ian Hacking, unpublished manuscript, "Psychopathology and Social Construction," presented at the APA Symposium, Atlanta, 30 December 1996, "Social Construction and Psychological Kinds."

4. See Lieslotte Steinbrügge, *The Moral Sex*, trans. Pamela E. Selwyn (Oxford: Oxford University Press, 1995).

5. Julia Penelope, "The Lesbian Perspective," in Jeffner Allen, ed., *Lesbian Philosophies: Explorations* (Palo Alto, Calif.: Institute of Lesbian Studies, 1986).

6. Sandra Bartky, "Foucault, Femininity, and the Modernization of Patriarchal Power," in Irene Diamond and Lee Quinby, eds., *Feminism and Foucault: Reflections on Resistance* (Boston: Northeastern University Press, 1988).

7. Maxine Harris, *Down from the Pedestal: Moving Beyond Idealized Images of Womanhood* (New York: Anchor Books, 1994), 41.

8. See Georges Rey, *Contemporary Philosophy of Mind* (Cambridge: Blackwell's, 1997)

9. There are very intricate questions about the ontological status of either kind of representation, but these questions are irrelevant to this essay.

10. Churchland, "Neural Representation," 107.

11. Hume, *Enquiry Concerning the Principles of Morals*, in *Enquiries Concerning Human Understanding and Concerning the Principles of Morals*, 3d ed., ed. L. A. Selby-Bigge and P. H. Nidditch (Oxford: Clarendon Press, 1975), 270:218.

12. Baier, *Progress of Sentiments*, 153.

13. For an excellent discussion of the environmentalist/essentialist debate, see Moira Gatens, "A Critique of the Sex/Gender Distinction," reprinted in *Imaginary Bodies: Ethics, Power, and Corporeality* (New York: Routledge, 1996).

14. There is an interesting observation about the role of Virtue's attractiveness in Hume and how Immanuel Kant tells us, in the "Methodology of Practical Reason," in *The Critique of Practical Reason*, how one acquires the Moral Law. Briefly, Kant argues that there are a series of exercises that students need to be taught and to perform themselves in order for them to learn about and to acquire the Moral Law. There is a moment between the first and second exercise where the student must literally 'see' the beauty of the Moral Law (156:160). Such exercises, Kant writes, "[E]nables one to entertain himself with such judging and gives virtues or a turn of the mind based on moral laws a form of beauty which is admired but not yet sought (164:160)." It will be through the development, recognition and cultivation of moral beauty, at the end of the first exercise, that the Moral Law ultimately gains access to the student's mind. Thus, for Kant, the acquisition of the supreme moral principle is not through argument or "tests" such as those proposed in the *Grounding*; rather, it is through what one might call an '$aesthetic moment.'

15. Hume, *Enquiry*, 283:233.

16. Hume, *Enquiry*, 283:233.

17. Hume, *Enquiry*, 283:233.

18. Margaret A. Simons, "Two Interviews with Simone de Beauvoir," in Nancy Fraser and Sandra Lee Bartky, eds., *Revaluing French Feminism: Critical Essays on Difference, Agency, and Culture* (Bloomington: Indiana University Press, 1992), 29.

19. Simons, "Two Interviews," 29.

20. See Nancy C. M. Hartsock, "The Feminist Standpoint: Developing the Ground for a Specific Feminist Historical Materialism," in Nancy Tuana and Rosemarie Tong, eds., *Feminism and Philosophy* (Boulder, Colo.: Westview Press, 1995).

21. Hartsock, "Feminist Standpoint," 85.

22. David Hume, *A Treatise of Human Nature*, ed. L. A. Selby-Bigge; 2d ed. with text revised and notes by P. H. Nidditch (Oxford: Oxford University Press, 1978) Bk. III, Pt. I, Sec. XI, 486.

23. David Hume, *Essays, Moral, Political, and Literary* (London: Oxford University Press, 1966), 554–55.

24. Hume, *Treatise*, 488.

25. Hume, *Treatise*, 480.

26. Hume writes, "There is no passion, therefore, capable of controlling the interested affection itself, by an alteration of its direction. Now this alteration must necessarily take place upon the least reflection; since 'tis evident, that the passion is much better satisfy'd by its restraint, than by its liberty, and that by preserving society, we make much greater advances in the acquiring possessions, than by running into the solitary and forlorn condition, which must follow upon violence and an universal license . . . 'tis by establishing the rule for the stability of possession, that this passion restrains itself" (*Treatise*, 492–93).

27. Hume, *Treatise*, 488.

28. Maria C. Lugones and Elizabeth V. Spelman, "Have We Got a Theory for You," in Nancy Tuana and Rosemarie Tong, eds., *Feminism and Philosophy* (Boulder, Colo.: Westview Press, 1995), 500.

29. "Polyphonic narrative" is the result of my trying to find an unencumbered (or, at least less encumbered) concept to serve as the basis of a very inclusive feminist point of view that avoids placing people and their viewpoints in discrete theoretical fiefdoms in which there is little possibility of fruitful discourse and proper representation of the interests of many different groups of women. I sought to find a term that suggests how a theory can be created that incorporates aspects of various theories, thus demonstrating respect towards others' and their deeply held philosophical commitments and search for truth and demands that people are equally reflective about their own. I have

been reminded by David Sullivan of Julia Kristeva's use of the term "polyphonic discourse," which incorporates various aspects of Mikhail Bakhtin's thought. (See "Word, Dialogue, and Novel," in *The Kristeva Reader*, ed. Toril Moi [New York: Columbia University Press, 1986], 34–61.) Also, bell hooks uses the term "polyphonic" in discussing her style of writing and that of other black writers. hooks writes: "I don't sit around comparing my work to see which voice is better; to me they are different, and precisely because of that difference may appeal to different audiences. That's the joy of being polyphonic, of multivocality." (bell hooks, *Yearning: race, gender, and cultural politics* [Boston: South End Press, 1990], 228.) My use of polyphonic is limited to acknowledging more than two 'voices' or two perspectives through which a distinct narrative, representing the interests of all participants, explicitly present or not, will be constructed.

30. D. W. Winnicott, *The Child, the Family, and the Outside World* (Harmondsworth: Penguin Books, 1964), 88.

31. Ruth Garrett Millikan, "Pushmi-pullyu Representations," in *Mind and Morals* (Cambridge: MIT Press, 1996).

32. Hume, *Enquiry*, 271:225.

33. Two dear friends have noted: "Philosophy is a cooperative enterprise" and "Philosophy is an activity, not a theory." This essay has benefited from various forms of comment, criticism, and encouragement from Kate Abramson, Christine Korsgaard, Polly Radosh, David Sullivan, and Jacqueline Taylor. In particular, I thank Anne Jaap Jacobson for her generous help. She is an "honest woman" and a true "woman of sense and merit."

10

Humean Androgynes and the Nature of 'Nature'

Sheridan Hough

Hume's women have appetites. "What restraint, therefore, shall we impose on women, in order to counter-balance so strong a temptation as they have to infidelity?"[1] Like men, they can be gripped by desires for sex and power—"no passion seems to have more influence on female minds than this for power"[2]—and like men they use their reason to satisfy their passions. But, Hume insists, the all-too-human hungers of women are accompanied by a female 'nature,' one drawn to things pleasant and soft: "There are different trees, which regularly produce fruit, whose relish is different from each other; and this regularity will be admitted as an instance of necessity and causes in external bodies. But are the products of *Guienne* and *Champagne* more regularly different than the sentiments, actions, and passions of the two sexes, of which the one are distinguished

by their force and maturity, the other by their delicacy and softness?"[3]
These delicate creatures are more susceptible than men to the suasive
powers of the imagination. "The same infirmity, which makes them faint
at the sight of a naked sword, tho' in the hands of their best friend, makes
them pity extremely those, whom they find in any grief or affliction."[4]
And women have their own "point of honor," chastity, while men are
expected to display the virtue courage.[5]

What is the source of these "regularly different" actions and passions? Is
Hume claiming that women have a different nature from that of men, or
is this an account of how women are socialized? If it is a question of
education, what implications does this have for altering women's lot? The
question of alteration is itself complicated by Hume's various assertions
about the nature of our 'nature.' We are told that "human nature is too
inconstant to admit of any such regularity. Changeableness is essential to
it,"[6] yet we are also reminded that "(men) cannot change their natures."[7]
We must postpone this problem of inconstancy versus stability until much
later in this essay.

We will need a (rough) definition of 'human nature' before we can
think about where Hume places the origin of gendered behavior, and
what his claims may tell us about the possibility of altering that behavior.
Recent philosophical preoccupations are not necessarily well suited for
Hume's arguments;[8] still, his empirical account of human nature can be
usefully compared to the antiessentialism of thinkers such as Nietzsche,
especially when the role of habit and custom are being considered. After
establishing some features of Humean nature, I will look at one of Hume's
more 'frivolous' (his own word)[9] turns in order to speculate about what
Hume's women might hope for.

The key element in Hume's description of our nature is, of course,
regularity. Different trees regularly produce different fruit, and this difference reliably indicates something about what is causally necessary to
them. Despite considerable variation between cultures and over time,
human creatures are consistently moved by beauty and wealth, and
drawn, through the imaginative power of sympathy, to compare themselves to one another,[10] and to become prideful or humbled by so doing.[11]
In the Second Inquiry Hume makes this paradigmatic comment: "All
birds of the same species, in every age and country, build their nests alike:
in this we see the force of instinct. Men, in different times and places,
frame their houses differently: here we perceive the influence of reason

and custom."[12] Of this passage Christopher Berry remarks, "There is no attempt to avoid the evidence of the variety of fabrics etc., but within all this variety there are roofs."[13] Dwelling in shelters is a universal feature of human nature, and the tremendous diversity in the kind of houses we build is only evidence of contingent necessities and predilections. Such variety is entertaining to survey, yet it serves to underscore a fact about our nature, that we are enhoused creatures. So too with a long list of characteristics. We are informed by sympathy (more of this later), we are 'naturally' attuned to our lovers and our children,[14] we reliably and consistently seek riches, make moral judgments, and enjoy the society of our fellow creatures.[15] Our 'nature' is this dependable catalog of habitual behaviors, the frame for the local curiosities of our history.

Notice, though, that thus far this sketch of human nature does not include any gendered features. 'Generically,' we are social, passion driven, and myopic in our interests, partial to lovers and relations, yet brought by sympathy to a wider sense of our concerns (and so to justice). Nothing as yet has been earmarked as 'male' or 'female' in our nature, and yet Hume claims that female behavior is consistently sensitive and passive. This passivity is 'natural,' but it turns out that it is only via the interpretation of a fact of nature that we get female 'nature.' Nature is mute on this matter; culture and education provide an account of it.

That fact of nature is childbearing. We can always tell who a person's mother is; securing paternity can be difficult or impossible. Although no account of female nature is available at this level, at the level of her biology, Hume declares that certain tenets of the education of women necessarily follow from this feature of their bodies: "From this trivial and anatomical observation is deriv'd that vast difference betwixt the education and duties of the two sexes."[16] Hume takes it for granted that "there is no foundation in nature" for chastity and modesty, but it is nonetheless imperative that "education take possession of the ductile minds of the fair sex in their infancy."[17]

The importance of chastity turns on a psychological claim about men. They ('naturally') care more for their own offspring, and they will need reassurances that the children they raise are indeed their own.[18] Women will be trained to be ashamed of their polygamous sexual urges: "'Tis necessary, therefore, that, beside the infamy attending such licences, there shou'd be some preceding backwardness or dread, which may . . . give the female sex a repugnance to all . . . liberties that have an immediate relation to that enjoyment."[19]

What comes 'naturally' to women, their modesty and chastity, comes to them through their upbringing. Hume does not deny that women can behave as freely as (some) men do, he is merely advocating that they should not. One of Hume's most colorful women,[20] described in the *Essays*, has the wealth to remain single, and is enough of a freethinker to select a male solely for breeding purposes, rejecting him after she bears the child. Without the proper cultivation, the appropriate 'artifice,' women can comport themselves as freely as licentious men do. Women's 'nature' is thus, like justice, an artifice that is prompted by facts of biology and maintained by the activity of our (deeply seated) attitudes toward this fact.

So: is this Humean female 'nature' determined by (to put it crudely) 'nature' or 'nurture'? As we have seen, this contrast is not particularly useful. Simple facts of biology, 'nature,' lead ineluctably to an account of how females should be 'nutured,' but those conventions are in turn only related at one remove to the nature on which they are founded. One way to begin sorting this out is to focus on what it actually means to 'construct' this female 'nature,' and the kind of claims and assumptions this enterprise must involve.

One hundred and forty years later, Nietzsche makes a similar claim about the making of female 'nature' (and a comparison with Hume's account of female socialization is instructive). Nietzsche's renowned misogyny is of interest here not because of its violence (Schopenhauer clearly outdoes him on that score) but because of the view of human 'nature' that it assumes. Like Hume, Nietzsche sees modesty as a useful and essential artifice:

> [T]he "emancipation of woman," in so far as it has been demanded and advanced by women themselves . . . is . . . a noteworthy symptom of the growing enfeeblement . . . of the most feminine instincts. There is stupidity in this movement, an almost masculine stupidity, of which a real woman—who is always a clever woman—would have to be ashamed . . . to seek with virtuous assurance to destroy man's belief that a fundamentally different idea is wrapped up in woman . . . to talk men out of the idea that woman has to be maintained, cared for, protected, indulged like a delicate . . . agreeable domestic animal.[21]

Nietzsche argues that women themselves have a considerable stake in this educational 'veneer.' Hume is less convinced of any advantage to women in this training program. He seems to think that the training of women is a necessary, although in some cases disagreeable, social measure (e.g., women past the age of childbearing will still be expected to be chaste and modest even though the biological imperative is moot).[22]

Nietzsche's customary hostility toward women—a far cry from Hume's occasional antique gallantry—rarely abates. One exception is a curious passage in the *Gay Science* 71. In "Of Female Chastity" he remarks that "one cannot be too kind about women" precisely because of their education: "What could be more paradoxical? All of the world is agreed that they are to be brought up as ignorant as possible of erotic matters, and that one has to imbue their souls with a profound sense of shame in such matters . . . and then to be hurled, as by a gruesome lightning bolt, into reality and knowledge, by marriage."[23]

What is Nietzsche's view of female 'nature'? Clearly he agrees with Hume that many feminine manners are instilled through education (or, as Nietzsche would say, 'breeding'), but does he believe that this instruction is commanded by our biology?

The answer to this comes, as answers often do in the aphoristic maze of Nietzsche's writings, in several parts. First, the following passage from *Human, All Too Human*:

> Can women be just at all if they are so used to loving, to feeling immediately pro or con? For this reason they are also less often partial to causes, more often to people; but if to a cause, they immediately become partisan, therefore ruining its pure, innocent effect . . . what would be more rare than a woman who really knew what science is? The best even nourish in their hearts a secret disdain for it, as if they were somehow superior.
> *Perhaps all this can change; for the time being it is so.*[24]

The possibility of change makes this passage particularly interesting. But for the final sentence, Nietzsche would have us believe that his characterization of women reveals what women essentially *are*, rather than what they have become through an extensive history of socialization. Nine sections later Nietzsche clarifies this difference: "*Women's period of storm and stress. In the three or four civilized European countries, one can in a few centuries educate women to be anything one wants, even men*—not in the sexual sense, of course, but certainly in every other sense. At some point, under such an influence, they will have taken on all male virtues and strengths, and of course they will also have to take male weakness and

vice into the bargain."[25] Women (and presumably men as well) can create
new characteristics and features that may even contradict previously
existing characteristics and features. We are called to distinguish between
what women are presently like (in Nietzsche's case, the frail, faint
creature of nineteenth-century Europe) and what women can become.
Apparently, they are infinitely malleable. Hence Nietzsche's 'antiessentialism': human beings are either male or female, but this fact is never
'bare,' for it always exists in a cultural context, in which 'masculine' and
'feminine' have already been given very specific significance. Nietzsche,
unlike Hume, does not view our biology as the source of any necessary
cultural imperatives. Our bodies have been the site of a series of understandings of what it means to be male or female, but none of these
interpretations flow directly from our physical structure. On the other
hand, Nietzsche is not making the idealist claim that the way we see
ourselves determines what we are. A person's physical sex constitutes a
kind of natural boundary[26] on what one can become through cultural
evolution. The material provided by nature, however, is too thin to
determine any one way of understanding it, and so males and females
become the historical hosts for many attributes, not all of which (perhaps
none of which) can be true of them at all times. Nietzsche himself makes
a sizeable (and remarkably offensive) contribution to the category of
female attributes. Fortunately, Nietzsche, unlike Hume, seems to believe
that these characteristics are contingent, historical, and changeable.
Nietzsche does not, as Hume does, view the facts of human reproduction
as establishing a single directive of interpretation. Human beings can
reinterpret themselves. Women can emulate the empowered sex, namely
men, by adopting their attire, body postures, and so forth, until they too
comport themselves in business and society as 'men.' Since the essential
female nature is a 'fiction,' women—and men—can alter their traditional
identity, perhaps indefinitely.

Nietzsche clearly believes that human 'nature' can be altered, and in
fact this account of human beings reconceiving and refashioning themselves is perhaps the most familiar of his claims: it is familiar, and yet it is
widely misunderstood. Nietzsche does see human nature as plastic and
malleable, but this (slim) capacity is not the end of the matter. He also
enjoys describing the habitual failings of human beings, and he treats
these behaviors in a fairly Humean fashion. Certain individuals, groups,
and cultures can indeed be relied on to behave in certain ways. He calls
these regular practices "granitic':

Learning transforms us, it does that which all nourishment does which does not merely preserve . . . But at the bottom of us, "right down deep," there is, to be sure, something unteachable, a granite stratum of spiritual fate, of predetermined decision and answer to predetermined selected questions. In the case of every cardinal problem there speaks an unchangeable "this is I"; about man and woman, for example, a thinker cannot relearn but only learn fully—only discover all that is "firm and settled" within him on this subject.

How do we reconcile this "granite stratum" and "unchangeable 'this is I'" with our capacity to reinvent ourselves? How can a person's 'granitic' character ever be remade?

We need a better understanding of what this 'granite stratum' is. A fairly simple distinction is in order. In *Human, All Too Human*, in the section titled "On the History Of the Moral Sensations," Nietzsche remarks:

> *The unalterable character.*—In the strict sense, it is not true that one's character is unchangeable; rather, this popular tenet means only that during a man's short lifetime the motives affecting him cannot normally cut deep enough to destroy the imprinted writing of many millennia. If a man eighty thousand years old were conceivable, his character would in fact be absolutely variable, so that out of him little by little an abundance of different individuals would develop. The brevity of human life misleads us to many an erroneous assertion about the qualities of man.[27]

Here we have a model for thinking about the 'granite aspect' of our personalities. A person grows up in, and is shaped by, her parenting, her education, her genetic inheritance, her location in the prevailing class structure, and so forth, "the imprinted writing of many millennia." Many of the attitudes that shape a lifetime are formed long before that person is able to articulate and "own" those attitudes. And what of altering this "imprinted writing"? The suggestion here is that this business of refashioning ourselves is more arduous than we might have suspected. Conceiving of ourselves in a new way is easy; living this new life is a very different sort of task, and one of a different magnitude of difficulty altogether. The life of feeling is older than the life of reason, and reason can be a remarkably feeble tool when we attempt to dismantle our inclinations and aversions.[28] A person who lives for eighty thousand years certainly has the time to shift her deepest feelings. During that time the cultural norms would go through so many changes that she would be in a position to see, and more important, to *feel*, that such norms are transitory. Actual people, of course, can only experience such norms as absolute, which within the bounds of an average individual's life they usually are. In this sense a person's deepest feelings are a "piece of fate": "No one is accountable for existing at all, or for being constituted as he is, or for living in the circumstances and surroundings in which he lives . . . One is necessary, one is a piece of fate, one belongs to the whole."[29]

Nietzsche's claims about a person's "spiritual fate" can be understood as his apology (or at least his excuse) for the reprehensible remarks about women that follow it. Evidently he thought that his deepest feelings about women were "unteachable," and he completes passage 230 with the following comment: "I may perhaps be more readily permitted to utter a few truths about 'women as such'; assuming it is now understood from the outset to how great an extent these are only—*my* truths."[30] If his remarks about women are read without this preamble, they will certainly sound like truths, immutable truths at that; but, of course, Nietzsche denies that such truths exist.

We must recognize that Nietzsche is making different kinds of claims. His own "perspective"[31] is critical and tendentious. He argues that the emancipation of women will be a disaster for Europe: "This will be the age in which the actual masculine affect will be anger: anger at the fact that all the arts and sciences have been choked and deluged by an unheard-of dilettantism, philosophy talked to death by mind-bewildering babble . . . society in full dissolution, because the custodians of ancient morality and custom have become ludicrous to themselves and are striving to stand outside morality and custom in every respect."[32] These remarks, however, are made in the context of his antimetaphysical and skeptical agenda. Nietzsche does not approve of female suffrage, but he is clear that this is "his" truth, and that another perspective is no doubt waiting in the cultural wings. For Nietzsche, nothing follows ('essentially,' that is) from the facts of biology or the fact of universal male hegemony. We ('good antimetaphysicians') cannot make any inferences of an essential or foundational sort from biology or history. All we may say is that human bodies have a particular structure, and that history has offered up a series of understandings of this. Of course, each of us will have our own understanding of this history, and this "granitic" set of responses and habits is largely unalterable (although what can and cannot be altered in a person's character, and in the character of a culture, is always surprising and unpredictable).

Nietzsche's account of human nature combines two surprising claims (it is their juxtaposition that is the surprise). Human creatures have the beliefs and desires that they do because of a particular embodied understanding of what it means to be human. These interpretations of 'human being' can be scrutinized, reflected on, and altered: we can become artists of ourselves: "[W]e want to be the poets of our life—first of all in the smallest, most everyday matters."[33] However, Nietzsche also cautions us that even the poet himself forgets the source of his wisdom: "[F]rom his father and mother, from teachers and books of all kinds, from the street and especially from the priests; he is deceived by his art . . . whereas he is repeating only what he has learned."[34] A person is a cultural product, and as such a human being is remarkably stable. The contingent set of historical and linguistic circumstances that produce a person are very difficult to challenge and displace: hence, our "granitic fate." This "spiritual granite" is roughly analogous to Hume's biology. For Nietzsche, only the culturally interpreted body can render a set of reliable facts (and that is why, for example, Nietzsche has much to say about the behavior of the nineteenth-century European female). The body is not the source of female behavior: the cultural view of being female is.[35]

Hume, as we have seen, *does* believe that something follows from the biological facts (although just how closely the conclusion follows is a question that we will consider in a moment). Our biological makeup 'naturally' forces the question of paternity, which in turn creates a behavioral imperative for women. Female manners are thus created, and these habitual responses—chastity, modesty, softheartedness (and, in Hume's less charitable moments, softheadedness)[36]—constitute female nature: not a metaphysical essence, to be sure, but a necessary inheritance nonetheless. For Hume, what proceeds from the biological facts is the reliable manifestation of female comportment, and her subordination to the culture that has so educated her. It is much the same with the difference between day laborers and "men of quality." The difference is 'natural' and 'universal,' but what distinguishes them does not reside in their bodies, but in a universal pattern of social development:

> The skin, pores, muscles and nerves of a day-labourer are different
> from those of a man of quality: So are his sentiments, actions and
> manners. The different stations of life influence the whole fabric,
> external and internal; *and these different stations arise necessarily,*
> *because uniformly, from the necessary and uniform principles of human*
> *nature.* Men cannot live without society, and cannot be associated
> without government. Government makes a distinction of prop-
> erty, and establishes the different ranks of men. This produces
> industry, traffic, manufactures, law-suits, war, leagues, alliances,
> voyages, travels, cities, fleets, ports, and all those other actions
> and objects, which cause such a diversity, and at the same time
> maintain such an uniformity in human life.[37]

This chaos of human endeavor is produced by our social nature, which is
usually expressed in "different ranks." Difference is "necessary," yet the
determination of who shall labor and who shall govern is apparently a
matter of luck. So too with the "distinction" of women: a fact of their
biology is necessarily laden, by society, with rules of comportment, and it
is their ill fortune that this should be so.

This comparison with the day laborer reveals an important point about
the origin of difference. The laborer is shaped by his work, and his body
reflects his station in the social network. Male and female bodies are
distinct, just as laboring and lordly bodies are distinct, but of course the
former difference is not a social construct. The biological difference,
however, is *not* where the imperative to hobble the female originates (and
in this way the laborer and the female are alike: the body is not the
ultimate source of their condition). Again, it is a story of "the necessity of
rank." The fact of childbearing is decisive not in itself, but in relation to
male psychology, and to the needs of the male in establishing order. Since
men command the household, they are universally interested in maintaining that rule by, among other things, fixing their place as the
patriarch. The key idea here is the requirement of hierarchy in the social
order.

Hume and Nietzsche are fellow travelers in several respects, and it is
worth noting the place where they part ways. Both Hume and Nietzsche
acknowledge that women can comport themselves as men do; both argue
that feminine manners are the result of socialization, not a female
'nature.' Both agree that this state of affairs is (more or less) a salubrious
arrangement. The real difference between them, obviously, is what each

will count as a 'truth' about human nature. Nietzsche as "perspectivist" has the most complex (and vexing) view. He, like Hume, denies that a metaphysical substrate guides human development. He agrees that there are contingent, yet reliable and necessary, human traits. But Nietzsche will deny that a robust empiricism can deliver those traits to us: "—we are not 'knowers' when it comes to ourselves."[38] Hume insists that our history reveals a common human nature beneath its many decorative curiosities. Nietzsche argues that to flatten out the "curiosities" of history in order to discern a deeper structure is the very mistake made by generations of truth seekers. He repudiates this reductive move. In the preface to *The Genealogy of Morals* he remarks, "[O]ur thoughts, values, every 'yes,' 'no,' 'if,' and 'but' grow from us with the same inevitability as fruits borne on the tree." This Humean trope is sympathetic to the "regular fruit of *Guienne* and *Champagne*," but Nietzsche will refuse to gather up their produce under a common human rule. It is all fruit, certainly, but the variety of perspectives on these differences—so easily effaced in reflection—are substantive in practice. Different values will produce different habits, rituals, beliefs and desires, and hence different, and often competing, accounts of what is 'essential' and 'necessary' in human affairs.

Nietzsche urges his readers to think "genealogically" rather than historically. Any claim about human nature—even Hume's most self-evident ones—have a pre-history, a "genealogy," in the beliefs and desires of the philosopher advancing that claim. A genealogy considers why certain explanations are consistently preferred to others. For example, Nietzsche speculates about the motives of the English historians of ethics who argue that the moral judgment 'good' originated in actions that proved useful to the recipient, actions that became habitual and praiseworthy in their own right over time. "We can see at once: this first deduction contains all the typical traits of idiosyncratic English psychologists,—we have 'usefulness,' 'forgetting,' 'routine,' and, finally, 'error.'"[39] Nietzsche does not name Hume, although he may have had him in mind.[40] Nietzsche's own explanation of the provenance of 'good,' namely as the appellation of nobles who had the power to enforce their judgments, does not turn on any notion of utility.

Hume's story about the necessity of female chastity and modesty contains a claim that really does demand a kind of genealogical analysis. Why is it a universal and necessary fact that men need reassurances about paternity? Hume himself provides a counterexample to this psychological truism. In the essay "On Polygamy and Divorce" Hume describes the marital arrangements of the "ancient Britons": "Any number of them, as ten or a dozen, joined in a society together, which was perhaps requisite for mutual defence in those barbarous times. In order to link this society the closer, they took an equal number of wives in common; and whatever children were born, were reputed to belong to all of them, and were accordingly provided for by the whole community."[41] Even though Hume calls this arrangement "singular," it is curious that he would adduce what is clearly an exception to the "necessity" men feel when confronted with questions about who fathered their progeny. Why Hume found this description of the male psyche so attractive is a very Nietzschean question.

So: both Hume and Nietzsche provide psychological models in their ethical histories, but Nietzsche as genealogist will go on to analyze the appeal of certain psychological claims. A second, and perhaps more fundamental, difference between them is in their respective views of history. Our history, Hume argues, provides a reliable account of essential human characteristics, and we are advised neither to idealize the possibilities for humanity (as Plato does) nor to make matters more sordid and bleak than they actually are (as Hobbes does). Things really are as they seem: "There is a general course of nature in human actions, as well as in the operations of the sun and climate. There are also characters peculiar to different natures and particular persons, as well as common to mankind. The knowledge of these characters is founded on the observations of an uniformity in the actions, that flow from them; and this uniformity is the very essence of necessity."[42] Nietzsche, unlike Hume, does *not* believe that things are as they seem, since "seeming" is the very essence of getting and maintaining power. His explanation of the demise of noble valuation at the hands of Christian morality is a good example of this. Even though Christian sensibilities actually triumphed (through a cunning reversal of noble evaluation), Nietzsche insists that "slave morality" is still weaker, less robust, and less life affirming than the straightforward powers of the eclipsed nobles (he cites Napoleon as a latter-day eruption of this energy). Christian morality has won the day, but this victory is *not* evidence of its superior strength. Nietzsche predicts a recrudescence of ancient, unqualified, and unapologetic power in the waning of decadent "slave virtues."

This is how Nietzsche rewrites the traditional account of Christian, rational, and democratic values overturning all things pagan, irrational, and hierarchic. And what of women? Does Nietzsche's genealogical approach offer any way of reinterpreting the place of women in history?

The genealogist's claims are, as Nietzsche says, perspectival: "There is only a perspective seeing, only a perspective 'knowing'; the more affects we allow to speak about a thing, the more eyes, various eyes we are able to use for the same thing, the more complete will be our concept of the thing, our 'objectivity.' But to eliminate the will completely and turn off all the emotions without exception, assuming we could: well? would that not mean to castrate the intellect?"[43] In telling the hard truths about our history as knowledge seekers, as creatures with an intense desire for metaphysical certainties, the genealogist must also assert that every claim answers specific psychological and historical claims, and that each claim can expect to be adumbrated by future concerns:

> We cannot look around our own corner: it is a hopeless curiosity that wants to know what other kinds of intellects and perspectives there might be; for example, whether some beings might be able to experience time backward, or alternately forward and backward (which would involve another direction of life and another concept of cause and effect). But I should think that today we are at least far from the ridiculous immodesty that would be involved in decreeing from our corner that perspectives are only permitted from this corner.[44]

The genealogist speaks loudly about his view of our history, but admits that this view is limited. This limitation is not something to lament: in fact, by resisting this claim, we once again reveal ourselves to be driven by what Nietzsche calls the "will to truth"—our unconditional attachment to an final account of ourselves and the world—and as less concerned with the actual conditions of our lives as human creatures.

Hume's empirical survey is likewise kept free of the pursuit of absolute truths by his skepticism.[45] But his "uncertainty" about human behavior, unlike the perspectival possibilities of the genealogist, is only a kind of negative claim. Given the regularities of human conduct, we may be (relatively) secure in our predictions about what is to come. Human beings are quite complex and difficult to predict. Large-scale alterations in a person's character are possible, but unlikely. And what of ordinary inconstancy, the lapses and lacunae that figure in everyday life? In fact, this sort of changeableness turns out to be just one more of the regular features of our human constitution. At last we can see how it is that human nature is both "inconstant" and "unchanging." Our impressions

are constantly in motion, one giving way to another: "Grief and disappointment give rise to anger, anger to envy, envy to malice, and malice to
grief again, till the whole circle be compleated. . . . 'Tis difficult for the
mind, when actuated by any passion, to confine itself to that passion
alone, without any change or variation."[46] So *this* mutability is yet
another regularity of our nature. The configuration of impressions varies
widely over time, but their content and the connections between them
remain the same. Radical shifts in our habitual responses, including the
protean nature of our impressions, are for the most part ruled out.

The genealogist looks behind and beyond our habitual views of
ourselves, and the possibility of revolutionary change is left as an open
question. Is there any space in Hume's account for actively reconceiving
women and the roles given them? Hume's claim that "we can never free
ourselves from the bonds of necessity"[47] makes the chance seem slim.
Even so, the necessity that attaches to our biology is not the whole story.
Human creatures are also driven by sympathy, not only for one another
but for other living creatures as well. Human beings can imagine the pains
and pleasures of others, and these imaginings may bring about the social
changes that do take place. Society may be indispensably unequal and
divided, but the way in which the distinguishing lines are drawn is also,
necessarily, a matter that excites and provokes our sympathy.

Before considering the part that sympathy may play in the reevaluation
of gender roles, I want to look at what is perhaps Hume's most striking
plea for sexual equality. The essay "On Love and Marriage," written
shortly after the first publication of the *Treatise*, concludes with a fanciful
retelling of Aristophanes' speech from the *Symposium*. Hume begins by
calling on men and women to think of marriage not as a domain regulated
by the male, but as an equal partnership: "I could wish there were no
pretensions to authority on either side, *but that every thing was carried on
with perfect equality, as between two equal members of the same body*. And to
induce both parties to embrace those amicable sentiments, I shall deliver
to them Plato's account of the origin of Love and Marriage."[48] The story
that Hume tells only approximates Plato. He begins by describing these
female/male creatures as blessed by the gods. His "Androgynes" are utterly
happy: "[E]ach individual was in himself both husband and wife, melted
down into one living creature. This union, no doubt, was very entire, and
the parts very well adjusted together, since there resulted a perfect
harmony between the male and female."[49] These self-satisfied Androgy-

nes became "insolent through their good fortune, and "rebelled against the gods."

Two alterations of Plato's version are worth noting. First, Aristophanes offers us creatures of every sex combination: male-female (the actual androgyne), male-male, and female-female.[50] Hume's Androgynes really are just that, and their separation by Jupiter is meant to mark the origin of hostilities and misunderstandings between the sexes. This omission of homosexual pairs may be the work of Scottish prudery; then again, it echoes what Baier has described as Hume's familial metaphor.[51] Hume is interested in reproductive pairs, and in the fortunes of those who set up households in order to breed the next generation.[52]

Second, the larger concern in Hume's essay is very different from Plato's. Hume does not tell us why the smugly contented Androgynes foment revolution: what have they to gain? Plato, however, is clear about the intentions of his "circle people." They want to storm Olympus and to usurp the place of the gods in the cosmos.[53] Their punishment for rebelling is to be sliced in two. Divided in this way, the creatures spend their time searching for their other half, too preoccupied to have any thought of confronting the gods. Here is one reason why Aristophanes' story is not the last word on love in the *Symposium*: clearly, when the circle people become whole again, they will be back to their old tricks. Human beings desire to find a mate, their "other half," but they ultimately desire immortality, and a glimpse of the Good itself. In the Platonic account, finding your soul mate is only a prelude to the higher task of correcting and purifying the soul.

Hume, of course, is not bothered about the state of his Androgynes' souls. He wants quotidian happiness for these sundered pairs, but the road to conjugal reunion is made difficult by Pleasure and Care (roughly, sex vs. hearth and home). Hume remarks that getting a couple suitably matched in one dimension often disrupts arrangements in another (as in the blissful love affair that is hardly bliss for the actual spouses of the two people involved). When both Care and Pleasure "consent to the con-junction," the restored Androgyne may expect to prosper (again, no hint of unsatisfied Olympian urges). "Where this order is strictly observed, the Androgyne is perfectly restored, and the human race enjoy the same happiness as in their primeval state. The seam is scarce perceived that joins the two beings; but both of them combine to form one perfect and happy creature."[54] What these Androgynes achieve is a happy society, one free of the anguish of illicit love and the torpor of a cold bed. The home is stable and pleasure is secure within it. More important, since the "husband-wife" are equal partners, the abuses that can attend patriarchal authority have been emended: there are "no pretensions to authority on either side."

The formation of a happy society is absolutely central in Hume's interests. The key element of human nature in its construction is sympathy: "No quality of human nature is more remarkable, both in itself and in its consequences, than that propensity we have to sympathize with others, and to receive by communication their inclinations and sentiments, however different from, or contrary to, our own."[55] Sympathy is the emotional mechanism that makes human community possible. Hume notes that we are naturally sensitive to the emotions of others, and that a person may "catch," be infected, by another's mood: "A chearful countenance infuses a sensible complacency and serenity into my mind; as an angry or sorrowful one throws a sudden damp upon me." The passions of the people around us can become our own. We not only recognize that a loved one is suffering; through sympathy, we may feel (our own version of) that pain. "The idea is presently converted into an impression, and acquires such a degree of force and vivacity, as to become the very passion itself."[56]

Sympathy is essentially an exercise of the imagination. As such, it not only produces fellow feeling, it instructs us about the misfortunes of others. When, for example, we observe a city destroyed by fire, we "there enter so deep into the interests of the miserable inhabitants, as to wish for their prosperity, as well as feel their adversity."[57] Feeling a semblance of what others feel starts a series of impressions and ideas, a series that suggests ways to ease the suffering being sympathetically observed. By feeling a copy of a like impression, and by asking myself what I would want and need in similar circumstances, I can do more than simply feel with another: I can take action.

Not every action prompted by sympathy, of course, will be a moral one. Lovers and parents are notoriously apt to ignore what is just when their sympathies for their lover or child are aroused. (Hume claims that women are especially liable to feel that a criminal on his way to execution is "uncommonly handsome and well-shaped.")[58] Sympathy is not the emotion of morality; rather, it is a precondition for moral behavior. Through fellow feeling we can deliberate about what actions are appropriate, and our own sympathetically produced feelings of hurt or rage can motivate us to act. Sympathy is the dispositional response that may ultimately produce moral feelings. It can only do so if the person has adopted what Hume calls the "general view, an objective assessment of human behavior. As Philip Mercer remarks, "Sympathy . . . is capricious and lacks principle";[59] without the corrective of the general survey, we will be hopelessly tendentious in our sympathetic responses.

Justice, then, is not merely a sympathetic response: but justice is, according to Hume, strangely indebted to sympathy. Our sympathy for others imparts virtue to justice. Hume's account of this is roughly the following. Justice is, as we know, an artificial virtue, because it requires a rule or convention about the public good. Thus the point of individual acts of justice cannot be seen except by reference to a rule or convention that was initially the product of self-interest, a means of protecting our property and our lives. So described, just actions sound "selfish," since people are obeying the rule in question as a means of self-preservation. Hume observes that this cannot be the whole story, since this reductive account of moral virtue (virtue rendered only in terms of self-interest) fails to explain our interest and approval of moral acts that have nothing to do with us.[60] Justice is established through an artifice, a rule, but our approval of just acts is wholly natural. We are by nature, via sympathy, drawn to qualities of character that are "agreeable," either "in themselves" (not for the sake of some other end), or in their capacity to advance the good of society (for the sake of utility). Sympathy is the quality that makes morality more than an exercise in prudence or rule following. When we see someone injured or cheated, we understand our social obligation to correct matters; when we *feel* for that injured person, and sympathetically join him in his suffering, our actions become virtuous as well as just. Hume concludes: "[W]e partake of their uneasiness by sympathy; as every thing, which gives uneasiness in human actions, upon the general survey, is call'd Vice, and whatever produces satisfaction, in the same manner, is denominated Virtue; this is the reason why the sense of moral good and evil follows upon justice and injustice . . . Thus self-interest is the original motive to the establishment of justice; but a sympathy with public interest is the source of the moral approbation which attends that virtue."[61] Sympathy can mislead us when persons close to us are involved, but when we adopt the "general view" our response to others' misfortune is virtuous: we take pleasure in just acts and feel "unease" when a wrong is done.

Would a sympathetic review of women's lot in society create the possibility for change? Certainly, without adopting the "general view" it is all too likely that men will be swayed by the advantages of male dominance. Then again, once the convention of the just treatment of women is established, both men and women should be attracted to it through the native response of sympathy. The mechanism of sympathy is relevant here: "[W]e must be assisted by the relations of resemblance and contiguity, in order to feel the sympathy in its full perfection."[62] We are inclined to favor that which is familiar and near: a lover in tears seated next to us is more gripping than a news report about a stranger's broken heart. Male hegemonic society must first recognize the "nearness," the close relation of the unequal treatment of women to its own concerns, and to the pursuit of justice itself.

Which brings us back to the—perhaps—not entirely frivolous story of the Androgynes. What, after all, is more contiguous, or bears a greater "resemblance" to a person, than a part of one's own body? Consanguinity, says Hume, creates the most powerful bonds between people;[63] his Androgynes are quite literally tied by blood. This fanciful creature is receptive—perforce—to the needs and troubles of men and women, and has a stake in making sure that both parties are content. This exercise in imagination nullifies all questions of paternity, and denies essential differences between men and women. These women/men are (quite literally) joined in their parental roles and duties.

The Androgyne also serves as a handy emblem of the origin of culture in the "natural appetite betwixt the sexes" which "unites them together, and preserves their union, till a new tye takes place in the concern for their common offspring. This new concern becomes also a principle of union between the parents and offspring, and forms a more numerous society."[64] Society begins with the sexual bond between mates, and is indebted to this most fundamental aspect of our nature.

The Androgynes suggest and indeed elaborate on several important Humean concerns. Even though Hume removed this account from the final editions of the Essays (something worth speculating about), many other passages are equally intriguing (if not as much fun). I conclude with one such remark. In Book III of the *Treatise* Hume reminds us that patriarchy, the father's authority, is not the origin of social relations. He claims that "the American tribes, where men live in concord and amity among themselves without any establish'd government; . . . *never pay submission to any of their fellows*, except in time of war."[65] Submitting to the father is not the only "instruction of nature": a loving sexual bond is as well. The sympathy that sexual ties can create is not an answer to the unequal treatment of women, but it is at least the promise of a start.

Notes

1. David Hume, *A Treatise of Human Nature*, ed. L. A. Selby-Bigge (Oxford: Clarendon Press, 1978), 571.

2. David Hume, *Essays, Moral, Political, and Literary* (Oxford: Oxford University Press, 1963), 552.

3. Hume, *Treatise*, 401.

4. Ibid., 370.

5. Ibid., 570.

6. Ibid., 283.

7. Ibid., 537.

8. Annette Baier writes eloquently about this problem in *A Progress of Sentiments* (Cambridge: Harvard University Press, 1991). She remarks that Hume is neither utilitarian nor contractarian in his account of the 'laws of nature', despite many attempts to so render him (250).

9. In a letter to Adam Smith, Hume remarks, "I had resolved to throw out [the 6th and 7th essays] as too frivolous for the rest . . . but Millar, my bookseller, made such Protestations against it . . . that the Bowels of a Parent melted, and I preserv'd them alive" (*Letters of David Hume*, ed. J. Y. T. Grieg, vol. 1 [Oxford: Clarendon Press, 1969], 168).

10. Hume, *Treatise*, 291: "We likewise judge of objects more from comparison than from their real and intrinsic merit."

11. E.g., Ibid., 281.

12. David Hume, *An Inquiry Concerning the Principles of Morals* (Indianapolis: Library of Liberal Arts, 1957), 33.

13. Christopher Berry, *Hume, Hegel, and Human Nature* (The Hague: Martinus Nijhoff, 1982), 59.

14. Hume, *Treatise*, 352.

15. Berry provides an excellent list and discussion of these universal characteristics in *Hume, Hegel, and Human Nature*, 63.

16. Hume, *Treatise*, 571.

17. Ibid., 572.

18. Annette Baier notes that Hume himself suffered a bout of paternity anxiety. In 1734 Agnes Galbraith named Hume as the father of one of her illegitimate children ("Hume on Women's Complexion," in Peter Jones, ed., *The Science of Man in the Scottish Enlightenment* [Edinburgh: Edinburgh University Press, 1989], 51). This essay provides a very helpful discussion of the psychological claims employed in the 'argument from paternity'.

19. Hume, *Treatise*, 572.

20. See Annette Baier's careful examination in "Hume on Women's Complexion," 44.

21. Nietzsche, *Beyond Good and Evil*, trans. R. J. Hollingdale (New York: Penguin Books, 1973), 239. (All numbers refer to section or aphorism number, not page.)

22. Hume, *Treatise*, 573.

23. Hume gives this cheerful account of the virgin bride: "[she] goes to bed full of fears and apprehensions, tho' she expects nothing but pleasure of the highest kind, and what she has long wish'd for" (ibid., 447).

24. Nietzsche, *Human, All Too Human*, trans. R. J. Hollingdale (Cambridge: Cambridge University Press, 1986), 416, emphasis mine.

25. Ibid., 425, emphasis mine.

26. Although in the case of, e.g., hermaphrodites and sex changes the natural boundary is itself under dispute.

27. Nietzsche, *Human, All Too Human*, 41.

28. Cf. Nietzsche, *Daybreak*, trans. R. J. Hollingdale (Cambridge: Cambridge University Press, 1982), 34, 35, 81, 99, and 103.

29. Nietzsche, *Twilight of the Idols*, "The Four Great Errors," trans. R. J. Hollingdale (New York: Penguin Books, 1968), 8.

30. Nietzsche, *Beyond Good and Evil*, 231.

31. Of which there is much to be said, most of it outside of the scope of this essay.

32. Nietzsche, *Human, All Too Human*, 425.

33. Nietzsche, *The Gay Science*, trans. Walter Kaufman (New York: Random House, 1974), 299.

34. Nietzsche, *Assorted Opinions and Maxims*, trans. R. J. Hollingdale (Cambridge: Cambridge University Press, 1986), vol. 1, pt. 1 of *Human, All Too Human*, 176.

35. For a more extensive treatment of Nietzsche's view of the self, see my *Nietzsche's Noontide Friend: The Self as Metaphoric Double* (University Park: Penn State Press, 1997).

36. E.g., the opening remark of the essay "Of the Study of History": "There is nothing I would recommend more earnestly to my female readers than the study of history . . . much more instructive than their ordinary books of amusement" (Hume, *Essays, Moral, Political, and Literary*, 558).

37. Hume, *Treatise*, 402, emphasis mine.

38. Nietzsche, preface to *On the Genealogy of Morals*, ed. Keith Ansell-Pearson (Cambridge: Cambridge University Press, 1994).

39. Nietzsche, *On the Genealogy*, Essay I, Sec. 2.

40. Not that this is a particularly accurate rendition of Hume. For Hume, our original judgments about *justice* are distinctively rooted in (social) utility, but our judgments about what is good are a product of natural sympathetic responses to qualities that may not have any relation to, nor have any usefulness in, our particular, local situation. The important Nietzschean point here has to do with the act of naming. To call a quality or an act 'good' is to perform a powerful act of classification, and Nietzsche argues that, in the beginning, only those human beings with superior physical force could so name. In other words, the 'nobles' called only those qualities 'good' that were relevant to their own pursuits, without any (sympathetic) thought about the appeal of those qualities outside their sphere of concern.

41. Hume, *Essays*, 186.

42. Ibid.

43. Nietzsche, *The Genealogy of Morals*, Essay III, Sec. 13.

44. Nietzsche, *The Gay Science*, 374.

45. Hume, *Treatise*, 271–74.

46. Ibid., 283.

47. Ibid., 408.

48. Hume, *Essays*, 555, emphasis mine.

49. Ibid.

50. Plato, *Symposium*, trans. Alexander Nehamas and Paul Woodruff (Indianapolis: Hackett, 1989), 190b.

51. Baier remarks, "'Liveliness' (or 'vivacity') and 'force' are the dimensions along which perceptions are assessed. The more lively perceptions are fertile; they can pass on their life, can produce resembling 'copies' of themselves in ideas . . . Passions 'attend' one another, give life to

their resembling successors, or deal death to opposing rivals . . . The ties between perceptions seem to be biological and social ties, writ small in the soul" (A Progress of Sentiments, 29–30).

52. Of course, today many same-sex couples do take part in creating the next generation, but this social innovation was seriously beyond Hume's ken.

53. Plato, Symposium, 190c.

54. Hume, Essays, 557.

55. Hume, Treatise, 316.

56. Ibid., 317.

57. Ibid., 388.

58. Ibid.

59. Philip Mercer, Sympathy in Hume's Moral Philosophy (Oxford: Oxford University Press, 1972), 53.

60. "We frequently bestow praise on virtuous actions performed in very distant ages and remote countries, where the utmost subtlety of imagination would not discover any appearance of self-interest or find any connection of our present happiness and security with events so widely separated from us" (Hume, Inquiry, 44).

61. Hume, Treatise, 499–500.

62. Ibid., 318.

63. Ibid., 352.

64. Ibid., 486.

65. Ibid., 540, emphasis mine.

11

False Delicacy

Christopher Williams

I. A Problem Concerning Morality and Aesthetic Enjoyment

When does a spectator's failure to enjoy a literary or dramatic work indicate a defect in the work or an incapacity in the spectator? This is a general question, but it seems to have a peculiar pointedness when we think about works that are made at one cultural moment and are objects of appreciation at another. For example, a Victorian play or novel or a 1950s television show may present us with female characters who are frivolous, merely decorative beings, and portrayals of such characters may understandably be morally offensive to present-day readers or viewers

I wish to thank Anne Jaap Jacobson and Annette Baier for their comments on a draft of this paper.

(especially if they are at all reflective). A feeling of displeasure could either be evidence of a laudable refinement, an unusual sensitivity; or be evidence of a false refinement, a blameable unwillingness to make due allowance for cultural differences. Our problem is then to determine whether this response is defensibly enlightened or indefensibly prudish.

Those who are polemically concerned with the evolution of our moral sensibility—those who seek to promote desirable changes in our attitudes toward women, racial minorities, or homosexuals—have reason to worry about this problem, since it would be helpful to know what basis we have for drawing a line between enlightenment and prudishness. I want to approach this issue through the distinction between a work-flaw (which moral enlightenment could reveal) and a reader-flaw (which would convict its possessor of prudishness), and will focus on our attitudes toward women.

Our problem, it is worth noting, is closely allied to perennial difficulties in the philosophy of art having to do with the distinction between pornography and erotica, or between propaganda and politically self-conscious art. With pornography and propaganda we have some inclination to say that our enjoyment of particular instances (if we do enjoy them) tells us more about ourselves than about the work, and that our failure to enjoy (if we do not enjoy) is beyond reproach, since propaganda and pornography lack the subtlety or grace of aesthetically significant work. On the other hand, if the object of appreciation is an erotic or politically self-conscious work of significance, our inclination is to say that the failure to enjoy is the phenomenon calling for special explanation in extra-aesthetic terms: the tendency is to say that a viewer or reader who recoils *here* is merely squeamish, immature, or conventionally minded—unwilling to look the hard (and often disturbing) facts of life squarely in the face, as works of truly enduring significance commonly invite us to do.

In the remainder of this paper I wish to begin an investigation of our problem by examining what appears to be Hume's solution to one version of it.[1] Although his discussion is brief, Hume is one of the few major philosophers to address the problem explicitly.[2] I shall suggest, however, that his solution is unsatisfactory, notwithstanding its attractions (which feminist ethical theory may help us to recognize). I shall propose a better solution, one that is both faithful to the larger spirit of Hume and consistent with vanguard cultural criticism. This solution should also lead us to question whether a theoretical framework is the best framework for dealing with the problem.

II. Hume's Semiofficial Solution

Hume's discussion is found near the end of his essay "Of the Standard of Taste," where he turns his attention to "the celebrated controversy concerning ancient and modern learning" (Es 245).[3] This controversy, which may initially seem quite ancient itself and interesting only to antiquarians, in fact displays a structure that matches that of our problem.[4] For the partisan of the ancients must offer excuses whenever an ancient author expresses an "absurdity" (to use Hume's word), and ask for the modern reader's indulgence as compensation for that absurdity, whereas the partisan of the moderns must hold that the absurdity vitiates the work. To be sure, only someone intent on maintaining the superiority of either ancient or modern letters would feel much necessity in saying either thing, but even without having a stake in the wholesale superiority of either the ancients or moderns we may well wonder what our response to particular instances of absurdity should be.

Hume thinks that "the proper boundaries in this subject have seldom been fixed between the contending parties" (ibid.), and in his attempt to fix the boundaries he tries to give something to both sides. If the source of our displeasure is a difference in manners on which the moral sense[5] is silent, such as those customs that Hume has just described (which include the sight of "princesses carrying water from the spring, and kings and heroes dressing their own victuals"), then our displeasure reveals a "false delicacy and refinement" (Es 246).[6] But if the source of displeasure is some practice that affronts our moral sense, as is the case when we survey the "want of humanity and decency" in the "rough heroes" of the Greeks (Es 246), then our taking offense reveals (or so it would appear) a true delicacy and refinement. Our moral feelings, and only our moral feelings, furnish us with the means of determining whether the work or the spectator is flawed: for Hume takes pains to insist that intellectual differences between ourselves and the author provide no just cause for complaint, provided that the sentiments of the author's heart have not been perverted by the author's intellectual commitments (as can happen when the commitments are to a religious system). Thus, insofar as there has been moral progress, Hume in effect sides with the moderns, but otherwise he is prepared to follow the partisan of the ancients in seeking indulgence for absurdity.

We might think that the division of manners into innocent peculiarities and blameable differences will not take us very far unless we know why the division is made as it is—that is, why the moral sense weighs in when it does. Hume does not tell us very explicitly what the basis of the division is, but we can piece together an explanation from what he does say, which yields what I shall call his semiofficial solution to our problem.

At first glance, it would seem that the explanation of the division has to do with the changeableness of the manners that are innocent, in comparison with the settledness of our moral feelings: customs are in "continual revolution," together with fashions in "speculative opinions," but the heart remains largely the same across time. However, the fact of change, the mere fact, cannot give us the explanation we seek, and there are two reasons why it cannot.

The first is that the heart does change a bit, by Hume's own lights, where the moral sense is concerned, and there need to be changes in order to generate our problem. When Hume asks rhetorically whether we must throw aside the pictures of our ancestors on account of the ruffs and farthingales that they wore, the answer is clearly that we should not. But we must throw aside, as it were, the author whose moral sense is at odds with our own, or at least point out the discrepancy as a blemish on the author's work. To the extent that we do encounter this discrepancy, we might say that we have evidence of a revolution, however modest; and thus a change in moral sentiment, while less likely than a change in speculative opinions, can still occur.[7]

The second reason is that the mere fact of change is really beside the point, since it is possible to make imaginative compensations more easily for certain changes rather than for others. The degree of imaginative *resistance* we encounter in grasping the changes is the proper locus for the explanation.

To see why, let us examine the answer to Hume's rhetorical question about our ancestors' quaint clothing more closely. We do not think that a painting is impaired by ruffs and farthingales, and we would consider a person foolish who thought that it was. Part of the reason may be due to the medium, since it could be argued that pictures, which present the visual surfaces of the objects they represent and which do not involve words (the medium of our thought), present fewer obstacles to appreciation. (It is striking that the ancestor's portrait is Hume's one example of pictorial art in an essay otherwise devoted to the verbal arts.) But the main reason, it would seem, is that ruffs and farthingales are extraneous appurtenances of a person, which we can easily alter in our imagination, and so it takes no great effort to imagine a recognizable person, one of us, in that strange garb. It will be harder, but only slightly, to imagine a person whose particular intellectual commitments are also strange. The imagining of different feelings will be harder still, but when we come to the moral feelings the difficulties will be insuperable. For we cannot imagine what it would be like to divest ourselves of our sense of right and wrong: this is the farthingale we find that we cannot remove, or perhaps can remove only if we also lose some sense of who we are.[8]

Hume hints at an explanation along these lines when he says that "a very violent effort of imagination is requisite to change our judgment of manners, and excite sentiments of approbation or blame, love or hatred, different from those to which the mind from long custom has been familiarized" (Es 247). Hume says that our judgments are slow to change, and presumably this slowness just tracks the imaginative inaccessibility of alien moral sensibilities. Although "the fancy runs from one end of the universe to the other in collecting those ideas, which belong to any subject" (T 24), it does not evince a similar facility in traversing moral space—so little facility that we may not find the language of a *moral space* helpful. For our moral sense may just accompany our imagination through whatever spaces it does run.

Another passage that reinforces the resistance explanation occurs in the section on liberty and necessity in the first *Enquiry*. After arguing that actions must be connected with a person's character if the person is to be responsible for them, Hume raises the theological worry that if this view is correct, and if God's character is implicated in everything that happens, then we have a dilemma: either God is the author of evil, since some of the events that happen are evil, or else God is not the author of evil, and so evil exists in our perception merely, as incompletely glimpsed good. Hume spends virtually all of his time ruling out the second horn of the dilemma, and his argument has the following shape: we cannot think that what we call evil is really good if seen from a revisionary perspective because "the affections take a narrower and more natural survey of their object" (E 102) and the revisionary perspective is not one that we can occupy, except in the occasional fleeting moment of speculation. But this is just to say that the alternative morality that the theodicy proposes is so inaccessible for us that we are unable to regard the alternative even as an intelligible option in thinking about morality. We are close to the limit of imaginative accessibility, and so there is something wrong, it appears, with the revisionary perspective, rather than with us for failing to occupy it.

We can say that Hume's semiofficial view is that to the extent that a difference between ourselves and a represented character is genuinely traversable by (some of) us in our imagination, then the inability of a person to bridge the gap points up an incapacity in the person. But if the difference is not so traversable, then there need be nothing amiss in the person; the work is simply alien, and a person should have no misgivings about occupying her accustomed point of view.

III. The Apparent Virtues of Hume's Account

This account of the distinction between work-flaws and reader-flaws should be congenial to some feminists who want to question the very propriety of literary canons as such.[9] If we regard a canon as an exclusionary device to enshrine the Dead White Male, then what Hume says can furnish us with a way of understanding why the exclusions occur and why canon-distrust is fitting. Here is how that understanding might be made available:

As enlightenment proceeds, as our consciousness of sexual injustice and inhumanity is raised, we find that we lose the spontaneous ability to make imaginative contact with superseded moral notions. As a result, it is possible that certain esteemed works of the past will no longer command a following, or the same following. Similarly, it is possible that formerly unesteemed works that anticipate the course of enlightenment will acquire their rightful audience in the proper season. In other words, Hume's account will lead us to champion the ethical "moderns," whoever they might become and wherever in history they might be found. And there is something in this picture that is inimical to one conception of canonical literary merit, the conception of the masterwork whose glory cannot fade, whatever the vicissitudes of history. But we could obtain a new conception, according to which (and this is a necessary condition only) the canon consists of those works that, by our best current moral lights, conform to those lights.

In the passage I have been examining from "Of the Standard of Taste,"

Hume does not present himself as advancing a moving-target conception of literary merit. Indeed, he motivates his question about the ancestor's portrait by saying, in an elegiac tone, that the poet's monument more enduring than brass would disappear if we did not make allowance for changes in fashion and for other changes that behave in a fashionlike way. Even so, the logic of his position is that insofar as there are changes in moral sensibility, these changes ought to be reflected in changed views of literary merit.

Another aspect of Hume's account should be congenial to some— perhaps the same—feminist tempers. Regarding the writer whose moral feelings we do not share, Hume says that "we cannot prevail on ourselves to enter into his sentiments, or bear an affection to characters, which we discover to be blameable" (Es 246) and that, consequently, we should be "jealous" defenders of our moral standard and so not "pervert the senti- ments of [our] heart for a moment, in complaisance to any writer whatsoever" (Es 247). Thus, when our moral sense is offended, we should refrain from criticizing the feeling, and not attempt to indulge the writer; when no offense is given, criticism of the feeling may be in order, and hence we might attempt to look at matters through the writer's (quite possibly very male) eyes. We thus might suppose that what is true of the moral sense generally is true of the vanguard moral sense, and we could then conclude that we might invoke the new light we have on sexual injustice and inhumanity to block suspect imaginative contacts.

Yet this account is seriously defective. What appear to be its selling points—its moving-target conception of merit, and its invitation to acquiesce in moral displeasure—are not really selling points at all, and we can embrace this verdict even if we think (as I do) that our moral sensibility is evolving in ways that are consonant with a broadly feminist interpretation of that evolution. This account is also difficult to square with Hume's general philosophical commitments, and the difficulties here arouse the anxieties that, as Mary Mothersill has said, are not far away from us in "Of the Standard of Taste."[10] I shall discuss four difficulties involved with accepting or applying the account.

IV. Why the Apparent Virtues Are Merely Apparent

1. *Too much jealousy.* We can agree with Hume that our moral feelings are not subject to our imaginative control: we cannot imagine ourselves

wearing different moral costumes as easily as we can imagine ourselves living in an exotic geographical location or traveling through time (a possibility that science fiction routinely exploits).[11] But this is not to say that our moral feelings are insusceptible to change, nor that they ought not to change; it only means that *we* are not, and cannot be, the agents of change. Of course, our moral feelings do change, and on any reasonable history of moral development these changes ought to occur. And we need not assume, for the sake of telling or believing this history, that moral progress is simply inevitable, nor that progress has to be conceived in any robustly transcultural way, for we might say merely that morality "progresses" in the sense of becoming progressively better adapted to the historical contingencies in which human beings find themselves.

Hume should not dispute these claims.[12] That being so, we might have expected Hume to say that works of imagination have a role to play in the evolution (a better word, indeed, than revolution) of our moral sensibility. To acknowledge this role, we do not need to suppose, as Martha Nussbaum has done, that literature purveys fine-grained moral insights that are not independently available.[13] This is a strong view, and it raises difficult questions about why the content of these insights must have a literary vehicle. A more modest, and adequate enough, view of the moral role of literature results if we note that imaginative enjoyments, because of their relative freedom from practical exigency, allow us to entertain sensibility-altering viewpoints that we might not otherwise occupy. Reading a literary work can be like listening to the king's fool, though we should not think that some unwelcome news has to be conveyed to the king (or queen). The very liberty of the mind at play, the mind without an ulterior agenda, advances our moral refinement.

The evolution of sensibility cannot be the work of a single person, or a single group of like-minded persons, and however much intentional activity may consolidate our awareness of the changes taking place, it is doubtful whether such activity could originate real changes. This evolution is always the work of many insensibly converging influences. Abstruse metaphysical reasonings did not convince our culture that slaves were persons, or that women should have the same life-opportunities as men (though such reasonings do serve a need). Rather, the culture gradually discovers, or realizes, that the weight of moral feeling is no longer with the enshrined practices, and that it is inescapably incumbent on its members—some earlier, some later—to reform them. This picture I am sketching is Humean, for Hume is both distrustful of what unassisted intellects can do and notably sanguine about social achievements that are not traceable to anyone person or group.[14] And for this very reason, we should expect imaginative literature to play a role in the cultivation of our moral sensibility.

With this stage setting in place, the first difficulty with the semiofficial account is the following. If we think moral enlightenment ought to preclude us from enjoying morally discredited works, we shall be endorsing a view whose acceptance will make it difficult for us to be imaginatively receptive to literature. The same openness or liberty that makes it possible for us to go against the grain in the cases where we think, on independent grounds, that going against the grain is salutary is also operative in the cases where we think it is not. It does not seem that we can have one possibility without the other.

Hume's recommendation to guard jealously the moral standard of which we are confident meets with a fate similar to that which befalls the assorted philosophical "maxims" that Hume's Sceptic (of the eponymous essay) retails to hilarious effect.[15] The Sceptic tells us that a common misfortune of philosophers' recommendations is that if they were to have any success at all in controlling a wayward passion, they would do so only at the price of mortifying desirable passions as well (cf. Es 173ff). It would be better, then, to think that we ought not to be too concerned about the rectitude of our moral standard when we approach a work, and that we should not try willfully to resist imaginative contact with unshared moral feelings when the work successfully secures such contact.

2. *A misconceived threat.* A more searching criticism concerns the internal coherence of the account. On the one hand, we are told that we cannot easily change our moral feelings, and the difficulty of changing our accustomed point of view is presented as a reason for thinking that our inability to enjoy moral absurdities does not reflect poorly on us; on the other hand, we are to be justly jealous of our morality and should not "enter into" the sentiments of the alien writer. These two sets of ideas do not fit together comfortably.[16] If we are slow to take on new points of view, then the language suggestive of temptation is inapposite: work and reader, we surmise, would pass each other by. It would be strange to cite the *inaccessibility* of an alternative morality as a reason to avoid *seductive* contact with it.

The ideas here fit together without strain if we add two theses. The first is that what is *otherwise* inaccessible becomes accessible to the mind in imaginative play. (We may call this view, crudely, the Platonic thesis.)

The second is that to do something in the mind is tantamount to doing the very same thing outside the mind. (We may call this view, crudely again, the Christian thesis.) The Platonic and Christian theses jointly give us reason to worry that if we read a literary work, we may encounter bad moralities that are imaginatively occupiable, and that if we do occupy them we in effect trade our own better morality in order to make the occupation. So there would then be a basis for talk of jealous guardings of our moral standard.

It is difficult to see how this talk could even get off the ground without the two theses. But more to the point, their invocation does not help salvage the account. The Platonic thesis can be platitudinously true: literature can bring alien viewpoints to life for us. Yet it is another step, requiring argument, to say that the artificially accessible is malignly accessible; and that extra step is needed to motivate jealous self-protections. The Christian thesis might give us some materials for that step, but the Christian thesis seems, when we state it crisply, to be just wrong.[17]

In any event, acceptance of the theses seems to reinstate the perception of a necessary warfare between higher and lower faculties within a person. The tenor of Hume's philosophical psychology is to reject a necessary warfare.

3. *A narrow conception of morality.* A third difficulty with Hume's exemption of morality concerns morality itself, and the extent to which inaccessible viewpoints are possible within it. Granted that there are genuine and even intractable moral disagreements between members of the same culture, and between cultures, we should not let these conflicts blind us to the fact that disputants must share a great deal of common ground with one another. In practical terms, the common ground may not be helpful in resolving a dispute (and in the really difficult problems, such as abortion, it certainly is not). Nevertheless, this common ground shows that the morality of the other is not inaccessible to us.

The mistake of overemphasizing moral difference is one that Hume is anxious elsewhere to expose. In "A Dialogue" Hume's irreverent (and "modern") interlocutor, Palamedes, presents an assortment of cultural practices that, under veiled and context-insensitive descriptions, seem repellent or just bizarre. We then learn that these are the practices of the esteemed Greeks and Romans, whom Hume is called upon to defend. Hume's strategy is to try to get Palamedes to see that the ancients led lives that are morally comprehensible to us if we take a charitable view of them. The "Greek loves," to take an example of a practice about which

Hume appears, or affects, to be a bit squeamish, originated in innocent gymnastic exercises and were reinforced by the conviction that they were "the source of friendship, sympathy, mutual attachment, and fidelity; qualities esteemed in all nations and ages" (E 334). In such a light Greek homosexuality begins to lose its alienness, if it does seem alien.

It would be wrong to conclude that this strategy foists on us a denial of the reality of moral progress. This was definitely not Hume's own view, as the *History of England*, which charts a slow, uncertain, but still real progress from barbarism to civility, makes clear. But the strategy does require us to look at people generously, and to be prepared to stretch our conception of the moral so as to secure an imaginative fit with them.

Why Hume does not pursue this sensible strategy in the essay on taste is a mystery. He is seemingly willing to grant indulgences to historical Greeks that he advises us to withhold from their literary counterparts.[18] It may be that the differential treatment is traceable to an unexpressed view that the historical record deals with hard facts about people that it is the business of inquirers to know, and to accommodate as sympathetically as they can, whereas literature is gratuitous fantasy, the work of "liars by profession" (T 121). Or it may be due to the expressed view that the study of history is just more instructive and less likely to abet vice (cf. Es 567), and so indulgences can be granted with a clearer conscience. (These views may come to the same thing.) However, the very gratuitousness of literature ought to make our imaginative approach to it less worrisome, not more (unless we import Platonic assumptions about hidden psychological malignancies attendant upon the approach). Or, finally, it may even be that the treatment is not differential, that Hume is concerned, in the essay, with differences that remain *after* all allowances of the sort implicitly recommended in the dialogue are made. But then the residuum of imaginatively untraversable difference would hardly justify the practical stance Hume recommends in the essay.

4. *Bypass of the work itself.* There is another criticism of Hume's account that does not depend on the morality exemption at all. This criticism concerns the role that degrees of imaginative accessibility can be called upon to play in an account that seeks to identify shortcomings, or for that matter strengths, in a work.

The problem is that accessibility, of whatever degree, is a relation that holds between the reader and a merely intellectually graspable subject matter rather than between the reader and the features that a work, as imagined, possesses. We can sit in our studies, without a book in our hand, thinking about various scenarios involving different subject matters with equal—equally abstract—facility; but if we try to occupy a point of view attaching to these scenarios—to imagine the scenarios, in other words—we discover few or many impediments, the kind and the number depending on who we are and how well we imagine. But we have not made a work, nor interacted with one already made. It is therefore difficult to tell how the accessibility of the subject (as I shall call the subject matter for short) could reflect on the work, for good or for ill.

We might lose track of this truth if we focus too narrowly on accessible subjects that present hurdles to readers that are felt prior to the reading. Books that offend, or anticipatorily disengage, their readers merely because of what the book is about (as with, for example, subjects that are provocatively sexual, or perceived to be blasphemous) pose a hurdle for their readers or nonreaders, but the hurdle arises directly from the subjects, and only derivatively from the work. Of course, actually reading the offending book is not likely to win over many of these people. But for just that reason we should take care not to blur the distinction between the work and its subject. Even if these readers do read the book, there is a sense in which they will respond only to the subject.

We want to say that such readers are plainly not ideal: we say that they are not open minded or receptive, that they are not giving the work a fair chance. There is a genuine problem with the reader here, but we should not conclude that if the subject is accessible, the work itself is successful. At best, a *handicap* for enjoying the work is merely out of the way. And by the same token, a subject that is relatively inaccessible does not thereby guarantee that *any* work dealing with that subject is flawed.

Because the recalcitrance of a work and the recalcitrance of a work's subject are different things, Hume's account has the wrong shape. By appealing to the inaccessibility of subjects to demarcate work-flaws and reader-flaws, that account ultimately leaves the work itself out of the picture: at most it might show that some subjects are not worth thinking about (whatever that might mean exactly).

V. A New (but Nevertheless Humean) Solution

These last observations suggest that the right place to begin attacking our original problem is with the work rather than with the reader. We need to have an account of what it is for a work to be successful, first, and then we shall be able, if the work is successful, to attribute a reader's displeasure to an incapacity in the reader.

Let us say that a work is *realized* if it makes vivid, or lifelike, or true to life, the experience or point of view that it represents. (I believe that this family of notions also applies to works that are not standardly thought of as "realistic.")[19] The terms 'vivid' and 'lifelike' apply, as Ryle taught us, to imaginings, not to the visual experiences corresponding to them, and these terms, and their conceptual cognates, are indispensable to us when we try to explain what distinguishes a successful work from an unsuccessful. To bring out the force of these terms, let us conceive a highly inartistic work.[20] We could just think about a subject for a story, and then, after committing to paper our idea, decide to pass off the description of the subject as the story itself. The proposal for the story, so to speak, would be no more a story (if we mean something psychologically compelling or imaginatively satisfying), than the mere thought of the subject. In a realized work we have more than a description of some experience; we additionally have a hypothetical presentation of an experience. To separate cleanly the descriptive elements from the hypothetical presentation may be impossible, but the distinction as such between content and presentation is nonetheless real. In a work that "works" or "comes together" (our language is impressionistic, and probably unavoidably so), we feel that the characters or the authorial viewpoint have the ring of truth, the grain of reality. Such works are true to life, in harmony with our experience, even though we would never ordinarily take the experience of the work's content to be a life experience in the usual sense.

If the characters' points of view do not convince us that the characters are true to life, we say that they are wooden, lifeless, cardboard, mere vehicles for the author's ideas, or that the *author* wants to attain a certain end which the *work* fails to achieve. The works of which we speak in this fashion are not realized. We know well enough what events these works are representing, but the representations do not have the character of felt experience: they have a willed air about them that felt experience lacks.

This distinction is drawn by Hume, though not quite in the same way. In his essay "Of Simplicity and Refinement in Writing," Hume invidiously contrasts the sort of author that we can reread with pleasure many times with the sort whose pleasures are exhausted on the first reading. (For the sake of simplicity in this piece of writing, I will schematically treat the contrast as simple and absolute.) The rereadable authors, such as

Catullus, are those whose works please in "each line, each word," whereas with once-only authors, such as Martial, "the first line recalls the whole; and I have no pleasure in recalling what I know already" (Es 195).[21] The reason that the first line suggests the rest is that the "merit of the composition lies in a point of wit"—a mere conceit, or touch of cleverness, that impresses by its cleverness but which leaves us unmoved. With the more lasting pleasers, however, there is "nothing surprizing in the thought" once we state what the thought is. And so, we have a contrast between the satisfying work that speaks to the homely affections and the satisfying work that addresses a more fanciful and novelty-loving part of ourselves.

In his discussion Hume aligns wit with imagination, which (he says) is incompatible with passion, and thus he arrives at what we might regard as the deep explanation of our contrary responses to Catullus and Martial. Yet I would say that the merely witty work is not imaginatively realized, and this language, at least, seems to be at odds with Hume's view. Yet we have no real conflict.

There is a straightforward sense of 'imagination,' to be sure, according to which the clever conceit counts as imaginative. It is this sense that Hume invokes in the "Conclusion" of Book I of the *Treatise*, when he writes that "nothing is more dangerous to reason than the flights of imagination" and that "men of bright fancies may . . . be compar'd to those angels, whom the scripture represents as covering their eyes with their wings" (T 267). For we reveal one kind of imaginativeness when we excogitate airy systems of thought that stand paradoxically at a distance from the judgments of common life, inasmuch as we think of imagination as mental activity that does not conform to routinized and prosaic patterns of thought. "Wit" is imaginative in this sense.

This style of imagination is not one that we praise very warmly, except indirectly (we might think, for instance, that a few men of bright fancies are worth having around for their amusement value, or because one of their wild ideas might have some payoff). Mere fancifulness is mere fancifulness, yet when we praise a composition for being a work of imagination we are not complimenting it for being airy. We do expect such a work to be out of the common run, but only in the unobviousness (as Hume, following Addison, would say) with which it presents material that already seems natural to us. And this is not an easy thing for an author to do: this achievement—not the dreamchild of bright fancy—discloses the true, aesthetically relevant effort of the imagination. Hume may not use the word 'imagination' for this effort, but he has the concept.

Why is it that the first line of Martial recalls the whole? If we assume that the work is an elaborate conceit, the answer is not far to seek. Conceits, like the perfect rationalistic system, have an intellectually unified structure: to grasp the part is to grasp the whole implicitly. Hence, it would not be surprising for the mind, upon being reacquainted with the work, to recollect the sequel from the first line. A unified structure may not be undesirable if we are perusing a theory, but that is not what we are dealing with here. We want a reading that rewards us as we proceed, whose pleasures are not localized in, or at least not confined to, the grasped-in-advance thought.

And why does Catullus please us in the unfolding whole, and not merely in anticipation? It cannot, of course, be that we simply forget what we read on the first reading, so that the subsequent readings are, for all the world, as good as the first phenomenologically. A better explanation is to suppose that a realized work affects us in a way that is similar to the way that life, as opposed to a mere description of lived experience, affects us. In that experience we do not meet with tidy interconnections between things or fully spelled-out relations, but with much that is impalpable and opaque. A powerful work of literature re-creates our experience, thematizes certain of its aspects, and does not explain it; in that respect, a work is true or lifelike. In grasping that which is lifelike we do reap a recognitional pleasure not to be found in life itself, and this pleasure can be renewed on subsequent readings—and need not be diminished even if we know what is going to happen next.

We can say, then, that a work is flawed to the extent that it fails to realize the experience it represents. A failure of realization is the problem with the authors whom Hume thinks of as overly "refined," though perhaps his terminology is misleading. For a work could be satisfyingly refined in the sense that the impressions it evokes are nuanced, and our ability to register nuance presumably presupposes what Hume calls delicacy of taste. Works that are refined in this way need not have anything "surprizing in the thought," however. Consequently, the contrast between refinement and simplicity may be better articulated as a contrast between intellectualism and nonintellectualism. So viewed, Hume's discussion of the two kinds of author may supply us with a usable account of a work's success or failure.[22] And on that basis, we can say that it is a reader-flaw if the reader is unable to enjoy a realized work.

VI. A Worry About Reactionary Aesthetics

The notion of a realized work has implications for our understanding of progress in the arts, and these are worth considering. If the structure of the work, rather than the imaginative abilities of the reader, is the proper point of departure for thinking about the work, then we are committed to the view that the aesthetic success or failure of the work can obtain independently of the vagaries of particular readers. That is, we would want to say that a successful work was true to our ongoing experience, as the enjoyment of successive generations of appreciators should attest. And this, we might note, is just the "ancient" position on literary history, which Hume did not want to embrace where morality was concerned and which, in any of its present-day analogues, gives many people pause. The ancient position, these people will say, seems to lead to an excessively traditional conception of aesthetic greatness, or to a disingenuous aestheticism that deems our moral convictions irrelevant to our appreciation of a work. Such consequences may seem intolerable.

And so they are, but they do not in fact follow from the ancient position properly understood. Some of the discomfort arises from the confused idea that having a test of time entails that the test has been completed, and that the results are in. (Aesthetic conservatives who think that there is nothing new or valuable under the sun seemingly fall prey to such a confusion.) Some discomfort is problematic in a less obvious way. If the analysis is correct that a literary work vividly intimates the experiences it represents, then the thought that literature does not progress, far from being a prop for a reactionary aesthetics, is a mere truism. Art does not progress because our experience itself does not progress. What we think about, or the conclusions that we draw from, our experience may indeed progress, as our thinking about anything can, but it is really quite unintelligible to think that experience as such admits of being progressive (or regressive). Experience just happens.

We may have particular trouble appreciating this point in the case of literature, which is an extension, however eccentric at times, of our experience. Nevertheless, when we talk about art generally we often vacillate between idioms that are simply representational and those that call attention to the thingliness of the representation. This vacillation is discernible in Plato, who wants to think of the artist's painting of a bed sometimes as a painted (and intellectually inferior) representation of a bed and sometimes as a bed-made-of-paint. Now although it has seemed self-evidently false to some that the painter makes a (peculiar sort of) bed, Plato's thingly idiom itself embodies an important insight about our relationship to works, and I doubt whether we could (or should) ever eliminate it. Speaking of a work as a special sort of thing calls attention to the experiential character of art, and having that character firmly before us should help us to see the nonprogressivist claim for the truism that it is.

Our moral convictions are no more irrelevant (whatever that might mean) to our aesthetic experience than they are "irrelevant" to our experience at large. We do not suppose either that our experience of other people will jeopardize our good convictions and give illicit reinforcement to the bad or that we must check our convictions wholesale at the door if we are to enjoy ("appreciate") others. To think that this disjunction exhaustively maps the available options for ordinary experience would be extremely strange, and yet this disjunction is sometimes thought to map our aesthetic options. On this point, however, we should not expect art and life to be so different. Our moral sense can be shaped by art as by life, but it is unmeaning to think that a literary work affords us a kind of moral theory that, in principle, either competes with the reader's or, by matching the reader's, encourages complacency about it.

To mobilize our moral convictions, prior to an engagement with a work, for or against some element of the imaginative experience that the work affords indicates an incapacity in the reader. But this position does not entail that there is no work for the morally enlightened critic to do. For moral enlightenment can, and should, have an impact on criticism, but not after the fashion that a moralizing philosopher intends. Let us consider, in conclusion, how this idea could be made out, and to do so I would like to return to, and make much more explicit, Hume's notion of *false delicacy*—though in so doing I shall make it a technical notion of my own.[23]

VII. Enlightened Criticism

Hume devotes a fair amount of attention in a few of the essays to "delicacy of taste," the ability to discern fine differences in objects of taste. These objects are not restricted to works of art, but include, notably, people as well; and the exercise of this ability is not a native endowment, but is attained through the refinement of cruder tastes. Thus, "the gaiety and frolic of a bottle companion improves with him [sc. the person whose taste is delicate] into a solid friendship: And the ardours of a youthful appetite become an elegant passion" (Es 8). We begin with tastings that are fairly undiscriminating, that satisfy basic human needs, and end with tastings that are much more selective and that do not satisfy needs, at least where needs are understood in primitively human terms.

How the mind passes from a cruder to a more delicate taste Hume does not explain, but we may surmise that this refinement of the mind, like other Humean refinements, takes place insensibly in propitious external circumstances and is not something we can directly aim at producing. Delicacy of passion, the ability to respond emotionally to a wide variety of stimuli, seems to be "originally connected" with delicacy of taste—at least this is the view Hume flirts with, and that he endorsed in a deleted passage[24] that says that women have both greater delicacy of taste and passion than do men—though it is also clear that the two are in tension with each other, since Hume recommends that we seek to cultivate our taste in order to silence our passions. It appears that a favorable, if not strictly necessary, condition for delicacy of taste is a relative immobility in the face of stimuli that are apt to sweep us along emotionally and deprive us of our self-possession.

All of this suggests that as the mind grows more collected it has more leisure to notice subtle perceptual phenomena that, because of their subtlety, would otherwise be lost in the mental shuffle. The mind in the growth of its tasting capacity is like a dull instrument that is transformed into an instrument of great precision. But if this characterization is correct, it comes as a mild surprise to find Hume speaking of "false delicacy and refinement" when he mentions the person who is shocked by innocent peculiarities of manners. How exactly does falsity enter the refinement picture? For all that Hume says elsewhere, our minds may just differentially, albeit accurately, register nuances. If we say that falsity enters with the judgments that we make about what we are registering, we should ask what sorts of errors these judgments involve and how we make them.

The notion of falsity is most easily approached, at first, through bodily taste. Although Sancho Panza's kinsmen detect different flavors in the same wine, they are both vindicated, Hume says, when a leather-bound key is found in the hogshead (Es 234–35). But let us suppose that just an unadorned key is found. In that event the kinsman who detects some-thing leathery in the wine might be accused of having a falsely delicate taste, of tasting something that is not really there (a false sensation perhaps akin to awareness of movements in a phantom limb). This model does not easily transfer, however, to the more mental taste that most concerns Hume. With that taste, it is less plausible to suppose that the taster is misclassifying a simple qualitative feature. Of course, it might be that the false delicacy Hume has in mind afflicts only those who merely have pretensions to refinement, who give themselves superior airs regard-ing their powers of discrimination, such that their claims to have detected nuances would collapse into misclassifications, leaving authentic (unpre-tentious) refinement beyond the pale of possible falsity. Yet however well this strategy might work for some cases, it is doubtful whether it could cover them all. Perversion of taste, not just (or not even) witting or unwitting hypocrisy regarding taste, is the problem that false delicacy poses.

Another model is needed. An initially promising candidate (and no more than that) is suggested by Hume's discussion, and partial defense, of luxury in "Of Refinement in the Arts." Luxury refers to "great refinement in the gratification of the senses; and any degree of it may be innocent or blameable, according to the age, or country, or condition of the person." Only a mind "disordered by the frenzies of enthusiasm" (Es 268) would hold that any refined gratification was in itself vicious, and such gratifi-cations only become vicious if they "entrench upon" some virtue, and so obstruct more "laudable pursuits" (Es 269). By analogy, a false delicacy of taste would then be a vicious delicacy, a gratification of a refined taste that is in some sense overdone.

In the case of luxury, overdoneness does not infect the exercise of taste as such, but results only if the exercise collides with other goods that we care about. That is, the taste is vicious only if, to put it crudely, its timing is off, if we insist on gratifying it when gratification is inappropriate because we are better advised to be doing something else. In cases of false delicacy, like that of the man who is shocked by innocent peculiarities, the issue of timing does not at all arise. For we are saying that his judgment is false irrespective of the external conditions under which he enjoys the object or offers the judgment. So we need to alter the model to accommodate the relevance of external conditions.

When a person's taste is false, there is disconnection between what the person perceives while she is in the taste situation and what she says about that perception. The disconnection can be hard to think about in the example of the falsely shocked man, since we may have difficulty thinking that such a person truly has taste. A more credible example would help.

Hume's Sceptic observes, "You will never convince a man, who is not accustomed to Italian music, and has not an ear to follow its intricacies, that a Scotch tune is not preferable" (Es 163). His point is that argument is useless here, but for our purposes we can regard the implied communication as an exchange between a refined and unrefined taste, in which falsity need not be a factor. We can make it a factor if we suppose that the man with the ear for Italian music is also unable to take pleasure in the Scotch tune. It is one thing for the Scotch tune to be thought inferior, on the basis of a musical experience more extensive than that which the naive listener brings to bear: we might find the tune a source of genuine pleasure, however limited the pleasure may be. It is quite another thing if the higher pleasure poisons the well of the lower, as it were, so that the tune no longer provides even the limited pleasure. This second possibility, I propose, illustrates false delicacy, which is essentially overintellectualized perception, and I want to suggest that this falsity can infect more than just our judgments of what is pleasurable. In the case of literary works, it can infect our judgment about the experience that a work mediates.

Works can be unrealized, but an appreciator may not have the right disposition to appreciate what a realized work offers, for an overly intellectualized perception may prevent him from seeing the work for what it is, from responding to the work, emotionally and imaginatively, as an extension of ordinary experience. And so, it is a mistake to think that a specific cause of failure to enjoy a work—moral friction, for example—can be assigned to a shortcoming in either the work or in the appreciator without the further information that practical criticism supplies. For there can be moral friction that results because the work is unrealized, in which case the felt difficulty is traceable to an underlying work-flaw, or because the work is realized, in which case we have a reader-flaw. Telling which is which is a project for criticism, not aesthetic theory.[25]

Enlightened criticism can help to expose the blindnesses that result from overly intellectualized perception. For example, one feminist literary critic has called into question the realization (as I would put it) of Dickens's Bella Wilfer in the following way: "The woman who knows beyond a doubt that she is beautiful exists aplenty in male novelists' imaginations; I have yet to find her in women's books or women's memoirs or in life."[26] Relying on all of our experience—women's as well as men's—enables us to see a character in the round, and we may find that, in certain cases, there is less of a character to see as we rely on that enriched experience more: what we thought was a realized character increasingly becomes for us an abstraction or artificial construction. Or criticism can change our understanding of how a work is realized, as with Charlotte Perkins Gilman's "The Yellow Wall-paper": awareness of women's historical domestic experience has helped to transform the work from a mere tale of horror to a more moving story of the infantilization of its female protagonist.[27] By performing such offices as these, what a gifted critic succeeds in showing us becomes part of the test of time that a work has traditionally been thought to pass or fail.

To be sure, not all feminist criticism exposes false delicacy; some criticism no doubt exemplifies it.[28] But this state of affairs is as it should be. The fallible task of seeing what there is to see takes time and patience to accomplish, and intellectualized blindness is no respecter of the sexes, or of other sources of division between people. And the persistence of that blindness, which only due receptivity to the work can remove, affords us one way of identifying the reason why criticism is perpetually necessary in the arts, and why a purely philosophical explanation of imaginative resistance in art distorts the issue it is called upon to explain.

Notes

1. Another version arises when we ask how closely a work can approximate the appearance of what it represents without giving offense, if the real thing is offensive. It is this version that Hume considers at the end of his essay on tragedy, where he inveighs against *The Ambitious Stepmother*, but I will not consider that version here.

2. As Richard Moran has said, "To my knowledge, the nature of . . . imaginative resistance does not receive much explicit discussion in the history of aesthetics, even though so many terms of aesthetic criticism (for example, the sentimental, the pretentious, etc.) can be seen as expressing judgments of this kind" ("The Expression of Feeling in Imagination," *Philosophical Review* 103 [1994]: 95). Moran then considers the passage in "Of the Standard of Taste" that will concern me, claiming that "Hume makes a few somewhat halfhearted attempts at explanation, but his answers are brief and do not appear to strike Hume himself as terribly persuasive" (98). It is difficult to say whether Hume's attempt is halfhearted, but it is an attempt, and as such is worth a careful examination.

3. In this essay I will use the following abbreviations for Hume's writings: Es (*Essays, Moral, Political, and Literary*), T (*A Treatise of Human Nature*), E (*Enquiries Concerning Human Understanding and the Principles of Morals*), D (*Dialogues Concerning Natural Religion*). The page references are to the Miller edition for the *Essays*, to Selby-Bigge/Nidditch for *Treatise* and *Enquiries*, and to Popkin for the *Dialogues*.

4. To avoid anachronism in what follows, I will confine my discussion to literary examples, though my remarks are meant to have application to any of the verbal media (such as film and television).

5. I am assuming throughout this essay that the portion of Hume's moral theory that is relevant to our purposes belongs wholly to the "moral sense" tradition. In this tradition our moral judgments themselves express the deliverances of taste, broadly understood: the general feelings of rightness or wrongness we have when contemplating practices or persons, and that we can reasonably expect others to share.

6. The relationship between delicacy and refinement is not readily apparent from this passage, but in another passage (from the *Dialogues*) Hume suggests that false delicacy is to be explained by false refinement. Philo supposes that the miseries of our existence are real and give rise to justifiable complaints, and then considers an imagined interlocutor who objects, "It is only a false delicacy . . . which a few refined spirits indulge, and which has spread these complaints among the whole race of mankind" (D 61). The account of false delicacy I offer in Section VII is faithful to this explanatory suggestion.

7. That "revolutions" in moral sentiment can occur within Hume's framework may come as a surprise, and I will say more about this in Section IV. I also think it a desirable feature of his framework that they are possible, since the moral sense turns out to have an implausibly ahistorical character if we think otherwise—and treating the moral sense as if it were not historically conditioned is one reason that talk of "our" moral sense can seem so clubby and hopelessly old-fashioned.

8. We can of course imagine different objects activating our sense of right and wrong. I will also take this up in Section IV.

9. It can be difficult to know what the main objection to a "canon" is. For one feminist discussion of the canon, see Lillian S. Robinson, "Treason Our Text: Feminist Challenges to the Literary Canon" in Robyn R. Warhol and Diane Price Herndl, eds., *Feminisms* (New Brunswick: Rutgers University Press, 1991), 212–26. An important question that Robinson raises is whether the canon "is to be regarded as the compendium of excellence or as the record of cultural history" (218)—important because we get different conceptions of literary study depending on which of these alternatives we endorse. I assume that the problem of this essay makes sense only if we regard literary works as candidates, at least, for aesthetic excellence (which is not to say that the study or cultivation of such excellence must always make sense).

10. "What one does come to see eventually is that the smooth Addisonian surface with its ornamental platitudes conceals deep intellectual conflict. Indeed, as conveying a sense of the turmoil and exasperation endemic to philosophical work, the essay has affinities with *Philosophical Investigations*" (Mary Mothersill, *Beauty Restored* [Oxford: Clarendon Press, 1984], 182). I will try to show that Mothersill's remark has particular application to the ancients-moderns passage, to which Mothersill does not give much attention, comparatively speaking.

11. It is possible to imagine, in an abstract way or in a make-believe setting, that we have different moral attitudes—a nonracist actor can convincingly play a KKK member (an example I owe to Anne Jaap Jacobson). It is much more difficult to imagine ourselves actually feeling differently *and endorsing* the differences, and it is with this more difficult feat that I am concerned.

12. This remark ideally calls for a detailed discussion, which I cannot undertake here, but some pertinent textual materials for it include the second *Enquiry*, Section III, the essay on polygamy and divorce, and the *History of England*. The suggestive *History*, in particular, deserves more attention from philosophers: reading it can help us to appreciate how respect for legal order and aversion to violence acquired its grip on the European moral sensibility over successive generations.

13. Nussbaum advances this line of thought in *Love's Knowledge* (New York: Oxford University Press, 1990).

14. In arriving at this view of Hume I myself have been assisted by Annette Baier, whose *A Progress of Sentiments: Reflections on Hume's "Treatise"* (Cambridge: Harvard University Press, 1991) develops this view in great detail.

15. I discuss this feature of philosophical passion-control, and Hume's essay, at length in *A Cultivated Reason* (University Park: Pennsylvania State University Press, 1999), chap. 3.

16. As Moran has also observed ("Expression of Feeling," 98–99). Moran does not explain why the two sets might appear together, however.

17. Richard Wollheim helpfully discusses what is wrong with it in *The Thread of Life* (Cambridge: Harvard University Press, 1984), chap. 7, sec. 6. Wollheim characterizes the denial of the importance between the inner and the outer as the "inwardness" of morality, which he associates with the self-lacerations of the Freudian superego.

18. Perhaps, as Robert Shaver has suggested, the literary characters are not true counterparts: the Greeks of "A Dialogue" may be historically later, and more civilized than, the Greeks who would be the proper counterparts to the Homeric heroes. I do not see evidence that Hume took such a contrast seriously, however, and do not think that it would matter much if he did, since the strategy of "A Dialogue" could with equal justification be applied to a more archaic phase of Greek culture.

19. Even a surrealist story, if successful, *rings* true. We might think of Kafka's *The Metamorphosis* in this regard.

20. That inartistic works are more easily summoned up than artistic ones for the sake of thought experiments indicates, as we shall see, an important difference between success and failure.

21. Whether we agree with Hume about Catullus and Martial is beside the point for my purposes, and the same is true of his comments (in "Of the Standard of Taste") on Corneille and Racine—which Mothersill, for one, finds "unpersuasive" (*Beauty Restored*, 203). That we can draw a distinction between rereadable (or good) authors and unreadable (or bad) is more important than how we draw it, which is a task for practicing literary critics.

22. There are familiar epistemological problems connected with the identification of successful works, but I shall not discuss them. I assume that they can be dealt with, but assume also that we shall not get anything like an external test for identifying successes. Some who are skeptical about the epistemology of taste may fuel their skepticism by requiring such a test.

23. For a discussion that raises some of the same issues as mine does, but which does not pick out the same problem exactly, see Jenefer Robinson and Stephanie Ross, "Women, Morality, and Fiction," in Hilde Hein and Carolyn Korsmeyer, eds., *Aesthetics in Feminist Perspective* (Bloomington: Indiana University Press, 1993), 105–18.

24. "For we may observe that women, who have more delicate passions than men, have also a more delicate taste of the ornaments of life, of dress, equipage, and the ordinary decencies of behavior. Any excellency in these hits their taste much sooner than ours; and when you please their taste, you soon engage their affections" (Es 603).

25. At the end of "Of the Standard of Taste" Hume writes that "it must for ever be ridiculous in Petrarch to compare his mistress, Laura, to Jesus Christ" (Es 248–49). It would be plausible to attribute Hume's singling out of the Jesus comparison to his generally hostile view of religion, which is also a moral view that Hume, following his own injunction, ought to be guarding jealously. If we accept his semiofficial account, we are obliged, if we are disposed to dispute Hume's literary judgment, to debate moralities with him. But it makes much better sense to say that the comparison adds nothing to our imaginative perception of Laura as a woman, and that for this literary-critical reason the comparison is "ridiculous."

26. Joanna Russ, "Aesthetics" (from *How to Suppress Women's Writing*), reprinted in Warhol and Herndl, *Feminisms*, 204.

27. The Gilman example is discussed by Annette Kolodny, "Dancing Through the Minefield: Some Observations on the Theory, Practice, and Politics of Feminist Literary Criticism," reprinted in

Warhol and Herndl, *Feminisms*, 97–116; it is also discussed by Robinson and Ross in "Women, Morality, and Fiction,"

28. A possible example: Judith Fetterley claims that Hawthorne's "The Birthmark" is "the story of how to murder your wife and get away with it" (introduction to *The Resisting Reader*, reprinted in Warhol and Herndl, *Feminisms*, 500) and faults Hawthorne for not diagnosing the male protagonist's real problem, which is sexual-political. It is not clear that such a claim helps us to see the characters of the story better, however applicable it might be to the situation with which the story deals.

12

"Manly Composition"

Hume and the History of England

Kathryn Temple

History is a manly composition, and
should accordingly be apparelled
with such ornaments as are consistent
with the boldness of its nature.
Lucian very aptly compares an History
effeminated by trifling, incongruous
Circumstances, to Hercules in a Woman's
Dress, submitting to the Dominion and
Discipline of his Mistress Omphale.
—Peter Whalley,
   "An Essay on the Manner of Writing History," 1746

When Peter Whalley rejected "effeminate" methods of writing history in 1746, he could not have known that he was accurately characterizing David Hume's historical method while pointing to its gendered implications. In the essay, written eight years before Hume's famous *History of England*, Whalley details the qualities necessary to the historian, qualities such as virtue, objectivity, and "Integrity of Heart."[1] He rejects the methods of the "romance" writer, arguing that while romance revels in "unwarranted Excess . . . which might be apt to descend to low Minutenesses," history should be "temperate and sparing."[2] Meanwhile, he

I wish to thank Cynthia Wall, Lindsay Kaplan, and Cynthia Herrup for their insightful comments on earlier drafts of this essay.

associates "ambitious ornaments" or "trivia," which he sees as typical of romance, with effeminacy. Choosing the overtly gendered "Hercules-Omphale"[3] trope quoted above (an ornamental device in itself), Whalley adopts Lucian's argument that historical facts should be "dressed" in an appropriately masculine style because Herculean history is somehow masculine, deserving of masculine attire. Rather than submit to the feminine—which becomes a catchall concept related both to romance and disruption—history should distance itself from what Whalley calls the confusion of "trifling, incongruous circumstances."

Whalley's tract, which purports to summarize general attitudes toward historical writing, attests not only to history's importance and popularity in the mid-eighteenth century, but also to its gendering. Moreover, his commentary suggests a model for the feminist analysis of a much more influential work, David Hume's tremendously popular *History of England*.[4] Like Whalley, Hume masculinized "proper" history and feminized romance, at times explicitly rejecting romance conventions as inappropriate for historical writing. But Hume's use of this dichotomy was far more ambitious than Whalley's. Deploying a more complex model on a grander scale, Hume used it to lend his *History of England* force in imagining Britain as a nation.[5]

As many commentators have noted, Hume's *History*, published between 1754 and 1762, made him "rich and famous";[6] its popularity made his "name familiar to all who could read."[7] Quite respected, The *History of England* became the standard historical source, informing public policy long after Hume's death.[8] In large part, critics have credited its success to Hume's appealing narrative style, noting also his "subtle and sophisticated historical reasoning."[9] Hume provided readers with a reassuring account of British history by reframing party politics in polite terms[10] and employing a powerfully unifying magisterial voice. Moreover, as Rodney Kilcup has pointed out, Hume's account of "historical flux" was stabilized by "a decisive and unchanging point of reference, universally constant human nature."[11] Thus, according to the critics, gender has little to do with Hume's national history, nor with its success.

As is common in political histories, women seldom appear in the *History of England*,[12] but ignoring gender altogether neglects Hume's well-documented concern with gender issues, a concern that permeates his *History*, his historiography, and his philosophy.[13] And focusing only on the absence of women, though important in itself, neglects Hume's reinscription of gender as a force in English national consciousness. My alternative reading of the *History of England* focuses on gender, suggesting that Hume associated gender with genre to reinforce Britain's emerging sense of national identity.

As Benedict Anderson, Eric Hobsbawm, Lauren Berlant, and other theorists of nationalism have pointed out, nations "imagine" themselves into being partly by claiming roots in the past. Hobsbawm observes: "[M]odern nations and all their impedimenta generally claim to be the opposite of novel, namely rooted in the remotest antiquity, and the opposite of constructed, namely human communities so 'natural' as to require no definition other than self-assertion."[14] The ability of the nation to construct itself as unified, whole, and rich with content, and thus "naturally" a "nation," depends in part on an implied continuity with a national past. Imagined wholeness and linear continuity become even more important during periods such as Hume's when rapid change threatens an emerging national culture.[15] In writing a national history, Hume created a sense of integrity and unity in part by rejecting "trifling, incongruous circumstances," in effect, by re-presenting British history through the lens of a mid-eighteenth-century desire for nation.

Hume accomplished this in part by following Whalley and distinguishing "history" from "romance." In the essay "Of the Study of History,"[16] Hume conflates romance and its debased subgenre "secret history," dismissing both as popular forms of no redeeming value. But in practice, he banishes neither romance nor secret history from history. Progressive historical narrative is masculinized, while historical moments that defy progressive explanation are contained in a feminized form of romance, simultaneously seductive and easily dismissed. Hume thus draws on both generic traditions, carving out a space for a history of the nation precisely by distinguishing it from what he defines as a disruptive counternational "romance"—a form associated since the late seventeenth century with both a generalized femininity and a specific female readership.[17]

Far from prescriptive, then, Hume's antiromance commentary must be understood as a conventional gesture that allows him to make use of the full range of generic devices while risking neither critical sanction nor the loss of readers eager for a reader-friendly, but identity-affirming, history of the nation. In this essay, I focus on Hume's compelling account of James I's court and the "notorious" Frances Howard[18] incident in the contexts provided by his philosophy and historiography. Rereading Hume's gendered rendering of James I's court reveals the complexity of Hume's efforts to inscribe a newly imagined national history in gendered generic terms.

The Gender of History

Hume's philosophical writing sheds light on the connections that he draws between gender and genre, between the disruptive feminine and the romance.[19] Far from being a stereotypical misogynist, Hume believed that men and women share a basic sexuality as well as similar intellectual potentials. Although he thought most Englishwomen to be poorly educated and thus poor companions, his intellectual relationships with French women demonstrated a deep respect for female intellect. But as Annette Baier has argued in an intriguing series of articles,[20] Hume also believed that social utility rather than natural difference required society to treat women quite differently from men. For instance, he grounded his demand for absolute female chastity not in any argument about the "essence" of women, but in an argument related to the proper functioning of society. In Hume's discussion of gender difference in the *Treatise*, the major concession to the natural or essentialized argument for gender difference involves biology as related to paternity: a woman will always know whether a particular child is genetically her own, while a man's knowledge must rest on women's protestations. If men cannot be sure that their children are their own, they will refuse to support them, thus destabilizing patrilineage and the structure of the family. As Hume posits, "From this trivial and anatomical observation is deriv'd that vast difference betwixt the education and duties of the two sexes."[21] The "trivial" nature of the distinction is belied by its impact on women and on society at large. For based on this difference, one that creates an "inequality of trust" between men and women and thus threatens to upset all of society, women must be held to a special, higher standard of chastity and modesty. Like men, women are not naturally chaste or modest, but unlike men, women (or at least most women—Hume creates an exception for prostitutes) must be socialized into absolute chastity lest men be discouraged from supporting children and society lapse into chaos.

Undergirding this utility-oriented theory of gender traits lies a more subtle association between women and disruption. In the *Treatise*, Hume ends "On Morals" by setting up a dichotomy that any late twentieth-century feminist will recognize. Remarking that the obligations of men "bear nearly the same proportion to the obligations of women, as the obligations of the law of nations do to those of the law of nature,"[22] he argues that male moral obligations in the sexual arena are much less necessary than female obligations. Here Hume compares women to nature, an entity that he has earlier described as disruptive in that it is "independent of our thought and reasoning."[23] Nature, it turns out, though composed of "but few and simple" principles,[24] resembles Whalley's version of history in that it "is compounded and modify'd by so many different circumstances, that in order to arrive at the decisive point, we must carefully separate whatever is superfluous."[25] The "laws of nature" are seen to govern the circumstantial superfluity that tends to blind us to them, just as moral obligations placed on women regulate feminine excess and irregularity and thus protect the institution of the family.

The association between masculinity and linearity, femininity and superfluity has obvious consequences for the writing of an historical narrative founded in a model of linear progress. As Luce Irigaray suggests, the oft-noted conflation of "void" with "feminine" elides the feminine's real consequences for historical linearity.[26] The masculinized tendency to equate woman with "lack" reveals anxieties about women's "insatiable hunger, a voracity that will swallow you whole," but simultaneously cloaks the far more threatening possibilities presented by female multiplicity—possibilities that, as we have seen, Hume refers to in his philosophical work. In "This Sex Which Is Not One," Irigaray tells us that "[female] desire . . . really involves a different economy more than anything else, one that upsets the linearity of a project, undermines the goal-object of a desire, diffuses the polarization toward a single pleasure, disconcerts fidelity to a single discourse."[27] Hume's commitment to "the linearity of a project" can be observed throughout his work, but he specifically rejects multiplicity in favor of linearity in several key discussions of historical method incorporated into the *History*. In his account of Henry III, Hume argues that "[h]istory also, being a collection of facts which are multiplying with out end, is obliged to adopt such arts of abridgement, to retain the more material events, and to drop all the minute circumstances, which are only interesting during the time. . . . What mortal could have the patience to write or read a long detail of such frivolous events . . . which would follow, through a series of fifty-six years, the caprices and weaknesses of so mean a prince as Henry?"[28] Hume deals with the anxiety about disruptive, and surprisingly, *reproductive*, "facts which are multiplying with out end" by advocating a historiography of elimination. In general, "minute circumstances" and "frivolous events"—both associated with the feminine—should be elided. The historian should focus on what

Whalley constructs as Herculean history and Hume calls "general theorems."[29]

To see this theory at work, we can turn to a crucial moment in the early chapters of Volume 5 of the *History of England*. Passing over the infamous physicality of James I's infatuation for Robert Carre, Hume dispatches in a few lines the rumors that "the monarch, laying aside the sceptre, took the birch into his royal hand, and instructed him in the principles of grammar." Rather than pursuing this interesting topic, Hume breaks off into a defensive explanation, abruptly announcing that "[s]uch scenes, and such incidents, are the more ridiculous, though the less odious, as the passion of James seems not to have contained in it any thing criminal or flagitious. History charges herself willingly with a relation of the great crimes, and still more with that of the great virtues of mankind; but she appears to fall from her dignity, when necessitated to dwell on such frivolous events and ignoble personages."[30] Here Hume equates a moment of homosocial disorder with the feminized fall of history. But he also demonstrates the contradictory complications involved in rejecting "frivolous" scenes. For here, as in Whalley's discussion of Omphale, the "ridiculous" image draws the reader's attention to its moral. By placing frivolity against the "dignity" of history, the "birch" against the "sceptre," Hume amuses readers while impressing upon them the seriousness, virtue, and centrality of his historical project.

Given this context, it is not surprising that Hume invokes a gendered model of historical study in "Of the Study of History," an essay addressed to "my female readers."[31] Here Hume reiterates his views of the purposes of history while emphasizing the disjunction between masculinized history and feminized romance. He argues that female students of history will be benefited "much to their quiet and repose" partly because they will learn that they have much less impact on men than romances and novels may have led them to believe. From reading history, women will learn that "love is not the only passion, which governs the male-world, but is often overcome by avarice, ambition, vanity, and a thousand other passions."[32] Men are motivated by desires, not necessarily virtuous, but certainly removed from female influence.

Although Hume suggests that both men and women can benefit from reading history, he creates of women a special case, detailing "how well suited it is to every one, but particularly to those who are debarred the severer studies, by the tenderness of their complexion, and the weakness of their education."[33] Without studying history, "a woman's "mind is so unfurnished, 'tis impossible her conversation can afford any entertainment to men of sense and reflection." Halfway through the essay Hume admits that these remarks constitute "raillery"[34] but the admission serves not to soften his message, but to underscore the boundary between the feminine, which prompts levity, and the historical, which does not. In the final section of the essay, Hume shifts to a masculine norm, suddenly remarking that "a man acquainted with history may, in some respect, be said to have lived from the beginning of the world." Leaving questions of female inadequacy behind and turning to Machiavel, Horace, and the generic "man of business" for his examples, Hume seems to forget the gendered theme with which he began.[35]

While Whalley finds redeeming characteristics in the romance, associating it with "fable" and the "greater Kinds of Poetry," Hume—at least in this essay—associates romance with novels and with the "secret history," a term loosely applied to the works of Madeleine de Scudéry, Delariviere Manley, and Aphra Behn.[36] As Hubert McDermott tells us, the secret history developed from the Greek heroic romance exemplified by Heliodorus's *Aethiopica*.[37] Significantly different from history, the romance valued intricacy of plot, often heightened by numerous interpolated tales, more than logical narrative progression. Generic conventions typical of the heroic romance included noble characters, love at first sight, and threats to that love from parents, rivals, and natural disasters such as storms and shipwrecks. As McDermott notes, the genre was distinguished by an almost ritualized series of conventions: "Hero and heroine fall madly in love with one another. . . . The romance details their numerous adventures from the time they meet until their eventual marriage. . . . The couple are invariably prevented from marrying by one, or several reasons—parental opposition, disparity in rank, the threat of incest, the machinations of villains and the intrigues of rivals. Natural disasters such as shipwreck, as of old, contrive to keep the lovers apart also."[38] What Hume calls secret history cannot be equated directly with the heroic romance. Rather he refers to a simplified, shortened, and sexualized subgenre, one that had been more popular in the early part of the century than it was in Hume's own day. The works forming the subgenre tended to focus on the seduction and eventual destruction of the heroine, sometimes represented as virtuous but misguided, and sometimes as sexually aggressive and malicious. Moreover, they often referenced prominent people, offering to a larger public detailed insight into the private or "secret" doings of the elite. While such stories appealed to readers titillated by accounts of sexual games in high places, writers justified their erotic content by claiming a higher moral purpose. Typically, authors claimed that the erotic content was secondary to a narrative that at least exposed vice if it did not punish it.

Ironically, Hume opens "Of the Study of History" with an interpolated example of the secret history:

> I remember I was once desired by a young beauty, for whom I had some passion, to send her some novels and romances for her amusement in the country; but was not so ungenerous as to take the advantage, which such a course of reading might have given me, being resolved not to make use of poisoned arms against her. I therefore sent her PLUTARCH's lives, assuring her, at the same time, that there was not a word of truth in them from beginning to end. She perused them very attentively, 'till she came to the lives of ALEXANDER and CAESAR, whose names she had heard of by accident; and then returned me the book, with many reproaches for deceiving her.[39]

Immediately following this inserted "teaser," Hume attacks the secret history for its falseness and triviality. But his use of its techniques and motifs—personalization of the famous, revelation of desire, a lexicon of potential seduction—in an essay that explicitly and emphatically denounces the form—suggests a dynamic similar to that relied upon by secret-history writers. Like them, Hume seduces his readers and then subjects them to moral didacticism. Like them as well, he relies on the implications of secret history to define its opposite. Although the essay places the trivialized interpolated romance against a linear and progressive discussion that associates history with truth, impartiality, virtue, and manliness, the seductive opening refuses erasure. In granting secret history a lingering presence, Hume reinforces proper history's seriousness and "manliness."

Hume's *History of England*: Reading Frances Howard

Hume presses gender into service throughout the *History of England*. Disorderly males may be feminized or disorderly events attributed to a feminine cause, while at times extreme chaos is indicated by recourse to anecdotes that position women petitioners, rioters, and hysterics as signs of societal disruption.[40] Such minute examples provide an implicit commentary on Hume's use of the genre-gender connection in the fifth volume of the *History*. The fifth volume was the first volume written by Hume. Covering the recent past rather than the ancient past, it begins with the ascension of James I in 1603 and ends with what Hume refers to as the "the dissolution of the monarchy in England," marked by the famously romanticized beheading of Charles in 1649.[41] Hume began the project with this period—despite the disadvantages of writing history in reverse chronological order—because he felt it essential to understanding not only his own age but also the previous history of the nation. Thus his early chapters—which are replete with gender references—serve to frame the rest of the *History*.

In the first volume, Hume makes brilliant use of gendered allusions. He represents what some historians have called the "traumatic" shift from Elizabeth's women-dominated reign to that of James I as "tranquil," celebrates the age as one that drew on the "manly virtues, which the Greek and Roman authors . . . recommend to us,"[42] and makes of Prince Henry a paragon of manliness.[43] But Hume's most compelling use of gender connects gender to genre as he displaces the many signs of chaos that accompanied James I's reign onto the secret history of the "notorious" Frances Howard.

David Lindley's *Trials of Frances Howard* offers a sophisticated twentieth-century analysis of her story.[44] As Lindley points out, very few of its "facts" are based on reliable evidence. Emotionally driven, misogynistic accounts of Howard's life and character—accounts that accuse her of sexual excess, sorcery, and poisoning—have come to dominate the historical record.[45] The essential details can be summarized as follows. The daughter of a prominent family with Catholic connections, she was married to the earl of Essex. Without consummating the marriage, she and her husband were separated for four years. Sometime before Essex's return, James I's favorite, Robert Carre, and Howard were reputed to have become lovers. In order to marry Carre, Howard sued for divorce based on Essex's supposed impotence. Despite James I's support, Essex was subjected to questioning regarding his virility, and Howard (or a cleverly disguised substitute) underwent a widely publicized physical examination by a jury of matrons. Meanwhile, Carre was thought to have intrigued to have Sir Thomas Overbury, who opposed the marriage, thrown into the Tower, where he was eventually poisoned. After Howard and Carre married, a conspiracy to poison Overbury was revealed, and the couple was charged with murder. In the end, James saved Howard and Carre from execution, but imprisoned them for six years and banished them thereafter. Living in isolation with a man she had grown to hate, Howard eventually died of uterine cancer, a fate that her contemporaries believed appropriate to the nature of her sins.[46]

Whether the most negative versions of the story were constructed from fragments of free-floating anxiety about poisoning, duplicity, Catholicism, the weakness of the king, and the excesses of the court, or simply gained greater credibility from this historical milieu, the story took on great cultural valence. As Lindley argues, Howard operated as an emotional vortex for "a hostility which frantically seeks to shore up the dominant ideology by demonizing the woman who confronted it."[47] Like many historians before him, Hume participates in this hostility. But his complex deployment of the narrative potential that Howard represented suggests that far more than a straightforward defense of the patriarchy was at stake. Instead, Hume seizes on the Howard story as a way of fulfilling several goals simultaneously. He not only uses the story to reinforce the gender-genre connection that validated masculinized history over feminized romance, but also relies on it to absorb the chaotic multiplicity that typified James's reign. By drawing on the outmoded form of secret history for the representation of disorder, Hume creates a chronological boundary that protects Britain's recent history from antinational disruption. The secret history of Frances Howard feels archaic, unrelated to England's recent history, because it is represented in an archaic form. Meanwhile, much like the interpolated secret history in Hume's "Of the Study of History," the Howard story intrigues and seduces readers, perversely attracting a readership with the very methods of seduction that Hume argued should be eliminated from progressive history.

Hume's observation that "the history of this reign may more properly be called the history of the court than that of the nation"[48] calls attention to how important it was that Howard's story absorb and contain the negative imagery surrounding James I. For where James is concerned, it seems no accident that Hume attempts to distance "court" from "nation." Even Hume's most rational, evenhanded, explanatory tone fails to cloak the many signs of instability that accompanied James's reign. The conspiracy to place Arabella Stuart on the throne, the Gunpowder Plot, and the plague constituted real-world disruptions mirrored and distorted in the frivolities of the court. By separating court from nation, Hume allows the court to absorb and contain these disorderly events, distancing them from his stately narrative progression; by displacing "court" to the story of Frances Howard, Hume doubly insulates the nation from the forces of disruption.

As David Lindley notes, James's court was "characterized by a dangerous femininity. . . . As a place of ease, of music and feasting, the court is intrinsically effeminate, subject to passions and pastimes rather than the nurse of heroic and manly virtues."[49] Moreover, James, enmeshed in a tangle of intricate personal passions, displayed an alarming "feminine" interest in what Whalley calls "trivia." Courtiers were warned to praise his ornate regalia,[50] and he displayed his love for the decorative by awarding titles so extensively that their value was questioned. Worse, his fascination for male "favorites"[51] seemed matched only by his unseemly interest in the private and romantic lives of his family and subjects.[52] Hume treats such excesses sparingly. He simply omits much personal detail about James, never mentioning, for instance, James's well-documented obsessive interest in fashion and dress. Although he notes the excessive awarding of titles—a "proliferation" so extensive that parodic notices were posted offering memory training—Hume attributes James's acts to kindness. And, as we have seen, Hume's reluctance to detail "caprices and weaknesses" curtails his discussion of the king's relationship with the prominent favorite Carre.

Hume renders the Frances Howard story in terms of radical disorder. Interior to the story of the court and thus doubly removed from "nation," the story contains and focuses national disorder while maintaining a safe distance from the national symbolic.[53] Hume's account is restrained compared to those of some of his predecessors; nevertheless he awards a prominent place in the narrative to what might, by rights, have fallen into the category of the trivial. But although Hume's extensive detailing of Howard's story may seem inconsistent with his historiographical principles, it participates in the established dichotomy between proper history and secret history, that in which the secret history absorbs the multiplicity and disruption inappropriate to proper history.

Hume relies on easily recognizable generic features to mark a gradual shift from "history" to "romance" to "secret history." Carre's relationship with the king, essential to the events that led to Howard's downfall, appears in a form that any reader of romance would have recognized. The two meet "at a match of tilting" when Carre, flung from his horse, is approached sympathetically by the king. As Hume relates: "Love and affection arose on the sight of his beauty and tender years; and the prince ordered him immediately to be lodged in the palace, and to be carefully attended. He himself, after the tilting, paid him a visit in his chamber, and frequently returned during his confinement. The ignorance and simplicity of the boy finished the conquest begun by his exterior graces and accomplishments."[54] As if uncertain that the "accident on horseback" trope would signal romance to his readers, Hume steps entirely if ironically into the role of romance writer when he introduces Frances Howard, noting that: "[t]o complete the measure of courtly happiness, nought was wanting but a kind mistress; and, where high fortune concurred with all the graces of youth and beauty, this circumstance could not be difficult to attain."[55] Yet romance deteriorates into secret history when Howard enters the narrative. As Hume relates, Carre's happy affair with the king is interrupted not by a "kind mistress," but by an encounter with Howard, an encounter that Hume tropes as a natural disaster, as "that rock, on which all his fortunes were wrecked, and which plunged him for ever into an abyss of infamy, guilt, and misery."[56] Images of disruption, chaos, and the watery void—long associated both with romance and with female disruption—introduce Howard as the focal point for disorder of every kind.[57]

Just as in the secret histories of Manley and Behn, Hume's romance characters (like few other characters in the usually eevenhanded *History*) are represented as one-dimensional, either entirely evil or entirely virtuous. Howard, in particular, appears to have no redeeming qualities. Indeed, the evil agency that Hume accords her drives the narrative. Other historians have held various views regarding her complicity in the events that led to her two trials, some blaming her family, some even suggesting that James manipulated her. Certainly, familiarity with her history suggests her entanglement in a complex web of court intrigue, royal manipulation, and political maneuvering. Hume uncharacteristically leaves such rational causes unexplained, blaming Howard's uncontrollable lust and anger for events that were probably well beyond her control.[58]

Hume's other characters seem drawn directly from the supply provided by secret-history writers. Carre, for instance, appears as little more than Howard's dupe. As Hume remarks, when Howard's "rage and fury broke out against Overbury, [Carre] had also the weakness to enter into her vindictive projects." Nevertheless, Howard was "not satisfied, till she should farther satiate her revenge on Overbury; and she engaged her husband . . . in the atrocious design of taking him off secretly by poison."[59] Mentioning but not judging Overbury's role in Howard's seduction (Overbury composed the love letters that first interested Howard in Carre), Hume characterizes him as a "judicious and sincere counsellor." In fact, Hume repeats Overbury's objections to the Howard-Carre marriage as if they were his own: "How dangerous, how shameful, to take into his own bed a profligate woman, who, being married to a young nobleman of the first rank, had not scrupled to prostitute her character, and to bestow favours on the object of a capricious and momentary passion."[60] Hume further connects the feminine, secret history, and disordered multiplicity in an aside about the trivial case of a "lesser criminal," Frances Howard's affiliate Mrs. Turner. Departing from the progressive relation of the story, he leaps from the guilt of Frances Howard to that of her agent: "It may not be unworthy of remark that Coke, in the trial of Mrs. Turner, told her, that she was guilty of the seven deadly sins: She was a whore, a bawd, a sorcerer, a witch, a papist, a felon, and a murderer. And what may more surprize us, Bacon, then attorney-general, took care to observe, that poisoning was a popish trick."[61] While Hume claims to quote Coke in detail to demonstrate the strength of prejudice against papists during James's reign, the rhetorical strength of the reference to "seven deadly sins" overwhelms its overt message against "bigotted prejudices." Coke's excessively expressed catalog of sins uncannily repeats the various concerns about the "sins" of James's reign—each word describes an unexpressed fear regarding James.

Howard's story absorbs the array of anxieties about James that float through the historical literature. Fears about the shiftiness of James's favorites and indeed about his own intentions reappear disguised as concern about Howard's duplicity, particularly in an aside regarding her use of a virgin "under a mask" during the hearing that tested Howard's virginity. Fears regarding the irrationality of the king's attachment to various young men reappear in Hume's note about the "ridiculous opinion of fascination or witchcraft" that accompanied Howard's first trial. Suspicions about the king's role in poisoning Henry, mentioned and dismissed by Hume in one paragraph, are displaced onto certainty regarding Howard's poisoning of Overbury.[62] Even the Gunpowder Plot resurfaces here, lent relevance by the Howard family's Catholic background and by the cultural connections between poisoning and Catholicism.[63]

Unmediated by the irony or the historical analysis present in his recounting of most other events, Hume's narrative suggests an underlying agenda that goes beyond titillating, shocking, or educating his readership. Full of "rage and fury," Howard cannot be "satisfied." Given the circum-stances—not one husband, but two, not merely the Tower, but poison—Hume's rhetorical emphasis on Howard's thirst for satiation invokes not only the evil heroine of secret history, but also Irigaray's discussion of women's "insatiable hunger, a voracity that will swallow you whole."

For Hume, Howard becomes the model for the sort of woman who creates an "imbalance of trust" in male-female relations. She interrupts the natural progression of events, the logic of natural science, and the lawful relations among people. Like the evil heroines of secret history, she disturbs homosocial and patriarchal relations, destroying the friendship between James and Carre and the fatherly relationship between Overbury and Carre. On a symbolic level, she destroys the law's ability to control private unions, and the king's role as keeper of law. Indirectly, she breaches the impenetrability of the Tower of London, sign of royal power, and even Overbury's very body through her association with the "poison" that killed him.

The conflation of Howard with all manner of evils shelters all male authority, especially royal authority, from blame for failing to control complex processes. Indeed, Hume's deployment of the story can be seen as a subtle defense of James: Howard's uncontrollable passions lead to the downfall of Carre; Carre is replaced by Villars; Villars spends extrava-gantly; James's "urgent wants" lead to the loss of what Hume calls his "most valuable possessions" and the "full liberty of the Dutch common-wealth."[64] Unexpected multiplying consequences never threaten the symbolic value of "nation" because they can be traced back to Howard.

Such a displacement allows Hume to contest the assessment of James levied by other historians. For when historians such as the royalist Peter Heylyn held James accountable for the problems of his reign they did so almost invariably in terms of chaotic multiplicity and the disruption of stable symbols. As Heylyn argues: "One might say (I fear too truly) that by putting off the majesty belonging to a king of England, that so he might more liberally enjoy himself, neglecting the affairs of state, and cares of government, to hunt after pleasure; deserting the imperial city, to sport himself at Royston, Newmarket and such obscure places . . . and finally by letting loose the golden reins of discipline held by his predecessors with so strict a hand, he opened the first gap unto those confusions, of which we have since found the miserable and woeful consequences."[65] Hardly recognizable to readers of Hume, Heylyn's James is described in the

feminized lexicon of confusion and pleasure taken in obscurity. In
comparison, Hume offers a lengthy appraisal of James's good and bad
qualities, not hesitating to criticize him in the midst of a general
rehabilitation.[66] Hume's criticism is mitigated both by his reference to the
influence of "factions" and by his very fairness. Immediately following a
reference to the "contagion" that James suffered from vice, Hume offers a
long balanced periodic sentence in which James's virtues become vices
only in that they are excessive. Perhaps most interesting is Hume's
displacement of James's vices to a sphere more appropriate to secret
history than to proper history. As Hume remarks, James's "intentions were
just; but more adapted to the conduct of private life, than to the
government of kingdoms." In Hume's final analysis, James's "capacity was
considerable; but fitter to discourse on general maxims than to conduct
any intricate business."[67] Here Hume places history and secret history in
close dialogue, as he represents James suffering "contagion," at once more
comfortable with the "private" of secret history and yet unable to manage
its "intricacy." The final appraisal retains credibility only because "intricacy" has been marginalized, subordinated to "general maxims" here just
as it was contained in the trivialized secret history of the Frances Howard
story in the larger narrative.

The displacement of multiplicity, of chaotic and uncontrollable circumstances, allows Hume to narrate James's death as a moment that
combines heterosexual virtue with patrilineal authority and national
unification. Hume narrates the deathbed scene as follows: "[James] sent
for the prince, whom he exhorted to bear a tender affection for his
wife, but to preserve a constancy in religion; to protect the church of
England. . . . He expired on the 17th of March, after a reign over
England of twenty-two years and some days. . . . In all history, it would
be difficult to find a reign less illustrious, yet more unspotted and
unblemished than that of James in both kingdoms."[68] For other historians, those "spots" and "blemishes"—banished from public view to secret
history—resisted total erasure. As Lindley reports, quoting Wilson, the
blemishes surfaced in stories of Howard's deathbed moments: "Her death
was infamous. . . . And though she died (as it were) in a corner (in so
private a condition) the loathsomeness of her death made it as conspicuous as on the house top: For that part of the Body which had been the
receptacle of most of her sin, grown rotten (though she never had but one
Child) the ligaments failing, it fell down, and was cut away in flackes,
with a most nauseous and putrid savour; which to augment, she would

roul her self in her own ordure in her bed. . . . Pardon the sharpness of these expressions."[69] Private and yet so loathsome as to become conspicuous, Howard's highly physicalized death conflates images of the uterine void with those of an overwrought complexity denoted by uncontrolled "ligaments" and "flackes." Rot, sin, even self-indulgence are condensed as economically as James's deathbed narrative condensed positive notions related to "Englishness."

That Hume omitted Howard's death scene suggests a delicate negotiation with secret history. The successful representation of Britain as "nation" required certain permissible images that make up the imagined nation to displace images of total degradation. Even images of disruption had to be domesticated and contained. Like Whalley's effemination of Hercules, Hume's interpolated secret history of Frances Howard must have exercised a peculiar power over readers. But in Whalley's extended metaphor, the compelling image of Omphale ruling a Hercules attired in "a Woman's Dress" displaces the argument for a "manly" history. Despite Whalley's intentions, "Mistress Omphale" comes to dominate Hercules—as the image dominates the reader. Hume's task required him to reverse this dynamic. To forward the emerging national identity of mid-eighteenth-century Britain, history must dominate the secret history of sexuality, irrationality, and disruption.

For the twentieth-century reader, however, the horrifying image of Howard's death suggests all that is false about the "imagined community" of national identity. By haunting Hume's magisterial description of James's final moments, it calls into question the rationalizing, progressive project of national history. Lingering in the historical record only to reappear sporadically, the image reminds us of the abjected "other," of all that must go unsaid in order to shore up the nation.[70]

Notes

1. Whalley, Peter, An Essay on the Manner of Writing History. London: Printed for M. Cooper, at the Globe, 1746, 10. Epigraph is from 22.
2. Whalley, An Essay on the Manner of Writing History, 20.
3. For an introduction to the Hercules-Omphale narrative, see the entry for "Hercules" in the Simon Hornblower and Antony Spawforth, eds., Oxford Classical Dictionary, 3d ed. (New York: Oxford University Press, 1996). Hercules was required to serve Omphale for a period of years to atone for acts that are described differently in different sources. She purportedly dressed him as a woman and required him to perform women's tasks. In some accounts, he claims to have worn a bra. This story

was recounted in various classical texts and was taken up by a number of artists and sculptors. At least one eighteenth-century play draws on the theme. See *Hercules and Omphale: A Grand Pantomimic Spectacle in Two Parts.* Composed by Mr. Byrn. London: Printed by H. Macleish, 1794; Karl Galinsky, *The Herakles Theme: The Adaptations of the Hero in Literature from Homer to the Twentieth Century* (Totowa, N.J.: Rowman and Littlefield, 1972); and Natalie Boymel Kampen, "Omphale and the Instability of Gender," in Natalie Boymel Kampen, ed., *Sexuality in Ancient Art: Near East, Egypt, Greece, and Italy* (Cambridge: Cambridge University Press, 1996).

4. All references to Hume's *History of England* are to *The History of England from the Invasion of Julius Caesar to the Revolution in 1688,* 6 vols. (Indianapolis: Liberty Classics, 1985). I have chosen this edition because it relies on the 1778 edition, the last edition reviewed by Hume, and because students will find it readily accessible.

5. Working at the intersection of national identity and gender, my reading of Hume relies on methodologies drawn from cultural studies, literary criticism (especially genre studies), and feminist psychoanalytic theory. For a cogent discussion of a methodology that analyzes "historical" texts from a literary perspective, see the introduction to Peter Burke's *Colonial Encounters: Europe and the Native Caribbean 1492–1797* (New York: Routledge, 1992). For a discussion of the application of psycho-analytic theory to history, see Ann McClintock's introduction to *Imperial Leather: Race, Gender, and Sexuality in the Colonial Conquest* (New York and London: Routledge, 1995). For a recent collection of essays on gender and nationalism, see Anne McClintock, Aamir Mufti, and Ella Shohat, eds., *Dangerous Liaisons: Gender, Nation, and Postcolonial Perspectives* (Minneapolis: University of Minnesota Press, 1997). For an influential discussion of issues in genre studies, see Adena Rosmarin, *The Power of Genre* (Minneapolis: University of Minnesota Press, 1985), 3–51. For an impressive traditional reading of Hume's *History of England,* see Rodney Kilcup's introduction to David Hume, *The History of England from the Invasion of Julius Caesar to the Revolution in 1688,* abridged (Chicago: University of Chicago Press, 1975). For overviews of Hume's life and work, see David Fate Norton, ed., *The Cambridge Companion to Hume* (Cambridge: Cambridge University Press, 1993) and John Valdimir Price, *David Hume,* updated ed. (Boston: Twayne, 1991). For the standard biography, see Ernest Moss, *The Life of David Hume* (Austin: University of Texas Press, 1954).

6. Price, *David Hume,* 15.

7. Mossner, 302.

8. For a discussion of the *History's* popularity and influence, see Nicholas Capaldi and David Livingston's preface to *Liberty in Hume's History of England* (Dordrecht: Kluwer, 1990). The preface notes that prominent readers of Hume included Louis XVI, Thomas Jefferson, and Winston Churchill, who "learned English history from a student's edition" (vii).

9. Nicholas Phillipson, *Hume* (New York: St. Martin's Press), 83.

10. Phillipson, *Hume,* 85.

11. Kilcup, introduction to Hume, *History,* xxviii.

12. Such an absence is representative, of course, of women's general erasure from official history, an erasure that has provoked much feminist commentary and "recovery" work. For a recent collection of some of the most compelling essays published on feminist history and gender studies, see Joan Wallach Scott, ed., *Feminism and History* (Oxford: Oxford University Press, 1996).

13. Jerome Christensen's *Practicing Enlightenment: Hume and the Formation of a Literary Career* (Madison: University of Wisconsin Press, 1987), offers a sensitive, complex, book-length discussion of Hume's relationship to the "feminine" and to gender.

14. Eric Hobsbawm and Terence Ranger, eds., *The Invention of Tradition* (Cambridge: Cambridge University Press, 1983). 15. See also Benedict Anderson, *Imagined Communities: Reflections on the Origin and Spread of Nationalism* rev. ed. (New York: Verso, 1991); and Lauren Berlant, *The Anatomy of National Fantasy: Hawthorne, Utopia, and Everyday Life* (Chicago: University of Chicago Press, 1991).

15. See Hobsbawm, 4. Hume's social, cultural, and economic context, including the national

threat posed by the Jacobite rebellion of 1745, and Hume's own unstable Anglo-Scottish position, no doubt increased the importance of linearity in the History.

16. David Hume, *Essays, Moral, Political, and Literary*, rev ed., ed. Eugene F. Miller (Indianapolis: Liberty Classics, 1987), 563–68. The essay first appeared in 1741, but was withdrawn after the 1760 edition of *Essays and Treatises on Several Subjects*. See Miller, 563 n. 1.

17. The term "romance" has been defined in many different ways with many different purposes in mind. For a discussion of the history of the term and its relationship to women readers and to the novel, see Laurie Langbauer, *Woman and Romance: The Consolations of Gender in the English Novel* (Ithaca: Cornell University Press, 1990). For two very different, but normative, approaches to the term, see Hubert McDermott, *Novel and Romance: The Odyssey to Tom Jones* (Totowa, N.J.: Barnes and Noble, 1989) and Northrop Frye, *Anatomy of Criticism: Four Essays* (Princeton: Princeton University Press, 1957), 186–206. I draw on both traditional and feminist approaches here, connecting "romance" to its generic predecessors while agreeing with Langbauer that it is most often used to establish the validity of its "other," whether that other is the novel or historical writing. For a collection of representative eighteenth-century romances by women and an introduction to the form, see Paula R. Backscheider and John J. Richetti, *Popular Fiction by Women: 1660–1730, an Anthology* (Oxford: Clarendon Press, 1996). Other important works include John J. Richetti, *Popular Fiction Before Richardson* (Oxford, Clarendon Press, 1969); and Rosalind Ballaster, *Seductive Forms: Women's Amatory Fiction from 1684–1740* (Oxford: Clarendon Press, 1992).

18. See Edward Le Comte, *The Notorious Lady Essex* (New York: Dial Press, 1969) for an account that covers the Overbury trial and gives Howard's first marriage "its indecent due" (vii). For a theoretically sophisticated account, see David Lindley, *The Trials of Frances Howard: Fact and Fiction at the Court of King James* (New York: Routledge, 1993). For the most recent history, see Anne Somerset, *An Unnatural Murder: Poison at the Court of King James* (London: Weidenfeld and Nicolson, 1997).

19. Much work has focused on the connections between Hume's philosophical and historical writings. See especially David Fate Norton, "History and Philosophy in Hume's Thought," in David Fate Norton and Richard H. Popkin, eds., *David Hume: Philosophical Historian* (Indianapolis: Bobbs-Merrill, 1965), xxxii–lv.

20. My account here is heavily indebted to Annette Baier's numerous articles on Hume. See "Good Men's Women: Hume on Chastity and Trust," *Hume Studies* 5, no. 1 (April 1979): 1–19; "Hume, the Women's Moral Theorist?" in Eva Feder Kittay and Diana T. Meyers, eds., *Women and Moral Theory* (Totowa, N.J.: Rowman and Littlefield, 1987), 37–55; and "Hume: The Reflective Women's Epistemologist?" in Louise M. Antony and Charlotte Witt eds., *A Mind of One's Own: Feminist Essays on Reason and Objectivity* (Boulder, Colo.: Westview Press, 1993), 35–48.

21. Annette Baier's work influenced my discussion of this passage. Baier, "Good Men's Women," 6–7; David Hume, *A Treatise of Human Nature*, ed. L. A. Selby-Bigge, 2d ed., rev. P. H. Nidditch (Oxford: Clarendon Press, 1978), 571.

22. Hume, *Treatise*, 573.

23. Ibid., 168.

24. Ibid., 182.

25. Ibid., 175.

26. Luce Irigaray, *This Sex Which Is Not One*, trans. Catherine Porter (Ithaca: Cornell University Press, 1985). For a selection of Irigaray's works, see Margaret Whitford, ed., *The Irigaray Reader* (Oxford: Blackwell, 1993). For a brief introduction to what has loosely been called French Feminism, see the entry "French feminist criticism," in Maggie Humm, ed., *A Reader's Guide to Contemporary Feminist Literary Criticism* (New York: Harvester Wheatsheaf, 1994).

27. Irigaray, *This Sex Which Is Not One*, 29–30.

28. Hume, *History of England*, 2:3–4. This frequently discussed passage was first brought to my attention by Price, *David Hume*, 89.

29. Hume, *History of England*, 2:3.

30. Ibid., 5:53.

31. Hume, *Essays, Moral, Political, and Literary*, 563–68.

32. Ibid., 564.

33. Ibid., 565.

34. Ibid.

35. Ibid., 566–68.

36. For representative examples, see Madeleine de Scudéry *Artamene, ou le grand Cyrus* (1649–53) and *Clelie* (1656–60). Aphra Behn's *The History of the Nun* (1689) and Delariviere Manley's *The Secret History of Queen Zarah and the Zarazians* (1705) are both collected in Backscheider and Richetti, *Popular Fiction by Women*.

37. For a recent, accessible translation, see Heliodorus, *An Ethiopian Romance*, trans. Moses Hadas (Ann Arbor: University of Michigan Press, 1957). For a discussion of the relationship between the ancient Greek novel and the British literary tradition, see Margaret Anne Doody, *The True Story of the Novel* (New Brunswick, N.J.: Rutgers University Press, 1996).

38. Ibid., 116–17.

39. Hume, *Essays*, 564.

40. See, for example, Hume, *History of England*, 2:3–4.

41. Although beyond the scope of this essay, Hume's use of romance has implications that extend beyond these early chapters to resonate in the final scenes of the volume. In narrating the execution of Charles as heroic romance, Hume draws on the gender-genre connections discussed in this essay. The death of Charles, presented as heroic romance, is marginalized, rendered archaic by its genre and told for its emotional power rather than for its contribution to the formation of nation. The gender-genre connection Hume establishes in the early chapters prepares readers to interpret Charles's beheading as extraneous romance rather than as a sign of national disruption.

42. Hume, *History of England*, 5:13.

43. As Hume says, Henry's "inclinations, as well as exercises, were martial. The French ambassador, taking leave of him, and asking his commands for France, found him employed in the exercise of the pike; *Tell your king*, said he, *in what occupation you left me engaged*" (ibid., 5:50).

44. I am much indebted to Lindley, both for this summary and for the complex understanding of the Howard story offered in *The Trials of Frances Howard*.

45. Lindley, *The Trials of Frances Howard*, 44ff.

46. Although I have consulted a number of sources for the Howard story, my summary here is largely indebted to David Lindley.

47. Lindley, *The Trials of Frances Howard*, 42.

48. Hume, *History of England*, 5:51.

49. Lindley, *The Trials of Frances Howard*, 61.

50. For only one of many examples, see the letter from Lord Thomas Howard to Sir John Harington, 1611, collected in Robert Ashton, ed., *James I by His Contemporaries* (London: Hutchinson, 1969), 234–35.

51. Hume, of course, discusses this. See also Osborne, *Traditionall Memoyres*, in *Secret History of the Court*, 1:274–76, collected and reprinted in Ashton, *James I by His Contemporaries*.

52. See Letter from John Chamberlain to Alice Carleton, 18 February 1616, reprinted in Ashton, *James I by His Contemporaries*, 101–2.

53. I borrow the term from Lauren Berlant's *The Anatomy of National Fantasy*. As she notes, the "national symbolic" refers to "the order of discursive practices whose reign within a national space produces, and also refers to, the 'law' in which the accident of birth within a geographic/political boundary transforms individuals into subjects of a collectively-held history" (20).

54. Hume, *History of England*, 5:52.

55. Ibid., 5:54.

56. Ibid.

57. As McDermott notes, the trope was well recognized by romance writers. He quotes Scudéry as follows: "the sea is the scene most proper to make great changes in, and that some have named it the Theatre of Inconstancy" (115).

58. George Macaulay Trevelyan, for instance, passes over the incident in two pages and places the blame on Howard's ambitious family, as does Christopher Durston. See Trevelyan, *England Under the Stuarts*, vol. 5 of *A History of England in Eight Volumes* (London: Methuen, 1904, repr. 1965), 106–7; Durston, *James I* (New York: Routledge, 1993), 17–20.

59. Hume, *History of England*, 5:56–57.

60. Ibid., 5:55.

61. Ibid., 5:62.

62. Ibid., 5:56–57.

63. See Lindley, *The Trials of Frances Howard*, 163–66, for an interesting discussion of the cultural valence of poisoning.

64. Hume, *History of England*, 5:66.

65. Quoted in John Kenyon, *The History Men: The Historical Profession in England Since the Renaissance*, 2d ed. (London: Weidenfeld and Nicolson, 1993), 27.

66. Hume, *History of England*, 5:121–22.

67. Ibid., 5:121.

68. Ibid.

69. Lindley, *The Trials of Frances Howard*, quoting Wilson, 192.

70. See Julia Kristeva's works for my use of the term "abjection," particularly *Powers of Horror: An Essay on Abjection*, trans. Leon S. Roudiez (New York: Columbia University Press, 1982); and *Strangers to Ourselves*, trans. Leon S. Roudiez (Columbia University Press, 1991). McClintock summarizes Kristeva's use of the term as follows: "Kristeva argues that a social being is constituted through the force of expulsion. In order to become social the self has to expunge certain elements that society deems impure: excrement, menstrual blood, urine, semen, tears, vomit, food, masturbation, incest and so on. For Kristeva, however, these expelled elements can never be fully obliterated; they haunt the edges of the subject's identity with the threat of disruption or even dissolution." *Imperial Leather*, 71.

13

Superstition and the Timid Sex

Jennifer A. Herdt

Hume very rarely focuses his attention specifically on the subject of women and religion, and where he does he seems at first glance only to be repeating cultural commonplaces, affirming a longstanding tradition of blaming women for religious error. One example of this comes in the *Natural History of Religion*, where Hume, in a throwaway comment, claims that the "weak and timid" sex is responsible for leading men into superstition.[1] Although on first reading this looks like a casual derogatory remark about women (and religion), when read in a broader context it can be seen to contain the seeds of a feminist analysis and critique of the ways in which religion reinforces the socialization of women into prescribed sex roles, as well as a critique of those sex roles themselves. Nevertheless, it must be recognized that Hume never develops this analysis and critique. His concern with social order leads him to suppress an inconsistency in his thought: he ultimately affirms the socialization that renders women "weak and timid" because he feels that this is necessary for the maintenance of social order, but at the same time he analyzes induced weakness and timidity as dangerous sources of superstition and eventually of religiously motivated violence.

I

The belief that a special affinity exists between women and superstition can be traced back to the ancient world; Hume supports his own comment by appealing to the authority of the renowned geographer Strabo. Before embarking on a conceptual analysis of Hume's views, it is worth pausing to look back not only at Strabo, but also at a few other significant points in the history of attitudes toward women and religion, as these help to give background and context to Hume's comments on the subject. In the course of his multivolume *Geography*, Strabo discusses a Germanic tribe of which it is said both that they are "god-fearing" and that the men live apart from the women. Strabo finds this utterly contrary to reason and remarks that such an idea "is much opposed to common notions on that subject; for all agree in regarding the women as the chief founders of religion, and it is the women who provoke the men to the more attentive worship of the gods, to festivals, and to supplications, and it is a rare thing for a man who lives by himself to be found addicted to these things."[2] Strabo supports his view of these "common notions" by appealing to the poet Menander, who in one play introduces men complaining of the money the women spend on festivals: "The gods are the undoing of us, especially us married men, for we must always be celebrating some festival." In his play *Misogynes*, Menander's "Woman-hater" complains that "we used to sacrifice five times a day, and seven female attendants would beat the cymbals all round us, while others would cry out to the gods."[3] Whether or not it is contrary to reason to think that a man could be attentive to the gods while living apart from women, it was in fact the case that women were disproportionately active within the mystery cults of the ancient world. This is hardly surprising, since these religions provided an arena in which women could exercise some independence and acquire positions of power and authority. Some religious cults, such as that of Isis, were confined to women, and men tended to find them suspect, speculating about the indecency of the secret rites carried out within such cults.[4]

Something analogous to Strabo's conviction that women are respon- sible for leading men into superstition is also a recurring theme in the Hebrew Scriptures; the men of Israel are warned, before they get to the Promised Land, of the dangers of taking foreign wives who will turn them from Yahweh to worship other gods.[5] Again and again, however, the men of Israel ignored this warning, married foreign wives, and ended up worshiping foreign gods. King Solomon, for instance:

> loved many foreign women . . . from the nations concerning which the Lord had said to the people of Israel, "You shall not enter into marriage with them, neither shall they with you, for surely they will turn away your heart after their gods"; Solomon clung to these in love. He had seven hundred wives, princesses, and three hundred concubines; and his wives turned away his heart. For when Solomon was old his wives turned away his heart after other gods; and his heart was not wholly true to the Lord his God, as was the heart of David his father.[6]

It is not clear by what means Solomon's women are thought to be so successful in drawing their husband to worshiping their own gods, but the fact that this is seen as one of the greatest threats to the survival and integrity of Yahweh's people is unambiguous.[7]

Interreligious marriage could upon occasion work in the other direction as well. At least some of the early Christians believed that a woman's behavior could succeed in drawing a husband into the Christian fold. The letter of 1 Peter urges, "Likewise you wives, be submissive to your husbands, so that some, though they do not obey the word, may be won without a word by the behavior of their wives, when they see your reverent and chaste behavior."[8] Women are here seen as drawing men into the true religion, rather than toward false gods, a notion that runs counter to the dominant tradition but that remains alive as a missionary strategy throughout the first millennium. Noteworthy is the fact that the author specifies that women accomplish this feat not through conversa- tion and rational modes of persuasion, but by their behavior, which exercises some sort of attraction over their husbands.

As the Christian tradition develops, particularly in its Platonic-

Augustinian strand, women (now women in general, not just wives) are again feared for their capacity to draw men away from true religion, rather than draw them to it, but the threat is conceived of rather differently. Women draw men away from the spiritual to the carnal and earthly, and do so primarily through their power to incite lust. It is not the gods women worship or the mode in which they worship that are a threat, but rather that women's very being interferes with the impulse to shed the material world and rise to the spiritual.[9]

During the eighteenth century, however, this longstanding perception of women as a hindrance to men's capacity to draw near to God, a perception that had pervaded Christian culture, was displaced, at least in England and France.[10] Within what has been aptly termed the "culture of sensibility," women were no longer seen as a threat to men's spiritual progress, but rather as naturally pious and as possessing the capacity to soften men's hearts and lead them into true religion, that is, heartfelt religious devotion.[11] Some of the very same features of women's character that had been regarded as weaknesses now came to be seen as moral strengths; their susceptibility to emotion, their delicate nerves, their tears. Detachment from the material world was no longer idealized; instead, emotional responses to that world were to be cultivated, especially pity in the face of suffering. These changes are associated with economic and social developments, such as the rise of a middle-class consumer culture, as well as with a concurrent shift away from Puritan religious ideals. The Latitudinarian Divines, reacting both against Calvinism's pessimistic view of sinful human nature and against Hobbes's claims of fundamental human egoism, preached the natural goodness of human nature. Their sermons pointed to sympathy with suffering as a prime indication of this natural selfless goodness, a goodness that testified, in turn, to the governance of a benevolent rather than a cruel and tyrannical Creator.

Novels gained a new respectability and came to be seen as a powerful school for virtue, one that threatened almost to displace sermons in that capacity.[12] Samuel Richardson, one of the most important sentimental novelists, wrote in 1740 that women, particularly mothers, are the "cause of Virtue and Religion." In his novel Clarissa, the heroine is depicted as possessing the power to convert and reform the rake Lovelace through her exemplary character, which works in concert with her physical beauty.[13]

Although women's power to convert and reform is valued within the culture of sensibility, there remains a fine line that must not be crossed: men's hearts must be softened and converted without being made effeminate and weak. Politeness and sensibility must not come at the cost of a loss of manliness. The loss of masculine strength and self-command would mean the downfall of the public sphere. So the traits for which women were now valued were often regarded as existing to excess in women; only men could possess them in the proper degree and therefore as virtues.

What remains constant from ancient thought through eighteenth-century sentimental novels is the belief that women have a certain power over men, a power not of rational persuasion, but an ability to draw men after them by means of appearance or behavior. What changes is that in the eighteenth century this power is seen as a positive means to lead men to Virtue and Religion, not away from true to false gods or away from spirituality to sinful sensuality, as had predominantly been the view in the past.

Hume is part of this culture of sensibility; he sees compassionate, feeling hearts as a social good, and praises commerce (i.e., social interaction) between the sexes for its capacity to engender such hearts of compassion in men. In "Of the Rise and Progress of the Arts and Sciences" (1742), Hume makes clear the social value of intercourse between the sexes. He sets a very high value on politeness and civility and gives gallantry a place of honor among various forms of polite manners. Whenever association between a male and female takes place, there is "a visible complacency and benevolence, which extends farther, and mutually softens the affections of the sexes towards each other" (MPL 131). Gallantry contributes to the "entertainment and improvement of the youth of both sexes" (MPL 134), but Hume's attention is focused on the benefit to men: "What better school for manners, than the company of virtuous women; where the mutual endeavour to please must insensibly polish the mind, where the example of feminine softness and modesty must communicate itself to their admirers, and where the delicacy of that sex puts every one on his guard, lest he give offence by any breach of decency" (MPL 134). For this reason, women should not be confined to the domestic realm, but should be brought out into the "polite world" and into "good company," where they can soften and polish the roughness of the public male-dominated realm—although this realm should continue to be male dominated.

Hume also (though in a tone of such gallantry that its seriousness seems suspect) suggests that "Women of Sense and Education . . . are much better judges of all polite writing than Men of the same Degree of Understanding," because of the "Delicacy of their Taste, tho' unguided by

Rules" (MPL 536). The importance of delicacy of taste is made clear in "Of the Delicacy of Taste and Passion" (1741). In this essay, although Hume says nothing of women, he does advocate the cultivation of delicacy of taste, which produces "sensibility to beauty and deformity of every kind" and which "improves our sensibility for all the tender and agreeable passions; at the same time that it renders the mind incapable of the rougher and more boisterous emotions" (MPL 4–6). Delicacy of taste is associated with the capacity for sound judgment of character as well as assessment of artistic productions. Thus, delicacy of taste, far from being an irrelevant feature of character, much less a weakness, is closely linked with central moral capacities.

Yet Hume is also a critic of the culture of sensibility, for he sees traditional religious piety as a threat to the public good of sociability, not an ally or an expression of it. In addition, he is sensitive to the underside of feeling, to the ways in which passions flare up in religious zeal and sectarian divisions. Within the culture of sensibility more generally, religion and virtue are almost synonymous; it is primarily men's manners that need to be "converted." For Hume, however, virtue and religion must be separated. Men's associations with women become a double-edged sword if women draw men not only into virtue, but also into superstition.

II

It is from within this social context, this ambiguous relationship to the conventionally religious "culture of sensibility," that Hume writes his *Natural History of Religion* and offers his comment about the "weak and timid" sex:

> What age or period of life is the most addicted to superstition? The weakest and most timid. What sex? The same answer must be given. *The leaders and examples of every kind of superstition, says Strabo, are the women. These excite the men to devotion and supplications, and the observance of religious days. It is rare to meet with one that lives apart from the females, and yet is addicted to such practises. And nothing can, for this reason, be more improbable, than the account given of an order of men amongst the Getes, who practised celibacy, and were notwithstanding the most religious fanatics.* A method of reason-

ing, which would lead us to entertain a very bad idea of the devotion of monks; did we not know by an experience, not so common, perhaps, in *Strabo's* days, that one may practice celibacy, and profess chastity; and yet maintain the closest connexions and more entire sympathy with that timorous and pious sex. (NHR 37; see also MPL 579)

The irony is so thick and tangled here that it is a challenge to unravel. "Superstition" has negative connotations, yet the broader context is a discussion of various things that bring "men to a due sense of religion"— not of superstition. The careful reader of the *Natural History of Religion* finds no real difference between "religion" and "superstition," but it is telling that Hume drops his mask when he talks of women, and not at some other point. Although he accepts the culture of sensibility's link between "timorousness" and piety, he uses this not to praise women, but rather to lay blame on them.

In some respects the real target of Hume's attack here seems not to be the women who "excite" men into superstition, but rather those other "leaders and examples" of superstition, the monks. Is Hume perhaps insinuating that monks' chastity is perhaps *only* professed, and their celibacy suspect? He may be taking advantage here of his readers' antipathy toward all things smacking of "papism." Surely many of his readers would with alacrity have accepted the hint that monks' associations with women were frequently more intimate than those countenanced by the official rules. They would also have seen monks' religiosity as superstitious. But that monks are targeted here does not mean women are not. Rather, it is women who are depicted as the primary source of superstition.

This is puzzling in light of arguments that Hume offers elsewhere that suggest that monks are devoted, even fanatical, in large part because they have been deprived of other more natural cares and interests in life, including connections with women and the possibility of marriage and children. In the *History of England*, Hume analyzes the way in which the Benedictine monks,

carrying farther [than had previous monastic orders] the plausible principles of mortification, secluded themselves entirely from the world, renounced all claim to liberty, and made a merit of the most inviolable chastity. . . . The Roman pontiff, who was making every day great advances towards an absolute sovereignty over the ecclesiastics, perceived that the celibacy of the clergy alone could break off entirely their connexion with the civil power, and, depriving them of every other object of ambition, engage them to promote, with unceasing industry, the grandeur of their order.[14]

Celibacy prevents the formation of the usual social ties, ties that give pleasure and create personal loyalties and commitment to the public good. Monks are left with nothing to which to devote themselves, nothing to which to give their loyalty, apart from the ecclesiastical realm.

The religious devotion of monks and priests is thus induced by their peculiar mode of life, more specifically by their *disconnection* from women and thus from family life. Why, then, does Hume blame women for leading monks into superstition? Perhaps his point is not so much that women are directly responsible for leading monks into superstition (although he could not resist a jab at monastic chastity). Perhaps the more serious point behind his claim that "one may practice celibacy, and profess chastity; and yet maintain the closest connexions and more entire sympathy with that timorous and pious sex" is to point out a special sort of "sympathy" that exists between monks and women. Although women often lead men into superstition, they need not lead *monks* into superstition, since monks get there by a different route. But there is a deep affinity between the feminine virtues and the character traits that the monks value and strive to embody—virtues such as chastity, modesty, humility, and passive suffering.

Before trying to make sense of these affinities and their significance, I pause to explore more fully the phenomenon of superstition and women's tendency toward it. Superstition, according to Hume, arises out of fear of evils and the unknown sources of those evils, and consists in attempts to appease or mollify the invisible powers that seem to play with one's destiny. Since these powers are unknown, the methods employed for this purpose are "unaccountable, and consist in ceremonies, observances, mortifications, sacrifices, presents, or in any practice, however absurd, which either folly or knavery recommends to a blind and terrified credulity" (MPL 74). In the paragraphs immediately preceeding his comment on the weak and timid sex, Hume has been discussing various factors that contribute to superstition. This makes clear that women are a contributing but certainly not the sole or primary cause of superstition, and it also contains important clues to deciphering women's "addiction" to superstition. During times of prosperity, Hume argues, superstition fades; prosperity "engenders cheerfulness and activity and alacrity and a lively enjoyment of every social and sensual pleasure" (NHR 36). Divines can effectively bring men to "a due sense of religion" only by "subduing their confidence and sensuality" (NHR 36).

When Hume thought of the efforts of divines to subdue the confidence and sensuality of their parishioners, he might well have been thinking of the edifying guidance of the *Whole Duty of Man*, that popular treatise according to which Hume had made his boyhood self-examinations. The *Whole Duty of Man* dwelt in particular on the sin of vanity. In order to combat this sin of sins, we must consider ourselves as "worms of the earth . . . polluted and defiled, wallowing in all kinds of sins, and uncleanness," in order to have "such a sense of our own meanness, and his excellency, as may work in us a lowly and unfeigned submission" to God's will and wisdom.[15] Hume did not find that the *Whole Duty of Man* was very successful at subduing his own confidence; Boswell relates that Hume found the task of examining himself according to the treatise "strange work; for instance, to try if, notwithstanding his excelling his schoolfellows, he had no pride or vanity."[16]

There is such tension between men's experience in the everyday world and the account of reality given in religion, that religious belief is hardly worthy of the name. Men, says Hume:

> disguise to themselves their real infidelity, by the strongest asseverations and most positive bigotry. But nature is too hard for all their endeavours, and suffers not the obscure, glimmering light, afforded in those shadowy regions, to equal the strong impressions, made by common sense and experience. The usual course of men's conduct belies their words, and shows, that the assent in these matters is some unaccountable operation of the mind betwixt disbelief and conviction, but approaching much nearer the former than the latter. (NHR 74)

Religion/superstition are thus clearly, for Hume, something artificially induced, which must compete, never with full success, with the natural confidence and sensuality of men.

Priests face a particularly pressing need to sustain their religious convictions. Celibacy may ensure that priests at least will be utterly devoted to clerical power, but the sincerity of their devotion to the spiritual realm is not so easily secured. "Though all mankind have a strong propensity to religion at certain times and in certain dispositions," writes Hume, "yet are there few or none, who have it to that degree, and with that constancy, which is required to support the character of this profession [of priest]" (MPL 199). (This makes one wonder about *womankind's* propensity to religion, a point to which I will return.) Priests find it necessary

> to feign more devotion than they are, at that time, possessed of, and to maintain the appearance of fervor and seriousness, even when jaded with the exercises of their religion, or when they have their minds engaged in the common occupations of life. They must not, like the rest of the world, give scope to their natural movements and sentiments: They must set a guard over their looks and words and actions: And in order to support the veneration paid them by the multitude, they must not only keep a remarkable reserve, but must promote the spirit of superstition, by a continued grimace and hypocrisy. This dissimulation often destroys the candor and ingenuity of their temper, and makes an irreparable breach in their character. (MPL 200)

Priests must be guarded and reserved in their behavior, constantly monitoring the way they are being perceived by others. Since their fervor is not always up to par, they must become hypocrites, pretending a devotion that does not match their inner states, their natural dispositions. This hypocrisy introduces a flaw that in turn warps their entire characters.

Superstition thrives where men are fearful and subdued, because fear gives birth to longing for a higher power on which to rely, and fosters an attitude of awe and submissiveness in the face of this power. Superstition undermines confidence in the value of the manly virtues, which come to seem too assertive, and the monkish virtues step in to take their place. "Where the deity is represented as infinitely superior to mankind," writes Hume, "this belief, though altogether just, is apt, when joined with superstitious terrors, to sink the human mind into the lowest submission and abasement, and to represent the monkish virtues of mortification, penance, humility, and passive suffering, as the only qualities which are acceptable to him" (NHR 62).

If superstition thrives among those who are fearful and subdued, it makes sense to expect it to thrive among the "weak" and "timid" or "timorous" sex. If these characteristics are natural to women, then here those divines who must work so hard to bring men to a due sense of religion will have an easy time of it. The natural diffidence of women will work in favor of superstition just as the natural confidence of men works against it. But are women's weakness and timidity natural? There are places where Hume asserts this, as in "Of the Rise and Progress of the Arts and Sciences," where he comments that "nature has given *man* the superiority above women, by endowing him with greater strength both of mind and body" (MPL 133). Elsewhere he refers to the "tenderness of [women's] complexion" (MPL 565) and "the inferiority of women's capacity," their faculties of both mind and body (MPL 193). But he also suggests that it would be wise if relations between men and women were conducted "with perfect equality, as between two equal members of the same body" (MPL 560). Would this simply be a prudent fiction, engaged in for purposes of harmony between the sexes? Hume has no clear answer to the question of whether the sexes are equal, and if so, in what respects. He does, however, offer something more important to the investigation of women's addiction to superstition: an analysis of the female virtues of chastity and modesty.

That chastity and modesty are artificial virtues, Hume takes to be obvious; "education takes possession of the ductile minds of the fair sex in their infancy."[17] In order that men may be certain that their wives' children are also their own children, men must have confidence in their wives' fidelity. Hume assumes that it would be natural for women to succumb to infidelity: "the temptation here is the strongest imaginable" (T 571). Whatever character traits women "naturally" possess, fidelity to the marriage bed is apparently not one of them. "'Tis necessary, therefore," says Hume, "that, beside the infamy attending such licences, there shou'd be some preceding backwardness or dread, which may prevent their first approaches, and may give the female sex a repugnance to all expressions, and postures, and liberties, that have an immediate relation to that enjoyment" (T 572). As in the case of the artificial virtue of justice, the pragmatic justification for the virtues of chastity and modesty becomes obscured, and they become valued for their own sakes, subject to *moral* approval. It is socialization, therefore, that fosters "backwardness or dread" in women, and this dread is not confined to illicit sexual intercourse. As Hume says, "when a general rule of this kind is once establish'd, men are apt to extend it beyond those principles, from which it first arose" (T 572). Women's "timidity," like their chastity and modesty, is artificial.

Divines must work hard to subdue the confidence and sensuality of men, in order to bring them to superstition. But women's confidence and sensuality have been quite effectively subdued from infancy on. Whereas what men are told from the pulpit fails to conform to the rest of their experience, when women hear the same thing it coheres very well with their self-concept as shaped by other sources of moral authority, from close family to public opinion at large. Religion reinforces the sex roles into which women are socialized. It would thus seem that one, like Hume, who wishes to eliminate superstition would therefore be well advised to give careful attention to the ways in which women are socialized to make them passive and dependent. If women were not socialized into timidity and weakness, they would lose their proclivity to superstition, and so become less likely to pull men into superstition after them.

III

What seems at first glance to be a passing insult to women thus can be interpreted instead as the kernel of a feminist critique of religion, a critique of the ways in which religion works to hinder the flourishing of women. Moreover, it provides the basis for a critique of the ways in which women are socialized into a communally as well as personally harmful addiction to superstition. Yet Hume's critique of religion has not, to my knowledge, been claimed by feminist theologians and critics of religion, who have tended to emphasize their indebtedness to and affinity with liberation and other political theologies. This is not to say, of course, that feminists have not mined other aspects of Hume's thought, including his epistemology and moral philosophy.[18] But the features of Hume's episte-mology and moral philosophy that have contributed most to feminist interest in his writings, that is, his emphasis on human sociability and relationality, on the positive role of the passions and emotions, and on the centrality of sympathy to the moral life, are not regarded as relevant to understanding Hume's critique of religion. The *Dialogues Concerning Natural Religion* and *On Miracles* are seen as epitomizing his approach to religion—that of the cheery skeptic, who delights in uncovering the self-contradictions in religious beliefs, of showing that natural religion and traditional theism are equally devoid of justification. Feminist writing on religion, in contrast, has been less concerned with the justification or critique of isolated religious beliefs in the abstract, and more concerned with pragmatic understandings of religious truth and with the ways in which religious beliefs, language, and activity *function*, in particular how they function to reinforce certain attitudes toward women and their proper role in society. Elizabeth Johnson, for example, writes that "in the course of this program [of feminist theology] one criterion recurs as a touchstone for testing the truth and falsity of theological statements and religious structures. This criterion, variously enunciated, is the emancipation of women towards human flourishing. As a gauge it is applied in a practical way, the adequacy of a religious symbol or custom being assessed according to its effects, for if something consistently results in the denigration of human beings, in what sense can it be religiously true."[19] Feminist religious criticism is, in the largest sense, ethical criticism of religion, (where "criticism" is to be understood as in "social criticism").

Given the traditional perspective on Hume's philosophy of religion, it is hardly surprising that it has not been seen as a resource for feminist thinkers wrestling with the multifaceted phenomenon of religion. It is of course recognized that Hume's interest in religion ranges beyond the issue of justified belief, but these other aspects of his reflection on religion are often seen as derivative. According to such an approach, Hume, having determined that religious beliefs lack justification, became curious about the causes that gave rise to these pseudobeliefs and about their capacity to influence society. The corpus of Hume's writings as a whole makes more sense, however, if his urgent concern with the social and political effects of religious belief is seen as the heart of his project.[20] His analysis of the causes of religious belief and of the self-contradictions inherent in religious belief are impelled by his anxiety about religious zeal and factional strife.

Along with other leading Scottish intellectuals of his day, Hume hoped to promote the transformation of Scotland from a poor and backward province to a civilized, cosmopolitan, and flourishing nation.[21] He regarded factions as one of the greatest threats to social peace and prosperity in general and as one of the most pressing dangers facing eighteenth-century Scotland in particular. Factions, he argued, invariably disrupt trade and destroy social peace and stability: "Factions subvert government, render laws impotent, and beget the fiercest animosities among men of the same nation, who ought to give mutual assistance and protection to each other" (MPL 55). Of all factions, Hume argued that those arising out of religious disputes were particularly pernicious. Religious controversies not only set off the wars that convulsed Europe throughout the sixteenth and seventeenth centuries, but also continued to trouble eighteenth-century Scotland, where rivalries between Moderates and Evangelicals within the Church of Scotland distracted attention from what Hume considered to be the urgent shared interests of the Scottish people.[22]

Much of Hume's critical intellectual reflection was devoted to understanding why groups who profess different religious beliefs tend to become inflamed into irreconcilable factions. "Though theological principles," Hume writes, "when set in opposition to passions, have often small influence on mankind in general, still less on princes; yet when they become symbols of faction, and marks of party distinction, they concur with one of the strongest passions in the human frame, and are then capable of carrying men to the greatest extremities" (H, vol. 2, chap. 68, 579). Human beings have a tendency to form factions based on interest and affection. These can lead to deplorable divisions in society, but there is at least a hope of keeping such divisions under control, or even of eventually resolving them, since they are based on real differences that might be amenable to adjustment.[23] For instance, Hume was convinced that the pursuit of personal wealth makes more resources available for taxation in time of need; hence, there is no real division of interest here between government and individuals.

The key to the intractability of religious factions lies, according to Hume's analysis, in the odd nature of religious belief. When it comes to religious factions, Hume finds no real differences of interest or sentiment to be settled between them, since "the controversy about an article of faith, which is utterly absurd and unintelligible, is not a difference in sentiment, but in a few phrases and expressions, which one party accepts of, without understanding them; and the other refuses in the same manner" (MPL 59). Banding together with others who share one's beliefs provides reinforcement for beliefs that cannot be adequately defended by reasons. Zeal emerges as a defense against the internal contradictions and instability that characterize religious belief; and confrontation with contradictory religious views, rather than destroying belief, as one might anticipate, tends instead to intensify this zeal and engender violent outbursts.

If societies are to be freed of the pernicious effects of religious factions, individuals must either be persuaded to give up their beliefs or they must come to hold these beliefs in a different way. Hume is more sanguine about the possibility of the latter than he is about the former. If only the people could be persuaded that religious belief is utterly irrelevant to practical matters, perhaps religion could be rendered safe, a matter for philosophical speculation or literary creativity rather than a matter for spite and warfare. Hume thinks this should be possible, as he takes it to have been the case in the past: "[R]eligion had, in ancient times, very little influence on common life, and . . . after men had performed their duty in sacrifices and prayers at the temple, they thought, that the gods left the rest of their conduct to themselves, and were little pleased or offended with those virtues or vices, which only affected the peace and happiness of human society" (E 341). The moral philosophy in the *Treatise* and the *Enquiry* is directed toward showing the possibility of understanding the moral sentiments solely in terms of "the peace and happiness of human society," and thus of suggesting that religion may be quite superfluous to morality.

Like feminist critics of religion, then, Hume holds that we must look at the roles played by beliefs within the social contexts in which they are held, seeing how these beliefs contribute (or fail to contribute) to human flourishing. We must not be content to extract these beliefs from their concrete contexts and play logical dissection games with them.[24] But there are other reasons that Hume's writings on religion have not been claimed by feminists. While Hume's approach to religion is in tune with that of feminist thinkers, and his critique of superstition contains feminist implications, he fails to develop these implications. Whereas he challenges the monkish virtues, saying that they should rather be considered vices, he allows chastity and modesty to retain the honorary title of virtues. Although they are artificial, they are, like justice, not to be thrown out on that account. Thus, Hume's critique of religion must itself be subjected to feminist criticism. His reflections on women and religion contain inconsistencies that, when explored, reveal the weakness of some of the elements of his analysis of religion.

IV

Hume's goal is the flourishing of human society, a goal that is shared by many feminist thinkers. Yet (as is understandable given his historical context) he is preoccupied with one particular aspect of that flourishing—lack of conflict. This is particularly evident in his political essays, as I indicated in the previous section, but it is also present within his moral philosophy. Sympathy is central to the development of moral judgment because it allows us to transcend the limited view of things in terms of competing interests. At the same time, our immediate sympathy for those we perceive as similar to ourselves will be stronger than for those we perceive as different, and thus sympathy will itself tend to reinforce factional divisions and conflict unless it is extended and corrected.[25] Our immediate approbation of traits that are useful or agreeable to ourselves or others is not always in agreement with the immediate approbation felt by others; Hume strives to show how properly moral judgments *naturally* emerge out of a process of conflict *avoidance* at increasingly reflective levels of moral judgment. The achievement of social stability and the achievement of stability in moral judgment are intimately linked in Hume's thought.

Hume is generally resistant, therefore, to changes in the status quo that will threaten or simply fail to help secure the goal of peace or absence of conflict. Since religious zeal and faction clearly threaten peace and security, he devotes considerable effort to understanding these phenomena and striving to diffuse them. Yet he does not fully appreciate the dangers that women's virtues pose to the social order. There is one point at which Hume seems to get a glimpse of this; it comes in his remarks on revenge: "Revenge is a natural passion to mankind; but seems to reign with the greatest force in priests and women: Because, being deprived of the immediate exertion of anger, in violence and combat, they are apt to fancy themselves despised on that account; and their pride supports their vindictive disposition" (MPL 201). The virtues inculcated in priests and women require the repression of anger and assertiveness, passions that can be expected to break out in other, often more destructive, ways. But the dangers posed by women's repressed passions are hidden from Hume by the fact that women do not form a faction or party; they are physically dispersed, attached to various households, and see their interests as lying with those of their household, not with other women. Hume looks to factions as the source of religious conflict, and thus underestimates the impact that women can have. Of priests, in contrast, he notes that "all wise governments will be on their guard against the attempts of a society, who will for ever combine into one faction, and while it acts as a society, will forever be actuated by ambition, pride, revenge, and a persecuting spirit (MPL 201).

Even more important, Hume is already persuaded that women's virtues have a positive, not a negative, social role to play. Chastity and modesty secure social stability by assuring men that their wives' children are also their own offspring and thereby inducing men to support these children and remain within the marriage bond. Since Hume is convinced that the way in which women are socialized reinforces peace and order, he fails fully to discern the implications of his own argument that the induced psychological weakness and timidity of women may well, through their consequent "addiction" to superstition, become a potent threat to social stability.

What Hume does not fully absorb is the fact that the same social practice may serve both to eliminate one potential source of conflict and to contribute to another source of conflict. There are two possible responses to this realization—one quantitative and the other qualitative. The quantitative approach would retain lack of conflict as the primary measure of social flourishing and would consider whether a practice contributes more to creating conflict or to easing conflict or consider whether a given set of practices leads to more or less conflict overall than a competing set of practices. In a case in which a practice contributed equally to engendering as to easing conflict, however, one would presumably have no way to decide for or against the practice. This points to the inadequacy of lack of conflict as the criterion of flourishing and suggests that what is needed is a qualitative rather than a quantitative response.

On the qualitative response, one would attend to the salient differences between different kinds of conflict and conflict-free states. Does existing conflict reflect attempts by some individuals or groups to challenge social inequities or to draw attention to issues that are being ignored? Is conflict absent because some individuals are being deceived by others or by themselves? Is conflict absent because some individuals are too afraid of repercussions to speak up and assert themselves? Or is conflict absent because all members of the society can contribute freely and meaningfully to shared goals? This approach would lead in the direction of concluding that the sort of peace that is constitutive of human flourishing is a *just* peace, not a mere absence of conflict. Without a capacity for qualitative, that is, normative, evaluation of social practices in light of more than the single value of absence of conflict, blind spots such as Hume's will be impossible to avoid.

Hume does offer an additional way in which to distinguish between ways of life that contribute to human flourishing and those that do not. In taking conflict as a criterion of evaluation, one looks at the consequences of a social practice. One can instead, Hume suggests, consider whether a person or set of persons is living an "artificial" or a "natural" form of life. This is to look not at consequences of practices, but rather at their source. Living an artificial life is radically different from living a life in which artificial virtues have a role to play. The artificial virtues, justice most centrally, are human conventions that arise directly "from the circumstances and necessities of mankind" (T 477) and that respond in useful and beneficial ways to these circumstances and necessities. Hume remarks that "mankind is an inventive species; and where an invention is obvious and absolutely necessary, it may as properly be said to be natural as any thing and proceeds immediately from original principles, without the intervention of thought or reflexion. Tho' the rules of justice be *artificial*, they are not *arbitrary*. Nor is the expression improper to call them *Laws of Nature*; if by natural we understand what is common to any species, or even if we confine it to mean what is inseparable from the species" (T 484). In certain key respects, therefore, the artificial virtue of justice is natural: it is obvious, absolutely necessary, requires no thought, is not arbitrary, and is common to the species. The same cannot be said for artificial lives.

The notion of artificial lives is most fully discussed in the "Dialogue," which Hume appends to the *Enquiries Concerning the Principles of Morals*. A discussion of the diversity of manners and morals leads Hume to respond to his skeptical interlocutor with the familiar Humean claim that all virtues are either useful or agreeable to the possessor or to those connected with the possessor: "For what other reason can ever be assigned for praise or approbation? Or where would be the sense of extolling a *good* character or action, which, at the same time, is allowed to be *good for nothing*? All the differences, therefore, in morals, may be reduced to this one general foundation, and may be accounted for by the different views, which people take of these circumstances" (E 336). It must be conceded that this view leaves room for very significant differences in morals. Hume's basic suggestion that good things must be good for something is almost as formal and empty as Kant's categorical imperative, or the first principle of practical reason in Aquinas's natural law: Good is to be pursued and evil is to be avoided. We need not assume that Hume is resting here on a substantive account of human nature, from which one might attempt to derive a list of virtues. But his principle does, he believes, exclude a certain class of candidates for the title "virtue."

It is here that artificial lives enter in. Palamedes, the skeptic, suggests to Hume that "What you insist on . . . may have some foundation, when you adhere to the maxims of common life and ordinary conduct. Experience and the practice of the world readily correct any great extravagance on either side. But what say you to *artificial* lives and manners?" (E 341). By "artificial lives," Palamedes explains that he means ancient philosophical schools, on the one hand, and modern religion, on the other. Both seek to regulate human conduct, and do so on the basis of abstract speculative principles that have no immediate connection with concrete human existence and that are applied with an inflexibility that frustrates the pursuit of the concrete goods of ordinary life. Hume's reply is that "when men depart from the maxims of common reason, and affect these *artificial* lives, as you call them, no one can answer for what will please or displease them. They are in a different element from the rest of mankind; and the natural principles of their mind play not with the same regularity, as if left to themselves, free from the illusions of religious superstition or philosophical enthusiasm" (E 343). There is no limit to what may be prescribed and praised when directives for ordinary life are derived from speculative systems, and the prescriptions claim finality and infallibility, since they are rooted in the metaphysical rather than the changing physical realm. Hume is confident that when the "natural principles" of the mind are followed, in contrast, there is room for change and development in one's moral judgments, room for responsiveness to changing circumstances, room for fallibilism, room for acceptance of variations—except for those dictated by abstract speculation. Most important, artificial lives, in contrast with natural lives, are good for nothing; the virtues they embody are neither agreeable nor useful to anyone.

This conviction of the artificiality of religious lives is at the heart of Hume's well-known critique of the monkish virtues; "where men judge of things by their natural, unprejudiced reason, without the delusive glosses of superstition and false religion," they will see that the monkish "virtues" are really vices, since they are neither useful nor agreeable.[26] Hume observes that the monkish virtues "serve no matter of purpose; neither advance a man's fortune in the world, nor render him a more valuable member of society; neither qualify him for the entertainment of company, nor increase his power of self-enjoyment. . . . We observe, on the contrary, that they cross all these desirable ends; stupify the understanding and harden the heart, obscure the fancy and sour the temper" (E 270).

Crucial to Hume's critique of these virtues is his claim that no superstition has "force sufficient among men of the world, to pervert entirely these natural sentiments [that is, sentiments that the monkish virtues are really vices]" (E 270). This fact proves to Hume that the monkish virtues find their place only in artificial lives.

The monkish virtues do after all serve a purpose, though (just not one that Hume appreciates): prescribed by a certain set of speculative beliefs, they act in turn to reinforce these beliefs and reduce the sense of conflict between the "usual course of men's conduct" and their religious beliefs. Monks lack the usual human ties to spouses and children; this serves to reinforce their ties to fellow monks and to the church. Even then, the conflict continues, and zeal is a likely outcome, compensating in its intensity for the instability of belief. Another likely result is violent opposition to differing beliefs—one fights on behalf of that for which one lacks good reasons. The artificiality of religious lives thus leads us back to the problem of conflict.

When we turn to consider the situation of women within the Christian tradition, rather than that of Hume's not-so-generic "man," it becomes much more difficult to distinguish the "usual course of [wo]men's conduct" from their speculative religious beliefs, and thus more difficult to differentiate natural from artificial lives. This is captured vividly by Mary Daly's critique of Christian morality:

> There has been a *theoretical* one-sided emphasis upon charity, meekness, obedience, humility, self-abnegation, sacrifice, service. Part of the problem with this moral ideology is that it has become accepted not by men but by women, who hardly have been helped by an ethic which reinforces the abject female situation. Of course, oppressed males are forced to act out these qualities in the presence of their "superiors." However, in the presence of females of the oppressed racial or economic class, the mask is dropped. Basically, then, the traditional morality of our culture has been "feminine" in the sense of hypocritically idealizing some of the qualities imposed upon the oppressed.[27]

Since women actually embody the moral values, such as chastity and modesty, to which men give only lip service, corresponding religious beliefs (representing God as an all-powerful monarch, in contrast to whom human beings are utterly weak, passive, and evil) can be expected to come more "naturally" to women. As long as this is so, women will be less likely than men to feel a sense of conflict between their self-understanding in an everyday and in a religious context. Their religious beliefs will be more sincere, less "hypocritical" than those of men, including those of priests. This may mean that they are less likely than men to resort to zeal and violence to reinforce their beliefs, but it will also mean that the distinction between artificial and natural life may not seem clear to them. "Common sense and experience" reinforce the former to such an extent that the latter will have to be constructed, not discovered. An appeal to nature is inadequate; creative imagination must provide assistance in envisioning the "nature" of a flourishing life for women. Complicating matters here is the fact that women are not cut off, as are priests and monks, from familial relationships. Quite the contrary, women's virtues are particularly suited to the sphere of the family, to tending selflessly the needs of husband and children. This makes their role and its virtues seem much more natural than the monkish virtues. Attending to the case of women's "addiction" to superstition thus helps to reveal the inadequacy of Hume's assumptions about the possibility of distinguishing natural from artificial lives. Normative assessments of virtues and forms of life are not as simple as the categories "natural" and "artificial" seem to suggest.[28]

Just as with the monkish virtues, the virtues embodied by women do serve a purpose; they help to reinforce patriarchal power and make that power seem natural—inevitable and benign. Hume is occasionally able to see male claims of authority over women as neither benign nor inevitable. In a passage I cited earlier from "Of Love and Marriage," for instance, he first chides women for their lust for power, then suggests that this is only a reaction against the tyranny of men: "Tyrants, we know, produce rebels; and all history informs us, that rebels, when they prevail, are apt to become tyrants in their turn. For this reason, I could wish there were no pretensions to authority on either side; but that every thing was carried on with perfect equality, as between two equal members of the same body" (MPL 560). But this is a passing comment, and Hume is not one to advocate thoroughgoing social change—for such change would undoubtedly engender conflict.

If Hume has only glimpses of the problematic nature of hierarchical relationships between women and men, he mounts a more forceful critique of hierarchical thinking about the deity. "Where the gods," in contrast, "are conceived to be only a little superior to mankind . . . we are more at our ease in our addresses to them, and may even, without profaneness, aspire sometimes to a rivalship and emulation of them. Hence activity, spirit, courage, magnanimity, love of liberty, and all the virtues, which aggrandize a people" (NHR 62–63). But Hume fails to notice what Daly points out, that the Calvinist insistence on the sovereignty of God creates a hierarchical paradigm within which men are given license to play God with respect to women. Since he overlooks this hidden payoff to men, he fails to understand why men cling to hierarchical thinking about God with such tenacity.[29] Do men really want women to aspire to "rivalship and emulation" of men? "Activity, spirit, courage, and magnanimity" are certainly not among Hume's list of approved feminine virtues.

There is another twist to the hierarchy question that neither Hume nor Daly appreciates. God as transcendent sovereign not only provides a model for male sovereignty, but also a basis for critique of all human authority. Insisting on God's sovereignty can, that is, be a way of calling into question all human claims of sovereignty. No man really is like God in the relevant respects (omniscience, omnipotence, benevolence), and thus men are not justified in asserting authority over women. How is this to be factored into the broader analysis of hierarchical thinking? Is hierarchy, like conflict and artificiality, inadequate as a criterion for assessing human flourishing?

A feminist analysis of Hume's critique of religion thus brings to light several flaws in his assumptions and approach. First, using lack of conflict as a criterion for human flourishing is insufficient. Some forms of conflict may enhance human flourishing, and even more important, lack of conflict may sometimes mask situations of injustice. Second, using a distinction between artificial and natural lives in order to critique religious ethics is inadequate. On the one hand, it simply allows Hume to reject any supposed form of life that does not meet his own criteria for usefulness and agreeability. On the other hand, not everything that appears to be a natural form of life is worthy of reflective approbation. Finally, Hume fails to follow through on his critique of hierarchical relations and thus does not perceive the structural role played within patriarchy by hierarchical conceptualizations of the divine-human relationship. Identifying these flaws helps us understand why Hume, despite the fact that so many elements of his thought resonate with feminist philosophers, himself held rather ambiguous views on women and their capacities.

There are aspects of Hume's analysis of religion that are of considerable value for feminists. His analysis and critique of religion and of society at large is, like that of feminists, directed toward the end of enhancing human flourishing. His achievements and blunders in this regard can help others reflecting on how such flourishing is to be understood and pursued. Most important, Hume offers a paradigmatic investigation of the significance of religious socialization in shaping character and society and prepares the ground for exploring the role that gender plays in this complex process.

Notes

1. David Hume, *The Natural History of Religion and Dialogues Concerning Natural Religion*, ed. John Vladimir Price (Oxford: Clarendon Press, 1976), 37. (Subsequent references will be given parenthetically and the work's title abbreviated as "NHR.") Similarly, in "Of Suicide" Hume notes that the gaiety and sweetness of temper commonly possessed by the "fair sex" are often marred by superstition. In *Essays: Moral, Political, and Literary*, ed. Eugene F. Miller (Indianapolis: Liberty Classics, 1985), 578–79. (Subsequent parenthetical references will be to "MPL".)

2. Strabo, *Geography*, Loeb Classical Library, 1924, 7.3.4.

3. Menander, cited in Strabo, *Geography*, 7.3.4.

4. Michael Massey, *Women in Ancient Greece and Rome* (Cambridge: Cambridge University Press, 1988), 10–11; 28–29. See also Gillian Clark, *Women in the Ancient World* (Oxford: Oxford University Press, 1989), 33–37.

5. See Deut. 7.4, 17.17. The prophets Ezra and Nehemiah invoke these warnings and explain Israel's troubles by reference to them: Ezra 2.3, 10.44; Neh. 13.23–27.

6. 1 Kings 11.1–6.

7. Scholars have argued that these foreign wives came from matrilineal societies. In introducing the worship of their gods, they were also introducing matriliny. This was a great threat to the patrilineal structures of the tribes of Israel. See Nancy Jay, *Throughout Your Generations Forever: Sacrifice, Religion, and Paternity* (Chicago: University of Chicago Press, 1992), chap. 7.

8. 1 Peter 3.1–2.

9. For discussions of images of women within the Christian tradition, see Barbara J. MacHaffie, *Her Story: Women in Christian Tradition* (Philadelphia: Fortress Press, 1986) and the essays in Rosemary Radford Ruether, ed., *Religion and Sexism: Images of Women in the Jewish and Christian Traditions* (New York: Simon and Schuster, 1974).

10. A parallel development in Germany is discussed in Robert Norton, *The Beautiful Soul: Aesthetic Morality in the Eighteenth Century* (Ithaca: Cornell University Press, 1995). I am indebted to Jan Lüder Hagens for this reference.

11. See G. J. Barker-Benfield, *The Culture of Sensibility: Sex and Society in Eighteenth-Century Britain* (Chicago: University of Chicago Press, 1992), 217–58.

12. In this regard, it is worth noting how many female novelists there were at this time. Thus, women played an active role in shaping the culture of sensibility. See Barker-Benfield, *The Culture of Sensibility*, xvii.

13. Ibid., 250.

14. David Hume, *The History of England* (Philadelphia: M'Carty & Davis, 1836), vol. 1, chap. 2, 52. (Subsequent parenthetical references will be to "H".)

15. [Richard Allestree,] *The practice of Christian graces or the Whole Duty of Man* (London: D. Maxwell for T. Garthwait, 1658), Pt. II, § 1–3.

16. James Boswell, *Private Papers of James Boswell*, vol. 12, ed. Geoffrey Scott and Frederick A. Pottle (Mount Vernon, N.Y.: W. E. Rudge, 1931), 227–28.

17. David Hume, *A Treatise of Human Nature*, ed. L. A. Selby-Bigge, rev. P. H. Nidditch (Oxford: Clarendon Press, 1978), 572. (Subsequent parenthetical references will be to "T".)

18. See, notably, the writings of Annette Baier, especially "Hume, the Women's Moral Theorist?" and "Hume; The Reflective Women's Epistemologist?" both in *Moral Prejudices: Essays on Ethics* (Cambridge: Harvard University Press, 1994), 51–94.

19. Elizabeth A. Johnson, *She Who Is: The Mystery of God in Feminist Theological Discourse* (New York: Crossroad, 1992), 30. See also Rosemary Radford Ruether, *Sexism and God-Talk* (Boston: Beacon Press, 1983), 18–19.

20. For a more fully developed argument in support of this claim, see my *Religion and Faction in Hume's Moral Philosophy* (Cambridge: Cambridge University Press, 1997), introduction and chap. 5.

21. See Phillipson's works, particularly his essays "Towards a Definition of the Scottish Enlightenment," in Paul S. Fritz and David Williams, eds., *City and Society in the Eighteenth Century*, 125–47 (Toronto: Hakkert, 1973) and "Culture and Society in the Eighteenth Century Province: The Case of Edinburgh and the Scottish Enlightenment," in Lawrence Stone, ed., *The University in Society*, vol. 2, *Europe, Scotland, and the United States from the Sixteenth to the Twentieth Century*, 407–48 (Princeton: Princeton University Press, 1974). The essays in Istvan Hont and Michael Ignatieff, ed., *Wealth and Virtue: The Shaping of Political Economy in the Scottish Enlightenment* (Cambridge: Cambridge University Press, 1983) are also relevant.

22. Richard Sher and Alexander Murdoch, "Patronage and Party in the Church of Scotland, 1750–1800," in Norman MacDougall, ed., *Church, Politics, and Society: Scotland 1408–1929* (Edinburgh: John Donald, 1983), 213. See also Callum G. Brown, *The Social History of Religion in Scotland Since 1730* (London: Methuen, 1987), 22–32, and Ian D. L. Clark, "From Protest to Reaction: The Moderate Regime in the Church of Scotland, 1752–1805," in N. T. Phillipson and Rosalind Mitchison, eds., *Scotland in the Age of Improvement: Essays in Scottish History in the Eighteenth Century* (Edinburgh: Edinburgh University Press, 1970), 200–24.

23. John Robertson, "The Scottish Enlightenment at the Limits of the Civic Tradition," in Istvan Hont and Michael Ignatieff, eds., *Wealth and Virtue* (Cambridge: Cambridge University Press, 1983), 154.

24. Such games might nonetheless have a place—they are a useful tool to deploy against those whose chief delight is in such games. This is the role played, I would suggest, by writings such as the *Dialogues Concerning Natural Religion*. The *Dialogues* will keep the philosophical theists busy and distract them from attempting any concrete expression of their religious beliefs. See Jennifer A. Herdt, "Opposite Sentiments: Hume's Fear of Faction and the Philosophy of Religion," *American Journal of Theology and Philosophy* 16 (1995): 245–59.

25. See my *Religion and Faction in Hume's Moral Philosophy*, chaps. 2 and 4.

26. David Hume, *Enquiries Concerning Human Understanding and Concerning the Principles of Morals*, ed. L. A. Selby-Bigge, rev. P. H. Nidditch (Oxford: Clarendon Press, 1975), 270. (Subsequent parenthetical references will be to "E".)

27. Mary Daly, *Beyond God the Father: Toward a Philosophy of Women's Liberation* (Boston: Beacon Press, 1973), 100–101.

28. I do think that Hume does, in other contexts, move towards developing more fruitful approaches to comparative moral assessment. His claims about artificial lives constitute one of the more vulnerable parts of his moral philosophy. See my *Religion and Faction in Hume's Moral Philosophy*, esp. chap. 4.

29. Johnson argues that traditional speech about God is idolatrous: "Insofar as male-dominant language is honored as the only or the supremely fitting way of speaking about God, it absolutizes a single set of metaphors and obscures the height and depth and length and breadth of divine mystery. Thus it does damage to the very truth of God that theology is supposed to cherish and promote" (*She Who Is*, 18). According to Johnson, such speech about God impairs human flourishing *and* damages the truth of God. Hume, of course, thinks that human flourishing is best secured without any God-talk at all. Johnson might argue that this demonstrates a lack of creativity on his part; he sees no other way of talking about God than those ways of the past that have impeded human flourishing. But to enter on this would be to raise the possibility of a *religious* critique of Hume's thought, which is not the subject of this essay.

Bibliography

Publications on Hume of Interest to Feminist Philosophers

Baier, Annette. "Good Men's Women: Hume on Chastity and Trust." *Hume Studies* 5 (April 1979): 1–19.

———. "Hume, the Women's Moral Theorist." In Eva Feder Kittay and Diana T. Meyers, eds., *Women and Moral Theory*, 37–55. Lanham, Md.: Rowman and Littlefield, 1987.

———. *Moral Prejudices.* Cambridge: Harvard University Press, 1994.

Bar On, Bat-Ami. "Could There Be a Humean Sex-Neutral General Idea of Man? *Philosophy Research Archives* 13 (1987–88): 367–77.

Battersby, Christine. "An Enquiry Concerning the Humean Woman." *Philosophy* 56 (July 1981): 303–12.

Bell, Linda A. "Gallantry: What It Is and Why It Should Not Survive." *Southern Journal of Philosophy* 22 (Summer 1984): 165–74.

Bracken, Harry M. "Essence, Accident, and Race." *Hermathena* 16 (Winter 1973): 81–96.

———. "Philosophy and Racism." *Philosophia* 8 (November 1978): 241–60.

Burns, Steven. "The Humean Female." *Dialogue* 15 (September 1976): 415–24.

Immerwahr, John. "David Hume, Sexism, and Sociobiology." *Southern Journal of Philosophy* 21 (Fall 1983): 359–70.

———"Incorporating Gender Issues in Modern Philosophy." *Teaching Philosophy* (September 1990): 241–52.

Kenelly, Laura B. "Women, Religion, and Zeal: Hume's Rhetoric in the *History of England.*" In Kevin L. Cope, ed., *Compendious Conversations: The Method of Dialogue in the Early Enlightenment.* Frankfurt am Main: Peter Lang, 1992.

Korsmeyer, Carolyn W. "Hume and the Foundations of Taste." *Journal of Aesthetics and Art Criticism* 35 (Winter 1976): 201–15.

Levey, Ann. "Under Constraint: Chastity and Modesty in Hume." *Hume Studies* 23 (November 1997): 213–26.

Lloyd, Genevieve. *The Man of Reason: "Male" and "Female" in Western Philosophy.* 2d ed. Minneapolis: University of Minnesota Press, 1993.

Marcil-Lacoste, Louise. "The Consistency of Hume's Position on Women." *Dialogue* 15 (1976): 425–40.

Sapp, Vicki J. "The Philosopher's Seduction: Hume and the Fair Sex." *Philosophy and Literature* 19 (April 1995): 1–15.

Publications Discussing the Nonskeptical Interpretation of Hume

Baier, Annette. *A Progress of Sentiments: Reflections on Hume's "Treatise."* Cambridge: Harvard University Press, 1991. See also the Baier works above and her essay in the present volume.

Capaldi, Nicholas. "The Dogmatic Slumber of Hume Scholarship." *Hume Studies* 18 (November 1992): 117–35.

Garrett, Don. *Cognition and Commitment in Hume's Philosophy.* New York: Oxford University Press, 1997.

Jacobson, Anne Jaap. "Inductive Scepticism and Experimental Reasoning on Moral Subjects in Hume's Philosophy." *Hume Studies* 15 (November 1989): 325–38.

King, James T. "Despair and Hope in Hume's Introduction to the 'Treatise of Human Nature.'" *Hume Studies* 20 (April 1994): 59–71.

Loeb, Louis E. "Stability, Justification, and Hume's Propensity to Ascribe Identity to Objects." *Philosophical Topics* 19 (Spring 1991): 237–70.

McIntyre, Jane L. "Hume: Second Newton of the Moral Sciences." *Hume Studies* 20 (April 1994): 3–18.

Norton, David Fate, ed. *The Cambridge Companion to Hume.* Cambridge: Cambridge University Press, 1993.

Owen, David. "Philosophy and the Good Life: Hume's Defence of Probable Reasoning." *Dialogue* 35 (Summer 1996): 485–503.

Penelhum, Terence. *David Hume: An Introduction to His Philosophical System.* West Lafayette: Purdue University Press, 1992.

Read, Rupert, and Kenneth Richman. *The New Hume.* London: Routledge, 2000.

Stewart, M. A., and John P. Wright, eds., *Hume and Hume's Connexions.* University Park: Pennsylvania State University Press, 1995.

Swain, Corliss Gayda. "Being Sure of One's Self: Hume on Personal Identity." *Hume Studies* (November 1991): 107–24.

Wright, John P. "Hume's Academic Scepticism: A Reappraisal of His Philosophy of Human Understanding. *Canadian Journal of Philosophy* 16 (September 1986): 407–35.

Notes on Contributors

ANNETTE BAIER is Distinguished Service Professor Emerita at the University of Pittsburg. Author of many contributions to the philosophical literature, she has been, among other things, president of the American Philosophical Association. Her recent publications include *The Commons of the Mind* (*the Paul Carus Lectures*) (Open Court, 1997), *Moral Prejudices* (Harvard University Press, 1994) and *A Progress of Sentiments: Reflections on Hume's "Treatise"* (Harvard University Press, 1991).

JENNIFER HERDT is an assistant professor of religious ethics at New College of the University of South Florida. She is the author of *Religion and Faction in Hume's Moral Philosophy* (Cambridge University Press, 1997), which explores Hume's concept of sympathy in relation to tragedy, taste, history, and religion. She has published articles in the *American Catholic Philosophical Quarterly*, the *American Journal of Theology and Philosophy*, the *Journal of Religion*, and *Soundings*. She received her B.A. from Oberlin College and her Ph.D. from Princeton University and was a postdoctoral research fellow at the University of Notre Dame.

NANCY J. HIRSCHMANN is associate professor of government at Cornell University, and a fellow at the Institute for Advanced Study in Princeton for the 1998–99 academic year. She is the author of *Rethinking Obligation: A Feminist Method for Political Theory* (Cornell University Press, 1992), co-editor with Christine Di Stefano of *Revisioning the Political: Feminist Reconstructions of Traditional Concepts in Western Political Theory* (Westview Press, 1996), and co-editor with Ulrike Liebert of *Between the Cradle and the Grave: Feminist Theoretical and Empirical Perspectives on the Social Welfare State* (Rutgers University Press, forthcoming). She is currently finishing her latest book, which is a feminist analysis of the concept of freedom, and co-editing, with Kirstie M. McClure, *Feminist Interpretations of Locke* for the Re-reading the Canon series.

SHERIDAN HOUGH is assistant professor of philosophy at the College of Charleston, where she also serves as editor of the women's studies magazine *The Forum*. She has published articles on a variety of topics in nineteenth-century philosophy and phenomenology, and her most recent work focuses on the very notion of female *nature*. She is the author of *Nietzsche's Noontide Friend: The Self as Metaphoric Double* (Pennsylvania State University Press, 1997).

ANNE JAAP JACOBSON, former president of the Northeast Society for Eighteenth-Century Studies, is an associate professor of philosophy at the University of Houston, where she is founding chair of the Cognitive Science Initiative. Her B.Phil. and D.Phil. are from Oxford University, at which she also held two research fellowships. Her published work is on epistemology, philosophy of mind, metaphysics, and early modern philosophy. In several recent papers she has argued against central aspects of the cognitivist program in cognitive science.

JOYCE JENKINS is associate professor of philosophy at the University of Manitoba. Her main interest is political philosophy. Her recent publications include "Art Against Equality" in *Philosophy and Literature*.

GENEVIEVE LLOYD is professor of philosophy at the University of New South Wales, Sydney, Australia. She is a graduate of the University of Sydney and Oxford University and is a fellow of the Australian Academy of the Humanities. She is the author of *The Man of Reason: 'Male' and 'Female' in Western Philosophy* (Methuen, 1984; 2d ed. Routledge, 1993), *Being in Time: Selves and Narrators in Philosophy and Literature* (Routledge, 1993), *Part of Nature: Self-Knowledge in Spinoza's Ethics* (Cornell University Press, 1994) and *Spinoza and the Ethics* (Routledge, 1996).She has published articles on seventeenth- and eighteenth-century philosophy, on philosophy and literature, and on feminist philosophy. Her book, jointly authored with Moira Gatens, *Collective Imaginings: Spinoza, Past and Present*, is forthcoming with Routledge (U.K.) She is currently editing a four-volume collection of papers on Spinoza in the Routledge Critical Assessments series.

SUSAN MARTINELLI-FERNANDEZ earned a Ph.D. from the University of Chicago. She is assistant professor of philosophy at Western Illinois University and is currently vice president of the Illinois Philosophical Association. She teaches courses in applied ethics, the history of ethics, and feminist theory. She is co-director of the Program for the Study of Ethics and coordinator of "Workshop on Education and Moral Development," an interdisciplinary workshop. Her main interests are the works of Hume and Kant (moral and political philosophy, moral education, and moral psychology) as well as their relationship to feminist theory and issues and has delivered papers in these areas. She has completed grant-funded research on seventeenth- and eighteenth-century role models in literature and is working on a book-length manuscript based on this research.

ROBERT SHAVER is professor of philosophy at the University of Manitoba. His main interest is ethics. His recent publications include *Rational Egoism* (Cambridge University Press).

AARON SMUTS is a graduate student in philosophy at the University of Texas at Austin. He graduated from the University of Houston in 1996 with a double major in philosophy and history. Primarily he is interested in the philosophy of art and American cultural history and plans on pursuing a Ph.D., specializing in classical Hollywood cinema and the analytic philosophy of film.

CHRISTINE SWANTON is a professor of philosophy at the University of Auckland, New Zealand. She has published a number of papers in ethics and political philosophy. She is currently writing a book on virtue ethics. Her book, *Freedom: A Coherence Theory*, won the Johnsonian Prize.

KATHRYN TEMPLE teaches eighteenth-century literature and culture at Georgetown University. She is currently finishing a book called *Literary Scandals: Authorship and National Identity in Eighteenth-Century Britain* and has published articles in the *Yale Journal* and *Law and Humanities*. She is the recipient of an American Council for Learned Societies research grant, of a Folger Shakespeare Library seminar grant, and of a American Society for Eighteenth-Century Studies research grant. Her Ph.D. is from the University of Virginia; she also has a law degree from Emory University School of Law.

JACQUELINE TAYLOR is assistant professor in the department of philosophy at Tufts University. Her current research centers on Hume's ethics and moral psychology and on the implications of feminist thought for virtue ethics.

CHRISTOPHER WILLIAMS is associate professor of philosophy at the University of Nevada, Reno. He is the author of A Cultivated Reason: An Essays on Hume and Humeanism (Pennsylvania State University Press, 1999). His interests are in aesthetics, ethics, and the philosophy of mind.

Index

tion of reason and, 100–101; justice discussed in, 139–43; reason and nature metaphor in, 94–96, 219–20; religion discussed in, 300–305; sensible knave and honest man in, 201–5; skepticism in, 77–78, 85–86; *Treatise* compared with, 96–98; Virtue prototype in, 202–5, 216n.14; women discussed in, 146–53

environmentalists, moral education and, 195–98, 203–5, 216n.13

"Epicurean, The," 50–52

epistemological theory: feminist morality and, 176–78; Hume and, 19–36

Essays, 35, 135n.28

essentialism: ethics of care and, 176, 191n.5; Hume on, 11; justice and, 207–10; moral development and, 195–97, 203–5, 216n.13

Essex, Earl of, 271–72

ethics: feminist theory and, 10–11; of virtue, 156–72

ethics of care: Humean sympathy and, 175–78; Hume's philosophy and, 9–10, 152, 155n.26, 157–72

exemplars, Hume's use of, 201–5

experience: Humean sympathy and, 179–85; feminism and, 177–78

external world, Hume's concept of, 7, 60, 71–75

fact-value distinction, in Hume's work, 17, 107–33

Falk, David, 123

falsity, Hume's discussion of aesthetics and, 241–44, 255–59, 260n.6

familial metaphor in Hume, 232, 237nn.51–52

familiarity, role of, in intellectual life, 48–49

"Feminism, Ideology and Deconstruction," 90

feminist standpoint theory, 206–7, 211–12

feminist theory: aesthetic criticism and, 255–59; cognitive science and, 64–67; connected knowing and, 176–78; epistemological aspects of Hume, 19–36; equality of taste and, 131–33, 136n.43; essentialism and, 195–97; history and gender studies and, 266–78, 279n.12; Humean reconstruction and, 185–91; Hume's philosophy and, 56–58; ideal of pure reason and, 61–83; metaphor and, 89–90, 105n.14; moral education and, 211–12; religious philosophy and, 294–97, 302–5; resources on, 5–13, 17n.14;

scholarship on Hume and, 1–5, 13–17; social construction in Hume and, 194–215; sympathy and empathy in Hume and, 175–78, 180–91; virtues and, 17, 18n.24; Western canon and, ix–xi

Fetterly, Judith, 262n.28

fiction, Hume's historical writing and, 265, 280n.17

Flew, Antony, 70

Foot, Philippa, 9, 165, 173n.10

Forbes, Duncan, 179, 181–82

Foucault, Michel, 33

foundationalism, Hume's philosophy and, 3–4

Fragmentation of Reason, The, 65

freedom, Hume's defense of, 33

Freeland, Cynthia, 105n.15

Freud, Sigmund, 66

Galbraith, Agnes, 236n.18

gaming metaphor, Hume's use of, 47–56

Gauthier, David, 153nn.5 and 6, 154n.15

Gay Science, 222

gender: in historical writings of Hume, 12, 264, 266–78; Hume on origins of, 218–19; of imagination and reason, 98–101; justice and, Hume's theory of and, 9; metaphors concerning, 7, 15–16, 85–90, 105n.15; moral obligation and, 195–97, 266–67; national identity and, 264, 279n.5; natural boundaries of, 223, 236n.26; nature of nature for Hume and, 220–21; object relations theory and, 176; skepticism of Hume and, 85–103; social construction of, 198–200

gender-genre connection, in Hume's work, 271–78, 281n.41

Genealogy of Morals, 228

"Gentleman's Companion to Hume, The," 2

Geography, 284

Gilligan, Carol, 10, 175–76, 195, 213

Gilman, Charlotte Perkins, 259, 261n.27

Goodman, Nelson, 89, 104n.11

government: consent theory and role of, 191n.1; Humean sympathy and role of, 184–85; right of resistance and, 187–91

Greek literature: heroic romance, 269, 281n.37; Hume's discussion of, 248–49, 261n.18

Guetti, James, 89

Gunpowder Plot, 272, 275

women: Beauvoir's concept of, 205–6; as cultural property, 131–32; culture of sensibility and, 286–88; in historical writings of Hume, 264–78, 279n.12; Hume's treatment of, 11, 14–15; metaphor of Nature as, 93–96, 105n.17; nature of nature in Hume and, 220–35; tyranny over, Hume's description of, 23, 25, 35–36, 145–53, 155n.20, 208–10

Woolf, Virginia, 105n.17, 107–8
works of art, Humean aesthetics and, 22, 250–53, 261n.20
Wright, John, 70

"Yellow Wall-paper, The," 259

Zeno's paradox, 100